CZECHOSLOVAKIA IN TRANSITION:

Politics, economics and society

Sharon L. Wolchik

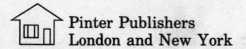
Pinter Publishers
London and New York

To Michael, Andrew, Annie, and John

© Sharon L. Wolchik 1991

First published in Great Britain in 1991 by
Pinter Publishers Limited
25 Floral Street, London WC2E 9DS

British Library Cataloguing in Publication Data

A CIP catalogue record for this book is available from the
British Library
ISBN 0 86187 408 0 (hb)
    0 86187 409 9 (pb)

For enquiries in North America please contact
PO Box 197, Irvington, NY 10533

Library of Congress Cataloging-in-Publication Data

Wolchik, Sharon L.
  Czechoslovakia in transition / Sharon Wolchik.
    p. cm.
  Includes bibliographical references and index.
  ISBN 0—86187—408 0
  1. Czechoslovakia — History. I. Title.
DB2063.W65 1991
943.7—dc20

                      91—17022
                      CIP

Typeset by Mayhew Typesetting, Bristol, England
Printed and bound in Great Britain by Biddles Ltd, Guildford and Kings Lynn

Contents

List of tables

Preface and acknowledgements

When I began this book, there were few observers who could see any hope for even limited political change in Czechoslovakia. Although Miloš Jakeš had replaced Gustáv Husák as head of the Communist Party, Czechoslovakia seemed immune from the upheavals that characterized Poland's political history in the communist period and the move toward a negotiated compromise with the opposition that the slow unravelling of the Kadar compromise in the face of economic failure brought in Hungary. But, as the pages to follow make clear, the outlines of the political and economic crises that weakened the communist system and the growth of the opposition that would oust that system and then lead the country in the transition to democracy and the market were evident in the last years of communist rule despite the surface stability.

As the result of the events of November 1989, what was to have been a study of Czechoslovakia's politics, economics, and society in the communist period became the far more interesting and rewarding task of analyzing the initial stage of the post-communist period. Given the magnitude of the changes in the last year and a half, many of the theoretical approaches and analytical tools we used to study economic, political, and social developments in Czechoslovakia are no longer useful. But, as the pages to follow illustrate, despite the important changes that have occurred in all areas of life as the result of the end of the Communist Party's monopoly of power, the legacy of communist rule continues to shape developments in Czechoslovakia. It is thus impossible to understand the transition that is taking place at present without reference to the policies and patterns of organization of the communist period. That period in turn was influenced in important ways by the country's pre-communist history.

This book thus begins with a look at the history of Czechoslovakia prior to the institution of a communist system. It then discusses the main developments in the country's politics, economics, society, and a number of important aspects of public policy during communist rule and the changes that have occurred in each area in the early post-communist period as the transition to democratic rule and a market economy continues.

The writing of this book has had something of the quality of trying to catch a fast-moving train about it. The exhilaration of witnessing the end of communist rule and the rebirth of democracy in Czechoslovakia has been accompanied by the frustrations that attend any effort to analyze ongoing processes of change and transformation. The rapid pace of change and uncertainties in both the political and economic spheres in the Czech and Slovak Federative Republic today make it impossible to come to any definitive conclusions concerning the outcome of the transition under way. As the final chapter of this book discusses in further detail, there are many reasons to be optimistic. However, as developments since November 1989 illustrate, the process of overcoming the legacy of 40 years of communist rule is an extremely complex and difficult one.

I have benefitted greatly from the help, support, and criticism of a large number of people in the Czech and Slovak Federative Republic and elsewhere during the writing of this book. I would like to thank the many Czech and Slovak colleagues and friends who contributed to this effort, including Jitka Havlová and Eduard Urbanek, whose task it was to be responsible for me as a research scholar during a period when contact with American scholars was risky; Jarmila Gabrielová and Eda Kriseová, who have offered warm friendship and encouragement; Miloslav Petrusek, Ivan Gabal, and Ivan Tomek, who have been indefatigable in providing me with sources difficult to obtain and sharing their own perspectives on current developments; and Karel Dyba, who found the time, not only while a guest scholar in Washington, but also while a minister in Prague, to help me come to grips with the changes under way in the economy at present. I am also indebted to Jan Urban, Daša Havlová, Ivan Havel, Jiří Musil, Martin Bútora, Soňa Szomolányiová, and Andrej Bartoscziewicz for sharing their perspectives on political and economic developments. Stefan and Nellie Korec, and Pavol Demeš also deserve my thanks for their viii *Preface and acknowledgements*

help in arranging my travels and meetings in Czechoslovakia in 1990, as do Ivana Mazalková and Pavlina Fabianková for their help in obtaining Czech and Slovak materials. Theodore and Sally Russell, Mark Bessinger, and Thomas Hull of the American Embassy in Prague were also very helpful.

My thanks are also due to colleagues and friends in the United States who have offered helpful comments on all or part of this manuscript and in other ways contributed to the project. Jane Curry, Hugh Agnew, Owen Johnson, Valerie Bunce, Gretchen Sandles, Ronald Linden and Michael Kraus deserve special thanks. Study and conversations with the late Václav Beneš, as well as with Zvi Gitelman, Alfred Meyer, Robert Putnam, William Zimmerman, and Walter Connor shaped my perspectives on politics in Czechoslovakia, mass-elite relations in communist states, the study of political elites, and social issues in Central and Eastern Europe. I am also deeply indebted to H. Gordon Skilling for the contribution his work has made to my understanding of developments in Czechoslovakia and for the friendship that he and his late wife Sally extended so freely. I would also like to thank Bogdan Szajkowski and Heather Bliss for their comments on an earlier draft of this volume. I am grateful to Nicola Viinikka for her editorial assistance and to Frances Pinter for her support of this project.

I would also like to acknowledge the financial support provided by the International Research and Exchanges Board, which awarded me a travel grant to Czechoslovakia. The George Washington University Committee on Research and the Institute for Sino-Soviet Studies of the Elliott School of International Affairs provided summer support and research assistance.

Many of the ideas that form the basis of this book were first tested on my students in the Russian and East European Studies Program at George Washington University and the Advanced Area Studies Program of the Foreign Service Institute of the Department of State. I would also like to thank Michael Kienbaum, Richard Grimes, Kirsten Holmes, Dominic O'Brien, Daina Stukuls, Gary Thomas, Susan Oh, Nina Jurewicz, Janine Valentine, Martina and Hana Neovesky, Tereza and Magdalena Platzová, and Craig Seibert for their research and clerical assistance.

Finally, I would like to thank my husband, John, and children, Michael, Andrew, and Annie, for their love, support and patience as mommy spent yet another Saturday in her study writing this book. My parents, Leon and Olga Wolchik, sisters Sharlene Wolchik and Shelley Cacchione, and Anita Juberts were, as always, important sources of support and encouragement. Maryanne Varnum and Candida Gargiulo deserve special thanks for helping to keep home and children on an even keel throughout the writing of this book.

I gratefully acknowledge the assistance I have received from these individuals and institutions. Of course all erroneous interpretations or significant omissions must be laid at my door.

Washington, DC
April 28, 1991

1 History

In November 1989, thousands of citizens of Czechoslovakia took to the streets to demand the end of Communist Party rule and the restoration of a democratic government. With this step, which soon resulted in the resignation of the conservative Communist Party leadership and the Communist Party's renunciation of its leading role, they began the process of recreating a democratic political system. The efforts that have followed to resurrect democratic political life, deal with the country's economic crisis, and rejoin Europe continue to be shaped by the economic and political impact of communist rule. But they are also influenced in important ways by the values and political traditions embodied in the country's pre-communist past.

Conditions in Czechoslovakia prior to the establishment of a communist system differed in many ways from those in pre-revolutionary Russia and the other European states that became communist after the Second World War. Reflected in the country's level of economic development, social structure, culture, political organization and traditions, as well as in the values, attitudes, and beliefs of the population, these differences had an important impact on the way in which the communist system was set up in Czechoslovakia. Although certain elements changed during the course of communist rule, the distinctive features of the country's past influenced the options open to political leaders and the way in which the population responded to elite initiatives.

As they seek to overcome the legacy of four decades of communist rule, the leaders and citizens of Czechoslovakia have turned once again to the values and traditions of the country's past. As has been true in many other European countries, Czechoslovakia's history during the twentieth century has been characterized by major discontinuities. Czech and Slovak leaders faced many of the same challenges, including the formation of a new state, its occupation and dismemberment in the Second World War, and the imposition of a communist system, that confronted other states in the region. The country's history has also been shaped by its position at the heart of Europe and the need to take developments in the broader international arena into account. At the same time, the common experiences noted above have been mediated by the country's particular ethnic composition, level of economic development, social structure, and political values and traditions.

Interwar Czechoslovakia

Many of the ways in which Czechoslovakia differed from its neighbors during communist rule were also evident during the interwar period, when Czechoslovakia first came into being as a unified independent state. The result of the work of Czech and Slovak leaders at home and abroad during the First World War and Allied desires to find a replacement for the Austro-Hungarian Empire, the new state brought political independence to the Czechs and Slovaks, who had been part of larger empires for centuries. It also brought together groups that differed from each other in many important ways, in part as the result of very different experiences under foreign rule. These differences, which were a persistent source of conflict during the interwar period and also left their imprint on Czechoslovakia during the communist period, spanned many areas, including levels of economic development, religious and cultural traditions, and political experiences. They also were evident in the different timing and pace of national movements among the two groups (see Korbel, 1977, pp. 12-37; Olivova, 1972, pp. 23-100; Mamatey, 1973b, pp. 3-38, 1979, pp. 75-88; and Perman, 1962).

In contrast to the situation in Russia before the Revolution and in the other Central and East European states created after the First World War which were predominantly if not overwhelmingly agrarian, Czechoslovakia had a relatively highly developed economy at the outset of its existence as an independent state. Thus, while political leaders elsewhere in the region began programs to industrialize their countries, industrialization was already well under way in Czechoslovakia. Levels of urbanization and the social structure, particularly in the Czech Lands, were more similar to those of the developed West European countries than to those of Czechoslovakia's Central and East European neighbors. Whereas from 75 to 80 percent of the population in Albania, Bulgaria, Romania, and Yugoslavia remained dependent on agriculture in 1930, and from 52 to 59 percent in Poland and Hungary in 1930, for example, only 35 percent of the population earned a living in this sector in Czechoslovakia in that year; approximately equal numbers were engaged in industry (see Janos, 1979, p. 208; Beneš, 1973, pp. 42-3). Czechoslovakia was also more urbanized than its neighbors. Approximately 48 percent of the population lived in cities of five thousand and over in 1930, compared to approximately 15 percent in Albania, from 20 to 22 percent in Romania, Yugoslavia, and Bulgaria, 27 percent in Poland, and 36 percent in Hungary (Janos, 1979, p. 208). Czechoslovakia also had much higher levels of literacy than other states in the region. By 1930, for example, the illiteracy rate was only 4.1 percent of the total population age ten and older (UNESCO, 1950, p. 19; see also Wolchik, 1985b, p. 33). As the pages to follow illustrate, these differences were especially evident in the Czech Lands (Bohemia and Moravia), which were considerably more developed during this period than in Slovakia and Ruthenia, in which conditions more closely approximated those in the other states in the region.

Czechoslovakia also diverged from the other Central and East European states in the political realm during the interwar period. The country's multiplicity of political parties, system of proportional representation, and resulting need for coalition governments posed many of the same potential threats to political stability as existed elsewhere in the region (see Korbel, 1977, pp. 67-71; and Beneš, 1973, pp. 67-8). However, although all of the new or recreated states set up in the region after 1918 were constitutional monarchies or republics, democratic government survived until ended by outside actors only in Czechoslovakia. The explanation for this persistence lies partly in the fact that Czechoslovakia had more of the social prerequisites for democracy than other countries in the region. A large middle class, the absence of a native aristocracy after the defeat of the Czech nobility at the Battle of White Mountain in 1620, a predominantly literate population, and, in the Czech Lands in particular, a citizenry with a tradition of autonomous, pluralistic group activity and some experience in limited self-government, all created better conditions for the maintenance of democracy than existed elsewhere in the region (see Beneš, 1973; Mamatey, 1973b; and Anderle, 1979, pp. 89-112).

The persistence of democracy in Czechoslovakia was also facilitated by the values and actions of many Czech and Slovak political leaders. Personified in the figure of Tomáš G. Masaryk, the first President of the Republic, whose tireless work to establish and then lead the new state made him the dominant figure of the period of independence, these values included a deep attachment to and respect for the institutions and procedures of self-government, as well as long-standing ties to Western culture and a commitment to social justice (see Korbel, 1977, pp. 38-40; Beneš, 1973, pp. 87-9; Anderle, 1979, pp. 96-8; and Szporluk, 1981, for discussions of Masaryk and his influence). The influence of these values was reflected in the willingness of party leaders to compromise and cooperate in the coalition governments the electoral system necessitated. It was also evident in the industrial and agrarian reforms begun soon after the establishment of the state, as well as in the decision to enact substantial changes, including land reform and nationalization of certain services, in order to deal with pressing social and economic problems and thus defuse popular discontent (see Beneš, 1973, pp. 89-91; Korbel, 1977, pp. 38-62; and Anderle, 1979).

Respect for democratic procedures and awareness of the necessity of compromise in a democracy were reflected in the stability of the multiparty government coalitions during this period. These values were evident in the ability of the leaders of the 'Petka,' as the five parties that formed the majority of the governments throughout the interwar period except between March 1926 and November 1929 were called, to maintain party discipline and honor the agreements they made. These values thus contributed to the continuity of policy and political direction in the new state. They also helped leaders incorporate diverse groups of citizens into the new political system and fostered allegiance to the Republic (see Mamatey, 1973a, pp. 99-

166; Beneš, 1973; and Anderle, 1979, for detailed discussions of these and other aspects of interwar political developments).

Czechoslovak democracy also benefitted from the fact that there were fewer severely alienated groups in Czechoslovakia than in many other Central and East European countries. The Czechoslovak Communist Party (*Komunistická strana Československa*—KSČ) was legal throughout the existence of the Czechoslovak Republic and attracted a sizeable degree of support. Founded in 1921, the Communist Party of Czechoslovakia grew out of a longstanding socialist movement that had substantial public support before the country gained its independence. Evident in the activities of the Czech-Slav section of the Austrian Social Democratic Party under the Dual Monarchy, this support was channelled into the Czechoslovak Social Democratic and Socialist Parties that continued to be active after 1918. When Soviet leaders called for the formation of separate communist parties in Europe, the more radical members of the Czechoslovak Social Democratic Party, led by Bohumír Šmeral, broke with the right and center of the party and joined with representatives of leftist parties in Slovakia and Ruthenia to establish the KSČ. This action was taken only after a long period of hesitation due to the difficulties of organizing a unified leftist party in a multiethnic society such as Czechoslovakia and the reluctance of certain elements in what later became the party (including its first leader, Bohumír Šmeral) to join the Comintern (Suda, 1980, pp. 44-5). The conflict between the reality of the situation in Czechoslovakia and Soviet or international considerations that would plague the party throughout its history was thus evident from its inception.

The fact that it existed in what was to remain the only functioning democracy in the region was a mixed blessing for the leaders of the Communist Party of Czechoslovakia. Because it was the only communist party in Central and Eastern Europe to remain legal until outside actors suspended the activities of all parties, the KSČ had better opportunities to organize its followers and gain popular support than communist parties elsewhere in the region, which were outlawed or suppressed early in the interwar period. At the same time, the necessity of operating in an electoral environment put certain constraints on the party and led it to adapt its structure and actions to its environment to some extent (see Suda, 1980, ch. 2).

Although communist leaders often used non-parliamentary means to further their cause during this period, the party's structure, base and activities were influenced by the need to compete for support in a democratic society. Thus, particularly before 1929, the year in which Klement Gottwald came to head the party, the KSČ was a large, mass-based party that bore little resemblance to a standard Leninist cadre party. Although it was not part of the government, its leaders participated in Parliament. The need to compete with other parties for electoral support and the fact that class conflict in Czechoslovakia had been defused to some degree by the government's efforts to promote social justice and progressive social welfare policies also moderated the party's position. These positions changed somewhat after 1929, as Gottwald attempted to follow Soviet directives to Bolshevize the party. With Gottwald at the helm, Czechoslovak communists became more militant in their activities domestically. The party's policies also came to correspond more closely to those of the Soviet Union after this time (see Suda, 1980, pp. 1-119; and Korbel, 1959, pp. 1-40).

However, even after this change, the activities of the Communist Party were less threatening to Czechoslovak democracy during the interwar period than problems that arose from other sources. Chief among these were ethnic issues. Challenges arising from the conflicting aims and perspectives of the country's different ethnic groups were less successfully dealt with than those based on economic grounds, and it was ethnic conflict that ultimately provided the pretext for the breakup of the Czechoslovak Republic in 1938. As was the case in Yugoslavia, the new Czechoslovak state brought together several ethnic groups in a common state for the first time. The political tensions and issues that arose from conflict between the Czechs and the Slovaks (who together accounted for 66 percent of the population in 1921), were complicated in the interwar period by the different interests and activities of several sizeable minorities, including Germans (who comprised 23.4 percent of the population in 1921), Hungarians

(5.6 percent), and Ruthenians, Ukrainians and Russians (3.5 percent) (Beneš, 1973, p. 40).

It was the situation of the Sudeten Germans that ultimately provided Hitler with a tool to dismember Czechoslovakia. However, Czech and Slovak relations were the more central and conflictual political issue during most of the interwar period. The roots of this conflict, which was reflected in the party system and colored political debate and discussion during this period, may be found in the disparate experiences of the two groups during centuries of foreign rule. As a result of these differences, Czechs and Slovaks entered the new state with very different levels of economic development, political experiences, national traditions, and histories. The cultural heritages of these two peoples who speak mutually intelligible languages also differed substantially.

One of the most noticeable and in many ways most troubling of these differences was evident in the economic area. The center of the Austro-Hungarian Empire's industrial development, the Czech Lands were far more developed economically than Slovakia or Ruthenia. They were also more urbanized. In 1921, for example, 336.4 of every 1,000 inhabitants in the country as a whole were employed in industry, and 395.6 in agriculture. Approximately 406 per 1,000 inhabitants in Bohemia and 378 per 1,000 in Moravia-Silesia worked in industry during that year, but only 175 in Slovakia and 104 in Ruthenia. Much larger proportions of citizens living in Slovakia (606.3 per 1,000) and Ruthenia (676.3 per 1,000) worked in agriculture in that year (Beneš, 1973, p. 43; and O. Johnson, 1985, p. 77). Literacy rates also differed considerably in different parts of the country. Although illiteracy rates of the population as a whole approximated those of the more developed West European countries (4.1 percent by 1930), illiteracy was somewhat higher in Slovakia, where 8.1 percent of all inhabitants ten years and older were illiterate, and much higher in Ruthenia, where 30.8 percent of the population in this age group were illiterate in 1930. By way of contrast, only 1.2 percent of all persons in Bohemia and 1.5 percent in Moravia were illiterate in that year (Státní úřad statistický, 1937, p. 12; and UNESCO, 1950, p. 19).

The political experiences of the population prior to independence also differed in the two parts of the country. Ruled from Vienna, the Czech Lands benefitted from the moderation of Austrian rule that occurred in the second half of the nineteenth century. As a result, Czech politicians and citizens had an increasing number of opportunities to participate in public life within the framework of imperial and regional institutions. They also benefitted from a nationalities policy that exhibited a fair degree of toleration of the language and cultures of non-dominant nationalities. In Slovakia, on the other hand, as in other areas under Hungarian rule, there was little room for non-Magyars to play any role in public life. Slovaks also faced much greater pressure to give up their ethnic identity altogether and assimilate to the dominant nationality.

These differences were reflected in the development of national movements among Czechs and Slovaks. In both cases, nationalist leaders first concentrated their efforts on the revival of the Czech and Slovak languages and the development of national literatures. Poets, linguists, and other writers played a large role in this process among both groups, particularly in the early period. In the Czech Lands, the role that scholars such as Josef Dobrovský and Josef Jungmann played in codifying a written Czech language was supplemented by the efforts of others, such as the historian František Palacký and the journalist Karel Havlíček to foster a sense of separate ethnic identity among Czechs. In Slovakia, early efforts by Catholics such as Father Anton Bernolák to create a literary Slovak language were not accepted by Protestant Slovak intellectuals. Several of these, including the Protestant poet and theologian Jan Kollár and Pavel Josef Šafárik, wrestled with the issue of how to ensure that the developing Czech literary language reflected Slovak influences even as they contributed to the Czech national movement and the development of Pan-Slavism. A younger generation of Slovaks, led by Ludevít Štúr succeeded in developing an independent literary Slovak language that was eventually accepted by Catholics and Protestants alike in Slovakia in the mid-1800s (Agnew, 1991a; see also Kerner, 1949, p. 38; Thomson, 1953, pp. 258-75; Brock and Skilling, 1970; and Agnew, 1981, pp. 201-26). The Czech and Slovak national revivals also resembled each other, and differed from those of many other

Central and East Europeans, including the Poles and Hungarians, in that they were not led by a native aristocracy (see Thomson, 1953, ch. 9; Kerner, 1949, ch. 3; and Agnew, 1986, pp. 577-97 and 1991b for discussion of the role of the Bohemian nobility in the Czech national movement. See O. Johnson, 1985, ch. 1, on the development of Slovak national consciousness). However, the social bases, content, and degree of success of the two movements differed.

Conditions for the development of nationalism were much more favorable for the Czechs than for the Slovaks. In part, this situation reflected the differing strategies for dealing with nationality issues and incorporating diverse national groups in the two halves of the Austro-Hungarian Empire. The efforts of Joseph II and other Habsburg rulers to create a centralized, German-speaking state were eventually replaced by concessions to the other nationalities under Habsburg rule. Vienna did not yield to Czech demands for autonomy similar to that which was granted to the Hungarians by the compromise of 1867; Czech-German conflict in Bohemia, as well as in Vienna, grew more acute and characterized the final years of the Empire. However, the Habsburgs did tolerate the formation and activities of nationally oriented groups in Bohemia and, particularly in the latter years of the nineteenth century, provided opportunities for participation in limited forms of self-government. With the exception of the period from 1871 to 1879, Czech leaders participated in the Diets in Bohemia and Moravia, as well as in the Parliament in Vienna (Kerner, 1949, pp. 43-5). Although the numbers and influence of the Czech deputies were very small, they were able to achieve certain changes, such as the division of the university in Prague into a Czech university and a German university, that were beneficial to the further development of Czech culture and the Czech national movement (see Thomson, 1953, pp. 216-23; Campbell, 1975, pp. 1-12; and Freeze, 1974).

These factors, coupled with the growing industrialization of Bohemia, created favorable conditions for the consolidation of ethnic loyalties among the Czechs and the flowering of Czech culture in the late nineteenth century. Together with the expansion of education and the creation of Czech language schools, they also allowed the development of a mass base for the Czech national movement.

Thus, Czechs were able to participate in a wide variety of voluntary, self-help, and charitable associations as well as in more partisan political organizations by the turn of the century (see Thomson, 1953, pp. 222-33; and Brock and Skilling, 1970). The development of mass political parties after the adoption of universal male suffrage in 1907 increased these opportunities (see Kerner, 1949, p. 46; Thomson, 1953, pp. 230-3; and Garver, 1978).

In contrast to these conditions, which allowed the development of a rich associational life and opportunities for broad segments of the population to participate to some degree in the public life of the nation, in Slovakia the population faced heavy pressure to give up its national identity. This pressure, which also existed in other areas ruled by Hungary after 1867, was evident in the restrictions placed on use of Slovak in public life and in the educational system, as well as in the severe limitations on political activity based on national grounds. Slovak national leaders, who were also handicapped by the relatively low levels of literacy and urbanization in Slovakia during this period, thus worked under very difficult conditions to prevent the total denationalization of Slovaks. At the time when Czech activists were able to form patriotic associations and eventually win certain concessions from the Austrians, Slovak national leaders saw the reversal of many of the gains they had made in the mid-1800s. As part of the Magyarization campaign, the few high schools permitted to teach in Slovak were closed in 1874; steps were also taken to discourage the use of Slovak in church education as well as in primary public education (O. Johnson, 1985, pp. 30-1). The main Slovak cultural association, *Matica slovenska*, established in 1863, was forced to close in 1875. Leaders of the emerging Slovak national movement persisted in their efforts to maintain Slovak national identity, despite the handicaps posed by these policies (O. Johnson, 1985, pp. 29-30). But the national movement remained weak and relatively small throughout the last years of the Austro-Hungarian Empire. Suffrage restrictions also kept most Slovaks from participating in the broader political life of the region under the Hungarians (see O. Johnson, 1985, pp. 15-49; Thomson, 1953, pp. 260-75; and Brock, 1976).

The Czechs and Slovaks who came together in the interwar

republic were also separated by religious differences, which in turn influenced the political ideals and values of each group. Although the majority of both peoples were nominally Catholic, the nature of Catholicism differed among the two groups, as did the relationship of religion and nationalism and the impact of religion on politics. Although most Czechs were Catholics, a more secularized culture had come to predominate in the more developed Czech Lands before independence, and the Catholic Church played a negligible role in the political life of the Czechs during the interwar period. In addition to stressing Catholic figures such as St. Václav and the patron saints of the lands of the Czech crown, Czech national consciousness also came to include a strong Protestant and anticlerical strain. Catholicism thus was not tied to the sense of Czech national identity that grew out of the efforts of Czech national leaders in the eighteenth and nineteenth centuries in the same way that it was to the development of Slovak national identity. Leaders such as Palacký looked back to the distant past, when Jan Hus, a Bohemian priest, defied the authority of the Church and began what proved to be an early attempt to reform the Church. Although Hus was burned at the stake as a heretic in 1415, his teachings provided the spiritual inspiration for the religious and political movement that dominated Bohemian life for much of the fifteenth century and brought Bohemia and Moravia into conflict with much of the rest of Europe. The defeat of the Czech nobility at the battle of White Mountain in 1620 by the Habsburg Emperor Ferdinand II led to the decimation of the native nobility and the flight of many Protestants. The Czech population was forcibly re-Catholicized after the end of the Thirty Years War in 1648. However, the Hussite tradition and Protestant experience remained an important part of the nation's past (see Thomson, 1953, pp. 69-119 and 257-9).

Slovakia also developed a Protestant tradition during the Reformation. The counter-reformation was not as thoroughgoing in Slovakia as in the Czech Lands, due to the fact that many of the Magyar nobles were Protestant. Protestant intellectuals also played a prominent role in early efforts to develop a national movement in Slovakia. However, despite the continued importance of Protestantism in Slovakia, the Catholic Church came to exert a much stronger influence on the personal lives, and political beliefs and behavior of Slovaks. Given the lower urbanization and literacy levels in Slovakia, the Catholic clergy were important public figures. As the interwar period progressed, clerics, including Father Andrej Hlinka of the Slovak People's Party, used their traditional authority as the base for developing a more explicitly political role. Giving voice to mounting Slovak resentment, they became leaders of the movement to promote Slovak national aims (Thomson, 1953, pp. 334-5; see also Hoensch, 1973, pp. 271-7).

The impact of the differences between the two main groups in the country became evident soon after the establishment of the new state. Slovak expectations of autonomy in the Republic were disappointed by the unitary state structure adopted, as well as by what was perceived as the domination of Slovak economic and political life by Prague. The fact that policies adopted by the central government were implemented by a bureaucracy comprised largely of Czechs added to Slovak resentment, as did the impact of Czech and Moravian competition in the industrial area (see Korbel, 1977, p. 106). Efforts to industrialize Slovakia, which, had they been successful, would have reduced the disparity in levels of development and social structure in the two regions and might have mitigated the growing sense of distrust and the betrayal of national hopes, also failed, in part as the result of the world depression. The Depression also had an impact in the Czech Lands, but its repercussions were particularly great in Slovakia, where it compounded the already poor economic conditions and further fueled Slovak emigration. Czechoslovakia's economy recovered to some degree in the mid-1930s, but Slovakia's level of development remained far below that of Bohemia and Moravia as the interwar period drew to a close (see Pryor, 1973, pp. 188-215; and Teichová, 1988, pp. 17-86).

Economic trends obscured the substantial progress made in Slovakia in the educational and cultural areas during this period. Although Slovakia's economy stagnated, the newly established educational system produced a substantial decrease in illiteracy among Slovaks and a significant improvement in the educational levels of the population. It also allowed the creation of a national intelligentsia in Slovakia. The extension of educational opportunities

in Slovak to the mass public and the new freedom of Slovak intellectuals to write and publish in Slovak without the restrictions
experienced under Hungarian rule led to a revival of Slovak culture
during this period (see O. Johnson, 1985; and Korbel, 1977, pp.
105-6). The creation of a more urbanized, educated population also
provided resources which could be mobilized by Slovak national
leaders (see Rothschild, 1981, for an analysis of the impact of these
and other factors on the development of nationalism).

Despite the gains made in Slovakia in these areas, they were not
enough to outweigh the effects of economic hardship and Slovak
perceptions of injustice. In this situation relations between Czechs
and Slovaks became increasingly bitter. Economic grievances and
continued insistence on centralism by Prague also provided fertile
ground for the action of Slovak nationalists who, breaking with the
primarily Protestant Slovak intellectuals who counseled continued
cooperation with Prague, called for autonomy. These demands were
embodied in the platform of the Slovak People's Party, which was
led by Father Andrej Hlinka until his death in 1938 and later by
Josef Tiso. Influenced by the growing power of Nazi Germany and
the extremist views of radical nationalist leaders such as Vojtěch
Tuka, the activities of the People's Party paved the way for the
establishment of the Slovak state under Nazi tutelage in March 1939.
For all practical purposes a puppet of the Reich, the new Slovak
Republic nonetheless did go a certain way toward satisfying the
desires of some Slovaks for their own state. It also created expectations for new state arrangements that would give Slovakia greater
autonomy in the post-war period (see Rothschild, 1974, pp. 117-21;
Korbel, 1977, pp. 153-6; Hoensch, 1973; Jelinek, 1976; and Thomson, 1953, pp. 416-19, for discussions of the Slovak state).

Although Czech-Slovak relations remained problematic throughout the interwar period, the pretext for the breakup of the interwar
Czechoslovak state was provided not by Czech-Slovak tensions but
by the grievances of the German minority. Comprising 23.4 percent
of the population in 1921 and 22.3 percent in 1930, the Sudeten
Germans, as they were called in reference to the area of the country
in which the largest number lived, were the descendants of groups
that had come to what was to become Czechoslovakia centuries

earlier. Long-term residents of the area for the most part, they were part of the dominant German element of the Austro-Hungarian Empire prior to the establishment of independent Czechoslovakia. The conflict that developed during the interwar period thus had its roots in the interplay of Czech and German culture that had occurred in the region for several centuries. However, two new elements came into the picture during this period. The first arose from the fact that the Germans, long used to being part of the dominant culture, now found themselves in the position of being a minority in a Slavic state. Czech-German relations also came to be tied very closely to events outside the country's border, particularly the development of Nazism in Germany proper (see Campbell, 1975, pp. 1-41; Wiskemann, 1938; and Luža, 1964, pp. 1-46).

Occupying areas of the country that had substantial resources, the Sudeten Germans shared a number of grievances that were increasingly exploited by militant nationalists and agents of Hitler as the interwar period progressed. Certain of these were economic. Because they were among the wealthiest of the new Czechoslovak state's citizens, the Sudeten Germans were disproportionately hit by the land reform and other redistributive policies of the new government (Korbel, 1977, p. 116; and Luža, 1964, pp. 6-13). Although most of the large estates confiscated for redistribution were German, most of the land was given to Czechs. Ties to German banks and a heavy export orientation also made industries in this area more vulnerable than industry in the rest of the Republic to the impact of the Depression and to the actions of outside powers. Other grievances included the policy of making financial assistance from Czech banks to Sudeten industries conditional upon the hiring of Czech workers and the resultant migration of Czechs to traditionally German areas, and efforts to make the borders more secure by Czech settlements (Luža, 1964, pp. 13-16; and Korbel, 1977, p. 116).

These grievances outweighed the guarantees of minority rights in the areas of education and culture enjoyed by the Germans and served as issues which extremist groups could use to mobilize antagonism to the Czechoslovak Republic. Although there were democratic German political parties whose representatives took part in Parliament after 1926 and which supported the continuation of the Republic, they proved unable to stem the movement toward extremism in the region. Nazi influence grew with Hitler's success in Germany and was reflected in the increase in mass support for the Sudeten German Party, founded by Konrad Henlein, which became an increasingly militant voice for German demands *vis-à-vis* the central government. Coordinating their actions with Hitler's plans, leaders of the German minority thus provided the excuse for Hitler's dismemberment of the Czechoslovak state. While outside forces, including Nazi Germany's desire to take over Central and Eastern Europe and the Western allies' policies of appeasement, ultimately were responsible for the overthrow of democratic government in Czechoslovakia, its heterogeneous ethnic composition and policies in regard to ethnic issues were the weak spots that paved the way for such actions (see Rothschild, 1974, pp. 122-9; Korbel, 1977, pp. 116-20; and Luža, 1964, especially pp. 24-184; and Campbell, 1975, chs. 3-6).

Munich and the Second World War

Abandoned by its Western allies as the result of the Munich Agreement of September 29, 1938, the government of Czechoslovakia submitted to Hitler's demands that it cede the Sudetenland to Germany on September 30 without armed resistance. The capitulation of President Edvard Beneš and other Czechoslovak leaders to German pressure and this ultimatum was but the first step in the dismantling of the interwar Czechoslovak state. Slovak nationalists under the leadership of the Slovak People's Party established an autonomous Slovak government in October 1938 and, under the threat of Hungarian invasion, declared Slovakia an independent Republic in March 1939. Ruthenia, which had gained autonomy at the same time as Slovakia, was soon taken over once again by Hungary. Czecho-Slovakia, as the truncated Czechoslovak state was termed between October 1938 and March 1939, was further subjected to Hitler's control in March 1939, when Beneš' successor, Emil Hacha, was forced to accept the establishment of a German Protectorate of Bohemia and Moravia, and Germany occupied the country (see Korbel, 1977, pp. 121-49; and Rothschild, 1974, pp. 129-32, for discussions of the actions of Beneš and other Czechoslovak leaders during this period. See Luža, 1964, chs. 5 and 6; and Anderle, 1979, pp. 107-10, for overviews of this period and references to the vast literature on the Munich Agreement).

The experiences of Czechs and Slovaks during the Second World War differed substantially. These differences reinforced those already evident in the interwar period; they also created new issues and conflicts for the government that came into being after the Second World War. In the Czech Lands, German occupation was directed at extinguishing all vestiges of Czech culture and political values. Although human losses among the population as a whole were not on the order of those in countries such as Poland, the Jewish community in the Protectorate was virtually destroyed. The rest of the population, while spared physically, was subject to the violence and random terror associated with Nazi rule elsewhere. As occupied regions whose task was to produce industrial products for Germany and the war effort, Bohemia and Moravia also suffered heavy economic losses (see Korbel, 1977, pp. 157-60; Luža, 1964, chs. 7-10; Mastny, 1971; and Taborsky, 1979).

In contrast to the situation in Bohemia and Moravia, where the suspension of democratic freedoms and normal cultural life came about as the result of the actions of an outside occupier, in Slovakia they occurred as the result of actions by Slovak leaders. Initially welcomed by certain groups of Slovaks as the realization of their national aims, the Slovak state set up in 1939 emulated Nazi Germany in its policies as well as organization. An extreme nationalist ideology and anti-Semitism were reflected in the persecution of Czechs and the deportation of Slovak Jews to concentration camps (see Korbel, 1977, p. 160; Rothschild, 1974, pp. 133-4; Steiner, 1973; and Jelinek, 1976).

At the same time, it was in Slovakia that the most dramatic resistance occurred. While Czechs engaged in acts of passive resistance and risked their lives by staying in touch with and carrying out the orders of the government-in-exile led by Beneš in London, there was little open resistance to the occupation (see Korbel, 1977, pp. 160-4; and Mastny, 1971). In Slovakia, on the other hand, it was possible for opponents of the regime to organize more effectively. Democratic and communist forces cooperated to plan and stage an armed uprising in August 1944. The Germans eventually reasserted their control over the territory freed by Resistance forces, but it took them four months to do so. Although the Slovak uprising was not successful, it gave Slovaks who did not support the extremism and actions of the Slovak state a claim to consideration in the post-war order. The participation by communist leaders in this event also provided the basis for the later claims by Slovak communists that they had defended Slovakia's honor in a period of national shame (see Josko, 1973, pp. 362-86; Jelinek, 1976, pp. 125-8, and 1983, pp. 69-77).

1945-1948: modified pluralism and the institution of communist dominance

Czechoslovakia's political organization and political life also differed considerably from those that prevailed in the other states in the region immediately after the Second World War. Although liberated in large part by Soviet troops, Czechs and Slovaks managed to retain some freedom of action and a political system in which non-communist groups played a significant role longer than any other country in the region. From 1945, when the country was liberated, to February 1948, Czechoslovakia enjoyed a modified form of pluralism. During this period, which coincided with Soviet toleration of a fair degree of diversity in political structures and policies throughout Central and Eastern Europe, Czech and Slovak as well as other communist leaders talked of the need to take national circumstances into account (see Brzezinski, 1967, pp. 18-19; and H. Seton-Watson, 1956, pp. 339-71, for overviews of this period. See Korbel, 1977, pp. 218-52; Zinner, 1963, pp. 106-10; Taborsky, 1961, pp. 15-24; and Korbel, 1959). In contrast to many of the other Central and East European countries, which had governments clearly dominated by the Communist Party from the time of the end of hostilities on their territories, in Czechoslovakia the Communist Party shared leadership of the state with representatives of other parties. Prominent non-communist political figures, including the pre-war President, Edvard Beneš, returned to the country to play major roles in public life.

From the beginning of the post-Second World War period, however, the Communist Party enjoyed certain advantages over its democratic opponents. These included the psychological and other benefits derived from the Party's association with the liberating Soviet forces and the nearby presence of the Red Army. The communists were also the beneficiaries of several aspects of the political agreements between Beneš and the Soviets that preceded his return to Czechoslovakia, and of the provisions of the 1945 Košice Government Program, which became the basis for the newly reconstituted Czechoslovak state. Among the most important of the latter was the agreement to simplify Czechoslovakia's party structure. Justified in part by the argument that those parties that had collaborated with the Germans and the Slovak state should be excluded from the new system, the agreement in effect limited the number of legitimate parties to four Czech and two Slovak parties. These included, in addition to the Communist Party of Czechoslovakia, the National Socialist Party, the Czechoslovak People's Party, and the Social Democratic Party in the Czech Lands and the Communist Party of Slovakia and the Slovak Democratic Party in Slovakia (see Suda, 1980, pp. 178-84). According to the provisions of the Košice Government Program, which also formalized the political structure of the new state, all parties were to be part of the government coalition. There was thus no true opposition (see *Košický vládní program*, 1974).

The Communist Party also benefitted from the fact that it controlled numerous key ministries in the new Czechoslovak government, including the Ministries of Information, the Interior, Education, and Agriculture. These positions allowed the Party to have a disproportionate influence on the availability of information and control of the police, as well as to garner popular support by distributing confiscated German lands and controlling admission to educational institutions. The communist leaders also sponsored measures, including efforts to recover from the effects of the Second World War, which appealed to the patriotism of the population and had genuine popular support.

As a result of these factors, as well as the opportunism of those who saw the communists as the most likely victors in the struggle over the direction of the country's development in the post-war period and the renewed activism of party members who survived the war, the Communist Party's membership increased substantially, and reached over a million in 1946 (Suda, 1980, p. 195). The party also enjoyed a good deal of support from non-members in the early post-Second World War period, particularly in the Czech Lands. This support was reflected in the 1946 elections, in which the Communist Party gained 37.9 percent of the vote, the largest share obtained by any party (see Suda, 1980, pp. 195-201; and Korbel, 1977, pp. 234-7. See also Burks, 1976, p. 215).

The uneasy truce between the Communist Party and other political forces in Czechoslovakia came to an end in February 1948. The immediate catalyst for the institution of a government clearly dominated by the Communist Party was a crisis over control of the police that led to the resignation of the non-communist ministers in the government. Their actions, which were designed to force President Beneš to dissolve the government and call for new elections, backfired as Beneš yielded to the threat of civil unrest posed by communist-organized demonstrations and manipulation of public opinion (see Korbel, 1959, pp. 210-20).

Faced with the *de facto* control of an increasing number of public institutions by 'Action Committees' created by the communists, an armed and mobilized workers' militia led by the communists in Prague, and organized, militant demonstrations against the actions of the democratic ministers, and hampered in his ability to respond to threatened violence by communist influence in and control over the police and army, Beneš eventually accepted the resignations of the democratic ministers. This step, which has been the subject of fierce controversy in Czechoslovakia and elsewhere, opened the way for the formation of a reconstituted government composed of members of the Communist Party and selected sympathizers in other parties. Although other parties continued to be nominally represented in the government, it was clearly controlled by Klement Gottwald and the Communist Party. The May 1948 elections, which offered voters only those candidates approved by the Communist Party, reflected the new political realities. The resignation of President Beneš in June, which was followed by his death three months later, was further testimony to the end of the post–Second World War coalition.

These events, which were the culmination of the tensions that were inherent in the political situation after the Second World War in Czechoslovakia, took place in the context of domestic and international developments that made a continuation of the uneasy truce between communist and democratic forces in Czechoslovakia increasingly unlikely. On the domestic front, the Communist Party's support, which reached a high point in the May 1946 elections, was widely perceived to be declining (Korbel, 1959, pp. 198–200, and 1977, p. 244). The threat this decline posed to the party's campaign to come to power by the ballot box was reflected in increasing militancy on the part of party leaders and intensified efforts to ensure communist dominance in positions of power in the state bureaucracy and police force.

The stability of the coalition government in Czechoslovakia was also threatened by changes in the international arena in 1947 and 1948. The deterioration of relations between the Soviet Union and the Western allies in the late 1940s was reflected in Soviet insistence that the Central and East European countries support Soviet aims and yield to Soviet desires on issues of foreign policy. It was also evident in the increasing similarity of political institutions and policies in the region. In the case of Czechoslovakia, Soviet pressure on the Beneš government to withdraw from discussions concerning Czechoslovakia's participation in the Marshall Plan in July 1947 foreshadowed later developments. The creation of the Cominform in 1947 also did not bode well for continued Soviet toleration of diversity in the region.

1948–1962: Stalinism implemented

After February 1948, the leadership of the Czechoslovak Communist Party began implementing the Stalinist model of political organization, social transformation, and economic development in earnest. As in other Central and East European countries, Klement Gottwald and the other Communist leaders attempted to destroy the country's existing institutional and value systems and reintegrate the populace into new structures. They also sought to inculcate new political and social values and foster new patterns of behavior in many other areas of life (see Gitelman, 1970, for a discussion of elite strategies in this respect).

Paradoxically, the democratic nature of the interwar political system in Czechoslovakia did not moderate, but rather seemed to intensify the efforts of Czech and Slovak Communist Party leaders to transform the country along Soviet lines once they came to power. The desire to emulate the Soviet experience, even though, or precisely because, it conflicted with the dominant political and cultural values of the country, was evident in the severity of the purges and the terror that accompanied the imposition of communist rule.

In the political realm, earlier efforts to discredit and reduce the power bases of non-communist actors were stepped up, as were measures designed to strengthen the organizational base of the Communist Party and ensure its domination of political life. This process, which began during the coalition period, involved the political use of justice and propaganda campaigns against leaders of other parties, who were soon forced to leave their posts in the mass organizations as well as in their own parties (see Korbel, 1977, p. 255; and Zinner, 1963, pp. 196-223). Political measures were supplemented by economic policies including further nationalization of industry, severe restrictions on private inheritance, and currency reform, designed to remove the economic power base of non-communist elites (see Korbel, 1977, pp. 260-8).

The party leadership also embarked on a renewed campaign to strengthen the Communist Party's organizational base. Membership in the party, which had increased greatly in the years immediately after the Second World War, reached two million by spring 1948, when approximately one out of five adults in the country was a member of the Communist Party. Recruiting campaigns supplemented the influx of members from the former Social Democratic Party and further diversified the Communist Party's social composition by bringing in large numbers of middle-class and white-collar members (Suda, 1980, pp. 225-6).

The imprint of Soviet experience was soon evident in the

institutional structure of Czech and Slovak society, which was simplified to conform to the Soviet pattern and ensure the political control of the Communist Party. It was also reflected in the policies adopted by the post-February government. The formal governmental structure of the country remained relatively unchanged by the new constitution enacted in May 1948. However, governmental organs at every level were supervised by and effectively subordinated to the corresponding Communist Party body. The country's party system, which until February 1948 reflected, although in truncated form, the multiparty system that had characterized political life in Czechoslovakia in the interwar period, also changed. All political parties with any potential for challenging the communist order were neutralized. The Social Democratic Party was forced to merge with the Communist Party; the National Socialist and Slovak Democratic Parties were disbanded; the latter was replaced by the Slovak Revival Party. The People's Party in the Czech Lands, and the Slovak Party of Freedom, which was formed in 1946, were allowed to continue to function after substantial changes in their leaderships. However, their activities were confined largely to mobilizing their members to support the aims and policies of the Communist Party (see Zinner, 1963, pp. 224-5; and Taborsky, 1961, pp. 144-5).

The associational life of the country, which had reflected both the tradition of pluralism and the multiparty nature of the political system in the interwar period, was simplified further. The country's voluntary associations, including trade unions, student groups, and women's associations, had been centralized to some extent since the early post-Second World War period as the result of the requirement that they be part of nationwide umbrella organizations and the National Front. After 1948, the non-communist groups were dissolved, and the unified mass organizations were subordinated to the Communist Party.

The Czechoslovak leadership also set up institutions similar to those which existed in the Soviet Union to direct a centrally planned economy. Earlier measures to nationalize large industries were supplemented by policies designed to increase central control over the economy. Eventually, legislation was passed that eliminated virtually all private ownership (see Korbel, 1977, pp. 38-41;

Teichová, 1988, pp. 87-100; Stevens, 1985, pp. 7-11; and Luža, 1973, pp. 387-415, for brief discussions of social and economic changes enacted between 1945 and 1948. See Zinner, 1963, pp. 226-8; Korbel, 1977, pp. 261-268; and Teichová, 1988, pp. 101-48; and chapter 4 in this book for further details concerning post-1948 economic policies).

These measures were accompanied by the strengthening and expansion of the central planning mechanism, and the adoption of a series of five-year economic plans. As in the Soviet Union and other Central and East European countries, economic planners adopted ambitious programs of rapid industrialization based on the mobilization of all available labor resources. Heavy industry in particular was emphasized, to the neglect of agriculture and Czechoslovakia's traditional strength, light industry. The country's foreign trade, which had been heavily oriented to Western Europe in the interwar period, was redirected toward the Soviet Union and other Central and East European communist countries.

The agricultural sector was also transformed. The collectivization drive, which began in earnest in Czechoslovakia in 1950, used a mixture of material incentives and coercion to induce farmers to join collective farms and succeeded in greatly increasing state control over agriculture. By 1960, over 90 percent of all farmland in Czechoslovakia had been collectivized (Korbel, 1977, p. 261; see also Taborsky, 1961, pp. 382-423; Stevens, 1985, pp. 16-57; and Wadekin, 1982).

The Czechoslovak leadership also followed Soviet experience in attempting to promote social and value change during this period. Efforts were made to restructure the stratification hierarchy and change the status of disadvantaged social groups by manipulating wage policies as well as by controlling access to secondary and higher education. Communist officials used the centrally controlled mass media as well as the newly established system of censorship to discredit members of the old elite and promote new images of manual laborers and agricultural workers. They also attempted to change certain aspects of women's roles. The leadership gave particular emphasis in this regard to convincing women to join the labor force (see Wolchik, 1979, pp. 583-603, and 1981c, pp. 123-42).

Czechoslovakia's communist leaders also mounted a concerted campaign against religion during this period. Seminaries and religious schools were closed and church property was confiscated. Priests were subjected to political controls and their numbers reduced. People known to be believers were harassed, and outward manifestations of religious belief, including church attendance, participation in religious ceremonies to mark important life events such as baptism, marriage, and death, declined (see Ramet, 1989, pp. 277-8). Efforts were also made, through organized 'schooling' sessions, as well as through the use of the media and educational system, to wean Czech and Slovak citizens away from previous political beliefs and to socialize them to new values, including allegiance to the new political order and belief in Marxism–Leninism. The arts and cultural life, as well as leisure-time activities, were affected by these efforts, as political leaders attempted to politicize all aspects of life. In this area, as in others, Soviet experience was taken as the guide, and previous links to the rest of European culture were disregarded.

As in the Soviet Union and elsewhere in Central and Eastern Europe, Czech and Slovak leaders increasingly relied on coercion to implement these policies. Despite the fact that there had been some genuine support for the Communist Party in Czechoslovakia in the interwar and immediate post-Second World War periods and not-withstanding the lack of any serious challenge to the institutions of the new system after 1948, Czechoslovakia also experienced political purges and the widespread use of terror as the Stalinist system was consolidated. The purges within the Communist Party, which began in 1949 with the wholesale replacement of members of several regional party organizations and soon moved to the top layers of the party, were among the most severe in the region. Eventually they came to involve numerous top party officials, including Rudolf Slanský, then Secretary-General of the party. The Slovak Communist Party was particularly hard hit by the purges, which involved show trials of numerous Slovak communist leaders, including Gustáv Husák who later led the party, on charges of bourgeois nationalism (see Pelikán, 1971, pp. 37-147; Skilling, 1976, ch. 13; and Suda, 1980, pp. 233-57 for analyses of the trials. See

Loebl, 1976, for a more personal account).

In contrast to the situation in Hungary and Poland, the Stalinist system persisted relatively unchanged in Czechoslovakia after Stalin's death in March 1953. Workers' riots in Plzen over economic issues failed to spread to other areas of the country and were quickly suppressed. Antonín Novotný, who became First Secretary of the Communist Party, and Antonín Zapotocký, who became President after the death of Klement Gottwald in 1953, continued Gottwald's policies in most areas.

Khrushchev's denunciation of Stalin and his crimes at the Twentieth Congress of the Communist Party of the Soviet Union in 1956, which ushered in an era of de-Stalinization in the Soviet Union and led to dramatic challenges to the communist system in Hungary and Poland, had little impact in Czechoslovakia. There was little change in the top leadership aside from minor personnel shifts and the division of certain top positions. Czech and Slovak leaders gave lip-service to other elements of de-Stalinization, such as the need to respect socialist legality, but the secret police remained an extremely important institution, and there was little change in the relationship of the Communist Party to the populace or in the style of rule.

The persistence of the Stalinist system in Czechoslovakia until the mid-1960s can be traced to a number of factors that differentiated Czechoslovakia from its neighbors. These influenced both the pressures for change from below and the willingness of the party leadership to initiate change from above. One of the more important of these was the fact that, due to its higher level of development prior to the imposition of communism, the Czechoslovak economy was not as severely affected by the Stalinist model of development as those of countries such as Poland and Hungary by the mid-1950s. The relatively good performance of the economy during this period meant that the Soviet leadership did not push Czech and Slovak leaders to institute changes to the same extent it did Hungarian and Polish leaders. It also meant that economic discontent, one of the primary reasons for mass pressure for change in Poland and Hungary in 1956, was not as pervasive in Czechoslovakia at this time. The Stalinist leadership also benefitted from a loyal intelligentsia. There was thus less pressure for change from communist and non-party intellectuals than in Hungary and Poland at this time. The party also benefitted from the fact that there was no strong historical animosity toward Russia or the Soviet Union in either the Czech Lands or Slovakia.

The severity of the purges and the high level of political control in Czechoslovakia also inhibited change at this time. The harshness of the Stalinist system prevented opponents of the regime from mounting a political challenge. The personal involvement of Novotný and many of his colleagues in the purges also strengthened the leadership's resistance to change. Czechoslovakia's multiethnic composition contributed to the maintenance of Stalinism. Political leaders were able to deflect dissatisfaction with the system toward other ethnic groups. The differences in cultures, levels of economic development, and historical experiences of the Czech Lands and Slovakia also inhibited the development of a unified opposition (see Brzezinski, 1967, ch. 8, for an overview of developments in the region).

1962–1968: rethinking the basis of socialist society

Change in this state of affairs came about as a result of changes in the international arena, as well as in economic performance and ethnic relations in Czechoslovakia. Although the overtly political aspects of the reform only came into the open after January 1968, when Alexander Dubček replaced Antonín Novotný as head of the Communist Party, the reform movement that came to be known as the effort to create Socialism with a Human Face or the Prague Spring was preceded by a lengthy period of debate, discussion, and preparation. To some extent the reform effort that culminated in 1968 can be seen as a process of delayed de-Stalinization. The process was shaped by the particular problems the Stalinist model created in Czechoslovakia. It was also shaped by the different political histories and national traditions of the Czechs and Slovaks.

The reform effort in Prague thus differed in many important ways from the events that followed Stalin's death and attempts to change the political system in other Central and East European communist countries. Thus, in contrast to most other movements for change prior to 1989, which were sparked by the actions of dissatisfied masses or intellectuals outside the Communist Party, in Czecho-slovakia the original impetus for change came from within the party itself. Ordinary citizens and non-party intellectuals eventually became involved in the process, but it was initiated by the leadership of the Communist Party and intellectuals affiliated with the party. The forms of popular participation and the content of the demands for change in 1968 were also influenced by the democratic heritage of Czechoslovakia and the country's ethnic composition. These factors also were reflected in the different course of the reform in the Czech Lands and in Slovakia.

The events that developed into the Prague Spring in 1968 had their roots in several areas of life. These included changes in the economic situation in the early 1960s; new tensions in the relation-ship between Czechs and Slovaks; growing restiveness and the rebirth of a critical spirit among the country's intellectuals and students; and increasing division within the Communist Party leadership itself concerning the best way of solving these problems. New signals from Moscow in the early 1960s also proved to be important in allowing the process that led to the reform to develop in its early stages.

The earliest and in some ways most significant of these deve-lopments arose in the economic sphere. By the early 1960s Czechoslovakia's economy, which had maintained a relatively high growth rate throughout the 1950s, despite the deformations caused by Stalinist economic policies, began to fail. The problems associated with central planning and unbalanced investment elsewhere in the region, including poor labor morale, the failure of prices to reflect the costs of production, imbalances in supply and demand, poor management, lack of material incentives for both workers and managers to produce quality goods, and sporadic shortages of basic commodities due to imbalances in the resources allocated to various economic sectors, began to be evident in Czechoslovakia as well. By 1963, the situation had deteriorated to the point that Czechoslovakia had a negative growth rate.

Although it at first resisted the idea of economic reform, in 1963 the party leadership appointed a team of economic experts, headed by Ota Šik, an economist who was also a member of the Central

Committee of the Communist Party, to devise a method of improving the economic situation. Šik and his team developed a proposal for economic reform that formed the basis for a series of measures for economic change approved at the 13th Congress of the Communist Party in 1966 (Skilling, 1976, pp. 58-9; see also chapter 4). Many of the suggestions of the economists were watered down in the final version of the reform package, whose implementation nonetheless created substantial resistance within the bureaucracy. The incomplete and halting implementation of the reforms over the next two years was one of the factors that contributed to the political changes attempted in 1968, for it led some of the economists who supported the reform to argue that it would be impossible to reform Czechoslovakia's economy without change in the political sphere as well (see Skilling, 1976, pp. 57-63; Korbonski, 1971; and chapter 4 of this work).

The new spirit of criticism that animated reform economists in the early and mid-1960s also found echoes in other areas of life. In part a response to Khrushchev's renewed denunciation of Stalin at the 22nd Party Congress of the CPSU in 1962, this attitude also reflected a maturing of the generation of young communists who had joined the Communist Party in their early 20s at the close of the war or soon after the party's rise to power in 1948 and who were approaching or had achieved positions of some influence in their professions.

Creative intellectuals were the first to challenge the regime and the prevailing intellectual orthodoxy. Writers and dramatists denounced party control of cultural life and, at congresses of their unions and in the cultural periodicals, criticized the effects of Stalinism on culture. They also called for greater freedom of expression for themselves and other citizens (see Skilling, 1976, pp. 62-72; Hamšík, 1971, pp. 25-73; Jancar, 1971, pp. 195-201; and Kusin, 1971, especially ch. 5; see also chapter 5 of this work). Less visible but equally important changes occurred during this period in other areas as other intellectuals began to question and in many cases renounce established dogmas.

This spirit of questioning, which ultimately provided the theoretical foundation for the political reform that came into the open in early 1968, was evident in all areas of intellectual life. It was particularly acute among those intellectuals such as philosophers, historians, and social scientists whose work was heavily influenced by official views concerning the nature of socialist society (see Kusin, 1971; and Golan, 1971). Led by loyal Communist Party intellectuals in many cases, these individuals participated in a rethinking of the basic nature of socialist society. Their reformulations, particularly those concerning the persistence of conflict among the interests of different social groups even under socialism, the requirements of the scientific-technological revolution, the need to reconcile democracy and socialism, and the need for new forms of political representation in developed socialist societies, formed the basis for many of the political reforms discussed in 1968.

The critical tendencies evident in debates and discussions remained confined largely to the elite level during this period. They did have some impact on other groups in society, including young people, who also began to voice their discontent with the regime. Student radicalism, which arose from student concern over problems in their own situation, including housing, poor employment prospects, and the nature of the educational process, soon came to reflect the new thinking of the older intellectuals concerning the need for political change (see Skilling, 1976, pp. 72–82; and Kusin, 1971, pp. 125–42).

Reformist tendencies also became evident in the activities of certain mass organizations, most notably the women's organizations, during the mid- and late 1960s. Led by intellectuals affiliated with the Communist Party, members of the National Women's Committee, for example, began to question party dogma concerning the position of women under socialism. Refuting the official notion that women were equal in socialist Czechoslovakia, they drew attention to unresolved issues in women's lives. Once a mass women's organization was re-created in 1967, its leaders used the formulations discussed above concerning the need for particular social groups to have organizations to defend their interests even in socialist societies to justify acting as an interest group to defend women's interests (see Scott, 1974; Wolchik, 1978, chs. 6 and 7; Heitlinger, 1979; and Wolchik, 1981a and 1981c). For the most part, however, such activities and criticism remained confined to intellectuals and members of the political elite. With the exception of new developments in culture and the arts, the mass public was little involved at this stage of the process.

Changes in Slovakia and Slovak desires for greater parity in the Czechoslovak state also contributed to the growing pressure for change in the late 1960s. The broken promises of autonomy for Slovakia made by Czech and Slovak communists after 1945 and the fate of indigenous Slovak communist leaders, including Vladimír Clementis, the former Foreign Minister who was executed in 1952 and Gustáv Husák, who was jailed on charges of 'bourgeois nationalism' in 1951, contributed to dissatisfaction among Slovak leaders and intellectuals with the state established after 1948. Slovak desires for greater recognition of Slovak interests within the common state continued to grow during the 1950s and 1960s. First evident in the writings of Slovak experts and intellectuals, these desires were expressed with greater frequency and increasingly openly in the 1960s. In part a reflection of the general intellectual ferment that occurred in the country during this time, Slovak calls for better treatment also expressed continued frustration at the remaining inequalities in living standards and development levels in the two parts of the country, despite investment patterns that gave Slovakia an edge in capital investment. The ability of Slovaks to translate these desires into political claims also reflected the impact of the degree of development and equalization that had occurred, as Slovak leaders had greater resources to use to press ethnic claims than in the past and also a more receptive, because more urbanized and literate, population of co-nationals (see Skilling, 1976, pp. 49-56; Kusin, 1971, pp. 69-75, and 1972, pp. 145-61; and Leff, 1988. See Rothschild, 1981, for discussion of factors that condition the political expression of national issues).

The sense of deepening crisis and growing awareness of the need for change evident in broad segments of Czechoslovakia's intellectual community in the 1960s eventually came to be reflected within the leadership of the Communist Party itself. Although Antonín Novotný maintained his position and the leadership's composition remained relatively stable, divisions developed between those who wanted to preserve the status quo and others, including Alexander

Dubček, the Slovak party leader whose name became synonymous with the reform process in 1968, who supported economic or political change. Party leaders were divided over the best strategy for overcoming the economic crisis and differed on issues such as how to deal with restive writers and other intellectuals, how far to go in re-examining violations of socialist legality and repudiating other aspects of Stalinism, and how to accommodate Slovak desires for a greater role in the state. The leadership was also split concerning the need for substantial political reform. These divisions, which crystallized quite late in Novotný's tenure and did not come into the open until after January 1968, had an important impact on the events which occurred after that time. As in other communist countries, they allowed actors beyond the small circle at the top of the Communist Party greater latitude in the options and issues they could discuss. Disunity at the top also created conditions that made it more likely for groups and individuals other than top party leaders to have an impact on public policy (see Skilling, 1971, pp. 3–18; and Wolchik, 1983b, pp. 111-32).

1968: 'Socialism with a Human Face'

Opposition to Novotný and his policies within the party leadership came to the fore at the October and December 1967 meetings of the Central Committee. In January 1968, Novotný was forced to relinquish his post as head of the Communist Party to Alexander Dubček (see Skilling, 1976, ch. 6). Although it was not immediately apparent at the time, Novotný's removal signalled the broadening of participation in the debate and discussion about change in Czechoslovakia beyond the elite level.

As the top leadership began to call for more participation by citizens and to discuss the need for far-reaching changes in the operation of the political system, debate over the nature of socialism in Czechoslovakia increasingly came to be reflected in the mass circulation media and in the cultural area. Once censorship effectively ceased to exist in March 1968, the way was open for free expression of a kind unseen in Czechoslovakia since 1948. In the course of eight months, Czechs and Slovaks challenged the shibboleths of the

Stalinist system and formulated plans for dramatic change in public life. A reflection of the rethinking and renewal that had taken place among party intellectuals in the preceding years, this process, which came to be known as the attempt to create 'socialism with a human face,' was aimed at correcting the abuses of the old system. It was also an effort to devise a form of socialism better suited to Czechoslovakia's democratic traditions, historic links to West European culture, and advanced level of economic development.

At the elite level, the process focused on several key issues. These included the attempt to come to terms with Stalinism and a reexamination of the purge trials; efforts to prevent future abuses of socialist legality and to institutionalize guarantees of free expression and other civil liberties for citizens; a redefinition of the proper role of the Communist Party and other political and social organizations; attention to Slovak grievances; and economic reform. Although not at the center of the party leadership's concern, the process also involved an expansion of the limits in the cultural sphere and consideration of the proper degree of autonomy and function of culture and the arts under socialism (see Komunistická strana Československa, 1968 for a summary of these points).

One of the most important and controversial of these issues was the effort to define new roles for the Communist Party and other political and social organizations. As would be the case with Gorbachev's reforms in the 1980s, the changes envisioned by the reformers within the Communist Party stopped short of a renunciation of one-party rule. Dubček and other leaders were steadfast in maintaining that the leading role of the party was not to be abandoned; they also refuted the idea of establishing a true multiparty political system with an opposition outside the Communist Party. However, they envisioned a less dominant position for the party and a corresponding increase in the role of other political bodies, including the government and social organizations. Divisions within the Communist Party and particularly within the top leadership over this and other issues related to the reform persisted and intensified during this period, as many of those who remained within the leadership had been close colleagues and collaborators of Novotný (see Skilling, 1976, pp. 208-20 and ch. 16).

As intellectuals pushed back the limits on free expression, broader groups of citizens became involved in the process. The established mass organizations, including the women's organization, student and youth leagues, and official trade unions, stopped functioning as instruments solely to mobilize the population to fulfil elite deter-mined objectives and began acting as interest groups in the Western sense of the word. Other groups, including KAN (The Club of Engaged Non-Party Persons), and Club 231 (former political prisoners who named their group after the number of the law under which many of them had been sentenced) formed outside the officially permitted organizations. The other political parties and lower levels of the Communist Party also began to awaken (see Skilling, 1976, pp. 200-4 and 232-6).

At first wary of what seemed only another change at the top, the population gradually came to take advantage of the new freedom to criticize past mistakes and discuss public events. Free from the restraints of the past two decades, Czech and Slovak citizens aired grievances and called for changes that in many cases went beyond those the party leadership was willing to entertain (see Skilling, 1976, pp. 196-201; Golan, 1971; Jancar, 1971; and Kusin, 1972. See Piekalkiewicz, 1972, for excerpts from public opinion polls taken during this period). The growth of pressure from below for further democratization was most noticeable in the Czech Lands. In Slovakia, national issues took precedence for the population as well as for many Communist Party leaders (see Skilling, 1976, ch. 15).

As the reform progressed, Dubček and other reformists within the leadership found it increasingly difficult to restrain their mass supporters from moving in more radical directions. Their options in dealing with unorthodox critics who went beyond what the leader-ship desired were limited by their new strategy of rule. In contrast to the strategy to keep the population in line used during much of the communist period in Czechoslovakia and in most of the rest of the communist world, the Dubček leadership attempted to increase the legitimacy of the system by allowing more genuine participation by ordinary citizens. But, while they refrained from harsh measures that would have undermined the sense of trust they were trying to cultivate, their inability to control events within the country fully made it difficult to reassure their increasingly worried socialist comrades outside the country.

These conflicting demands were reflected in the actions of the Dubček leadership in the late spring and summer of 1968. As it attempted to implement the principles for reform embodied in the Action Program adopted by the Communist Party at its April 1968 plenum (see Remington, 1969, pp. 88-136, for an English version of the text), the leadership faced challenges within the country from both conservatives who resisted change and those who called for more fundamental change in the political system and urged the leadership to move ahead more quickly. Expressions of the latter attitude, as in the celebrated 2,000 Words manifesto, in turn served to heighten the fears of Soviet and other Central and East European leaders that the Czechoslovak Communist Party was losing control of events.

In the end, it was the Dubček leadership's inability to reassure Czechoslovakia's external allies that brought about the end of the experiment. Alarmed at what they perceived to be a serious challenge to the leading role of the Communist Party and concerned lest the political innovations under discussion in Czechoslovakia spill over into their own countries, the Soviets and conservative Central and East European leaders warned Dubček of the need to change course. When their warnings, voiced in the official media and reiterated in a series of meetings with the Czechoslovak leadership during the spring and summer of 1968, failed to achieve the desired results, Soviet leaders resorted to a military invasion to bring the Czechs and Slovaks back in line on August 21, 1968 (see J. Valenta, 1979; and Hodnett and Potichnyj, 1970).

Although there was little armed resistance to the invading troops, both the reformists in the leadership and broader groups of Czech and Slovak citizens attempted to preserve as much of the reform momentum as possible. When the Dubček leadership, which was forced to go to Moscow immediately after the invasion, returned to Prague, Dubček and his supporters vowed to remain true to the post-January course. At the same time, they warned the population about the need to take the new situation into account (see Mlynář, 1980).

In the days immediately after the invasion Czech and Slovak citizens engaged in numerous forms of passive resistance. The activities of the underground radio in particular served to mobilize the population and kept alive the hope that the reform effort could be salvaged. Supporters of the post-January course, with the help of Prague workers, were able to convene the Extraordinary 14th Party Congress clandestinely, virtually under the eyes of the occupying forces. The radical changes in the composition of the Communist Party's leadership made at the Congress came too late, however, to influence the course of events (see Skilling, 1976, pp. 764-72; Eidlin, 1980, pp. 93-156; and Jancar, 1971; see also Wechsberg, 1969).

Leaders of the mass organizations, who had begun to transform their groups into interest groups similar to those that exist in democratic societies, condemned the invasion and reaffirmed their commitment to the reform process (see Jancar, 1971; and Wolchik, 1981b, pp. 123-42). The populace, which had exhibited some skepticism about the proposed reforms in the pre-August period, united behind Dubček, who came to symbolize the country's hopes for change and national pride. The prevailing attitude of passive resistance to the invaders was punctuated by isolated cases of more dramatic opposition and scattered acts of resistance throughout the last months of 1968 and early 1969, including the self-immolation of a young Czech student, Jan Palach, in Prague in January 1969. The efforts of both the reformist leaders and the population were increasingly hampered, however, by the growing influence of the hardliners within the Communist Party leadership.

1969-1985: 'normalization'

Political developments in Czechoslovakia from 1969 to the end of the communist period were dominated by the state of the Czechoslovak economy and the legacy of 1968. Thus, while Czech and Slovak leaders faced many of the same problems as leaders in other communist countries, their responses to these problems were influenced heavily by the end of the 1968 reform process and its economic and political repercussions.

The effort to roll back the clock to the pre-1968 period and return

Czechoslovakia once again to its position as the Soviet Union's most loyal ally intensified after the ouster of Dubček as head of the party and his replacement by Gustáv Husák in April 1969. A reflection of the growing influence of hardline elements within the Czechoslovak leadership and, perhaps, of the growing impatience of the Soviets with the actions of the leadership to that date, the change in top leaders was soon followed by a concerted effort to stamp out or reverse as many of the changes begun in the reform era as possible. This process, which became known as 'normalization,' occurred most quickly in the political and cultural areas, but it eventually affected economic policies as well.

In the political realm, 'normalization' included efforts to reassert the leading role of the Communist Party, the reinstitution of control of the media and other forms of information, massive personnel purges, and a change in the political formula. Explicitly disavowing the 'post-January course' of the party, the leadership took steps to reduce the influence of non-party groups and individuals in politics and restore party discipline. They also presided over a crackdown on independent groups and a cleansing of the Communist Party's membership. Dubček's supporters were removed from positions of influence in the party and elsewhere, to be replaced by people who had either opposed the reform or remained uninvolved. The impact of these changes on the composition of the Communist Party was heightened by the voluntary resignations of others who had been supporters of the reform.

Similar changes were made in the leaderships of the mass organizations, whose activities were redirected along more traditional lines, and in the universities and research institutes. The centers of intellectual life were particularly hard hit by the personnel changes, as many of the most capable authorities in many fields lost their positions. These changes, which are estimated to have involved approximately half a million people during the 1969-70 period (Kusin, 1982b, p. 29), were more far-reaching in the Czech Lands, where larger numbers of party officials and intellectuals had been involved in the democratizing aspects of the reform, than in Slovakia, where many of those who supported Dubček were concerned primarily with national issues. The personnel purges had long-term repercussions in Czechoslovakia, for they depleted the talent the post-reform leadership could draw on to formulate public policies in all areas of life. Thus, although the policy of relying more heavily on the input of experts and specialists in policy-making begun in the period leading up to the reform continued, the level of expertise and talent available to the leadership declined (see Kusin, 1971; Wolchik, 1983b; and Wolchik and Curry, 1984, for discussions of the role of these actors).

'Normalization' also involved a change in the political formula. The Husák leadership repudiated the earlier attempt to foster legitimacy and create genuine citizen support through opportunities for greater involvement by broader groups of people in the political process. Instead, it reverted to the strategy, much more common in communist countries, of gaining citizen compliance through a combination of material rewards and coercion (see Gitelman, 1970, pp. 235-64, for a discussion of these strategies).

This strategy proved to be successful in preventing any open manifestation of dissatisfaction in Czechoslovakia for almost a decade. At the mass level, improvements in the standard of living, including the greater availability of consumer durables and items previously considered luxuries, such as automobiles and summer cottages, as well as increases in social welfare benefits and their extension to previously uncovered groups of the population such as collective farmers, appeared to have bought the quiescence if not the support of much of the population. The impact of these measures was supplemented in Slovakia by the benefits, symbolic and otherwise, the Slovaks received from federalization as well as by the perceived increase in Slovak influence in Prague after Husák's elevation to the position of top party leader (see Wolchik, 1983a, pp. 249-70, and 1987, pp. 35-60).

The leadership relied on similar measures, as well as on the selective use of coercion, to neutralize any overt opposition by intellectuals during this period. More directly affected by the personnel purges and reinstitution of party control than other segments of the population, many Czech and Slovak intellectuals joined other citizens in pulling away from the political realm and retreating to private concerns (see Ulč, 1979, pp. 201-14). Once the personnel changes were accomplished and the policies of the reform era repudiated, the leadership also sought to co-opt those intellectuals who retained their positions in the universities, state and party bureaucracies, and cultural organizations by allowing them somewhat greater professional autonomy and increasing their role in decision-making in many areas (see Wolchik, 1983b, and Wolchik and Curry, 1984).

As the emergence of Charter 77 in January 1977 and events in 1988 and 1989 indicate, this strategy did not eliminate all organized opposition and dissent in Czechoslovakia. Despite persistent harassment of those who signed or served as spokespersons of the Charter, the group continued its activities. Encompassing ex-reformers from 1968 and dissidents from a variety of other perspectives, the Charter championed human rights from its inception. Charter spokespersons repeatedly called on Czech and Slovak leaders to adhere to international agreements guaranteeing human rights, as well as Czechoslovak law, and publicized violations of human rights. The Charter also came to serve as the focus of a growing and increasingly vigorous independent or 'second' culture and as an alternate source of information and views within the country (see Skilling, 1985, pp. 32-49; and 1981; Henecka, Janouch *et al.*, 1985; Havel, 1990; see also chapter 3).

Although the Charter was important as a symbol of hope and as a focus for non-conformist activity and thought, it did not pose a real threat to political stability in Czechoslovakia until the late 1980s. The persistent risk of reprisals for participation in Charter activities limited the number of people who were willing to support its activities openly. The Charter's impact was also limited by its social and ethnic composition and by the fact that, in contrast to the situation that emerged in Poland in the late 1970s and early 1980s, the Chartists were not successful in forging an alliance with broader groups in society, such as the workers, until external factors changed (see Connor, 1980, pp. 1-17, for an analysis of the dissident-worker alliance in Poland).

However, as the events of 1989 were to show, the Charter's activities helped to undermine support for the communist regime. While a relatively small number of people (approximately 2,500 by late 1987) signed the Charter, its influence on perceptions of public issues and thinking in Czechoslovakia was much wider. Charter activists played pivotal roles in the Civic Forum, the organization that emerged to lead the revolution in November 1989, and in the non-communist government that emerged in December 1989.

Important as the opposition would prove to be, the main threat to the persistence of the political formula employed by the Husák leadership and political stability in the late communist period came from the results of 'normalization' on economic performance and from developments outside the country. Chief among the latter was the selection of Mikhail Gorbachev as head of the Communist Party of the Soviet Union.

1985-1989: Gorbachev and the fall of the communist system

Gorbachev's rise to power in the Soviet Union at first had very little impact on developments in Czechoslovakia. Although Gustáv Husák and other leaders gave lip-service to the positive nature of the changes being proposed in the Soviet Union, they were noticeably less enthusiastic about following the Soviet example than usual. They were particularly hesitant to enact any changes that would signal the dawning of an era of *glasnost* in Czechoslovakia (see Wolchik, 1989a; and Sobell, 1988 for further discussion).

In the political realm, *glasnost* at first had few echoes in Czechoslovakia. Scattered incidents, such as the lenient sentences given the leaders of the Jazz Section who were tried and convicted for their independent cultural activities, and the fact that Charter 77 activists were allowed to assemble at the grave of one of the movement's founders, Dr. Jan Patočka, without harassment in March 1987, indicated that there was some degree of division among the leadership regarding how to treat dissent. They also raised hopes that *glasnost* in the Soviet Union would lead to a similar loosening of the reins in the political sphere in Czechoslovakia. Charter activists publicly supported Gorbachev's policies and called on Czech and Slovak officials to emulate them. They also issued statements which evaluated conditions in the country as ripe for increased activity on the part of the Charter in 1987. Developments in the Soviet Union in 1987 also encouraged a group of former communist officials removed after 1968 to make a statement expressing their desire and willingness to join the current leadership in efforts to restructure the economy and to democratize society.

However, as later reprisals against religious believers and other dissidents illustrated, the leadership was not willing to allow any real discussion of political reform. Clearly afraid of a repetition of the events leading up to 1968, when economic reforms spilled over into the political realm, the Husák leadership continued to set strict limits on political debate. Although control over the press loosened somewhat, there were still many subjects that could not be openly discussed. There was also relatively little turnover of personnel in the Communist Party or the state until mid-1988, despite the lip-service given to the need to eliminate corruption and rejuvenate party cadres at all levels.

The first area in which Gorbachev's policies in the Soviet Union had an impact in Czechoslovakia was the economy. Prodded by continuing poor economic performance, and Soviet emphasis on *perestroika*, the Husák leadership adopted a new approach to economic change at the January 1987 meeting of the Central Committee of the Communist Party. As chapter 4 will discuss further, the measures adopted by the party leadership endorsed substantial changes in the organization and management of the economy. Central measures of the reform were to include a sizeable reduction in the role and size of the central planning apparatus, with a corresponding increase in the powers of enterprises; greater worker input in the selection of managers; greater use of the profit motive and other incentives for both workers and managers; and price reform as well as change in the organization of the foreign trade system. The approach to economic issues articulated by the leadership in 1987 thus differed substantially from that which informed efforts to improve economic performance in the early 1980s. In contrast to these efforts, which attempted to make the centralized planning system work more efficiently, the changes proposed in 1987 were similar in many respects to those which economists who eventually came to support the political reform of 1968 formulated in the early 1960s (see chapter 4 for further information).

The similarity between the economic reforms proposed in the 1960s and in 1987 was acknowledged by the leadership only indirectly, but it was reflected in discussions of the 1968 experience. Leaders such as Štrougal continued to condemn the political elements of the 1968 events. However, in contrast to the period from 1969 to 1987, political leaders and experts alike talked openly again of the need for substantial, rather than minor, change in the economic organization of society, and reform was once again a permitted term.

As chapter 4 will discuss in greater detail, the general nature of the economic reform measures adopted in 1987 and the gradual time-table envisioned for their implementation raised the possibility that opponents of change would sabotage any significant reform before it was put into practice. There were also numerous problems with the nature of the proposed reforms themselves. Many economists expressed serious doubts concerning their efficacy (see Dyba, 1989a and 1989b; Dyba and Kouba, 1989; and Myant, 1989, pp. 250-2). In the event, few of the proposed changes had been implemented prior to the end of the communist system.

The policy of caution adopted by the Husák leadership was continued to a large extent by that of his successor, Miloš Jakeš. Chosen to replace Husák as head of the Communist Party in December 1987, Jakeš did not depart in any dramatic ways from the policies of his predecessor. Long rumored to be the most likely candidate to succeed Husák and responsible for economic affairs for the decade prior to his selection as top leader, Jakeš appeared to be somewhat more supportive of the idea of economic change than Husák. However, his experience in overseeing the verification campaign within the party that accompanied 'normalization' indicated that he would not be likely to support any far-reaching changes in the political realm.

Although there was no parallel in Czechoslovakia to the political developments that took place in the Soviet Union after Gorbachev's rise to power, the late 1980s witnessed a number of important political changes. The collapse of the communist system in Czechoslovakia in November 1989 was precipitated by events outside the country. The negotiated end of communism in Poland and Hungary and the fall of the hardline Honecker regime in East

Germany after mass protests were important catalysts in bringing about the end of communism in Czechoslovakia. But, while these developments, which ultimately can be traced to change in Gorbachev's policies toward Central and Eastern Europe, were critical, the events of 1989 reflected the underlying crises and widespread dissatisfaction of the people of Czechoslovakia with the communist system. They also were conditioned by important changes that occurred at both the mass and elite level between 1987 and 1989. Overshadowed by the more dramatic events taking place in the countries bordering Czechoslovakia, these changes were nonetheless significant in light of the political stagnation of much of the post-1968 period.

They also foreshadowed the dramatic end of the communist regime in 1989 and are crucial to understanding political developments since that time. The first, and in many ways most important of these changes was evident in the new willingness of the population to challenge the regime by organizing independent groups and taking part in unauthorized demonstrations and protests (see chapter 2). In the first area, the late 1980s saw the emergence of nearly a dozen new independent groups. Although their numbers did not begin to approach those of the informal groups that appeared in the Soviet Union in the late 1980s or the estimated 1,200 such groups that emerged in Hungary in the last two years of communist rule, these groups represented a significant increase in unofficial associations in Czechoslovakia. There was a certain degree of overlap in the membership of the new groups, and most shared a common commitment to free expression and human rights. However, the groups differed in their emphases. Several, including the Helsinki Committee, founded in May 1988, and the Initiative for Social Defense, founded in October 1988, built on the tradition of the Charter and VONS (the Committee for the Defense of the Unjustly Persecuted), and focused largely on human rights issues.

Others, including the Movement for Civil Liberties, founded in October 1988, and the Democratic Initiative, founded in 1987 with a reported 200 members, were more directly political and had programs that called for political pluralism, intellectual and religious freedom, and democracy. Still others, such as the Association of

Friends of the USA, founded in March 1988, the T.G. Masaryk Association, founded in October 1988 to spread knowledge about the political, social, and cultural legacy of the founder and president of the first republic, Tomáš G. Masaryk, and the Masaryk Society, founded in early 1988 to foster scholarly research in the spirit of Masaryk's inquiries, drew their inspiration from political philosophies and aspects of Czechoslovakia's history that challenged the existing order.

Reform communists, including Jiří Hájek, who was Foreign Minister during the Dubček era, and other officials who played key roles in 1968 also formed an independent group, *Obroda*, in 1989. Supportive of Gorbachev and his efforts to promote political and economic change in the Soviet Union, members of this group announced their willingness to work with the Jakeš regime to move ahead once again with reforms along the lines of those attempted in 1968 (see Pehe, 1988).

In addition to these groups, many of whose leaders were Chartists or other long-time dissidents, several independent groups emerged in 1988 and 1989 among young people. The first of these, the Czech Children, was founded in May 1988. Although its founding manifesto was at first considered a prank, members of the group played a key role in organizing mass demonstrations to commemorate important anniversaries in 1988 and 1989. Young people also created the Independent Peace Association, founded in April 1988 to work for recognition of the right to conscientious objection and the demilitarization of society, and the John Lennon Club, devoted to preserving the memory of the assassinated Beatle. A number of other groups also emerged during this period, including a group representing the interests of the Hungarian minority, an independent ecological group, and several religious groups, including the Association of Believing Catholic Laymen, a group whose twelve-point program included demands for religious freedom (see Pehe, 1988).

The increase in the number of dissident groups in the late 1980s was paralleled by an increase in the number and size of independently organized mass demonstrations and protests. These included a demonstration in March 1988 in Bratislava demanding religious freedom, and pilgrimages in Slovakia and Moravia that began in the mid-1980s and came to include an estimated 700,000 participants by 1989.

The year 1988 also saw the re-emergence of mass demonstrations focused on openly political issues. The first of these was the demonstration on the twentieth anniversary of the 1968 invasion in Prague that drew an estimated 100,000 people, despite the efforts of the authorities to prevent it. This demonstration, which grew spontaneously from the efforts of a small number of dissidents, was followed by a commemoration of the founding of the First Republic in October 1988, which had approximately 5,000 participants, and an independently organized peace demonstration in December that the authorities eventually permitted. Further demonstrations in Prague on the twentieth anniversary of the suicide of Jan Palach followed. Harshly broken up by the police, the January 16, 1989 commemoration was followed by several days of demonstrations that led to the arrest and criminal trial of approximately 40 leading dissidents, including Václav Havel and several of the leaders of the new youth groups that emerged in 1989 (see Vladislav and Prečan, 1990).

To a certain extent, these activities were a continuation of the tradition of dissent evident in Czechoslovakia after the founding of the Charter. However, there were several aspects of the resurgence of dissent in the late 1980s that were new. These, in turn, presaged the dramatic events of November 1989. The first, and in many ways most significant, of these was the role that young people played in founding new dissident groups and organizing public demonstrations that challenged the regime. This awakening of political interest in a generation many observers thought largely lost to political concerns surprised the leadership in Czechoslovakia, as well as many other citizens.

Another significant aspect of the activities of dissidents in the last years of communist rule was the relatively limited appeal of the ideals of 1968 or of reform communism. Aside from the *Obroda* group and certain members of the Charter who had been active in the reforms of 1968, interest in resurrecting the effort to create 'socialism with a human face' was very limited. Certain dissident groups endorsed *perestroika* and *glasnost* as goals, and many undoubtedly hoped that Gorbachev's policies in the Soviet Union would lead to change in Czechoslovakia. However, most dissidents had gone beyond these experiences as goals and called instead for a return to 'real', i.e. Western-style, democracy. The content of this concept was seldom spelled out very explicitly in the programs of these groups, which were still in the process of defining themselves when the communist system was overthrown in 1989. However, many of their manifestos and documents called for the freedoms and civil liberties found in Western democracies. Many of these groups, then, clearly found greater inspiration in Czechoslovakia's own democratic past than in foreign experiments with socialism.

In 1988 and 1989 opposition also began to move out of the intellectual ghetto to which it was confined for much of the last twenty years of communist rule. Although most of the leaders of the newly organized groups and the organizers of the demonstrations were intellectuals or students, ordinary citizens, including blue-collar workers, became more involved. The letters of support workers sent to Václav Havel after his arrest and trial in early 1989, as well as the numbers of workers who joined the August and October 1988, and January 1989 demonstrations indicated that the gap between the activities of the dissidents and the concerns of ordinary citizens had narrowed somewhat. The number of new organizations with signatories and members in Moravia and Slovakia, as well as in Bohemia, reflected the increased willingness of members of other ethnic groups in addition to the Czechs to be more open in expressing their dissatisfactions and desires for change.

A final change in the nature of dissent highlighted by the events of 1988 and 1989 was the spread of non-conformity to the official world itself. Contacts between dissidents and intellectuals who were part of the official establishment existed throughout the post-1968 period. However, until the late 1980s, there was little reflection of these contacts in the actions of those who remained in the good graces of the regime. The communist leadership thus was able to count on those in official positions to support its condemnations of dissident activities. As the letters of support and petitions circulated in the wake of Václav Havel's trial in February 1989 illustrated, by early 1989, many of the country's leading artistic and cultural figures were willing to take a public stand in defense of opposition activists. Many also were among the 30,000 individuals who signed the manifesto 'Several Sentences' that called for political freedom and an end to censorship in the summer of 1989 (see 'Několik vět,' 1989).

These developments were paralleled by the awakening of intellectuals in the official world in the late 1980s. This process was to some extent similar to the process of theoretical renewal and ferment among Czechoslovakia's intellectuals in the early to mid-1960s that preceded the political reforms of 1968. Thus, particularly after 1987, social scientists and creative intellectuals began to challenge accepted doctrines in many areas; they also began to voice their criticism of official policies more openly. Economists and other specialists centered in the Institute for Forecasting headed by Valtr Komárek, Deputy Prime Minister in the non-communist government formed in late 1989, for example, openly criticized many aspects of the new program of economic reform the government adopted in January 1987 (see Komárek, 1988a, 1988b, and 1989, for examples of these views). Members of the Institute and others also began to debate other previously untouchable issues, such as the need for a reorientation of the country's external trade patterns, the role of the world market in socialist countries, and the need for steps to legalize certain aspects of the unofficial economy (see chapter 4; see also Dyba, 1989a, and 1989b; Komárek, 1988a, 1988b, and 1989; Reboun, 1988; and Myant, 1989, ch. 10).

Creative intellectuals also began to take a more critical stance toward official cultural policies. Thus, leaders of the official Writers' Union decided in October 1988 to begin rehabilitating some of the many writers whose works were banned after 1968; they also began discussing the need to heal the schism between official and *samizdat*, or unofficial, literature and reintegrate works by writers living abroad into the mainstream of Czech and Slovak culture. These discussions, which continued in the first half of 1989, were followed by plans to publish the works of certain previously unmentionable and unpublishable authors (see chapter 5). Similar trends were evident in the world of film and in music, where several previously banned artists were allowed to perform in 1989. In Slovakia the numbers of people still in the official world who engaged in non-conformist activities increased, and many began to express their disagreement with the regime's policies more openly. Thus, there were numerous signs in 1988 and 1989 that many of the country's intellectuals, perhaps emboldened by developments in the Soviet Union and elsewhere in the region, were no longer willing simply to follow the lead of the political leadership. In contrast to the situation in the 1960s, however, when reformist intellectuals were supported by reformist elements within the leadership of the Communist Party, in the late 1980s, they received little open support from the few members of the party leadership willing to admit the need for change.

As chapter 2 will discuss in greater detail, there were also major changes in 1988 and 1989 within the leadership of the Communist Party. Although there were few personnel changes in the Czecho-slovak party in the early Gorbachev period, there was substantial turnover in top party bodies in 1988 and 1989. The process of change began in December 1987, when Miloš Jakeš, who became a member of the Presidium in 1981 but had a career in the party apparatus dating back to the 1960s, replaced Gustáv Husák as First Secretary of the party.

Jakeš' elevation was followed by the removal of many of the full members of the Presidium. As will be discussed in chapter 2 in greater detail, these changes were reflected in a decline of the average tenure in office and ages of the leadership. The career patterns and social backgrounds of the new members did not differ to a great degree from those of their predecessors. However, the new members of the party leadership were younger and, therefore, less personally responsible for and committed to the policies of 'normalization.' They were also less experienced than their predecessors. The turnover at the top also increased the divisions within the leadership. In addition to those who were elevated to their positions in the late 1980s, there was a core of holdovers from the Husák era, many of whom had been in power since the early 1960s (see Wolchik, 1991b; and chapter 2, for further information).

The impact of these divisions at the top was reflected in regime response to the growing challenge from below. Despite the heavy-handed reaction to the demonstrations in January 1989, which appears to have been calculated to increase and clarify the cost of dissent, especially for the generation of young activists who were not traumatized by the end of the 1968 reform, the pattern of the leadership's response to dissent changed to some degree. Thus, rather than automatically opting for swift and harsh repression of all non-conformity as the leadership had for the past twenty years, the Jakeš leadership demonstrated greater vacillation in its response to dissent in the late 1980s. Reflected in the permission granted to Alexander Dubček to travel to Italy to accept an honorary degree, the regime's more lenient attitude was also evident in its toleration and eventual sponsorship of a commemorative concert by the John Lennon Club in December 1988. It was also reflected in the discussions that the leadership held with members of the Independent Peace Association regarding conscientious objection in 1988 (see Kusin, 1989; and Pehe, 1989c, for brief analyses of these actions).

However, the regime did not hesitate to revert to its earlier tactics on occasion. The reprisals against participants in the August 1988 demonstration; the preventive detention of many known dissidents in October 1988 before anticipated demonstrations and the jailing of certain people who participated in those events; and the harsh response to the January 1989 commemoration of the death of Jan Palach all demonstrated that the Jakeš leadership had not foresworn repression as a tool, despite the fact that such actions were in stark contrast to the treatment of dissidents in Hungary, Poland, and the Soviet Union at the time.

Thus, although political developments in Czechoslovakia in the late communist period were not as dramatic as those in Hungary or Poland, changes at both the mass and elite levels in the late 1980s had undermined the stability of the system. Coupled with the ongoing economic crisis, these changes limited the capacity of the communist leadership to deal with increasing challenges from within and outside the country.

These developments had an important impact on the events of November 1989 and their aftermath. In contrast to the situation in Poland and Hungary, where reformists within the party leadership negotiated the end of communist rule in discussions with the opposition over a period of several months, the communist system fell in the space of 23 days in Czechoslovakia. The use of force against peaceful student demonstrators on November 17, 1989 was followed by a wave of mass demonstrations. Angered by the brutality of the police attack and emboldened by the collapse of the Honecker regime in East Germany, hundreds of thousands of citizens took to the streets to demand political change. As it attempted to deal with the spread of protests, the Jakeš leadership was hampered by its internal divisions and inexperience. Although certain individuals, including Ladislav Adamec, who replaced L'ubomir Štrougal as Premier in 1988, attempted to serve as mediators, the Communist Party's options were limited by the fact that, in contrast to the situations in Hungary and Poland, where communist reformists helped ease the transition to multiparty rule, there had been no clearly identifiable reformist faction in the leadership in Czechoslovakia for over 20 years. Unable to regain the initiative from the opposition once it became clear that Soviet forces could no longer be counted upon, the party leadership quickly acceded to the main demands of the opposition, including the end of one-party rule (see Halada and Ryvola, 1990; Birgus, 1990; *Nežna revolúcia*, 1989; Ash, 1990; Luers, 1990; Holubec, 1989; and Wolchik, 1990b).

When the police attack on student demonstrators galvanized the nation in November 1989, the links that had been forged between well-known dissident activists, student leaders, and critical intellectuals in the official world allowed them to organize quickly to direct the growing demonstrations and use the momentum generated to press for the end of the communist system. The umbrella organizations that emerged to negotiate with the government, Civic Forum (*Občanské forum*) in the Czech Lands and Public Against Violence (*Verejnost' proti nasiliu*) in Slovakia, had their roots in the opposition movement that had developed over the preceding decades. However, opposition leaders and activists were also taken by surprise at the speed with which the old system fell and by the extent of the changes they were able to achieve.

The transition to democracy and the market

Although Czechoslovakia lagged behind some of its Central European neighbors in challenging the communist system, once the process of change began, the old system was swept away very quickly. The 'Velvet Revolution,' as the mass demonstrations that brought down the communist system came to be called, led to the resignation of Jakeš and the rest of the Communist Party leadership, the renunciation of the party's leading role, and the formation of the country's first non-communist government in 41 years. The victory of the revolution was capped by the election of dissident playwright Václav Havel as President of the Republic in late December 1989. Because the old system collapsed so quickly, opposition activists had to take responsibility almost immediately for running the government as well as instituting fundamental political and economic reforms. The non-communist Government of National Understanding formed in late 1989 thus began the arduous process of restoring multiparty democracy, recreating a market economy, and reorienting the country's external relations.

Czechoslovakia's new leaders face many of the same political and economic problems that confront other post-communist leaders. In the political realm they must re-establish the rule of law; find new leaders to replace old officials; reform old institutions and establish new ones; deal with the remnants of the Communist Party's power and the legacy of the communist period on popular values and expectations; and find a way of channeling popular desires for change into coherent political directions and policy orientations. They must reshape the structure of the country to satisfy the national aspirations of Czechs, Slovaks, and other national groups and deal with the accumulated social, environmental, and other problems that are the result of over 40 years of communist rule. They must also deal with the economic legacy of communism. Political changes have thus been accompanied by steps to recreate a market economy and reorient the country's external economic relationships. The country's new leaders have also reasserted Czechoslovakia's independence in foreign policy.

As chapter 2 will discuss, the end of the Communist Party's

monopoly of power was followed by a rapid repluralization of Czechoslovakia's associational and political life. The unified official mass organizations have been replaced by a wide variety of interest groups, charitable, patriotic, religious, and professional organizations, and independent unions.

The period between November 1989 and June 1990 also saw the proliferation of political parties. As chapter 2 will discuss in greater detail, over 60 political parties and non-party political groupings were registered by late February 1990, and 23 fulfilled the conditions necessary to participate in the June 8 and 9 elections. These included the Communist Party and the two minor parties, the Czechoslovak Socialist Party and the Czechoslovak People's Party, which had been allowed to exist under the control of the Communist Party during the communist period, and asserted their independence after November 1989. A number of parties with roots in the interwar period; nationalist parties, such as the Slovak National Party, and the Movement for Self-Governing Democracy— Association for Moravia and Silesia; and political groupings and citizen initiatives formed around new issues, such as Civic Forum and Public Against Violence also competed in the elections (see 'Czechoslovakia Parliamentary Elections,' 1990; and *Jak a koho volit?*, 1990, for a brief summary of the platforms of the individual parties).

Many of these parties were winnowed out, at least for the near future, by the results of the June 1990 elections which resulted in a Civic Forum-Public Against Violence victory at the federal level. However, a number of other parties continue to be important political actors at present (see chapter 2).

Civic Forum received 50.0 percent of the votes to the House of Nations and 53.2 percent of the vote to the House of the People of the Federal Assembly. With 49.5 percent of the vote, Civic Forum also emerged as the dominant force in the Czech Republic. Its primary election rival in the Czech Lands, a union of Christian Democratic parties, was badly hurt at the end of the campaign by charges that Josef Bartončík, leader of its main political force, the Czechoslovak People's Party, had collaborated with the secret police and received only 8.7 percent of the vote to the Federal Assembly.

In Slovakia, Public Against Violence did better than expected in the elections to federal bodies, winning 33 percent of the vote for the House of the People and 37 percent for the House of Nations. However, the Christian Democratic Party, led by former dissident and, as of April 1991, Prime Minister of Slovakia Ján Čarnogurský, remained a strong political force in Slovakia, where it won 19 percent of the vote to the House of the People and 17 percent to the House of Nations. It received approximately the same proportion of the vote for the Slovak National Council (19.2 percent), compared to 29.3 percent for Public Against Violence ('Výsledky voleb,' 1990, p. 4).

The Communist Party won 13 percent of the vote to the Federal Assembly and emerged as the second strongest party in the Czech Lands and the third in Slovakia. Several nationalist parties also elected representatives to the Federal Assembly in the June 1990 elections. In the Czech Lands, the Movement for Self-Governing Democracy—Association for Moravia and Silesia won 7.9 percent of the votes to the House of the People and 9.1 percent to the House of Nations. In Slovakia the separatist Slovak National Party, formed in April 1990, won 13 percent and 11 percent of the vote. Neither the Social Democrats nor the Greens received enough votes to seat deputies (see 'Výsledky voleb,' 1990; and Boguszak and Rak, 1990a, Table 2).

The June elections thus validated the policies adopted by the first post-communist government and legitimized the new government that was formed afterwards. At the same time, because the elections took place while the electoral system, as well as the broader political environment, were themselves still very much in flux, their results are not necessarily predictive of future political alignments.

The dominant political forces in both the Czech Lands and Slovakia, Civic Forum and Public Against Violence, provided umbrellas for a wide variety of groups and individuals with varying political views and policy preferences in the first year of post-communist rule. Several groups that originally were part of these organizations broke away in the second half of 1990, as political views and policy preferences became more differentiated. The election of Václav Klaus as Chairman of Civic Forum in October

1991 and the decision to transform the Forum into a more hierarchically organized political party taken at its January 1991 congress were followed in February by a split between the two wings within the organization. The two groups, the Civic Democratic Party headed by Klaus and the Civic Movement, whose spokesperson is Pavel Rychetský, are united by a loose coordinating body in order to preserve the governing coalition and maintain rights to Forum's assets. Serious divisions also emerged within Public Against Violence in early 1991. Supporters of Vladimír Mečiar, then Premier of Slovakia, created a new organization, Platform for a Democratic Slovakia, in early March 1991. Conflict between the two factions of PAV concerning Czech-Slovak relations and a number of Mečiar's actions, including allegations that he met secretly with Soviet generals during a trip to the USSR in mid-March 1991, was one of the factors that led to the removal of Mečiar and several other members of the Slovak government on April 23, 1991.

Voter preferences and party identification are also quite fluid at present. The results of the local elections held in November 1990 illustrate these tendencies. Civic Forum retained its dominant position in the Czech Lands, with 35.4 percent of the vote. However, in Slovakia, Public Against Violence ran second, with 20.4 percent of the vote, to the Christian Democratic Movement, which received 27.4 percent of the vote. The Slovak National Party, which public opinion polls indicated was the strongest party in Slovakia during much of the fall of 1990, received a mere 3.2 percent of the vote in November (see '1. KDH, 2. VPN,' 1990). The fact that support for the Communist Party increased in the Czech Lands (to 17.4 percent) and slightly (to 14 percent) in Slovakia is a further indication of the volatility of voter preferences at present.

Although it is unlikely that the Communist Party will play any significant role in Czechoslovak politics in the near future given the dramatic rejection of communism and socialism in all forms evident in the events of 1989 and 1990, it may continue to play a small role in a democratic Czechoslovakia. The 13 percent of the vote the party received in the June 1990 elections is very similar to its levels of support in the interwar period. Support for the party appears to be drawn largely from older people as well as from those so compromised by their roles in the old system that they have nowhere else to go politically. The party may also gain support as a result of fear of change and the negative impact of economic reforms in the future. But, at present, it is not a viable alternative to the government in power, and thus cannot serve as a responsible opposition. The task of creating stable political organizations and orientations, then, remains to be completed in Czechoslovakia as elsewhere in the region.

As they seek to build new institutions and create or resurrect values that will support democratic rule, Czechoslovakia's new leaders continue to struggle with the issue of how to prevent the Communist Party from translating its previous advantages into undue power in the new system. Popular resentment over the large number of party members and former party members who remained in important economic and political positions at the local level was reflected in President Havel's call in August 1990 to rout old 'mafias' in a number of areas.

The new leadership in Czechoslovakia stated at the outset that there would be no wholesale purges in the governmental or economic sectors. Labor legislation that in effect required that workers and employees receive five months' notice before they were fired and the difficulty of finding qualified replacements further slowed personnel changes. As a result, in many areas new officials comprise only a thin layer at the top of organizations with largely unchanged staffs. Efforts to reform the bureaucracy thus must include an attempt to reshape the work habits and expectations of employees in these institutions in such a way as to overcome the legacy of their earlier experiences, as well as more extensive personnel changes.

Czechoslovakia's new leaders also are attempting to counter the impact of the communist period on the political attitudes and values of the population. As in other countries in the region, Czech and Slovak leaders and citizens have turned to their pre-communist past as they replace communist political institutions and attempt to create new political values and symbols. As discussed earlier in this chapter, in Czechoslovakia the dominant value system during the interwar period was democratic. However, as chapter 2 will discuss in greater detail, citizens' political values and attitudes continue to reflect the experiences of communist rule.

The democratically elected government of Czechoslovakia is also faced with the economic, as well as political, legacy of 40 years of communist rule. The impact of communist policies on the country's economy and the difficulty of the transition to a market economy were expressed succinctly in President Havel's comment in his 1991 New Year's Day address that what they thought was a 'neglected house a year ago is, in fact, a ruin' (Havel, 1991, p. 13). Although there is a general consensus on the need to move toward a market economy, important divisions have occurred among political leaders and experts concerning the pace and extent of economic change that should be enacted. These differences were resolved to some degree by the decision to move ahead more rapidly to liberalize prices, encourage demonopolization, and privatize the economy.

As chapter 4 will discuss in greater detail, a series of laws dealing with private ownership and private enterprises, the running of state enterprises, the use of land, joint ventures, foreign exchange, joint stock companies, and foreign trade was adopted in April 1990 to lay the basis for the return to a market economy. Under pressure from numerous political groups, including the Civic Forum, the government adopted a program for economic reform prior to the June elections that was a victory for those, including Finance Minister Václav Klaus, who advocated a rapid, radical reform. The proposal for economic reform submitted by the Federal, Czech, and Slovak governments to the Federal Assembly in early September 1990 reflected this perspective. Its key elements are privatization of the economy by use of domestic and foreign capital; a reduction of subsidies and deregulation of prices; and internal convertibility of the crown. Other aspects of the general program of reform adopted by the government include a restrictive monetary policy and institutional changes designed to simplify the economic ministries and planning apparatus and increase the responsibility of enterprise management (Dlouhý, 1990, p. 3).

Plans for economic reform also include a substantial reorientation of the country's external economic relations away from the very high level of dependence on the Soviet Union and other CMEA countries toward the West (see chapter 4). As chapter 5 will discuss in greater detail, in 1990 Czechoslovakia rejoined the IMF and World Bank and was granted most-favored-nation status by the United States. The positive responses and promised aid from democratic governments in Western Europe and the United States have been coupled with increased interest on the part of Western investors. This approach is part of the broader shift in the foreign policy commitments involved in reasserting the country's sovereignty and rejoining Europe. At the same time, Czech and Slovak leaders have had to deal with the negative economic impact of changes in Soviet economic policies toward the region and the disruption of economic relations with many other trading partners, including the former GDR, as well as with the impact of the Gulf Crisis (see 'Suroviny za zboží,' 1990, pp. 1, 8).

The end of censorship and control of the political agenda by the Communist Party has led to the emergence of new political issues and problems, and the re-emergence in new forms of old issues that could not be dealt with openly during the communist period. These include environmental issues, crime, and the need to reorient policy in almost all areas of life to remove the distortions created by communist rule (see for example, 'Kde se v teto,' 1990, p. 2; 'Výzva československé vláde,' 1990, p. 2; 'Konec mnoha fam,' 1990, pp. 1, 2. See also Merhaut, 1990, p. 6; Pospišílová, 1990, pp. 1, 2; Urban, 1990, pp. 26-7; and Mrazová and Kučerová, 1990, p. 4).

Ethnic conflicts are among the most important of these issues. As chapter 3 will discuss in greater detail, ethnic conflicts pervade discussion of most of the critical issues facing the current government. Evident in the prolonged debate over the name of the country, which was changed twice in the space of a month in early 1990, Czech-Slovak conflict increased throughout 1990. Ethnic tensions continue to complicate plans for economic reform as well as the process of constitutional revision now under way. The compromise concerning power sharing between federal and republic governments reached in December 1990 has been followed by renewed acrimony between Czechs and Slovaks over constitutional issues. Members of other ethnic groups, such as the Hungarians, Moravians, Ukrainians, and gypsies, have also organized around ethnic issues and are demanding greater rights (see Drábek, 1990, p. 1; Host'ovečka, 1990, p. 3; and Samková, 1990, p. 16). Moravian nationalism in particular emerged as a significant political force in early 1991, when thousands of Moravians protested to highlight their call for a federation that would recognize Moravian interests. The Movement for Self-Governing Democracy—Association for Moravia and Silesia withdrew from its coalition with Civic Forum in the Czech National Council in early 1991 and its deputies temporarily stopped participating in the work of the Council. As in the interwar period, then, the main threat to political stability and the success of Czechoslovakia's transition to democracy is likely to come not from anti-democratic forces, but from ethnic conflict.

Conclusion

As the preceding pages have illustrated, Czechoslovakia's history in the twentieth century has reflected the impact of its particular national traditions, social and ethnic composition, and level of economic development as well as the impact of events and forces originating beyond its borders. It has also been characterized by important disruptions and changes of regime that have led to discontinuities in the political experiences and values of the country's citizens. As they enter the last decade of the twentieth century, citizens of Czechoslovakia are once again experiencing a fundamental reordering of their economic, social and political institutions. As in the past, the success of the effort to deal with the legacy of communist rule and create new economic, political and social institutions will be determined largely by the actions of Czechoslovakia's citizens and leaders. The outcome of Czechoslovakia's transition to democracy will also depend on the impact of external developments. As has been the case throughout the country's history, the country's political and economic life will also be influenced by developments in the broader international environment and the actions of its neighbors. The impact of the Gulf crisis in 1990 and the ensuing war in 1991 and the economic dislocations that have resulted from the decrease in Czechoslovakia's trade with other formerly communist countries illustrate the vulnerability of Czechoslovakia to disruptions arising from external sources. These changes have been balanced to some extent by the positive responses and aid from other democratic European countries and the United States. Western aid, investment, and responsiveness to Czechoslovakia's initiatives to rejoin Europe and take its place as an independent actor in world affairs will continue to be important to the success of the transformation now under way. Given the high level of the country's economic ties to the Soviet Union and the presence of limited numbers of Soviet troops in Czechoslovakia and in neighboring countries, developments in the Soviet Union will also continue to have important repercussions in Czechoslovakia.

2 Politics and policy-making

Political life in Czechoslovakia has changed dramatically since November 1989. As in other Central and East European countries, the country's political organization and political values are in flux at present. The end of the Communist Party's monopoly of power has been followed by a rapid repluralization of political life, the emergence of new political leaders, and new patterns of mass-elite relations. There have also been important changes in political values and attitudes toward politics.

The end of the Communist Party's dominance has also had a major impact on the policy-making process. The end of censorship and the proliferation of new avenues of expression and channels of political action mean that many issues that could not be openly discussed and conflicts that were artificially submerged during the communist period have become legitimate topics of public discussion and political debate. New public policy issues arising from the political and economic changes under way have also emerged.

As political developments since November 1989 and the results of the June 1990 elections indicate, the initial stages of the transition to democracy proceeded very quickly and smoothly in Czechoslovakia. However, the process of recreating democracy in political life has not been completed. As noted in chapter 1, Czech and Slovak leaders face many of the same tasks as leaders in other formerly communist countries in the region (see also Wolchik, 1990a, 1991a, and 1991b). Political life also continues to be colored by the impact of four decades of communist rule (see Wolchik, 1990b).

From 1948 to 1989, political life in Czechoslovakia was conditioned by the fact that the country's political values and political structures were those associated with communist regimes. Thus, Marxism-Leninism was the official ideology, and the political system was effectively a one-party system in which the Communist Party was clearly the dominant political force. These features, which differed considerably from the value systems and institutions of democratic states, as well as from those that existed in Czecho-slovakia in the pre-communist period, determined the channels available to citizens to take part in politics; the prerogatives and responsibilities of political leaders; the legitimacy and utility of various tools of influence; and the way in which political issues got onto the political agenda. They also influenced the goals and values of political leaders and citizens and the way in which policies were made and implemented. At the same time, however, political life and political culture during the communist period continued to be deter-mined to some degree by Czechoslovakia's pre-communist history, culture, and level of economic development. The impact of these factors was evident in part in the political attitudes and values of the population. It was also reflected in the movements for change that arose when external conditions allowed national elements to come to the fore, as in 1968 and the late 1980s.

As the country's new leaders seek to create new institutions and legal codes appropriate to democratic political life and channel the massive desire for change evident in the events of late 1989 into viable political orientations and policy alternatives, they must also deal with the remnants of communist rule. These are evident in the political structure and political values of the country. The legacy of communist rule is also reflected in many of the political issues that face the current government.

The political framework: political structure

From February 1948 until late 1989, Czechoslovakia's state structure was characterized by the parallel government and party hierarchies that typically have been found in communist states. Thus, while the government formally wielded supreme power within the country, it was actually the corresponding Communist Party body at each level that was the more effective or powerful body. Differences in the functions and importance of government and party organs were evident in the length and frequency of their meetings and the timing of their consideration of topics, as well as in the social backgrounds and career patterns of officials in each group.

The renunciation of the leading role of the Communist Party that resulted from the November 1989 revolution has been followed by major changes in the organization of political life and the role of particular political institutions. One of the central features of these changes has been the rapid repluralization of political life. The role of the communist and other political parties as well as the functions of state, or governmental, bodies have also been redefined. To a certain extent, these changes are still in the process of being completed. The main task of the present national legislature, whose members were elected in June 1990 for a two-year term, is the drafting of a new constitution. The laws that govern the relationship of federal to republic and both to lower-level governments are likely to be revised further. The party system, which changed markedly between November 1989 and the June 1990 elections, is also still evolving. The institutional structures that will shape political life and safeguard democracy, then, are still in the process of being re-created. However, the fall of the communist system has led to a vast expansion in avenues of political expression and marked changes in the opportunities available to citizens to participate in politics. These changes have had a major impact on the way in which policies are made and implemented in all areas. Although the new system is not yet complete, the main outlines of the post-communist political order are in place.

The government

The formal or governmental power structure underwent a number of changes during the communist period in Czechoslovakia. The Constitution of 1948, enacted to replace the Košice Government Program which was the basis of the government from 1945 to 1948, reflected the new political realities in Czechoslovakia after February of that year. However, although many of the provisions of the Ninth of May Constitution, as it came to be known, echoed those found in the constitutions of the Soviet Union and other Central and East European countries at the time, it also retained certain features of Czechoslovakia's previous democratic constitution. In the Constitution adopted in 1960 to herald Czechoslovakia's passage to socialism, these distinctive features were replaced by institutional relationships and language closer to those of the country's socialist neighbors (see Taborsky, 1961, pp. 167-84). Although it was changed considerably by amendments, most notably those introducing and modifying federalization in 1969 and 1971, the 1960 Constitution remained the basis of government for the rest of the communist period. A new constitution was being prepared in Czechoslovakia prior to the ouster of the communist system in 1989. The new version of this document, which is currently being prepared and is scheduled to go into effect by January 1992, will differ fundamentally from the constitutions adopted during the communist period. One of the most important and controversial aspects of this process of redefining the constitutional basis of political life is the relationship between the federal- and republic-level governments.

As the result of constitutional amendments adopted in October 1968 which went into effect in January 1969, Czechoslovakia became a federated state. With this step it became one of only three European communist states (joining the Soviet Union and Yugoslavia) to recognize ethnic divisions by formally incorporating them into the state structure. The outgrowth of Slovak dissatisfaction with Slovakia's position in the unitary Czechoslovak state and one of the few lasting changes made during the reform period of 1968, Czechoslovakia's federal structure was designed to satisfy Slovak aspirations for parity in the state without relinquishing central control over critical matters of state security and economic planning (see Skilling, 1976, ch. 15 and appendix; and Leff, 1988, pp. 121-8). In its original formulation, federalization granted considerable powers to the republic level governments. However, these powers, particularly in the economic sphere, were reduced by a series of amendments introduced in 1971.

Determination of the extent to which the federal structure had an impact on the policy-making process and the division of political power between Czechs and Slovaks during the communist period is complicated by the fact that federalization was introduced at the same time that Gustáv Husák and numerous other Slovaks came to the forefront in the political sphere after the end of the reform period of the late 1960s. It is also hampered by the fact that there was little detailed study of the actual role of the various governmental bodies in policy-making in Czechoslovakia. While numerous Western scholars depicted the changes made in 1969 as largely window-dressing, others discerned a somewhat larger role for the republic-level governments in areas aside from the economy. From the evidence available, it appears that the Czechoslovak federation during the communist period fell somewhere between that of Yugoslavia and that of the Soviet Union. Thus, while the subnational units of government in Czechoslovakia were not as autonomous or powerful as they are in Yugoslavia, they had somewhat greater leeway in determining social, educational, and cultural policy than the Soviet republics prior to Gorbachev's rise to power (see Leff, 1988, pp. 243-73).

As developments since 1989 have demonstrated, many Slovaks in particular viewed the powers granted to the republic-level governments as insufficient. Nationalist forces within and outside of Slovakia have pressured the Slovak government to demand a much more substantial devolution of power to the republic-level governments. Support for an independent Slovakia has also grown. To date, the government of Slovakia remains committed to the federation. However, all political actors in Slovakia clearly want to see an increase in the autonomy and powers of the republic-level governments. Public opinion surveys conducted in mid-1990 found that only a small proportion (8 percent) of Slovaks favored two completely independent states. However, 41 percent of Slovaks (compared to 30 percent of Czechs) favored a common state with greater powers for the republic-level governments and 30 percent (compared to 16 percent of Czechs) a confederation (Beneš, 1990). These sentiments were evident in the discussions that led to the power-sharing agreement adopted in December 1990 and that continue to take place in the context of the revision of the constitution. Although the jurisdictions of the federal- and republic-level governments will be determined by the new federal and republic constitutions, the approaching introduction of the economic reform in January 1991 necessitated a temporary resolution of some of the issues involved. A provisional agreement concerning the division of power between the federal and republic governments was adopted by the Federal Assembly on December 12, 1990, by a vote of 237 in favor and 34 against, with 17 abstentions, after intense debate and extended negotiations between Czech, Slovak, and federal officials. This agreement represented a compromise between advocates of greater decentralization and those, including many members of the federal government, who wanted to see a stronger role maintained for the federal government. Controversial issues included the role of the central banking system, control of the postal service, control of gas and oil pipelines, and jurisdiction over nationalities policy ('Ústavní zákon,' 1990).

The compromise agreement resulted in a significant devolution of power to the republic level. The federal government retains jurisdiction over such all-state functions as defense, the currency, and foreign policy. It also will determine policy toward the churches and nationalities. All areas not specifically assigned to the federal level revert to the republics. The republic level governments thus have gained control over many economic decisions, although the federal government will continue to play an important role in the banking system and in areas essential to national security. The compromise reached in December 1990 averted a probable constitutional crisis. However, it was achieved by postponing decisions on many of the most controversial issues, including the decision over control of the gas pipelines. These issues will resurface as the process of rewriting the republic and federal constitutions continues. The proper relationship between the federal and republic levels thus continues to be controversial.

The federal government

During the communist period, sovereignty formally rested with the Federal Assembly. However, this body and other governmental organs were subordinated to the Communist Party. The democratic government that replaced communist rule continues to be a mixed parliamentary system. However, the functions of the legislature, government, and the presidency have changed dramatically, as the policy-making powers usurped by the Communist Party during communist rule have reverted to legitimate state institutions.

The presidency

The office of both the President and the Prime Minister were largely symbolic during the communist period. Those who held these positions were generally powerful, but their power derived not from their formal state positions but from their positions in the hierarchy of the Communist Party. The limited importance of the office of the presidency during this period was evident in the fact that Gustáv Husák was allowed to remain in that post after he was removed as head of the Communist Party in 1987.

The formal powers of the presidency remain limited in the new political conditions. However, although the government is charged with the day-to-day administration of the country, the President also plays an extremely important role at present. Chosen as President by the Federal Assembly when it was still dominated by communist deputies in December 1989 as the result of an agreement worked out between the party and the opposition, Václav Havel was re-elected to the presidency of the CSFR by the Federal Assembly on July 5, 1990. A dissident playwright who was jailed numerous times for his decades-long championship of human rights, Havel has emerged as the symbol of the country's hopes for democracy and a better future. As was the case with the country's presidents during the interwar period, particularly President Masaryk, he has become the dominant political figure in Czechoslovakia. Given his moral authority, which derives from his refusal to compromise with the previous regime, and the high regard in which the public holds him, his influence on policy-making far outstrips the formal powers of his office. In the early months of 1990, in particular, very few political decisions could be taken without his approval. However, apart from the circle of trusted friends and fellow dissidents who came to serve as his advisors, there was little formal provision for providing the President with the expertise needed to match the expanded demands of the office.

The reorganization of the President's office and expansion of his staff after the June 1990 elections was an attempt to remedy this situation. Headed by Prince Karel Schwarzenberg, who was named Chancellor, the staff was increased to include eight departments which deal with domestic and foreign policy, human rights, culture, legal and social affairs, economic policy, and press and information issues. Several of the advisors who accompanied the President to the Castle in December 1989 were named as heads of the newly created departments. They were joined by several former dissidents and activists from Slovakia, including Martin Bútora and Milan Šimečka, who died shortly after assuming the office of Chairman of the Council of Advisors to the President. Clearly needed to deal with the increased demands on the office of the President, this step nonetheless has been criticized as an effort to create a 'shadow cabinet' parallel to that of the government. It also highlighted the uncertain relationship between the President on the one hand and the government and parliament on the other under the existing constitution (see Mácha and Sirota, 1990, pp. 1,2. See Mežrický, 1990, for further discussion).

The potential difficulties that this situation poses came to the fore during the political crisis over the jurisdictions of the federal- and republic-level governments in December 1990. Noting that there was no political authority that was constitutionally authorized to resolve conflicts between the various governments that threatened to break up the state, President Havel called for the creation of a constitutional court to resolve such issues in the future. He also called for a strengthening of the powers of the Presidency, a step that provoked a great deal of controversy, particularly in Slovakia (see Adamičková, 1991b, pp. 1,2; and Šabata, 1990, p. 2). Public opinion polls conducted in late December 1990 found, for example, that approximately 76 percent of the inhabitants of Slovakia older than 15 did not approve of the President's request for greater powers (see Fuele, 1990; Šabata, 1990; and Hrčka, 1990, p. 13). Specific powers requested included the right to dissolve the Federal Assembly when it cannot pass laws; the power to call elections when the legislature cannot form a government or passes a motion of no-confidence in the existing government; and emergency powers to deal with serious internal or external threats to the state (Růžková, 1990). These powers, which continue to be controversial, are included in the proposal for the new constitution President Havel made in March 1991. At that time, he also called for the creation of a Federal Council of 20 to 30 members that would have the right to approve and endorse presidential decrees, return bills to the parliament, and elect the President jointly with the Federal Assembly ('Presidentův návrh,' 1991. See also 'Jedná otázka,' 1991, p. 4; 'Slezáková and Pokorný,' 1991; and Hrčka, 1991a, 1991b).

The results of polls conducted by the Institute for Research on Public Opinion illustrate the changes in popular perceptions of President Havel that occurred in the course of late 1989 and 1990. In late November 1989, only 10 percent of those polled identified Václav Havel as the political leader they trusted most, while 13 percent trusted him least. By late January 1990, 60 percent found him the most trustworthy, and only 4 percent least. By early April, 51 percent trusted him most and 5 percent least (Institut pro výzkum veřejného mínění, 1990b, p. 3). In both February and early May of 1990, 88 percent of a representative sample polled by the Institute for Public Opinion Research trusted President Havel (Institut pro výzkum veřejného mínění, 1990a). These levels were significantly higher than trust in the federal government, republic level-governments, the Federal Assembly, and local governments. Although most Slovaks as well as Czechs interviewed as part of a May 1990 survey felt that Havel should continue as President, levels of support were significantly lower among Slovaks (65 percent) than Czechs (81 percent) (Institut pro výzkum veřejného mínění, 1990c). Support for the President fell somewhat in the second half of 1990, particularly in Slovakia, but remained higher than that for most political leaders (see Boguszak, Gabal, and Rak, 1990c, p. 6). The impact of the crisis that arose over the power-sharing agreement in December 1990 was reflected in an abrupt drop in confidence in Havel in Slovakia from 74 percent in July 1990 to 43 percent in early December 1990 and the growth of those who expressed a lack of confidence from 17.8 percent to 43 percent. Levels of support for the President in Slovakia were considerably lower than for the Slovak Prime Minister Mečiar (80.3 percent) and Alexander Dubček (27.7 percent). Confidence in the federal government and the Federal Assembly also declined during this period (ČTK, December 11, 1990).

The government

Nominated by the President after his election by the Federal Assembly, the Prime Minister and members of the government now play active roles in determining the country's policies. They also have primary responsibility for implementing public policy. The interim Government of National Understanding which was formed to replace Communist Party rule in December 1989 consisted of 21 members. Nine of these were supporters of Civic Forum or Public Against Violence or independents; two were members of the People's Party and two of the Socialist Party; eight were members of the Communist Party. The Premier, Marián Čalfa, renounced his membership in the party as two other party members, Vladimír Dlouhý and Valtr Komárek, had earlier. Fifteen of the members of the government were Czech and six Slovak (see Sirota, 1989, pp. 1,3; and Martin, 1990d, pp. 3-4).

The government formed as the result of the June 1990 elections included eight members who had served since December 1989. These included Prime Minister Čalfa, Finance Minister Václav Klaus, Foreign Minister Jiří Dienstbier, Minister of Defense Miroslav Vacek, Minister of Social Affairs Petr Miller, Control Committee Minister Květoslava Kořínková, and two Deputy Prime Ministers for Economic Affairs, Václav Valeš and Vladimír Dlouhý. Two of the federal ministries were abolished and the remaining eight were filled by newcomers. These included Slavomír Stračar, as Minister of Foreign Trade; Josef Vavroušek, Minister of the Environment; Jiří Nezval, Minister of Transportation; Ján Langoš, Minister of Internal Affairs; Pavel Hoffman, Minister of Strategic Planning; and Theodor Petřík, Minister of Telecommunications. Pavel Rychetský and Josef Mikloško joined Jiří Dienstbier and Václav Valeš as deputy prime ministers. In October 1990, Miroslav Vacek was replaced as Minister of Defense by Luboš Dobrovoský. Ten of the members of the government are Czech, and six Slovak. Five of the ministers and deputy prime ministers are members of Civic Forum, and three of Public Against Violence. General Vacek, formerly a member of the Communist Party, resigned in February 1990. The Christian Democratic Movement is represented by two ministers. The remaining members of the government are independents.

The legislature

Although the 1960 Constitution retained the position of President of the Republic as head of state, it vested supreme state power in the National Assembly, or legislature (see Taborsky, 1961, Part II, for a discussion of the governmental system and the 1960 Constitution). A bicameral body as a result of changes made in connection with federalization, the Federal Assembly consisted of a 200-member Chamber of the People and a 150-member Chamber of Nations during the communist period. Deputies of the Chamber of the People were chosen on the basis of population; those of the Chamber of Nations were divided equally among the Czech and Slovak Republics. All deputies were elected every five years.

Both houses had equal powers, and the approval of both was required for all laws except those that affected only the internal functioning of a single Chamber. Required by law to meet at least twice a year, the Federal Assembly normally met for several days each session. In the interim between legislative sessions, the powers of the Federal Assembly were exercised by its 40-member Presidium. Each chamber elected a presidium, a president, and vice-presidents. There were also several parliamentary commissions attached to each House (see Chovanec, 1974, pp. 36-52, for further details).

The Federal Assembly also was charged with electing the President of the state, who in turn appointed the premier, deputy premiers, and ministers. Under the leadership of the premier, the executive branch was responsible for overseeing the implementation of government policies by the federal bureaucracy. It also coordinated and supervised the activities of the republic governments.

During the communist period, the Federal Assembly was a largely symbolic body whose primary tasks were to ratify decisions already made by the Communist Party and demonstrate support for the system. The largely symbolic role of the legislature was evident in the fact that it met infrequently and briefly; it was also reflected in its limited output and in the social backgrounds of legislators (see

Blondel, 1973, pp. 45-54, for a discussion of the significance of these factors). Although it was in theory subordinate to the legislature, the executive branch of the government, in conjunction with the top bodies of the Communist Party, played a much more important role in governing the country than the legislature, which was seldom in session. In the first ten years after federalization was adopted, for example, the Federal Assembly enacted a total of 130 laws. Six hundred fifty-one regulations and other normative measures were issued by the federal government and ministries during that period (Czafik and Virsík, 1980, p. 111).

The social backgrounds of deputies were a further indicator of the limited influence and importance of the Federal Assembly during the communist period. Although officials of the Communist Party, state, mass organizations, other political parties, and the military were well represented among the deputies (36.0 percent of all deputies in 1986), workers and agricultural workers accounted for the single largest occupational category (37.4 percent) (see Table 2.1). This pattern reflected the communist leadership's desire to ensure that this group, which was critically important from an ideological perspective, was well represented in the legislature. At the same time, however, the prevalence of workers meant that a large proportion of deputies did not have the political skills needed to be effective politicians. These tendencies were particularly evident among women deputies, over two-thirds of whom were workers or agricultural workers in 1986, compared to 25 percent of the male deputies (see Nelson and White, 1981, for a discussion of similar patterns in other communist legislatures. See Wolchik, 1981b, for further information on gender differences).

Important changes began to occur in the function and composition of the Federal Assembly soon after the fall of the communist government in 1989. The approximately 100 deputies who resigned or were removed from Parliament between December 1989 and the end of January 1990 were replaced by dissident activists and others by appointment. Certain other deputies remained in the Parliament, but renounced their links to the Communist Party. By the end of February 1990, 152 of the 350 members of the Federal Assembly were independents or supporters of Civic Forum and 138 deputies

Table 2.1 Occupations of deputies to the Federal Assembly, 1986

	Men	Women	Total
Workers	51 (20.0%)	60 (67.4%)	111 (31.7%)
Agricultural workers	13 (5.0%)	7 (7.9%)	20 (5.7%)
Enterprise directors, other executives, agricultural cooperative directors	17 (6.5%)	2 (2.2%)	19 (5.4%)
Officials:			
Communist Party	35 (13.4%)	0	35 (10.0%)
State	40 (15.3%)	0	40 (11.4%)
Mass organizations	20 (7.7%)	8 (9.0%)	28 (8.0%)
Other parties	12 (4.6%)	2 (2.2%)	14 (4.0%)
Military	9 (3.4%)	0	9 (2.6%)
White collar workers, intellectuals, professionals	58 (22.2%)	10 (11.2%)	68 (19.4%)
Retirees	4 (1.5%)	0	4 (1.1%)
Religious representatives	2 (0.8%)	0	2 (0.6%)
Totals	261 (74.6%)	89 (25.4%)	350 (100%)

Source: 'Poslanci federálního shromáždění.' *Rudé právo*, May 28, 1986, pp. 1-3.

were members of the Communist Party. The other minor parties that had been permitted to exist during the communist period held 27 positions, and the remaining mandates were held by newly appointed members of the recreated Social Democratic Party, the newly established Christian Democratic Initiative, the Christian Democratic Party, the Greens Party, and the Hungarian Independent Initiative. Six seats remained unfilled (see nig, 1990, p. 11).

Prior to the June 1990 parliamentary elections, the number of deputies in the House of the People was reduced to 150 in order to match that of the House of the Nations. Of the 300 seats filled in the June 1990 elections, Civic Forum and Public Against Violence hold 170 seats. The Communist Party holds 47, and the Christian Democratic Union and Christian Democratic Movement 40. Several smaller parties and movements hold the remaining seats, including

Table 2.2 Distribution of mandates in the Federal Assembly, 1990

	House of the People	House of Nations
Civic Forum	68	50
Movement for Self-Governing Democracy-Association for Moravia and Silesia	9	7
Christian Democratic Union	9	6
Public Against Violence	19	33
Christian Democratic Movement	11	14
Slovak National Party	6	9
Coexistence-Hungarian Christian Democratic Party	5	7
Communist Party	23	24

Source: From information in Obrman, 1990a.

the Movement for Self-Governing Democracy-Association for Moravia and Silesia (16), the Slovak National Party (15), and Coexistence-Hungarian Christian Democratic Movement (12) (see 'Výsledky voleb,' 1990, p. 4; and 'Volby 1990,' 1990; and Table 2.2).

The structure and staffing of the Federal Assembly have changed in important ways as it has changed from a rubber stamp of the Communist Party to a body whose actions determine national policy. The committee structure of the Federal Assembly has been simplified and the remaining committees have been given larger staffs and more resources to support their work. There are currently eight permanent committees in each house, including the Mandate and Immunity Committee, the Constitutional and Legal Affairs Committee, the Foreign Affairs Committee, the Planning and Budget Committee, the Defense and Security Committee, the Economic Committee, the Social Affairs and Culture Committee, and the Committee for the Environment. Representation on the committees is determined by the proportion of seats each group has in the assembly (see Pehe, 1990c, pp. 7–11, for further information and analysis). In addition to these bodies, numerous parliamentary clubs have been formed (see ada and nig, 1990a, p. 2).

In contrast to the situation in the communist period, when the Federal Assembly met briefly twice a year, the legislature is now clearly a working body and the position of deputy a full-time occupation. However, the move to create a more professional group of legislators, which began before the elections, has resulted in some controversy. After the June 1990 elections, the Federal Assembly approved higher salaries for deputies, as well as tax-free living allowances and additional funds to cover expenses related to parliamentary duties. Reduced from a proposed 17,000 crowns after criticism, the basic wage of 7,000 crowns is still approximately twice the average wage. The decision to recess the Federal Assembly for a month's vacation in the summer of 1990, despite the pressing concerns facing the country, also fueled criticism (see b, 1990b, p. 1; and Tréglová, 1990b, p. 5).

The primary task of the members of parliament elected in June 1990, who will be in office only two rather than the normal five years, is the rewriting of the country's constitution. In addition, deputies are continuing the process begun during the interim period between December 1989 and June 1990 of revising Czechoslovakia's legal framework to bring it into conformity with the requirements of democratic political life and facilitate the transition to a market economy. The Federal Assembly also must enact new laws that will eliminate the impact of communist rule in areas as diverse as culture and foreign policy.

Republic governments

The structure of the governments of the Czech Republic and the Slovak Republic parallels that of the federal government to a large degree. Thus the 200-member Czech National Council and the 150-member Slovak National Council are the highest government organs in their respective republics. The republic legislatures are unicameral bodies and elect their own presidiums.

Executive power rests with the prime minister who, with the deputy prime ministers, oversees the work of the republic-level ministries. During the communist period, many of the powers granted to the republic-level governments were curtailed by the constitutional amendments of July 1971. These gave the federal government the authority to override republic-level laws and also increased the scope of the federal government's economic responsibilities. However, republic-level bodies still played a role in determining social and cultural policies. They also were responsible for supervising the work of lower-level governmental units within their jurisdictions (Chovanec, 1974, pp. 90-3).

As the result of the law on the division of powers between the federal and republic governments adopted in December 1990, there has been a devolution of many of the tasks formerly reserved to the federal government to the republic level. Republic-level governments now have extensive powers over economic decision-making as well as social, cultural, and educational policies. They may also, with the knowledge of federal authorities, initiate actions in the international sphere. Both republics contribute to the budget of the federal government. However, in contrast to the situation during the communist period when revenues were sent to the federal government which then redistributed them, revenues from each republic remain in the republic that generated them and each republic government has the right to dispose of its own funds. Control of the communications networks also rests with the republics rather than with the federal government.

The impact of these changes was evident in the Slovak decision in early January 1991 not to close armaments plants as previously scheduled. As this very visible divergence in the policies of a republic level government illustrates, the new powers of the republics are likely to be reflected in policies that increasingly differ from each other in the Czech Lands and Slovakia.

At the republic level, Civic Forum, which received 49.5 percent of the vote to the Czech National Council formed a coalition with the Movement for Self-Governing Democracy-Association for Moravia and Silesia, which gained 10.3 percent of the vote. In Slovakia, Public Against Violence, which won 29.3 percent of the vote, entered into a coalition with the Christian Democratic Union, which received 19.2 percent of the vote, and the Democratic Party, which won 4.4 percent of the vote to the Slovak National Council (see Obrman, 1990a, p. 14; and Table 2.3).

Table 2.3 Distribution of seats in republic legislatures

Czech National Council

Civic Forum	127
Communist Party	32
Movement for Self-Governing Democracy-Association for Moravia and Silesia	22
Christian Democratic Union	19
Total:	200

Slovak National Council

Public Against Violence	48
Christian Democratic Movement	31
Slovak National Party	22
Communist Party	22
Coexistence	14
Democratic Party	7
Green Party	6
Total:	150

Source: Obrman, 1990a.

Lower level and regional government

The organization and functions of lower-level governmental bodies have also changed significantly since the end of communist rule. Governmental power at the lower levels in Czechoslovakia was exercised by regional, district, and local national committees during the communist period. These units, which had from 9 to 85 members at the local level, from 60 to 80 at the district level, 80 at the regional level, and from 80 to 130 in the major cities, elected a council, president, and vice-president to carry out their executive functions (Chovanec, 1974, p. 93). Charged with a wide variety of tasks, including ensuring proper economic, cultural, health, and social developments in their territories; creating and supervising economic enterprises, and cultural, health and social organizations; protecting socialist property; fostering socialist competition; and maintaining the defensive capabilities of the state, as well as implementing laws, the national committees at each level were subordinated to higher-level government units and unofficially to the Communist Party.

During the communist period, lower-level governmental units played an important role in carrying out the directives of higher governmental and party bodies, but had little autonomy of their own. Judging from the frequent published criticisms of these units, their ability to implement the policy directives handed down by higher authorities was limited. Headed by part-time officials and poorly staffed, lower-level government bodies were forced to rely heavily on volunteer citizen activists to carry out their programs. The impediments to effective implementation posed by the lack of resources and an inadequate number and variety of specialists trained to deal with the numerous social and economic issues they faced were compounded in certain cases by differences in local and central perceptions of local situations and needs (see Wolchik and Curry, 1984).

The results of a 1988 survey conducted by the Institute for Research on Public Opinion in Prague and made public in 1990 documented low levels of citizen interest in participating in the work of local governments and the low regard in which governments at this level were held by most citizens. Thus, although the majority of those surveyed indicated that they would be willing to participate in work to clean up their surroundings and improve the environment, far fewer either were serving or were willing to serve as a local deputy (14 percent), member of a local government commission (24 percent), or member of a committee for citizens' concerns (26 percent). When queried about the willingness of their neighbors and acquaintances, 39 percent thought they would be unwilling or very unwilling to do so. Two-fifths had not attended any meeting organized by the local government. The reasons given for lack of interest in such activities reflected low evaluations of the effectiveness of local governments and of citizens' possibilities to influence public affairs as well as negative experiences working with local government. Thus, 20 percent of those who indicated they were not willing to become officials of the local government stated that they had had negative experiences with local government and a further 47 percent indicated that they had no interest in such activities. Over 74 percent of those who had not attended any meetings organized by the national committee had no interest in such meetings or found them useless. The survey also found very low levels of political efficacy. Only 2 percent of respondents felt that they 'decidedly' influenced local affairs, and 14 percent felt that they had some influence. The vast majority of respondents indicated that they had rather little (42 percent) or decidedly little (42 percent) influence. Respondents were more positive about the possibilities of citizens in their neighborhood to influence public life but 42 percent judged these possibilities negatively and another 16 percent did not feel able to judge (Navářová, 1990, pp. 20-1).

Prior to the November 1990 elections, Czechoslovakia's new leaders enacted a number of important changes in the organization and functions of lower level governments. As the result of a constitutional amendment passed in July 1990, the national committees subordinated to higher bodies were abolished and replaced by a system of independent local governments effective November 31, 1990 (see 'V ČNR diskuse,' 1990, p. 1; dz, 1990a; 'Obce jsou schválený,' dz, 1990b, p. 1; vrz, 1990; and Fuk, 1990, p. 1). Their new powers include the authority to determine local budgets, make decisions on economic affairs and territorial changes, set up local organizations, and direct the police (Smola, 1990, pp. 1,5). No longer responsible to higher state authorities, the local government assemblies now elect a council and mayor.

The party system

Prior to November 1989, the Communist Party was the only effective political party in the country. The end of the party's monopoly of power has been followed by a proliferation of political parties, as well as interest groups and voluntary associations. This process of repopulating a political landscape dominated for over four decades by a single political force, which is a central aspect of the recreation of democratic government in Czechoslovakia, proceeded very quickly after November 1989. Over 100 political parties and groupings had registered by mid-1990, and 23 met the conditions necessary to field candidates in the June 1990 parliamentary elections. These ranged from the Communist Party to the Friends of Beer Party. The Czechoslovak Socialist Party and the Czechoslovak People's Party, which had been allowed to exist under the control of the Communist Party during the communist period, became independent parties. Several parties that had been active in the inter-war period resumed their activities. Nationalist parties, such as the Slovak National Party, and the Movement for Self-Governing Democracy-Association for Moravia and Silesia, and political group-ings and citizen initiatives formed around new issues, such as Civic Forum and Public Against Violence also competed in the elections (see 'Czechoslovakia Parliamentary Elections,' 1990, for a brief summary of the platforms of the individual parties).

Several general features of the party system stand out. First, it is clear that, as in the interwar period, Czechoslovakia will have a multiparty system. The requirement that political parties receive at least 5 percent of the vote to seat deputies in the Federal Assembly has eliminated many parties as serious political actors, at least for the time being. However, although relatively few of the registered political parties are represented in the federal- and republic-level legislatures, there are still several parties in both the Czech Lands and Slovakia that are credible political forces.

The results of elections held in 1990 reflected the dominance of non-partisan politics and the distrust of many citizens of organized political parties. Those political groups that did best were either non-partisan or new political groupings rather than more traditional parties with roots in the communist or pre-communist period. The decision by part of Civic Forum's leadership, headed by Václav Klaus, in January 1991 to become a hierarchically structured membership party reflected a belief that the time had come to regularize party structures. However, the breaking away of Klaus's opponents as well as the decision by part of Public Against Violence to remain a movement rather than a political party indicate that there is still considerable support for less traditional forms of political organization.

The party system in Czechoslovakia also differs from those that exist in many other Western democracies in that there is no strong social democratic party at present. Support for the several socialist parties and groups that exist has been very low to date (see Wolchik, 1990a). Thus, aside from the Communist Party, which cannot be a credible alternative at present, the political spectrum is tilted heavily to the center and center right. Supporters of *Občanské hnutí*, or the Civic Movement that formed after the split of the Civic Forum in February 1991, favor greater attention to social security and other positions that may lead to the elaboration of a program similar to those espoused by social democrats elsewhere. But the spokespersons for the group describe themselves as liberals in the American use of that term rather than social democrats at present.

Finally, although the outlines of the country's post-communist party system are evident, the positions of many parties and political movements are still evolving, and the political preferences and alignments of the population remain fluid. As the results of public opinion polls, the shifts in support for various parties between the elections of June and November 1990, and the differentiation that has taken place within organizations such as Civic Forum and Public Against Violence in late 1990 and early 1991, illustrate, a stable multiparty system is still in process of being created in Czechoslovakia. The most important parties and political groupings during the communist period and at present are discussed below.

Civic Forum and Public Against Violence

The development of the party system since the end of communist rule has differed to some degree in the Czech Lands and Slovakia. In the Czech Lands, Civic Forum was the dominant political force in 1990. Founded as an umbrella organization in November 1989 to coordinate opposition to the communist regime, Civic Forum emerged from the June 1990 elections with a majority of the seats in the Czech National Council (127 of the 200 seats from 49.5 percent of the vote), and the largest share (49.96 and 53.15 percent) of votes to the House of the Nations and the House of the People of the Federal Assembly. The beneficiary of popular support for the change of regime in November 1989, the Forum also gained support as a result of the fact that many well-known intellectuals and competent experts joined its ranks in late 1989 and early 1990.

Public support for Civic Forum decreased somewhat in late 1990. Evident in the results of the local elections in the Czech Lands, in which Civic Forum received 35.4 percent of the vote, the decline in support for the Forum is also reflected in public opinion polls. In part a reflection of the fact that the Forum is identified with the government, such attitudes also reflect growing popular impatience with the pace of reform, fear of the consequences of economic changes, and frustration that the economic situation will not be as easy to improve as many citizens had hoped and expected (see Boguszak, Gabal and Rak, 1990d; and ČTK, November 14, 1990).

The orientation and organizational structure of the Forum changed in the course of 1990 and early 1991. The Forum remained a loose grouping of diverse political forces for the first year of the post-communist period. The outgrowth of the opposition movement in the Czech Lands, it brought together individuals and groups with widely differing political perspectives. Thus, supporters of the Forum included dissident activists such as Václav Havel, who had never been a member of the Communist Party, reform communists, including the *Obroda* group formed in 1989, and others, such as Jiří Dienstbier, who had been forced out of the party after 1968, religious activists, radical socialists, free market advocates such as Václav Klaus, and numerous specialists and professionals.

United by their common opposition to the communist system, members of the Forum also shared a commitment to the broad principles of democracy, a belief in the necessity of economic reform, and a desire to see Czechoslovakia return to Europe. They nonetheless held diverse views concerning the concrete steps needed to achieve these aims and the nature of the society and economy to be created. They also differed in their opinions concerning the organization of the Forum itself. A sizeable number of the Forum's original leaders, including many of those who moved into government positions soon after the ouster of the communist government, distrusted partisan politics and argued that the Forum should remain a non-partisan citizen movement. Others, including Finance Minister Václav Klaus, favored a more orthodox, centralized organization.

The process of differentiation within the Civic Forum continued after the June elections and intensified once Václav Klaus was elected Chairman in late October 1990. In line with the move to make Civic Forum a more clearly defined right-wing political force, several left-wing groups that had been affiliated with the Forum, including *Obroda*, a group of reform communists and the Left Alternative, were expelled in late October 1990 (see Zeman and Mlynář, 1990, pp. 1 and 2; Marek, 1990, p. 2). Differentiation also occurred among the Forum's parliamentary deputies. The formation of the Inter-parliamentary Club of the Democratic Right was followed by the founding of the Interparliamentary Civic Association, and a Left and a Liberal Club of Civic Forum deputies. The latter included many former dissidents and members of the government close to President Havel, such as Jiří Dienstbier, Petr Pithart, Pavel Rychetský, Vladimír Valeš, Josef Vavroušek, Martin Palouš, and Dagmar Burešová (ds, 1990, pp. 1-2; Filip, 1990, p. 1; tma, 1990, p. 1; and 'Nesouhlasí s liberaly,' 1990, p. 3).

The growing divisions in Civic Forum ranks came to a head at its January 1991 congress. At that time, most of Klaus's opponents in the Coordinating Center of the Forum were removed from their positions, and the decision was made to transform the Civic Forum into a political party. According to the decisions adopted at the Congress, lower-level leaders were to be responsible to a Central Executive Council composed of representatives of the district organization and the Forum's parliamentary clubs. Civic Forum members were also to register as members and pay dues (Janyška, 1991a, p. 2; Pehe, 1991b, p. 3 and 'Občanské forum politickou stranou,' 1991, p. 1). The Congress also reinforced the position of those who wanted to see Civic Forum become a party of the center right, as the program adopted explicitly rejected all forms of socialism.

The continued dissatisfaction of those, including many members of the government, who disagreed with the results of the January congress led to an agreement to split the Forum. In mid-February 1991, the division within the Civic Forum was formalized. Supporters of Klaus formed the Civic Democratic Party. Members of the Liberal Club, led by Deputy Federal Prime Minister Pavel Rychetský, formed the Civic Movement. The Civic Democratic

Party will become a more formally organized political party with individual members only. The Civic Movement will retain a looser structure and will allow both individual and collective members. In addition to differences concerning political organization, the two groups also differ in their views concerning the responsibility of the government to moderate the negative effects of the shift to the market economy. The two groups are now loosely joined by a coordinating committee composed of equal numbers of supporters of each in order to preserve the governing coalition and control of the Forum's assets. Civic Forum as an organization is to be dissolved no later than the beginning of the next election campaign in 1992 (see Kryl, 1991, pp. 1,2; Šmidová and Veis, 1991; pen and la, 1991, pp. 1,2; 'jaš, jvs,' 1991, p. 2; ČTK, March 1, 1991; and Janyška, 1991b. See also Pehe, 1991b, pp. 1-3).

The Slovak counterpart of Civic Forum, Public Against Violence, was founded on November 20, 1989 in Bratislava. As in the case of Civic Forum, PAV had its roots in the growing circles of non-conformists that had developed in the later years of communist rule in Slovakia. Many of those who became leaders of PAV had been active in the ecological movement that was centered in the officially permitted Guardians of Nature organization during the communist period. A reflection of the different political climate in the Czech Lands and Slovakia, many of these individuals, including artists, social scientists, and other intellectuals, remained in their positions in the official world while engaging in non-conformist activities (Bútora, 1990; and Szomolányiová, 1990). Other supporters of Public Against Violence, including Miroslav Kusý, the philosopher later selected as rector of Comenius University, and Milan and Martin Šimečka, were open dissidents prior to 1989.

Public Against Violence emerged as the strongest political party in Slovakia in the June 1990 elections, and, with 37 percent of the vote to the House of Nations and 33 percent to the House of the People, formed part of the winning coalition at the federal level with Civic Forum. However, in contrast to Civic Forum, which did not face a strong opposition within the Czech Lands, PAV must deal with the challenge posed by the Christian Democratic Movement, which won a larger share of the seats in the local elections held in November

1990 (27.4 percent compared to 20.4 percent for Public Against Violence).

As the political force in Slovakia most committed to maintaining the federation, leaders of Public Against Violence have been faced with the need to balance the requirements of continued cooperation with Civic Forum at the federal level and the need to respond to growing nationalist pressure within Slovakia. Reflected in the growth of support for the Christian Democratic Movement and the more nationalistic Slovak National Party, this pressure has radicalized the positions of all Slovak leaders on the national issue.

As was the case with voters who supported Civic Forum in the Czech Lands, Public Against Violence supporters are drawn from a broad spectrum of social groups. But, although both groups have widespread support, the core of their adherents lies with better-educated, urban, white-collar workers and intellectuals (see Centrum pre výskum spoločenských problemov, 1990a, 1990b, 1990c, and 1990d).

Divisions within Public Against Violence came into the open in February and March 1991 when conflict between supporters of Premier Mečiar and those of Fedor Gál, head of PAV, intensified. Although both sides asserted their desire to avoid an open break, Mečiar and his supporters formed an Interparliamentary Club called PAV for Democratic Slovakia on March 6, 1991. Members of the two groups differ in their views on the federation and Slovak sovereignty (Čapko, Minárik, and Drábik, 1991; Hríb, 1991, and 'A Destabilizing Nervous Influence,' 1991, p. 2). As noted in chapter 1, conflicts within PAV were one of the factors that led to Mečiar's dismissal as Premier and his replacement by Ján Čarnogurský, leader of the Christian Democratic Movement. As noted in chapter 1, the two groups formally separated in April 1991.

The Communist Party of Czechoslovakia (KSČ)

From 1948 to November 1989, effective political power rested not with the state or governmental organs, but with the Communist Party itself. Identified in the constitution as the leading force in Czechoslovak society, the Communist Party of Czechoslovakia was the most important political organization in the country. It was also the center of actual policy-making. Party leaders at the national level determined the main outlines of national policy in all areas; they also set the country's political agenda. It was thus the members of the party's Presidium and executive committees at each level who were the country's effective, or actual, political elite.

The structure of the Communist Party of Czechoslovakia paralleled that of other communist parties in most respects while it was in power. According to party statutes, the most important party body was the party congress. Held approximately every five years, the congress was charged with electing members of the Central Committee, as well as with determining the main outlines of the party's activities in the upcoming period. In fact, during the period when the Communist Party was the dominant political force in Czechoslovakia, the congress sessions, which typically lasted several days, served largely to give formal approval to decisions already made by the executive organs of the party. It was the top party bodies, in particular the Presidium and the Secretariat, that determined the party's policies. Delegates to the party congress included members of the party's full-time apparatus, but the majority were not professional politicians or bureaucrats. Rather, they were exemplary workers and collective farmers, as well as other individuals chosen to represent a wide range of social categories and occupations.

When the party congress was not in session, party statutes stipulated that its authority was to be exercised by the Central Committee. This body, which met approximately once a month during the communist period to hear discussions of important political and economic issues by top party leaders, had little direct political role during periods of normalcy. However, in times of crisis or political change, the debates and decisions of the Central Committee had a decisive impact on political events (see Skilling, 1976, ch. 6). Members of this body, who numbered 135 in 1989, typically included individuals such as exemplary workers and collective farmers who were chosen primarily for their representational value. However, in contrast to both the legislative elites and delegates to the party congress, the majority of members of the

Central Committee were drawn from the party and state apparatus, as well as from leading economic, social, scientific, and cultural institutions.

During the communist period, the Presidium of the state-wide party was the main policy-making body of the Communist Party. Members of this body, which ranged in size from 13 to 18 in the last two decades of communist rule and had 13 full members and three candidates in early November 1989, also determined the main outlines of state policy in all areas. Although they often held important governmental offices simultaneously, their power derived from their party positions. The Secretariat, which included six secretaries and six members in addition to the First Secretary in late 1989, was the administrative center of the party. In theory elected by and responsible to the Central Committee, the members of the Secretariat were charged with carrying out the policies determined by the Presidium. They also directed the operation of the Central Committee's departments and supervised the work of lower levels of the party apparatus on a day-to-day basis.

After the events of 1989, the role of the Communist Party changed markedly. With the end of its monopoly of power, the party reverted to being one among many political parties. Its monopoly of political leadership in government bodies ended as well, as did the close intertwining of party and governmental structures and the subordination of the government to the party.

Czechoslovakia's new leaders have taken a number of steps to prevent the Communist Party from exercising undue power in the new order. One of the chief concerns was to prevent the party from translating its financial and organizational advantages into legitimate resources in the new system. Thus, the Federal Assembly enacted measures that required party leaders to relinquish property and assets. The inflated pensions of retired party leaders and other economic advantages of party leaders and members were also reduced. Early measures to force the party to restore property and assets to their rightful owners were followed in November 1990 by passage of a law confiscating all remaining assets of the party, with the exception of those allowed to all parties for their day to day operation (see 'KSČ vrátí majetek,' 1990, p. 1). This measure pre-empted the plan for voluntary surrender of assets proposed at the party congresses (see ada and nig, 1990b).

Party leaders including Vasil Mohorita, First Secretary of the Party from January to November 1990, and Ladislav Adamec, the former Premier and party leader who attempted to mediate between the government and the opposition in November 1989, tried to rally the party's supporters and define a role for it in the new circumstances. These efforts were hampered by the mass defection of party members and the overall impact of 41 years of communist rule.

In the early months of 1990, party leaders pledged their support for the effort to create a pluralistic society and articulated a role for the party as that of a constructive opposition. In September 1990, however, Mohorita called for open opposition to the government elected in June 1990 and a renewed struggle to take power (see Hvížďala and Vajnerová, 1990, pp. 1-2). This call was moderated somewhat by the victory of reformist leaders at the republic party congresses in October and the federal party congress in November 1990. The new leaderships of both the Czech and Slovak parties have rejected many of the central tenets of communism and pledged to transform their parties into modern left-wing parties. Individual party leaders, such as Jiří Svoboda, the 45-year-old film director who was elected Chairman of the Communist Party of Bohemia and Moravia, and the Slovak Party's congress document have expressed support for certain aspects of the economic reform program. However, party leaders questioned the orientation of the reform program and submitted the party's own proposal for large-scale privatization to the Federal Assembly. Communist leaders also expressed concern over anticipated increases in unemployment and other economic dislocations (see 'Sjezd KSČ,' 1990 and bč and nig, 1990. See also Pehe, 1990b, pp. 1-5).

The 18th Congress held in November 1990 also made important changes in the organization of the party. Prior to that time, there was a party organization at the republic level in Slovakia, but not in the Czech Lands. Established in May 1939, the Communist Party of Slovakia exercised a substantial degree of autonomy at various times, despite its formal subordination by party statute to the state-wide party (see Suda, 1980, pp. 124-30, 157-61, 179-80). The influence of the Slovak party was curtailed at the height of the Stalinist period when many Slovak leaders became victims of the purges. However, in the mid- to late 1960s, the Slovak party voiced Slovak national interests and championed federalization (see Skilling, 1976, pp. 203-4, 237-43, 280-3, 791-6; Golan, 1971 and 1973; and Jancar, 1971, pp. 177-9; Pergl, 1990, p. 1).

Discussion of the need to create a comparable Czech party organization in 1968 led to the creation of a Bureau for the Czech Lands within the Central Committee of the state-wide Communist Party in November 1968. However, although this body had the same status as the Slovak Communist Party in theory, it did not play a significant political role and was eliminated in May 1971. It was replaced by the Committee for Party Work in the Czech Lands, but this committee did not have its own Presidium or Central Committee as the Slovak party did. The existence of a separate party organization thus continued to provide Slovak communists with a forum and tools of influence which had no parallel in the Czech Lands.

In March 1990, the Communist Party of Bohemia and Moravia was created and the Communist Party of Slovakia, which changed its name to the Communist Party of Slovakia-Party of the Democratic Left and, in January 1991, to the Party of the Democratic Left, became an independent organization instead of a territorial unit of the larger party. The 18th Congress of the Party, held in early November 1990, completed the federalization of the party. Most of the powers of the federal-level party bodies have shifted to the two republic-level parties. The federal Central Committee has been abolished, and the newly named Federation of the Communist Party of Bohemia and Moravia and the Communist Party of Slovakia-Party of the Democratic Left is now headed by a 24-member council with 12 delegates from the Czech Lands and 12 from Slovakia. The chairmanship of the federated party is to alternate between representatives of the two republic parties on an annual basis (Bradáč, Pergl, and Růžička, 1990; Peryl, 1990; Bradáč, Krýl, and Pergl, 1990a).

As noted in chapter 1, the Communist Party won 13.5 percent of the vote in the June 1990 parliamentary elections and 17.4 percent

(Czech Lands) and 14 percent (Slovakia) of the vote in the November 1990 local elections ('Výsledky voleb,' 1990). Although a far cry from its previous dominant position, the levels of support for the Communist Party were similar to those it received in the interwar period, when it won from 10 to 13 percent of the vote. In contrast to the situation in Poland and Hungary, then, where the communist parties were seen as alien forces imposed from without throughout the communist period and where their successors currently play extremely small political roles, in Czechoslovakia the party, although in different form and with somewhat different policies, is likely to continue to be an important element of the political spectrum. Unable to serve as a credible opposition at present, it nonetheless retains the support of those whose personal fortunes were so closely tied to the old regime as to preclude any other political option. Although it is extremely unlikely that the party will once again dominate political life, it may be able to capitalize on fear of change among workers and other elements of the population, as well as on the negative impact of the economic reforms currently being enacted. It also continues to have certain organizational advantages over other political forces.

The size and social composition of the Communist Party have changed greatly since the end of communist rule. The KSČ was from its inception one of the largest communist parties. In 1950, for example, 22.7 percent of the population 18 years of age and older and approximately one-third of all males aged 18 and older, were party members (Wightman and Brown, 1975, p. 404). This proportion decreased somewhat in the 1960s (18 percent of the population aged 18 and older were party members in 1962, and 12 percent of the total population were members in 1966), and fell dramatically in the wake of the August 1968 invasion, when approximately 473,000 Czechs and Slovaks resigned or were expelled from the Communist Party (Wightman and Brown, 1975, p. 414). This decline in the party's ranks was reflected in the dramatic drop in the proportion of the population who were Communist Party members (to 8.5 percent of the total population in 1971) (Wightman and Brown, 1975, pp. 407, 413-14). Party membership increased gradually over the next two decades as these members were replaced. Numbering 1,717,000

Table 2.4 Membership of the Communist Party of Czechoslovakia
1945–90

July 1945	475,304
May 1946	approx. 1,100,000
November 1948	over 2,500,000
May 1949	2,311,066
August 1950	1,899,423
February 1951	1,677,443
June 1954	1,489,234
June 1956	1,417,989
January 1958	1,422,199
July 1960	1,559,082
October 1962	1,680,819
January 1966	1,698,002
January 1968	1,690,977
January 1969	1,671,637
May 1971	1,200,000
April 1976	1,382,860
1981	1,538,179
March 1986	1,675,000
May 1988	1,717,000
September 1990	800,000
November 1990	750,000

Sources: Wightman and Brown, 1975, pp. 397, 399, 405, 406; Taborsky,
1961, p. 26; Skilling, 1976, p. 499; Kusin, 1978, p. 184; 1981, p. 10;
1986, p. 13; 'Zpráva ze zasedání' p. 1; and Bradáč, Krýl, and Pergl, 1990a,
p. 1.

in mid-1988 (*Rudé právo*, 8 May 1988, editorial), the Communist
Party's members included approximately 11 percent of Czechoslovakia's total population, a proportion that was significantly higher
than that in the Soviet Union and most other communist countries.

Once the party's control of the political life of the country was
broken, large numbers of members renounced their membership. As
of November 1990, the party had a reported 750,000 members. Of
these, an estimated 200,000 were inactive in party affairs and had not
paid their dues (Bradáč, Krýl, and Pergl, 1990a, p. 1; Table 2.4).

The leaders of the Czechoslovak Communist Party typically released little information about the social composition of the party during the communist rule. That information which is available indicates that the party's social base changed somewhat in the course of the communist period. As in the Soviet and East German parties (Hough, 1977, p. 128-33; Ludz, 1972, pp. 180-1), better-educated people in more demanding occupations were better represented among party members than those in less demanding positions. In 1988, for example, every fourth technical-economic worker, compared to every eighth manual worker, was a member of the party (*Rudé právo*, 8 May 1988, editorial). However, although party membership was a prerequisite for advancement in most occupations, the Czechoslovak party's social composition differed to some extent from that of the Soviet and certain other Central and East European communist parties. The majority of members of the KSČ were workers, retired workers, or agricultural workers. Although the predominance of these social categories among party members decreased over time, the party still retained a strong working class core (see Wightman and Brown, 1975, pp. 400-9). In 1986, 44.6 percent of party members were workers and 6 percent agricultural workers (KSČ, 1986). This characteristic, which was evident in the KSČ throughout the post-Second World War period, reflected its strength among the working class in the interwar period, as well as the difficulties it encountered in attracting talented, educated young people.

As in other communist states, the KSČ's membership remained predominantly male. Women accounted for 28.9 percent of party members in 1986 (Komunistická straná Československska). Although this proportion represented an increase in women members in the late communist period, women comprised a higher proportion of party members in 1948 (approximately 33 percent) than at any time since that year (Wolchik, 1981b, p. 257).

The party also had difficulty in attracting younger members, particularly in the early post-1968 period. Efforts to attract young people to the party were somewhat more successful in the late 1970s and 1980s. In 1988, for example, over one-third of the party's members were under 35 years of age. In contrast to the situation in

1966, when a majority of members had joined the party at least 20 years earlier (Wightman and Brown, 1975, p. 415), approximately 51 percent of all party members in 1988 had joined the party after 1968 (*Zprava ze zasedání*, 1988, p. 2).

There have been marked changes in the social composition of the party since November 1989. As of September 1990, 31 percent of the party's members were workers, and 25.5 percent white-collar workers and intellectuals. The largest category of party members (36 percent) consists of pensioners. The membership of the party has also aged dramatically. Thus, only 6.3 percent of party members were younger than 30 by September 1990 (see Bradáč, Krýl, and Pergl, 1990a, pp. 1-2).

A similar pattern is evident in the party's electoral support. Public opinion polls and exit polls indicate that older, less-educated males were more likely to vote for the party than well-educated, younger men and women in all social categories. The party's high levels of support in Prague in all likelihood reflect the concentration of former members of the state and party apparatus in that city (see Centrum pre výskum spoločenských problémov, 1990a; and Boguszak and Rak, 1990a).

Other political parties

The end of communist rule saw the revival of the minor parties that had been allowed to exist during the communist period and the rebirth of a number of parties that had been active in the interwar period. New political parties and groupings also formed.

Several small non-communist parties were permitted to exist during the communist period. The largest of these were the Czechoslovak People's Party and the Czechoslovak Socialist Party, which were active primarily in the Czech Lands. The two minor parties permitted in Slovakia, the Party of Freedom and the Slovak Revival Party, were much smaller and appeared to draw their main support from the peasantry.

Allowed to exist primarily to mobilize segments of the population not likely to join the Communist Party or to support its initiatives, the minor parties had little, if any real political influence during the communist period. Their role in the political process was thus closer to that of the official mass organizations that also belonged to the National Front than to that of the Communist Party (see Skilling, 1976, pp. 543–5). In the last years of communist rule, officials of certain of these parties, most notably the Czechoslovak Socialist Party, began to play a somewhat more independent political role, but all remained subordinate to the Communist Party.

After November 1989, officials of these parties asserted their independence from the Communist Party and attempted to regain credibility as national political forces. The Czechoslovak People's Party in the Czech Lands, which formed an electoral coalition with several newly established Christian parties for the June 1990 elections, was the most successful of these. Public opinion polls prior to the elections indicated that the coalition had a sizeable degree of support in early 1990 (see Institut pro výzkum veřejného mínění, 1990d). However, as the result of allegations made in the closing days of the June election campaign that the leader of the People's Party, Josef Bartončík, had collaborated with the secret police, the party received only 8.7 percent of the vote to the Federal Assembly and 8.4 percent to the Czech National Council ('Výsledky voleb,' 1990; and 'Volby 1990,' 1990). Support for the party increased somewhat (to 12.1 percent) in the local elections held in November 1990, but it remains a minor player at present.

The Czechoslovak Socialist Party also attempted to revitalize its organization, but with less success. Neither it nor the newly re-established Social Democratic Party received enough votes to seat deputies in the Federal Assembly. In the latter case, the election of Jiři Horak, an *émigré* who had spent the last 40 years in the United States, as head of the party split the party internally (see Program Československé sociální demokracie, 1990 for the party's platform).

The small Freedom Party and Democratic Party which had been allowed to operate in Slovakia but had very little support during the communist period also continued their activities. Founded in April 1946, the Freedom Party emphasized the preservation of Christian traditions and moral values and supported equality for Slovakia within the federal state in its election platform. As it received only 1.44 (House of People) and 1.24 percent (House of Nations) of the vote in the June 1990 elections, it did not seat any deputies in the Federal Assembly. With only 1.77 percent of the vote, it was also excluded from the Slovak National Council. The Democratic Party, which was founded during the Slovak National Uprising in 1944 and received 62 percent of all votes in the May 1946 elections in Slovakia, was disbanded in 1948, and replaced by the Slovak Revival Party. In December 1989, the party returned to its previous name and articulated its support for democratic politics. The party received 3.7 percent of the vote in Slovakia to the House of Nations and 4.4 percent to the House of the People in the June 1990 elections. It received 4.39 percent of the vote to the Slovak National Council and became a part of the Public Against Violence-KDH coalition ('Volby, 1990,' 1990, pp. 31-2; 'Definitívné počty,' 1990; and Prague Domestic Service, June 10, 1990, pp. 32-3).

Several parties that had been active in the interwar period but outlawed after 1948 have also been recreated. The Czechoslovak Agrarian party, which had been a mainstay of the government coalitions in the interwar period, resumed its activities and participated in the June elections as part of a broader coalition, the Alliance of Farmers and the Countryside. The National Socialist Party was recreated by supporters who seceded from the Czechoslovak Socialist Party in September 1990. Its platform includes the preservation of a common state of Czechs and Slovaks, creation of a market economy with greater government action to keep a safety net for the population, and retribution against those who were responsible for the excesses of the communist period. However, as neither of these parties succeeded in seating deputies in the Federal Assembly, they play a negligible role in politics at present.

Thus, in the Czech Lands, there has been little credible opposition to the Civic Forum. In Slovakia, by way of contrast, the Christian Democratic Movement (*Krest'ansko-demokratické hnutie*, KDH) emerged as a strong counterweight to Public Against Violence. The KDH was founded soon after the November revolution of 1989, with the leadership of former dissident and later Deputy Prime Minister of Slovakia Ján Čarnogurský (who became Prime Minister of Slovakia in April 1990) and held its first congress in February 1990. Its political platform includes affirmation of Christian ideals, commitment to greater sovereignty for Slovakia within the federation, support for families and family values, independence of churches from the state, and the implementation of a market economy. Support for the KDH increased in Slovakia between the June 1990 elections in which it won 19.2 percent of the vote to the Federal Assembly, and the November local elections, in which it emerged as the victor in Slovakia, with 27.4 percent of the local seats.

Part of the governing coalition with Public Against Violence in Slovakia, the KDH has equivocated on national issues. Although the party's leaders supported the coalition position concerning the need to maintain the federation in the early fall of 1990, pressure from more extreme Slovak political groups pushed the KDH to emphasize the need for greater autonomy for Slovakia. The party's second congress, held in early November 1990, affirmed that sudden independence for Slovakia would not be in Slovakia's interest. However, the party supported the right of Slovakia to withdraw from the federation if necessary and pushed for a greater devolution of power to the republics (see ČTK, 3 November 1990a). KDH leaders also proposed several amendments to the economic reform in early 1991 in order to moderate its impact in Slovakia and on the weaker sections of society (Sirota, 1991, pp. 1,3).

Several new parties have been formed around national issues since the end of communist rule. The Movement for Self-Governing Democracy-Association for Moravia and Silesia (Hnutí za samosprávnou demokracii-Společnost pro Moravu a Slezsko), founded on January 23, 1990, has articulated Moravian and Silesian concerns about their status in the common state and called for greater attention to issues that concern these regions. With 7.9 percent of the votes to the House of the People and 9.1 to the House of the Nations, the Movement seated 16 deputies in the Federal Assembly ('Výsledky voleb,' 1990). Movement deputies also formed a coalition with Civic Forum in the Czech National Council. Candidates of this association received 4.7 percent of the votes in the local elections held in November ('Klidný průběh voleb,' 1990).

In early 1991, Movement leaders took the lead in pressing for greater autonomy for Moravia and the adoption of a form of federation that would recognize Moravia's interests. The Movement withdrew from its coalition with Civic Forum in the Czech government in February 1991 as a result of conflicting views on the future organization of the state (Gabrielová, 1991b, pp. 27-8; ij, 1991. See also st, 1991 and 'Žiadajú spolkovú,' 1991, p. 2).

Nationalist political parties have also formed in Slovakia. The Slovak National Party is the most important of these at present. Thought to be funded in part by Slovak *émigré* organizations outside the country, the SNS succeeded in sharpening debate about Slovakia's position in the federation and fueled separatist sentiment. A sponsor of the August 1990 declaration by nine political groups in Slovakia in favor of independence for Slovakia, the party opposed the compromise language bill enacted in October, 1990. Sharp divisions of opinion developed within the SNS in 1990 concerning the activities of one of its leaders, Vitazoslav Moric, and the organization's support of what some of its members perceived to be extremist tactics and positions (see 'O'prípadu Moric, 1990, 'Diferenciácia názarov,' 1990; and 'SNS je za Moricem, 1990, p. 3). Nonetheless, it continues to press for independence for Slovakia.

Other nationally oriented political groups in Slovakia include the National Salvation Front, an association organized to push for the Matica slovenska's draft law on language use, which would have made Slovak mandatory for official use by all citizens of Slovakia, including minorities, and Slovak independence. In November 1990 a more moderate group was created that explicitly rejects the SNS and National Salvation Front position and calls upon Slovaks to work toward their aims within the federation.

Hungarians in Slovakia have also formed political parties, including the Coexistence Party and the Hungarian Christian Democratic Movement, which formed a coalition for the June 1990 elections, and the Hungarian Democratic Initiative, which ran in coalition with Public Against Violence. Representatives of Coexistence also included members of the Ukrainian, Polish, and German minorities. Coexistence candidates received 6.3 percent of the vote in the November 1990 local elections in Slovakia (ČTK, 25 November 1990).

Several political groups have been created to represent the interests of the country's sizeable gypsy minority. The Party of the Democratic Union of Romanies in Slovakia, the Romanies Integration Party, and the Romany Civic Initiative all support greater recognition of the rights of gypsies as an ethnic group, the further development of the Romany language, and measures to upgrade the living conditions of gypsies. Not represented in the Federal Assembly, the Civic Initiative elected 63 candidates to local governmental positions in the November 1990 local elections (see Samková, 1990; and ČTK, November 15, 1990, p. 36).

In addition to these groups, numerous other parties and movements have been created around new political issues. Among the most important of these in early 1990 was the collection of groups devoted to ecological issues that coalesced into the Green Party. Founded on December 19, 1990, the party operated in both Slovakia and the Czech Lands. Although public opinion polls conducted in the Czech Lands in early 1990 indicated that the Greens were the second strongest party after Civic Forum, they did very poorly in the elections and did not seat a deputy in the Federal Assembly. Six Green deputies currently sit in the Slovak National Council. Hindered by the communist past of many of their leaders and followers, the Greens also were hurt by the fact that almost all political parties emphasized the high priority of attending to Czechoslovakia's ecological crisis as well as by the fact that many of the most important activists in the environmental movement ran as or supported Civic Forum or Public Against Violence candidates. As was the case with many of the smaller parties, candidates of the Green Party did better in the local elections, where they won 3.2 percent of the vote in the Czech Lands and gained 452 local government seats in Slovakia (ČTK, 25 November 1990; and čl, 1990, p. 1).

Several right-wing groups and coalitions have also formed. Most of these, such as the Free Block (*Svobodný blok*), a coalition of the Republican Union, the Constitutional Democratic Party, the Free Democrats' Party, and the Czechoslovak Neutrality Party, are very small, and none received enough votes to seat deputies in the federal legislature.

Other political organizations

The end of communist rule has also led to a repluralization of Czechoslovakia's associational life. In addition to the political parties discussed above, citizens may now join a wide variety of independent cultural, religious, professional, charitable, and other organizations. They may also form or join independent trade unions. These opportunities are in stark contrast to the enforced system of mass organizations controlled by the Communist Party prior to 1989.

As noted in chapter 1, Czechoslovakia's associational life was brought under Communist Party control after 1948. The 18 groups of the communist controlled National Front, which had 28 million members in 1988, included the trade unions, women's organizations, and youth leagues, as well as numerous special-interest groups, such as the Czechoslovak-Soviet Friendship Society and the Socialist Academy, in addition to the Communist Party and the minor political parties. From 1969 to 1990, when most of the official mass organizations were disbanded, each typically had Czech and Slovak branches at the republic level. The requirement that all organizations register and be accepted as part of the National Front was used to prevent the formation of independent groups that might challenge the officially sanctioned mass organizations.

The largest of these during the communist period was the unified Revolutionary Trade Union Movement (*Revoluční odborové hnutí*). Consisting of over 27,000 primary union organizations organized by branch of industry, the ROH encompassed over 97 percent of all those employed in the national economy. In the late 1980s, it had approximately 767,000 members (*Rudé právo*, 3 October 1987). As noted in chapter 1, the wave of reform that swept other mass organizations in the late 1960s also had manifestations in the official trade union organization. Change in the leadership of the union organization was accompanied by efforts to redefine its function from mobilization to acting as an interest group to defend workers' interests (see Skilling, 1976, pp. 579-84). 'Normalized' after the end of the reform era, the unions once again served largely to mobilize their members to achieve better economic performance and to support the initiatives of the political leadership. There was some discussion of the need for union organizations to be more responsive to the interests of their members in the wake of the development of the Solidarity movement in Poland in the early 1980s, but little actually came of these discussions.

There were also a variety of other mass organizations in addition to the official trade unions during the communist period. The most important of these were the youth organizations, the Socialist Youth League (*Svaz socialistických mládež*), and the Union of Czechoslovak Women (*Svaz Československých žen*). Established to replace the multitude of partisan and independent associations and organizations for youth and women that existed in the pre-communist and immediate post-Second World War period, these organizations also served largely to mobilize their members to carry out objectives determined by the Communist Party and socialize their members to accept the official value system. The youth organization, which had approximately 1,661,000 members and encompassed 45.4 percent of all young people between the ages of 14 and 29 in 1987 (ČTK *Dokumentační přehled*, 321 1987), placed a heavy emphasis on political education as well as on service to society in the form of volunteer labor. Membership in the youth league, which itself was a stepping-stone to party membership for young people, was a near prerequisite for secondary students who wished to go on to higher education. The impact of this factor was evident in the social composition of the SSM. In 1987, for example, industrial and agricultural workers accounted for only 21.6 percent of the organization's members in the Czech Lands and 25.6 percent in Slovakia. The different appeal and utility of membership in the group to different groups of young people was also evident in the fact that approximately 70 percent of the students in general secondary schools, which prepare students to go on to higher studies, were members of the organization in 1987, but only 30 percent of all workers 25 years of age or younger in the Czech Lands were members (*Mladá fronta*, May 22, 1987, p. 2; and *Smena*, May 12, 1987, p. 1). The women's organization, which was re-established as an organization with a mass membership again only in 1967 after a 17-year hiatus, served primarily as a locus for the political education of women. It also encouraged women to participate in volunteer activities for the good of society.

In the mid- to late 1960s, both of these organizations acted as interest groups in the Western sense of the term. Repudiating their functions as mobilizing agents, officials of both groups began to articulate and defend the particular interests of their members (see Scott, 1974; Heitlinger, 1979, pp. 68–76; and Wolchik, 1978, ch. 6, and 1981a, pp. 139–47; Skilling, 1976, pp. 596–9; and Kusin, 1972, pp. 127–42). Both organizations largely reverted to their former roles after the removal of those leaders who supported the reform movement of 1968. However, the women's organizations continued to pay more attention than during the period prior to 1968 to the particular interests of women. Officials of the organizations cooperated with social scientists who did research on women's situation and gender issues. In contrast to the silence concerning women's actual problems that existed in the 1950s, the state-wide organization's mass-circulation magazines continued to discuss certain problematic aspects of women's situation. As in the mid-1960s, leaders and intellectuals of the organization also participated in the debate about women's issues and policy toward women that began in Czechoslovakia in the late communist period (see Wolchik, 1981a and 1981c; Ondera, 1988, p. 2; and Krno, 1988, p. 5). The positions of the youth organization also began to change somewhat toward the end of communist rule. Leaders of the organization attempted to initiate a dialogue with independent youth groups in 1988 and 1989, for example, and argued for greater attention to the needs of young people.

Leaders of both of these organizations were represented in the leadership of the Communist Party. The heads of the state-wide and Slovak Women's organizations were members of the secretariat of the KSČ and the Slovak party from the early 1970s to the end of communist rule. Vasil Mohorita, the youngest member of the Secretariat in the late communist period and later head of the KSČ, was also the leader of the youth organization.

Another organization that played a large role in political socialization and also served to inform citizens of leadership initiatives during the communist period was the Socialist Academy. Organized after 1969 along republic lines, the Socialist Academies of the Czech and Slovak Socialist Republics organized numerous lectures, seminars, and discussion evenings on contemporary political, social and economic topics.

With the end of communist rule, most of the official mass organizations were abolished. The National Front suspended its activities in February 1990 and became the Association of Political Parties and Social Organizations (see Pehe, 1990a, pp. 7-10). The political organizations and groups that had been grouped in the National Front met diverse fates. Some have attempted to reorient their activities, while others, such as the official writers' union, have dissolved. In the case of the students' and women's groups, truncated versions of the unified organizations still exist, but a variety of independent, autonomous groups have also been created. The official student union, which was one of the sponsors of the demonstrations that sparked the ouster of the communist system, very quickly condemned the police action in November 1989 and began to change its statutes. Although the delegates to its January 1990 congress decided to continue and reform the organization, the many independent student organizations that formed during and after the events of November 1989 have been far more popular with young people (see Yazdgerdi and Obrman, 1990, pp. 22-3). The assets of the official youth organization were returned to the control of the government in early 1991 (ČTK, January 10, 1991).

A similar evolution has occurred in the case of women's organizations. The conservative leadership of the federal women's organization was removed soon after the events of November 1989, and the federal union itself was abolished in April 1990. As in the case of the youth organization, the activities of the republic women's unions which remain have been overshadowed by the growth of small, independent women's groups in both the Czech Lands and Slovakia. The activists of many of these groups are influenced by a reaction to the difficulties that the uneven pattern of change in women's roles during the communist period created for women and their families. Many thus focus on women's roles as mothers and homemakers (see ch. 3; and Wolchik, 1990b, 1991d, and 1991e). Discussion continues concerning the distribution of the official organization's property and assets (Yazdgerdi and Obrman, 1990, p. 24).

The unified Revolutionary Trade Union Movement was abolished in March 1990. Although there has been a proliferation of independent trade unions, and artistic and professional organizations, many have joined together voluntarily in a confederation in order to be more effective in dealing with governmental representatives (ČTK, 16 February 1990). The newly created Czech and Slovak Confederation of Trade Unions consists of 65 unions with more than 6.5 million members that have voluntarily associated themselves with the group, and is the largest union organization in Czechoslovakia. Representatives of the Confederation, which does not have the power of the old organization over its member unions, have criticized several aspects of the government's economic reform program and called for greater attention to the social dimension of economic change (John, 1991, p. 3; and ČTK, 6 December 1990d). In talks with the government in October 1990, the trade unions and the government agreed to cooperate to ease the uncertainties and difficulties of economic transition (ms, 1990b). Tripartite councils of representatives of the governments, employees, and trade unions were established to facilitate negotiations and discussion regarding controversial issues such as the laws on collective bargaining and collective contracts and the labor code ('Accord,' 1990, 'Rada vzájemné dohody,' 1990).

However, trade union representatives have come into conflict with government leaders on numerous occasions, despite this mechanism. Trade union representatives claimed in late 1990, for example, that the tripartite council was bypassed in a number of important areas, such as the plan for small privatization and the new labor code (Červenka, 1990). Trade union officials also demanded a higher minimum wage than that proposed by the government (zr, 1990a). Although the union leaderships have generally urged member unions to avoid strikes, the Confederation called a strike alert in late November 1990 to protest efforts by committees of the Federal Assembly to curtail the right of employees to participate in management that had been included in the proposed labor code as the result of negotiations between the government, employees, and the unions (see cka and zr, 1990, pp. 1,2; and ha and jop, 1990a, pp. 1,4). A general agreement between the federal government, the employers union and the Confederation of Trade Unions that binds all parties to agree to its provisions concerning employment, wages, and procedures, was signed in early 1991 (see 'Generální dohoda,' 1991, p. 3; am, 1991, p. 1; and Fiala, 1991, p. 2). Tensions between the new unions and the government are likely to continue as union organizations seek to protect workers' interests in the transition to a market economy.

The security forces

There have also been important changes in the role of the military and police forces in the period since 1989. In the military, these reflect the effort to depoliticize the army and transform it into a national force under the control of Czechoslovakia's civilian authorities. Important changes have occurred in the size, staffing, doctrine, deployment and international links of the army. These were begun by General Miloslav Vacek, a communist who was appointed Minister of Defense in December 1989 and was recalled from his position by President Havel after it was learned that he complied with orders directed at using the army against the population in November 1989 (jet, 1990a, pp. 1-2; 'Generál Vacek,' 1990; and M. Komárek, 1990, p. 2). Changes continued after Vacek was replaced by a non-communist civilian, Luboš Dubrovský, in October 1990. Competence testing of all soldiers was conducted in 1990 as part of an effort to upgrade the military's professionalism. Approximately 15 percent of those tested, or 9,380 of all professional soldiers had been discharged by early September 1990 (Valašek, 1990). The majority of these (51.6 percent) left the army at their own request. Approximately 23.6 percent (2,200) did not sign the new loyalty oath. These included slightly over one-half of all generals in the army. Two-thirds of all political officials also left military service, although approximately 1,500 career soldiers who worked in these positions remained (Königová, 1990, p. 5). The introduction of an alternative form of civilian service has further depleted the ranks of the military. Over 11,000 individuals, or approximately 6 percent of the total, had been released for such service by September 1990, and a further 13,855 had applied for such release (štp, 1990). By mid-December 1990, 16,477 soldiers had been released (Bratislava Domestic Service, 19 December 1990).

Czechoslovakia's leaders plan to reduce the number of soldiers by 60,000, for a total of 140,000 soldiers in the near future, and by two-thirds by the end of the 1990s (kčr, 1990, p. 7). Military service will be reduced from 18 months to 12 months in 1991. Plans are also under way to reduce major forms of equipment and weapons by 30 to 40 percent, in accordance with the 1990 Vienna Agreement and the November 1990 conventional arms reduction treaty ('Vláda o tancích,' 1991, and Prague Domestic Service, 3 January 1991). Discussion continues concerning a shift to a professional, or partially professional army. Ministry of Defense officials indicate that 43 percent of the army will be professionals by 1993, 60 percent by 1997, and 75 to 78 percent by the year 2000 (ČTK, November 7, 1990b; and ČTK, September 19, 1990. See also Ruttkay, 1990). Czechoslovak military officials have established ties to Western military establishments to improve the professional quality of the army. There have also been important changes in Czechoslovakia's military doctrines and deployment of troops. The doctrine of 'no potential enemy' elaborated in early 1990 was replaced in late 1990 by one that defined the primary mission of the army as defense of the country's sovereignty from any aggressor (kčr, 1990, p. 7). Czechoslovakia's military troops, which were stationed largely in the Western part of the country are to be redeployed more evenly throughout the country, including its eastern border (see ČTK, October 31, 1990). The 35 percent of total troops to be deployed in Slovakia will be housed in part in barracks vacated by departing Soviet troops (Fillo, 1990, pp. 1,3).

Steps have also been taken to decouple Czechoslovakia's army from connections to the Soviet army and Warsaw Pact structures. Over three-fourths of all Soviet troops had withdrawn from Czechoslovakia by the end of 1990. The last of these troops left Slovakia on December 22, 1990; the remainder are scheduled to leave by June 1991. Czechoslovakia's troops stopped taking part in large-scale Warsaw Pact military exercises in 1990. By late 1990, according to military officials, representatives of the Warsaw Pact's command headquarters in Czechoslovakia no longer had any contact with the Czechoslovak army (Hvížďala, 1990b, p. 3).

The developing ties to Western military establishments and aid from the latter to create a more professional military attest to the reassertion of national control over the military. Contacts with NATO military personnel and the participation of a chemical weapons defense group consisting of 179 volunteers sent to perform non-combat tasks with the coalition of international forces that opposed Iraq in the Gulf War in 1991 were further demonstrations of the reorientation of the military.

A new system of border guards, which is expected to be fully in place by January 1993, has begun operation (ČTK, 1 October 1990). Most of these units are currently concentrated on the country's western borders. However, new units will be created to deal with the anticipated emigration of large numbers of Soviets. Approximately 5,000 members of the border guards are currently being used to reinforce police units to deal with the increased crime levels (ČTK, 30 October 1990).

Czechoslovakia's parliament has taken steps to establish greater control over the military by civilian authorities by creating a General Inspector of the Armed Forces. The country's new leaders have also attempted to eliminate the influence of foreign intelligence operatives in the military. Military counterintelligence units which were transferred to the Ministry of Defense from the Ministry of the Interior in early 1990 were abolished by Defense Minister Dobrovský in October 1990 (ČTK, 29 October 1990). They are to be replaced by a smaller military defense intelligence system, consisting of approximately 50 people. This unit, which will be considerably smaller than its predecessor, is scheduled to have 150 members eventually, and will be directly subordinated to the Ministry of Defense (see Spurney, 1990, pp. 17-19; Hvížďala, 1990b, p. 3).

Efforts have also been made to restore popular trust in the army and resurrect some of its traditions from the interwar republic. The army, which was unpopular during the communist period as a result of its politicization and subordination to the Soviet Union (see Rice, 1984b; and Valenta and Rice, 1982), continues to suffer from its past image. Public opinion polls conducted in October 1990 found that only 67 percent of those polled supported maintaining the army, for example; 25 percent did not feel it necessary to have the army. Although a majority of respondents trusted the army, 30 percent did not ('Bez obav z nepřítele,' 1990). The army's prestige was further harmed in 1990 by rumors which were confirmed by a report released in mid-October 1990, that its leaders were prepared to use military force against demonstrators in November 1989.

There have also been major changes in the role and organization of the police. The security forces were an important support of the political leadership during the communist period. This role was particularly great during the Stalinist period. As the results of the investigations of the trials carried out in the 1960s revealed, members of the police forces participated in widespread violations of socialist legality and were, as a result of their connections with Soviet security forces, virtually outside the control of the Communist Party (see Rice, 1984a; Taborsky, 1961, pp. 207–8; and Pelikan, 1971). The decrease in terror and end of political trials that occurred in Czechoslovakia as well as elsewhere after the death of Stalin were accompanied by the restoration of party control over the police and a decrease in the political role of the security forces. However, these forces continued to play an important role in preserving political stability as well as in maintaining public order (see Rice, 1984a).

Many members of the security apparatus, which was one of the bastions of conservatism during the reform era in the late 1960s, willingly helped the post-reform leadership restore orthodoxy (see Skilling, 1976, pp. 407–8). In addition to harassing and repressing dissidents, members of the police also kept watch for signs of potential non-conformity or dissent in the population at large.

Efforts to curtail the power of the security forces were among the first steps taken by the non-communist government in early 1990. The secret police was disbanded, and many former members and officers of the police forces sent home to await their eventual firing. Czechoslovakia's new leaders also attempted to bolster the image of the normal police force, which was also linked in the public mind with the abuses of the past.

Access to the extensive files of the secret police has been one of the most difficult issues in this process. This issue became particularly critical in the context of the campaign for the June 1990 elections, when all candidates were subject to 'lustrace,' or perusal of their secret police files, if any, to insure that they were fit to stand for office. Several candidates, including Josef Bartončík, head of the Czechoslovak People's Party, and Ján Budaj, one of the leaders of Public Against Violence, were discredited by charges that they had agreed to collaborate with the secret police. Access to the secret police files became an issue once again in the fall of 1990, when candidates for election, as well as the members of the government, were screened. As a result of these screenings charges that certain members of the government, including Bedřich Moldan, the Czech Minister of the Environment, and several deputies of the Federal Assembly had collaborated with the secret police were confirmed.

The intelligence arm of the Ministry of the Interior set up by former Interior Minister Richard Sacher after the secret police units were abolished, the Office for the Protection of the Constitution and Democracy, was itself abolished in late December 1990 by Interior Minister Ján Langoš. It is to be replaced by a federal information service which will not be part of the Interior Ministry but rather will be subordinated to the Federal Assembly (rd, 1990; and jaD, 1990, p. 32). The new service will not have any police powers. It will thus not be able to interrogate individuals or conduct home searches as the secret police during the communist regime did. Its main focus will be on international crime, drugs, and terrorism (ČTK, 14 September 1990; and 'Šubert,' 1990). Controversy continues, however, concerning the organization, size and overall function of this body.

Discussion also re-emerged in late 1990 concerning the relationship between the Ministry of the Interior and the KGB. Presidential spokesman Michael Žantovský argued that a March 1, 1990 agreement of cooperation between the two bodies signed by then Minister of the Interior Sacher which envisioned further, although limited cooperation in certain specified areas, was in fact a 'dead letter' from the beginning and denied that any contact between the KGB and Czechoslovakia's security forces had taken place (ČTK, 3 December 1990; and V. Mlýnař, 1990, p. 2). However, reports that former members of the security forces have been hired by foreign intelligence services were confirmed by the director of the Office for the Protection of the Constitution and Democracy in December 1990 (ČTK, 5 December 1990). The reliability of former employees of the secret police who continue to work in this office and in the Ministry of the Interior also continues to be problematic (see Probostová and Kramer, 1990, p. 8).

Efforts have also been made to upgrade the position and authority of the ordinary police which were very low as the result of the association of all order-keeping forces with the abuses of the communist period (see 'Výskum naznačuje strach a obavy,' 1990, p. 2). In addition to reform in the administrative structure of the police, steps have been taken to deal with the very rapid increase in violent crime and the development of organized and drug-related crime. According to federal Interior Minister Ján Langoš, the crime rate rose by 41 percent in the first six months of 1990 (J. Tuček, 1990, pp. 1,2). Crime increased by a total of 122 percent in 1990. Of the serious crimes reported, the vast majority occurred in Prague ('Rok hledání,' 1991, p. 2; and mag, 1991, p. 4). Several special units were established in 1990 to patrol particularly crime-prone areas of large cities. However, the police forces in both the Czech Lands and Slovakia are still shorthanded (jet, 1990b, p. 8; Adamičková and Königová, 1990; and 'Serious Crime,' 1990). Substantial problems still exist, then, in creating security forces that will be both adequate to insure domestic order and protect the country from external threats and loyal to the new democratic government.

Political culture

As the preceding section has illustrated, the structure of political life has changed in important ways in Czechoslovakia since the end of communist rule. Although both the party system and the political structure of the state are still evolving, the outlines of a democratic political framework are in place. There have also been important changes in the political values and attitudes expressed by the population since the end of communist rule. However, the process of recreating a political culture that will be supportive of democracy is a complex one that will take longer to accomplish than changes in political structures.

The many ways in which Czechoslovakia differed from its neighbors during the interwar period, as well as the diverse histories of the Czechs and the Slovaks, continued to be reflected in the political values, attitudes, and opinions of the population during the communist period. However, as in other communist states, Marxism-Leninism was the official, explicit, value system in Czechoslovakia. It was also the only ideology that was legitimate.

Marxism-Leninism served several functions. As is the case with other ideologies, it expressed the official goals and values of the system. In theory, it also served to orient citizens to the world and their place in it. Thus, it justified the stratification system and the hierarchy of rewards and benefits; it also embodied expectations concerning the political system (including the rights and obligations of citizens), and the proper role of the state, and reflected judgments concerning what tools of influence were legitimate and other rules of the political game. Marxism-Leninism also served as a framework of analysis that influenced the way in which public issues and problems were conceptualized and determined which solutions could be considered. Finally, as in other communist countries, Marxism-Leninism acted as a language of political communication and was used to justify and legitimate policy choices made by political leaders (Lane, 1971, pp. 1-2).

Even prior to the collapse of communist rule, the functions of Marxism-Leninism had gradually changed in Czechoslovakia. As in other communist states, the role of ideology in determining the goals and public policies of the country declined. Thus, although the official ideology as interpreted by the leaders of the Communist Party served to make certain policy options difficult if not impossible to pursue, it was often of little relevance to the concrete decisions political leaders made (see Meyer, 1967; and Lowenthal, 1970, pp. 52-4, for discussions of the declining importance of ideology as a guide to policy-making in communist states).

In Czechoslovakia, as in other communist countries, the actual political beliefs, attitudes, and values of the population, i.e. the country's political culture, differed considerably from the official ideology during the communist period. These differences reflected the continued influence of the country's previous political history and pre-communist political culture, as well as the results of the population's experiences with the realities of political and economic systems dominated by the Communist Party. As the overthrow of communist systems throughout much of Central and Eastern Europe in 1989 and the course of political life since that time illustrate, the influence of the pre-communist value system remained strong in many of these countries. The particular amalgam of officially approved and other beliefs, values, and attitudes that made up each nation's political culture also reflected the different efforts political leaders made to change values. In Czechoslovakia, as in other communist countries, communist political leaders did not try to change all aspects of the pre-communist value system. Rather, their approach was a selective one. In some areas they attempted to eliminate pre-existing values and beliefs and replace them with new ones derived from Marxism-Leninism. In others, they sought to use traditional values and attitudes to support the communist system (see Gitelman, 1970; Jowitt, 1974; and Wolchik, 1978, chs. 6 and 7).

The extent of the gap between officially approved and actual values, attitudes, and beliefs was very difficult to determine with any degree of certainty in Czechoslovakia during most of the communist period. As Gail Lapidus has noted in the Soviet case, we know relatively little about this aspect of politics in communist states because very little empirical research was carried out on these topics in most of these countries, and much of what was done was not accessible to Western scholars (Lapidus, 1975, p. 91). Much more information about the political attitudes, values, and preferences of citizens became available in several of the European communist countries in the late 1980s. The expansion of public opinion polling and survey research on explicitly political topics in Poland and Hungary in the late 1980s and the creation of new centers for such research in the Soviet Union provided new and more systematic information on such topics. The results of these studies in Poland and Hungary in large measure confirm the more impressionistic picture one gains from observing the reactions of the Polish and Hungarian people to the crumbling of the Communist system in each case. In Poland, for example, the picture that emerges from public opinion polls and survey research conducted in the spring of 1988 is of a population that was deeply alienated from the ruling Communist Party and its leaders, but put high levels of trust in Solidarity and the Church (see Kwiatkowski, 1989). In Hungary, by way of contrast, the results of research conducted in the last several years of communist rule indicated a sharp decline in trust in and satisfaction with the Hungarian Socialist Workers' Party and its leaders and a deep-seated lack of sense of political efficacy. The majority of Hungarians studied, however, also distrusted most opposition groups and emerging parties (see Bruszt, 1988).

Unfortunately, given the impact of 'normalization' on social science research in Czechoslovakia after 1969, there is far less information available on political attitudes and values in Czechoslovakia during the communist period than in Hungary, Poland, or Yugoslavia. Nonetheless, information from a variety of sources, including public opinion surveys and social science research, *émigré* interviews, official commentary, personal observation, and political humor, provides some clues about the values of the citizens of Czechoslovakia during this time.

Czechoslovakia's political culture during the communist period reflected the influence of pre-communist traditions and certain aspects of Marxist-Leninist ideology. It also included values and attitudes that were not intentionally fostered by the political leadership but arose from the population's experience with the communist system. Several features of the country's pre-communist culture were of particular importance during the communist period. As noted in chapter 1, there was a great discrepancy between Czechoslovakia's dominant democratic political culture and Marxism-Leninism at the outset of the communist period. The experience of the citizens of Czechoslovakia with a functioning democratic system in the interwar period and, in the case of the Czechs in particular, the ability to participate in politics in the last years of Austrian rule, are often held to have fostered an abiding belief in political pluralism and attachment to democratic procedures (see Brown, 1979, p. 170 but also see Skilling, 1985, pp. 117-20 and Paul, 1985, pp. 135-40). The country also had a very strong social democratic tradition, which combined respect for political pluralism with a commitment to social justice. At the same time, however, there were other political traditions that contradicted the dominant democratic value system. The duality evident in the high levels of support for the Communist Party was paralleled by a certain level of support for authoritarian and fascist movements and policies, particularly in Slovakia. Finally, from the beginning of the country's existence as an independent state, there have been important differences in the political attitudes and values of Czechs and Slovaks (see Brown, 1979; Skilling, 1977 and 1985; and Paul, 1985).

The impact of these aspects of the pre-communist culture was evident in a number of ways during the communist period. The continued influence of the pluralistic elements of Czechoslovakia's political traditions was reflected in the reform movement of the 1960s. Although it was led by communist intellectuals and political leaders whose vision of political change did not encompass a renunciation of the Communist Party's monopoly of power, the reform movement of the 1960s evoked broader support for political pluralism among the larger population (see Piekalkiewicz, 1972; Brown, 1979, p. 170; Skilling, 1977; and Paul, 1979). Public opinion polls conducted during this period also found that many citizens, particularly Czechs, continued to view the interwar republic favorably. Many citizens also had high levels of respect for President Masaryk (Brown, 1979, pp. 178-9). The country's pre-communist social democratic traditions were reflected in high levels of support for egalitarianism during the communist period, as well as in expectations that the state would provide a high degree of social welfare (see Brown, 1979, pp. 173-4). As chapter 3 will discuss in greater detail, many Czechs and Slovaks appeared to accept the low wage differentials and the emphasis on the state's responsibility to provide for the social welfare of citizens that prevailed during the communist period.

Differences in the political values of Czechs and Slovaks also continued to be evident in a number of areas during this time. Studies conducted in the 1960s demonstrated the differing importance attached to national figures and those exemplifying traditions of political pluralism, as well as the far less positive views of most

Slovaks toward the interwar republic (Brown, 1979, pp. 163-9). As chapter 3 will discuss in more detail, members of the two groups also differed in the 'extent to which they adhered to religious beliefs during the communist period.

The participation of large numbers of citizens in the dramatic wave of demonstrations that led to the resignation of the Jakeš leadership in November 1989 was a clear indication of their dissatisfaction with the communist system and desire for political change. The rejection of the communist system evident in the mass actions of citizens at that time was presaged by the results of a number of public opinion surveys conducted in the late communist period. The results of these studies, which in many cases could not be published fully, but dealt with more controversial topics than had been permitted earlier, demonstrated high levels of alienation from the system. Large groups of citizens had little interest in political activities and many, including party members, expressed negative views about the Communist Party. Research conducted in 1989 by the Institute for Research on Public Opinion, for example, found that only one-third of respondents felt the leading role of the party was necessary. Nearly 50 percent felt it was not at all needed (Slavíková, 1989, p. 7). Surveys conducted by the Institute for Public Opinion Research in Prague in 1989 also illustrated decreased support for the notion that Czechoslovakia's foreign policy should continue to lean heavily on the Warsaw Pact. Whereas 85 percent of those questioned in 1987 agreed that membership in the Pact was important for the defense of Czechoslovakia, by mid-1989, this proportion had decreased to 47 percent. Significant proportions of citizens also disagreed with the view that Czechoslovakia should cooperate economically primarily with socialist states (Slavíková, 1989, pp. 8-9). The results of the study of citizen attitudes toward local governments discussed earlier in this chapter also demonstrated the low sense of personal efficacy of most citizens.

Studies of young people conducted in 1989 prior to the revolution also documented growing dissatisfaction with the communist system. Forty-four percent of young people surveyed in May 1989, for example, felt that the existing political system was not democratic. Approximately a third felt that the rights and freedoms of citizens were guaranteed only for a minority of the population or for no one. This survey also demonstrated a very low level of political efficacy and activity among young people. Only 12 percent, for example, felt they had great opportunities to take part in the leadership of society; more than a third stated that they had virtually no possibility of participating in decision-making on public issues. Over 80 percent indicated that they had no possibility of influencing the work or positions of political organizations. Two-thirds of the young people surveyed also felt that young people's representation in leadership positions was insufficient. The extent of youth's dissatisfaction with the existing system was evident in the fact that 90 percent of those surveyed felt further decentralization and fundamental economic change were necessary. Most were also highly dissatisfied with the pace of change and cynical about the outcome of official policies of 'přestavba' or restructuring. Increasing numbers of youth expressed critical views concerning the leading role of the Communist Party and the privileges that accrued to party members. This study also documented the instrumental function that membership in the Communist Party played for many people (Tomek, 1990b).

The failure of young people to internalize many of the officially supported values of the communist regime was also evident in the number (two-thirds), who indicated that they followed political events rarely or not at all (compared to approximately 50 percent of older citizens), and participated in regime activities because they were required to do so rather than of their own volition (50 percent) (Tomek, 1990b). These results confirmed those of other studies that found very low levels of involvement among young people in political actions (see chapter 3).

Similar glimpses of the extent of popular disaffection from the political system are evident in the results of a study of nationality relations conducted in April and May 1989. Approximately 53 percent of the respondents felt that they had good or rather good opportunities to participate in political decisionmaking, a decrease from the 80 percent who held these views in 1983. Levels of dissatisfaction in this regard were most noticeable among those with higher education. The decline in satisfaction was greatest among non-party members but fewer party members also felt they had the opportunity to participate in public life in 1989 than in 1983 (Mišovič, 1990, pp. 45-6). Although the majority of respondents indicated that they did not wish to live in another country, two-thirds of those studied stated that they were not proud to be citizens of Czechoslovakia. One-third indicated that they sometimes felt ashamed to be citizens of the country (Mišovič, 1990, pp. 50-2).

As chapter 3 will discuss in greater detail, survey research conducted during the communist period demonstrated low levels of political interest among women. Attitudes at variance with Marxism-Leninism were also evident in the continued religious observation of many citizens and in the persistence of attitudes concerning members of other national groups at odds with official views on this matter.

The latter differences were clearly reflected in a study of nationality relations completed in April and May 1989 and published in May 1990. Conducted by the Institute for Research on Public Opinion, the survey found that the majority of the inhabitants of both the Czech Lands and Slovakia felt that relations between Czechs and Slovaks were friendly or rather friendly (69 percent). This proportion was lower than the 79 percent of respondents in 1983 who evaluated these relations positively. Czechs were less positive than Slovaks (66 percent and 76 percent) (Mišovič, 1990, p. 12). Attitudes were less positive among Slovaks in regard to relations with Hungarians and Ukrainians and among Czechs with Poles (ibid., p.19). The majority of other national groups felt that their relations with gypsies were poor (ibid., p.20). Slovak respondents judged the contribution of the federation to the development of both Slovakia and the Czech Lands more favorably than Czechs (ibid., p.35). Each group felt the other to be overrepresented in political positions (ibid., p.37). As in earlier studies, Czechs and Slovaks identified different historical periods as most important and different historical figures as most worthy of respect (ibid., pp. 54-5).

The end of the Communist Party's monopoly of political power and the move toward pluralism in Central and Eastern Europe have been accompanied by the re-emergence of many pre-communist political symbols and the more open expression of certain pre-communist political values particular to each of the countries in the region. In Czechoslovakia, these symbols and values are those associated with the dominant pluralistic political culture of the inter-war period. Values related to national identity have also become more important, particularly in Slovakia. One of the central questions regarding the country's political culture at present is the amount of influence the country's democratic traditions have on the current political beliefs and values of citizens, given the interruption of the tradition for 50 years, and the fact that there are very few citizens left who have any personal experience with the democratic political system of the interwar period.

The numerous public opinion studies that have been conducted in late 1989 and 1990 illustrate the rapid shift in public preferences and political attitudes that has followed the end of communist rule. They also document the re-emergence of values supportive of democracy among sizeable groups of citizens. Thus, public opinion surveys confirm that there was widespread support for the change in political systems, as well as a favorable attitude toward democracy in late 1989 and early 1990. In the early weeks after the fall of the communist government, levels of political interest and involvement were very high. A survey conducted by the Institute for Research on Public Opinion in December 1989, for example, found that 84 percent of citizens discussed politics almost daily in the first week after November 17, and 87 percent in the second week (Herzmann, 1989, p. 5). Sixty-eight percent of a sample of citizens 15 years of age and older had participated in public manifestations and meetings in the previous three weeks, many more than once (Herzmann, 1989, pp. 5-6). Citizens from larger cities and supporters of Civic Forum were more likely to be involved in this way, but 17 percent of those who were Communist Party members also had participated in such activities.

A January 1990 survey conducted by the Association for Independent Social Analysis also documented high levels of interest and involvement among citizens. Fifty-four percent of those surveyed, for example, expressed a willingness to take an active role in political affairs, and 38 percent indicated that they would be willing to run for public office (Boguszak, Gabal, and Rak, 1990a). There was also a rapid decline in trust in the Communist Party and government and an increase in trust in representatives of Civic Forum and Public Against Violence. Thus, only 3 percent of the 746 citizens surveyed in December 1989 by the Institute for Research on Public Opinion trusted almost all of the representatives of the Communist Party and 7 percent trusted most of them. Three percent trusted most of the members of the government, and 9 percent some of them. Twenty percent trusted almost all of the representatives of Civic Forum and 27 percent most of them (Slavíková, 1989, p. 7). Levels of support for the newly created Civic Forum and Public Against Violence increased very quickly. As early as late November 1989, for example, 76 percent of those questioned indicated that they identified their hopes for the future with these movements. The newly created Green Party and independent unions also received high levels of support (58 and 59 percent), compared to the Communist Party (21 percent), and other established political organizations, such as the minor parties and official trade unions (Herzmann, 1989; and Slavíková, 1989, p. 9).

High levels of political mobilization were still evident in May 1990 when a survey conducted by the Institute for Research on Public Opinion found that 52 percent of a sample of 741 participated in a general strike on April 11, 1990 to support the demand that the Communist Party return its property. A further 17 percent of the respondents attended mass demonstrations although they did not strike and an additional 23 percent supported the demand symbolically (Dubský, 1990). Voters in Czechoslovakia also displayed high levels of interest in the election campaign. According to a representative survey of 2,004 citizens conducted in mid-May 1990, only 10 percent were not interested in the campaign (Tomek, 1990a, p. 1). Only 11 percent did not discuss the campaign with their neighbors and families (Tomek, 1990a, p. 2).

Citizens' optimism concerning the future of democracy and trust in leading figures in the new government increased in late 1989 and early 1990, as did support for more radical political and economic reforms. Thus, 86 percent of a sample of 2,400 respondents 15 to 69 years of age surveyed in January 1990 were happy with recent political developments. Most (83 percent) also believed that the

Table 2.5 Public representatives whom the public trusted, 1989—90

	11/11-12/1/89		12/9-12/12/89		1/31/89-2/5/90		3/27-4/4/90	
	Most	Least	Most	Least	Most	Least	Most	Least
V. Havel	10	13	18	11	60	4	51	5
M. Čalfa			4	1	8	7	10	3
V. Klaus					3	1	10	4
A. Dubček	2	2	2	1	7	3	4	3
Čarnogurský	0	0	1	1	0	0	2	2
M. Kňažko	3	2	2	1	0	0	0	0

Source: Institut pro výzkum veřejného mínění, 1990b, p. 3.

Table 2.6 Trust in leading organs and in the President of the Republic (%)

	Feb. 23-28, 1990			Apr. 23-May 5, 1990		
Trust	yes	no	don't know	yes	no	don't know
President of the Republic	88	9	3	88	10	2
Federal Government	83	11	6	81	16	3
Czech and Slovak Republic Govts	79	13	8	78	16	6
Federal Assembly	76	19	5	54	41	5
Local National Committees	31	58	11	31	60	9

Source: Institut pro výzkum veřejného mínění, 1990a.

political changes under way would lead not just to change of leaders but to a major transformation of the political system (c, 1990a, pp. 1,2).

As Table 2.5 illustrates, the extent to which the public trusted President Havel and other leading figures in the new government changed radically in the course of early 1990. Although trust in certain other prominent figures also increased, Havel's emergence as the most trusted public official is striking.

The research results summarized in Table 2.6 confirm the high regard in which the public held the President. They also illustrate the difference in popular trust in Havel and other institutions of government.

Further evidence of the resurgence of pluralistic values is seen in attitudes toward the Communist Party. Thus, a May 1990 survey conducted by the Institute for Public Opinion Research found that most citizens distrusted the Communist Party and felt that it would act in the same way it had in the past if it were to win the elections (63 percent). However, only 24 percent of those surveyed strongly favored a ban of the party. An additional 15 percent stated that they would agree with such a ban. The majority of citizens (60 percent) opposed such a step (c, 1990b, p. 18). Similar views were expressed in another survey conducted by the Institute for Public Opinion Research in May 1990 in which 72 percent of respondents thought that the Communist Party should have the same rights and responsibilities as all other parties (Dubský, 1990).

Public opinion surveys also illustrate the rapid shift in public preferences and political attitudes toward reform and the nature of society that followed the end of communist rule. Thus, only 3 percent of citizens questioned in late November 1989 and early December 1989 wanted to see Czechoslovakia choose a capitalist path of development. Forty-seven and 52 percent preferred something between socialism and capitalism, while 45 and 41 percent preferred a continuation of a socialist path (Herzmann, 1989, p. 7). There was a similarly high degree of reluctance to accept privatization of the economy. Approximately the same percentages of respondents were opposed or very strongly opposed (14 percent and 8 percent) to the privatization of large as well as small enterprises in December 1989 as in May 1989 (14 and 6 percent) (Herzmann, 1989, p. 8).

By early January 1990, 63 percent of respondents favored the development of a private sector and 43 percent indicated their willingness to tolerate a decline in the standard of living in order to create a market economy (Boguszak, Gabal, and Rak, 1990a). In May, 1990, 50 percent of the population was willing to tolerate such a decrease. Support also increased for a more rapid rather than slower reform between January 1990, when 42 percent of those questioned favored such an approach, and May 1990, when 58 percent did. Nearly 50 percent of respondents stated that they would approve of the sale of the enterprise in which they were employed in May 1990 (Boguszak and Rak, 1990a, pp. 25, 31).

The high levels of involvement in politics associated with the dramatic events of late 1989 and early 1990 declined significantly after the June elections. By October 1990, for example, only 4 percent of the population surveyed indicated that they were personally involved in politics (Ib, 1990). Levels of satisfaction with the government and optimism also decreased. Thus, by May 1990, 66 percent of the population was very or rather satisfied with the political situation. Nearly one-half (45 percent) of those surveyed felt that the November revolution had gone well in the beginning, but had 'somehow turned sour,' compared to 26 percent who were still satisfied with the results. Optimism concerning future political developments also decreased, to be replaced by the opinion that only individuals, not the system, would change (13 percent), and a more realistic assessment of the complexity of the situation. Although nearly one-half of respondents (43 percent) expected continued long-term progress toward a permanent democracy, only 5 percent expected such development to be rapid and without problems (c, 1990b, p. 7. See Institut pro výzkum veřejného mínění, 1990c, pp. 2-3, for similar results and variation in responses).

Approval of political leaders, including Václav Havel, also decreased somewhat. Lower levels of support for President Havel in Slovakia were evident in the smaller proportion (65 percent) of Slovaks than of Czechs (81 percent) surveyed in late April and early May 1990 who agreed that he should continue as President after the elections (Institut pro výzkum veřejného mínění, 1990c, and 1990d, p. 9). Although trust in the President continued to be very high in the Czech Republic, it declined significantly in Slovakia in the course of 1990. Thus, 90 percent of those polled in the Czech Republic in January 1991 expressed their confidence in the President, who ranked above the federal government and other governmental institutions. In Slovakia, however, the proportion of the population who trusted the President (60 percent) was substantially lower and also lower than the level of trust in the Slovak government (85 percent), the Slovak National Council (69 percent), and several Slovak politicians, including Vladimír Mečiar, then the Prime Minister of Slovakia, (Tomek and Forst, 1991a). Confidence in political leaders and institutions declined in both republics in the early months of 1991. In March, 48 percent of the population trusted the Federal Government and 39 percent the Federal Assembly. Trust in President Havel also declined (to 78 percent), but remained higher than that in the above institutions (Matuška, 1991).

Although the developments of 1989 and the emergence of political values since that time clearly illustrate the lack of legitimacy of communist rule in Czechoslovakia as well as elsewhere in Central and Eastern Europe, they do not necessarily mean the wholesale rejection of all of the beliefs and values promoted by the leadership in the communist period. (See the studies in Brown and Gray, 1979, for overviews of the political cultures of these countries prior to the collapse of communism.) As the results of surveys of Soviet *émigrés* illustrate, even those citizens dissatisfied enough to leave a state may have internalized certain elements of the approved value system (see Gitelman, 1977b; Millar, 1987; and White, 1979).

It is very likely, then, that the political culture that is emerging in countries in the region will include elements, both positive and negative, that can be traced to the influence of the official value structure of the last four or, in the case of the Soviet Union, the last seven, decades, as well as to the practical experience of living under communist rule. Certain of these values, including expectations concerning the responsibility of the state to provide social welfare benefits, free education and medical care, and full employment, will in all likelihood continue to color citizen expectations of the political authorities. Others, such as negative attitudes toward work and the view that it is not the responsibility of the individual to contribute actively to solving social problems, can be expected to create difficulties for whatever political and economic systems eventually evolve (see Musil and Linhart, 1990; and Slejška, 1990; Boguszak and Rak, 1990a; see Skilling, 1985 and Paul, 1985 for analyses of the factors that influence changes in political cultures).

Surveys of the population's attitudes toward economic change and its costs illustrate these trends in Czechoslovakia. In a survey conducted by the Association for Independent Social Analysis in early 1990, over 40 percent of all citizens identified economic reform as the main task facing the current government, compared with the 29 percent who felt environmental issues were most important, and 16 percent the continued development of freedom and democracy. Support for rapid steps to create a market economy even at the cost of a temporary marked drop in the living standard increased between January and June 1990 from 43 to 58 percent (Boguszak and Rak, 1990a, p. 17). However, most citizens, especially in Slovakia, underestimated the extent of the likely decrease in the standard of living and the time that will be needed for the transition (Boguszak and Rak, 1990a, p. 18). Over half of the citizens surveyed in January and 80 percent in May 1990 accepted unemployment as a necessary cost of the transition to a market economy. Only 24 percent of respondents felt that unemployment should be avoided even at the cost of ending economic reform (Boguszak and Rak, 1990a, Table 5). However, most citizens also supported maintaining a high level of social security. Respondents in the Czech Republic were considerably more willing to endure the loss of their present jobs (48 percent) than those in Slovakia (37 percent) (Boguszak and Rak, 1990a, Table 5). In the Czech Lands, acceptance of unemployment was lowest in Northern Bohemia, one of the regions most likely to be affected (Boguszak and Rak, 1990a, p. 20).

The impact of the communist period on popular expectations of the government is also reflected in the results of a May 1990 survey conducted by the Association for Independent Social Analysis which found that most citizens expect the state to continue to provide and finance basic health care and pensions (84 percent and 80 percent). Thirty-eight percent also want the government to take complete responsibility for ensuring a decent living standard for everyone. Significant proportions of citizens believe that the individual should take some responsibility in this area as well as in securing housing, but many want the state to continue its involvement in these areas (see Boguszak and Rak, 1990a, pp. 33-4). Those with lower education and skill levels are most likely to hold these attitudes. Such views are also more widespread in Slovakia than in the Czech Lands (see Table 2.7).

The impact of Czechoslovakia's egalitarian tradition and the important role the state played in economic life in the pre-communist as well as the communist period are also evident in attitudes concerning privatization of industrial firms. Forty-six percent of those surveyed in May 1990 stated that they would agree to the sale of such enterprises if they were unprofitable, but only 23 percent would approve of the privatization of large firms without consideration of their profitability to Czechoslovak citizens and 18 percent to foreign firms (Boguszak and Rak, 1990a, pp. 26-7).

The devastating impact of communist rule on work morale is also reflected in the results of this survey. Over 70 percent of those surveyed admitted, for example, that they could work more and improve their work performance, but most indicated that they had not changed their behavior in this respect. This pattern was most noticeable among higher professionals (83 percent) (Boguszak and Rak, 1990a, p. 30).

Significant differences also continue to exist in the attitudes of Czechs and Slovaks. These are evident in attitudes toward the political situation and economic reform, as well as in evaluations of public figures and institutions. Czechs and Slovaks also differ markedly in views concerning the best form of state arrangements.

Survey research conducted by the Association for Independent Social Analysis, for example, found that respondents in Slovakia were somewhat less likely (37 percent) than those in the Czech Republic (47 percent) to indicate that they were very satisfied with the current political situation in January 1990. By May 1990, 13 percent of Czechs and 11 percent of Slovaks were very satisfied. However, 41 percent of Slovaks, compared to 31 percent of Czechs were either dissatisfied or very dissatisfied (from data in Boguszak and Rak, 1990a, Table 1). As noted earlier in this chapter, Slovaks were also less eager to have Václav Havel remain President and had less favorable views of the President, although a majority (60 percent) of Slovaks still indicated that they trusted him in early 1991. Differences between the two groups in satisfaction levels and in their evaluations of public figures continued to grow in the last months

Table 2.7 Comparison of political and economic views of inhabitants of the Czech and Slovak Republics, 1990 (%)

	Czech Republic	Slovak Public
Satisfied with the current political situation	70	58
Agree that unemployment should be avoided even at the cost of significantly hindering or even suspending economic reform	19	34
Would select a harsher and more accelerated version of economic reform	61	51
Willing to accede to 50 percent price increases in essential goods	53	39
Willing to accept the loss of current employment	48	37
Fears about a decline in the standard of living	60	70
Would strike following a considerable increase in the cost of essential goods	37	50
Would strike if major cut in social security	62	61
Think that the state should bear complete responsibility for finding employment for every citizen	32	47
Think that the state should bear complete responsibility for ensuring a decent standard of living for each citizen	34	46
Willing to achieve a top level in job or occupation	39	44
Prefer being self-employed, intend to start a private enterprise	7	7
Plan to set up private enterprise	14	13

Sources: From Boguszak and Rak, 1990a, Table 1, and 1990b, p. 4.

of 1990. Slovaks also tended to be somewhat less interested and involved in politics in the immediate post-November 1989 period (see Dubský, 1990; and Herzmann, 1989, p. 5), although differences were not great.

A May 1990 survey conducted by the ASIA found that inhabitants of Slovakia were more likely to see the changes that had taken place since November as merely a reshuffle of people (18 percent), than those in the Czech Republic (11 percent). They also were less likely than Czechs (35 percent compared to 47 percent) to expect long-term development with constant and visible progress toward democracy (Boguszak and Rak, 1990a, Table 1).

The views of inhabitants of the Czech Republic and Slovakia on economic reform also differ in important ways. Although support for radical economic reform grew in both republics in 1990, residents of Slovakia are less enthusiastic about the need for such measures and less willing than Czechs to accept the negative consequences. A survey conducted by the Association for Independent Social Analysis in May 1990 found, for example, that 51 percent of Slovaks, compared to 61 percent of Czechs, supported a fast and radical reform with quick improvement rather than a 'soft' reform with more gradual improvement. Sixty-one percent of Slovaks, compared to 75 percent of Czechs, agreed that fundamental economic reform would be impossible without a temporary marked decline in the standard of living. As Table 2.7 illustrates, fewer Slovaks than Czechs were willing to accept a 50 percent increase in the price of basic goods if necessary or the loss of their current jobs. Fears concerning a decline in the standard of living, price increases, and unemployment were also greater in Slovakia than in the Czech Lands. These attitudes were related to a greater willingness to strike if the cost of essential goods were to increase considerably, although approximately equal numbers of Czechs and Slovaks indicated that they would strike if social security benefits were reduced markedly (Boguszak and Rak, 1990a, Table 1, p. 36; and Centrum, 1990a, p. 4).

Support for the view that the state should retain a high degree of responsibility for ensuring citizens' living standards and employment was also higher in Slovakia than in the Czech Republic. However, there were relatively small differences in attitudes concerning privatization, interest in starting a private business, or willingness to accept more important economic positions (see Table 2.8. See Boguszak and Rak, 1990b, for more detailed analysis).

Inhabitants of the Czech Lands and Slovakia also differ markedly in their attitudes toward the federation and the federal government. Thus, although only 8 percent of Slovaks (compared to 5 percent of

Tabe 2.8   Attitudes concerning the structure of the state, June 1990

In favor of:	ČSFR	Czech Republic	Slovak Republic
Common state, strong central government	33	42	16
Common state, strong republic government	34	30	41
Confederation	21	16	30
Two wholly independent Czech and Slovak states	6	5	8
Don't know, other	6	7	5

Source: L. Beneš, 1990, p. 1.

Czechs) surveyed in June 1990 were in favor of two wholly separate states, significantly more Slovaks (30 percent) than Czechs (16 percent) were in favor of a confederation. As Table 2.8 illustrates, Czechs were more likely than Slovaks to support a strong federal government. Slovaks were more favorable to a common state with considerable powers for the republic-level governments. A public opinion poll conducted in January 1991 found similar results. Inhabitants of the Czech Republic were more likely to favor a single state with one government (32 percent) or a federal state (33 percent) than a confederation (11 percent). Although the largest numbers of respondents in Slovakia also favored a federation (43 percent), a sizeable number (21 percent) favored confederation. Significantly more Slovaks (9 percent) than Czechs (3 percent) favored two wholly independent states. Support for separate states (5 percent overall) was higher in January 1991 than in June 1990, but had decreased from the 11 percent of all respondents who favored this option in October 1990 (Mišovič, 1991).

Similar attitudes are evident in the higher degree of trust Slovaks place in republic rather than federal institutions and politicians. Thus, a survey conducted by the Institute for Public Opinion Research in late January and early February 1991 found high levels of trust in the Czech Republic in the President (89 percent), Czech (67 percent), and federal governments (58 percent), as well as the Federal Assembly (62 percent). In Slovakia, however, trust was highest in the Slovak government (77 percent), and Slovak National Council

(67 percent), followed by the President (57 percent) and Federal Assembly (48 percent). More respondents in Slovakia distrusted the federal government (51 percent), than trusted it (44 percent) (Tomek and Forst, 1991).

The political values and attitudes of the population in Czechoslovakia, then, reflect the impact of the rapid and dramatic political changes of the recent past, as well as the legacy of communist rule. As analysts of the Association for Independent Social Analysis and other observers note, the political attitudes of many citizens are still very fluid at present. There are also many inconsistencies in the attitudes and values of individuals (Boguszak and Rak, 1990a). It is also not yet clear how important the legacy of the dominant democratic political culture of the interwar period will be. Although values supportive of democracy have re-emerged and gained widespread acceptance, it is too early to tell how lasting and deep the commitment to these values is among Czech and Slovak citizens. Popular political values and expectations of citizens and the state continue to be colored by the experience of communist rule to some extent, as well as, increasingly, by nationalist sentiments. As the movements for democratic change in East Germany, Poland, and Hungary suggest, the new amalgam of political values that emerges in these states may also include values and beliefs that have few if any roots in the country's previous political history and traditions.

Political elites

From February 1948 to November 1989, the effective political elite in Czechoslovakia consisted of those individuals who held the top positions in the Communist Party. This group, which at the national level included the members of the Presidium and the Secretariat, consisted of 20 individuals in late November 1989. The 197 members of the Central Committee, the 12 members of the Presidium and Secretariat of the Slovak Communist Party, and the 14 regional party first secretaries and first secretaries of the Prague and Bratislava party organizations formed a second level of the effective political elite.

Prior to the demonstrations of November 1989, the Communist Party leadership in Czechoslovakia appeared to be at the beginning of the second stage of what seemed likely to be a two-stage succession similar to that which we saw in the Soviet Union in the post-Brezhnev era. The first stage, in which Miloš Jakeš, who was 67 years old in November 1989, replaced Gustáv Husák (who was 76 in November 1989) as top party leader, brought a somewhat younger leader to power. However, given Jakeš's association with the policies of his predecessor and, in particular, the key role he played in the normalization of the party as the man who oversaw the exchange of party cards in 1971, it is not surprising that he did not spearhead any radical departures from his predecessor's policies.

The policies pursued by the Jakeš leadership from 1987 to 1989 were also conditioned by another factor, i.e. the extent of generational turnover within the top leadership. After a period of great stability in top party bodies, the late 1980s witnessed substantial changes in the composition of the Presidium, particularly among its full members. This process brought in somewhat younger leaders; it also brought individuals into the top leadership who were not directly involved in shaping and administering 'normalization'.

Although there were few personnel changes in the Czechoslovak party in the early Gorbachev period, there was substantial turnover in top party bodies in 1988 and 1989. The process of change began in December 1987, when Jakeš, who became a member of the Presidium in 1981, but had a career in the party apparatus dating back to the 1960's, replaced Husák as General Secretary of the party. Jakeš's elevation was followed by the removal of two long-time secretaries, Josef Haman and Josef Havlín, and a conservative member of the Presidium, Antonín Kapek, in April 1988. These changes were accompanied by the promotion of Jan Fojtík, journalist and ideologist, and Ignác Janák, first secretary of the Slovak Communist Party, from candidate to full membership in the Presidium, and of Miroslav Zavadil from a member of the secretariat to candidate membership in the Presidium. Miroslav Štěpán, head of the Prague city organization, and Vasil Mohorita, chairman of the Socialist Union of Youth, became members of the Secretariat at that time. Further changes followed in October, 1988, when František

Pitra lost his position as secretary but was elevated from candidate to full membership on the Presidium, and Peter Colotka and L'ubomir Štrougal, who had been members of the Presidium since 1969 and 1970 respectively, were removed from that body. Štěpán was elevated from membership in the Secretariat to membership in the Presidium, and Miroslav Zavadil was promoted from candidate to full membership in that body at that time. Jakeš's immediate successor as top party leader, Karel Urbánek, who had been head of the Central Committee department in charge of political and organizational matters and leader of the Czech party committee, was also added to the full membership of the Presidium. Changes in the leadership continued in December 1988, when hardliner Vasil B'ilak and Czech National Council Chairman Josef Kempný were removed from the Presidium, and Mikuláš Beno lost his position as secretary.

The changes that took place in 1988 and the first half of 1989 were reflected in a decline in the average tenure of full members of the Presidium from 17 years in 1985, when all but one full member had been on that body at least 14 years, to 7.6 in March 1989. The extent to which elements of the Husák leadership were still members of the top party elite prior to November 1989 is reflected in the fact that four of the members of the Presidium in March 1989 had been on that body for 18 to 20 years. However, six of the 11 full members of the Presidium had been members for a year or less at that time.

The average age of full members of the Presidium also decreased somewhat from 64 in the late Husák period (1985) to 56 in March 1989. Although the Husák leadership was not particularly old compared to the leaderships in certain other communist countries, such as the Soviet Union during the late Brezhnev era, most of its members were in their 60s, and only two of the candidate members were under 60. Husák, at 76, was the oldest member of the Presidium in November 1989, and seven additional full members of that body were in their 60s. However, all five of the full members added to the Presidium in 1988 and one of the candidate members were under 60 in 1989, and two of these additions were under 50 (48 and 45, respectively). There was less turnover among the few candidate members of the Presidium, a fact that was reflected in the slight increase in tenure at this level from 8 to 9.3 years from March 1985 to March 1989. The average age of the candidate members also increased slightly during this period, from 58 to 60. However, in contrast to the situation in 1985, when the youngest member of this group was 48, and most of its members were in their 60s, in 1989, one member, František Hanuš, was 46, and another, Vasil Mohorita was 37 (Wolchik, 1989a).

There was also a greater degree of continuity in the Secretariat than among the full members of the Presidium. As a result, the average age of members of this body did not change markedly from 1985, when it was 58.6, to March 1989, when it was 56.7. The elevation of Miroslava Němcová to replace Marie Kabřhelová in October 1989 reduced the average age of members of this body to 55.5.

The leadership that was in place in November 1989, then, included several members, particularly among the powerful full members of the Presidium, who either were not involved in any way in the normalization process, given their youth at the time, or who were active in the party, but at relatively low levels during the period when the main policies of the Husák era were being determined. Given this lack of personal responsibility for either the reforms of 1968 or the suppression of the reform effort, several of these newcomers were less personally attached to the policies of the Husák era and less fearful of reform and its potential political consequences than their predecessors.

The purge of most of the reformers associated with Dubček that occurred during 'normalization' simplified the division of opinion within the leadership group in Czechoslovakia. Common responsibility and experience in devising and implementing the policies that eliminated the reform and characterized political and economic life for nearly two decades were further threads that should have unified members of the leadership under Husák. Judging from their actions in regard to the populace and dissidents, there was a high degree of consensus within the Husák leadership concerning the general outlines of 'normalization' and, in particular, a shared view that efforts at political reform or a repetition of the events of 1968 should be avoided at all costs. However, beyond this consensus, the group appeared to be deeply divided along a number of lines. Thus, in addition to the divisions between those who were in the leadership prior to and during the reform era, members of the Husák leadership also had divergent views on the severity of the economic crisis as well as on the necessity or wisdom of economic reform or other measures to improve economic performance (see Kusin, 1982b; Kraus, 1985; Sobell, 1988; and Wolchik, 1987, pp. 46-7, and 1989a).

In December 1988 several of the most prominent hardliners in the leadership, as well as L'ubomir Štrougal, the former Prime Minister who, although part of the team that enacted 'normalization,' appeared to be the member of the leadership most receptive to the notion of economic and perhaps even political change, were removed. These changes and the influx of new members in October 1988 may have narrowed the divisions that characterized the leadership in the Husák era somewhat (see Wolchik, 1987, pp. 46-8; and Kusin, 1987).

At the same time, despite the high degree of turnover at the top in the period between 1987 and 1989, there were still holdovers from the old guard, including Husák, who retained his seat on the Presidium after relinquishing the top party post; Alois Indra, chairman of the Federal Assembly and one of the chief opponents of the 1968 reforms as they unfolded and afterwards; Karel Hoffman, who joined the Presidium in 1971; and Jan Fojtík, who became a full member of the Presidium in April 1988. The retention of Josef Haman, Vladimír Herman, and Miloslav Hruškovič as candidate members and of Zdeněk Hoření and Marie Kabřhelová as members of the secretariat provided further elements of continuity with the old leadership group (Wolchik, 1989a).

The extreme stability of the top leadership circles under Husák and the large number of changes in the late 1980s meant that there were marked differences in the degree of political experience and formative political experiences of old and new members of the leadership. Thus, although the poles of debate within the Jakeš leadership may have been closer than in the late Husák era, there was ample room for division and controversy. The vacillating response of the Jakeš leadership to the increase in dissent that occurred in 1988 and early 1989, which differed to some degree from the uniformly heavy-handed response of the Husák leadership, indicated that the underlying consensus regarding the need to preserve the political status quo that existed under Husák was disintegrating to some extent in the last years of communist rule.

These divisions were important, for they lessened the Communist Party's ability to control developments within the society and created greater opportunities for the growth of non-conformity (Wolchik, 1987, p. 46. See Skilling, 1976, especially chs. 3 and 5-7, for a discussion of the impact of this factor in Czechoslovakia in the 1960s). They also were reflected in the inability of the Jakeš leadership to deal effectively with the challenges to communist rule in November 1989 once it became clear that the Soviets would not back them up with force.

Social background characteristics and recruitment channels of Communist Party leaders during the communist period

As in other communist countries, individuals who reached the top in Czechoslovakia during the communist period did so by virtue of a long history of political activism and work, often within the party apparatus. The recruitment channels and social background characteristics of Communist Party leaders in Czechoslovakia thus resembled those that predominated in other communist countries to a certain degree (see Putnam, 1976, pp. 45-71). However, there were a number of features that distinguished the leadership cadre of this country from those in the Soviet Union and other Central and East European countries. The training and career patterns of the communist leadership in Czechoslovakia prior to the events of 1989 conformed to some extent to the trends toward increased educational levels and greater occupational experience outside the party apparatus found in other communist leaderships in the 1970s and 1980s (see Rigby, 1972, pp. 3-23; Hough and Fainsod, 1979, pp. 455-73; Kress, 1980, pp. 218-38; Bialer, 1980; Hough, 1977, pp. 1-16; and Blackwell, 1972, pp. 124-52, for the Soviet case. See Beck, 1970; and Bielasiak, 1980, pp. 345-69, for discussions of trends among Central Committee members in Central and Eastern Europe). Ten of the 13 full members of the Presidium, and two of the candidate members in mid-1989, for example, had some form of higher education. This pattern was a continuation of trends evident in the late Husák period, when nine of the 11 full members of the Presidium and all of the candidate members and members of the secretariat had some type of higher education. In contrast to the Soviet pattern, in which leaders increasingly have had higher technical education (Rigby, 1972, pp. 11-12; see Hough and Fainsod, 1979, pp. 469-70 for a discussion of the quality of these educations, however), only two full members and one candidate member of the Presidium under Husák had technical degrees in 1985. Three of the four other full members who had completed regular university programs did so in law, and the remaining full members, as well as candidates and members of the secretariat, attended higher party schools in Prague or Moscow (Wolchik, 1987, pp. 47-8).

This pattern continued to a large extent under Jakeš. Three of the full members of the Presidium had higher degrees in agricultural studies, and one of the candidate members as well as one of the members of the Secretariat had technical training. Four of the full members and two of the members of the Secretariat studied at higher party schools in Prague or Moscow. The remaining full members had degrees in law, philosophy, and education. One of the remaining candidate members graduated from the Leningrad Institute of Finance and Economy, and the other attended the Higher Party School in Prague.

Differences in the type and quality of education received varied to some extent by age and tenure on the Presidium. With the exception of Husák (76), who has a law degree, and Pitra (67), who graduated from an agricultural college, the older members of the leadership were also the least educated. Thus Presidium members Hoffman and Lenart, who were 65 and 66 in 1989, had only secondary education. Jakeš (67), Lenárt (66) and Secretariat member Kabřhelová (64) supplemented their training as apprentices and intermediate or secondary education with study at the higher party schools in Moscow and Prague. By way of contrast, six of the new members added to the Presidium and all four of those added to the Secretariat in 1988 and in 1989 prior to November had higher degrees. However, the type of education these leaders brought to office did not vary consistently by age. Two of the oldest in this group, Presidium members Pitra and Janák (59) had higher degrees in agriculture and another, Secretariat member Rohlíček (60), completed study at an economics college. At the same time, Presidium member Zavadil (57) and Secretariat member Mevald (57) received their training at the higher party school. A similar division was evident among the younger members of the leadership. Although several (Presidium members Knoutek, 53 and Štěpán, 45, and member of the Secretariat Hanuš, 46) received degrees in agriculture or a technical area in the course of normal university study, two of those added in 1988 and 1989, including the youngest, Secretariat member Mohorita (37), studied at higher party schools in Prague or Moscow. Thus, while the proportion of leaders who received non-political educations in the course of regular study was greater in the Jakeš leadership than in the past, there were still a large number of members who were educated at higher party schools.

The leadership of the Communist Party in Czechoslovakia as elsewhere has been predominantly male. With the exception of the early communist period, when women such as Marie Švermová played an important role in establishing a communist system in Czechoslovakia, few women have served in top party bodies. Women comprised 17.8 percent of members of the Central Committee (12.6 percent of full members, 29.3 percent of candidate members) ('Členové a kandidáti,' 1986) in 1986, for example, a proportion significantly lower than their share of party members. They also were underrepresented in central and line party positions. Marie Kabřhelová, who was head of the Union of Women, was a member of the Secretariat from 1974 to late 1989; Elena Litvajová, head of the Slovak women's organization, was a member of the Presidium of the Slovak party from 1971 until the end of communist rule. There were no women first secretaries in the important regional party organizations in the late 1980s. In a pattern common in other political systems, women's representation in central party bodies increased after the end of one party rule as the prestige and power of those bodies declined (see Jancar, 1978, pp. 88–99; and Wolchik, 1978, ch. 3, 1981b, pp. 459–62, 1981d, and 1990b).

Apart from those women active in the early post-Second World War years, most women who attained high positions within the Communist Party differed from their male counterparts in terms of social background characteristics and previous political experiences. At the level of the Central Committee, women members were far more likely than men to be workers or farmers. The few women who served in the Secretariat of the state-wide and Slovak parties after the early period had long records of activism as officials of women's organizations. The single woman on the Presidium of the Slovak party when the communist system was ousted, the one woman member of the Secretariat of the statewide party from 1974 to 1989, and Miroslava Němcová, who became head of the women's organization in 1989, replaced Kabřhelová as a member of the Secretariat in October 1989, and was elevated to candidate membership in the Presidium in late November 1989, had long records of public activism. However, in contrast to their male counterparts, whose careers were centered in the party apparatus, the women leaders rose to their positions by virtue of their roles in the official women's organizations (see Wolchik, 1978, ch. 3, and 1981d, pp. 159-60; Heitlinger, 1979, pp. 159-60; and Jancar, 1978, pp. 99-105, for discussions of these trends throughout the region.) Given the differences in career patterns and social background characteristics, women in both bodies had higher turnover rates, lower tenure, and, one may presume, less influence than many of their male colleague (see Wolchik, 1978, ch. 4, and 1981b).

The tendency for party leaders to be 'coopted' into full-time party work after extensive experience in professions outside the party apparatus found in other communist countries during various periods was evident to some extent in the top leadership in Czechoslovakia in the late communist period. Two of the full members and one candidate member of the Presidium in 1985, for example, had lengthy careers in industry and construction, and one full member pursued a legal career before moving into full-time party work. Four of the members of the Presidium and one of the three candidate members in 1989 worked in other areas (as educators, an agricultural technician, an agronomist, and an enterprise director) before becoming party bureaucrats, and an additional candidate member moved to the party apparatus only after seven years in the state hierarchy. The majority of the members of both the Husák leadership and the Jakeš leadership, however, were long-time party activists whose careers had been centered in the party apparatus or the mass organizations from the outset (see Fleron, 1970, pp. 108-39; Blackwell, 1972, pp. 124-52; Bialer, 1980; and Kress, 1980, pp. 218-38, for analysis of trends in the Soviet leadership. See Bielasiak, 1980, pp. 345-69 for an analysis of trends in Central and Eastern Europe). As in the early communist period, work in the mass organizations remained second only to a career within the party apparatus itself as a route to the top of the political hierarchy. Two of the members of the Presidium and two of the members of the Secretariat in 1989, for example, had careers centered in large part in the youth organization, and two additional members of the Presidium were active in that organization prior to moving to the party apparatus and other mass organizations. One of the candidate members combined work in the youth organization with activity in the trade unions, and another was active in the trade unions and the women's organization.

Four of the last six additions made to the Presidium and Secretariat during communist rule had substantial experience in other areas before entering the party apparatus. Two of the three members under 50 (Urbánek and Mohorita), as well as two of their older colleagues admitted in 1988, had careers centered entirely in the party or youth organization apparatus.

There are numerous limits to the inferences one can draw from the social background characteristics of leaders. As Alexander Dubček's actions in 1968 demonstrated, political actors often respond to situations once in office in ways that would not have been predicted, given their social backgrounds and previous experiences. There are also numerous constraints that will continue to condition the actions of new as well as present leaders. However, while it is thus impossible to determine the political preferences or concrete policy choices political leaders will make by reference to their social backgrounds and career patterns, such information gives us some idea of the skills political leaders bring to office and also may provide clues concerning their styles of analysis and the types of information or groups whose input they may seek or be responsive to in making decisions (see Putnam, 1976, pp. 40-4).

In the case of the Jakeš leadership, there was little reason to expect that the higher educational levels and career experiences of the leaders added to the Presidium and Secretariat in 1988 and 1989 would lead them to be markedly more interested than the Husák leadership or the older members of the leadership in promoting radical experimentation in the economic or political realm. Although they were better educated than their predecessors, most had followed career paths similar to those of older members of the leadership. At the same time, the fact that they were younger and thus less personally involved in implementing 'normalization' led several to adopt more flexible positions in dealing with the opposition and the implications of changes in the Soviet Union. As discussed in chapter 1, divisions within the Jakeš leadership were reflected in its vacillating response to the mounting challenge from below in 1988 and 1989. Internal differences also hampered the leadership in responding to the demonstrations of November 1989 and contributed to the inability of the party to regain control of the situation in the face of mass popular protest and the evident unwillingness of the Soviet Union to back them up with force.

The leaders who replaced the Jakeš leadership in late 1989 were largely unknown figures with little authority (see Pehe and Obrman, 1989b; and 'Výkonný výbor,' 1990). Ladislav Adamec, the former Prime Minister who negotiated with Civic Forum to end the communist era in November 1989 and took the newly created post of Chairman of the Party in March 1990, resigned from his position in September 1990. Changes in the organization of the party in late 1990 were accompanied by further changes in its leadership. Vasil Mohorita, the last member of the top leadership to have served in the party's highest organs during the communist period was replaced at the October 1990 Congress of the Communist Party of Bohemia and Moravia by Jiří Svoboda, a 45-year-old film director (Bradáč, Pergl, and Růžička, 1990, pp. 1,2; and 'Životopis J. Svobodý,' 1990, p. 2). Peter Weiss, who was elected head of the Slovak party in October 1990, and Pavol Kanis, who will serve as the first head of the National Council of the party at the federal level, both worked at the Institute of Marxism-Leninism of the Slovak Communist Party prior to their elections. Miroslav Grebeníček, who will replace Kanis next year, is an historian who taught at Masaryk University in Brno (Drábik, 1990, pp. 1-2).

Post-communist political leaders

Since the end of the Communist Party's monopoly of power, the holders of government office have become the effective political elite in Czechoslovakia. The new leaders who have come to power after November 1989 differ markedly from their communist predecessors.

One of the most striking differences is the large role that intellectuals play in the government and parliament at present. President Václav Havel, whose work as a playwright was widely acclaimed within and outside of Czechoslovakia long before he became President, is the most visible of these (see Kriseová, 1991). The Government of National Understanding that was formed in late 1989 included several communists members who had recently resigned from the Communist Party. However, the core of the new government consisted of former dissidents who were well-known to each other from their years in the opposition and had taken leading roles in the events of November 1989. Most were highly educated, but, due to their independent political activities or association with the reforms of 1968, had not been able to work in their original professions for many years. Many were employed in menial positions during the communist period. One dissident activist, Ján Čarnogurský, was on trial when the November demonstrations occurred. Several, including Foreign Minister Jiří Dienstbier, left their positions as stokers to become ministers. Others had held positions in the official world, but had been critical of government policies.

The federal government formed after the June 1990 elections also consists largely of intellectuals. The educational levels of Czechoslovakia's new leaders thus are similar to those of leaders in other democratic countries. All members of the governments have higher education; two of the members of the federal government were not able to complete their educations due to political reasons (Srb and Vaňo, 1990, p. 556). Many of the occupants of the 60 ministerial

138 *Czechoslovakia in transition*

Table 2.9   Educational specializations of members of the government

	Czechoslovakia	Czech Lands	Slovakia	Total
Technical	8	5	6	19
Economics	3	6	6	15
Law	2	2	5	9
Philosophy	—	3	3	6
Natural science	1	3	—	4
Art	—	—	1	1
Medicine	—	1	2	3
Veterinary sci.	—	1	—	1
None	2	—	—	2
Total	16	21	23	60

Source: Srb and Vaňo, 1990, p. 556.

posts in the Federal, Czech, and Slovak governments filled after the June 1990 elections have advanced degrees. However, their social backgrounds and career experiences differ from those of top political leaders in other democratic states in a number of ways that reflect both earlier Czechoslovak political traditions and the impact of the communist period. Thus, while the Prime Ministers of the Federal, Czech, and Slovak governments formed after the June 1990 elections and Ján Čarnogurský, who became Prime Minister of Slovakia in April 1990, as well as the Chairwoman of the Czech National Council were trained as lawyers, the majority of ministers of the three governments were educated in areas, including economics and the natural sciences, not usually found in the career backgrounds of members of West European governments. The government of the Czech Republic formed after the June 1990 elections, for example, includes two lawyers, two medical doctors, three doctors of natural science, one doctor of science, three unspecified Ph.D.s, and 11 experts whose title is engineer. Economists figure heavily in the latter group (from information in 'Most Members New,' 1990, pp. 1,2). As Table 2.9 illustrates, many members of the federal and republic governments have technical or economic training. Lawyers are particularly well represented in the Slovak government (see Table 2.9. See Tökés, 1990, for an analysis of new elites in Hungary).

As noted earlier in this chapter, 15 of the members of the federal government are Czechs and six Slovak. There was one Hungarian in the Slovak government formed in June 1990 (see Škorík, 1990, for a discussion of the representation of members of different ethnic groups at lower levels).

The members of the federal and republic governments are younger on the average than their communist predecessors. Three of the 17 members of the federal government, three of the 21 members of the Czech government, and seven of the 23 members of the Slovak government were born after the end of the Second World War. The average age of those named to the federal government in June 1990 was 50.8 years. The average age of members of the Czech Republic's government was 53.9, and the Slovak government 49.7 (Srb and Vaňo, 1990, pp. 555-6).

Members of the new legislative elite are similarly highly educated. As in the case of the governmental elites and those who serve in the President's office, many are former dissidents. In contrast to the pattern in most Western legislatures, numerous writers, artists, and other creative intellectuals currently serve as deputies (see 'Kandidát Občanského Fóra,' 1990).

As in the communist period, there are very few women among Czechoslovakia's new leaders. Despite the role that women played in organizing and supporting the mass demonstrations of November 1989, the political marginalization of women evident during the communist period continues. There is one woman among the ministers of the federal government and one in the Czech government. One of the members of the new Slovak government is a woman. Women are also poorly represented among the leaders of the federal and republic legislatures and chairs of legislative committees. Thus, there is only one woman among the 20 members of the Presidium of the House of the People and none among the 20 members of the Presidium of the House of the Nations of the Federal Assembly. One of the chairs of the 16 Federal Assembly committees is a woman. Women have fared somewhat better in the leading bodies of the Czech government. Dagmar Burešová, the activist lawyer who was Minister of Justice in the first non-communist Czech government appointed after the end of communist rule, was elected Chair of the Presidium of the Czech National Council. In addition, three of the 11 chairs of the committees of the Czech National Council and one of the remaining nine members of the Presidium of the Council are women (from information in b, 1990a, pp. 1,3; Macková, 1990, p. 6; and Čermáková and Navarová, 1990).

Elections to lower-level government bodies held in November 1990 also led to the replacement of large numbers of officials at that level. However, little information is available concerning these officials.

Citizen activism and participation

There has been a good deal of controversy among Western scholars about how to conceptualize mass political activity in communist states. Certain scholars have argued that the concept of political participation, which was developed to study Western, democratic political systems, has certain connotations, including voluntarism, efficacy, and the expectation that government will be responsive to citizen input, that make it inapplicable to communist systems (Sharlet, 1969, pp. 244-50). Others saw use of such a term in the communist world as 'concept stretching,' i.e. an effort that causes the term to lose its precision (see Sartori, 1970, pp. 1033-53). Still others have argued that the absence of legal opposition and the dominance of bureaucratic, as opposed to public, acts of participation resulted in fundamental differences in political participation in communist and democratic states (Rigby, 1976, pp. 258-61). Thus, many analysts of communist polities have tended to see a sharp distinction in the political activities of ordinary citizens in communist and democratic political systems. In the latter, citizens are thought to participate in political activities at their own initiative. Their actions can be expected to have an impact, and are based on the premise that the government has an obligation to and will in fact be responsive to its citizens. Citizen activism in communist states, on the other hand, is thought to be largely symbolic, i.e. to consist largely of mobilized actions that take place because the elite has organized them, and that do little beyond provide a symbolic reaffirmation of

Figure 2.1 Dimensions of citizen activism in Czechoslovakia during the communist period

Symbolic	*Effective*
Officially sanctioned acts	
Read and discuss political information	Join Communist Party
Vote	Participate as specialist or professional
Participate in election campaign activities	Participate in survey, public opinion research
Engage in volunteer labor	Withhold support
Join mass organizations	Implement policy

Write letters to editor
Participate in citizens commissions,
local government
Contact officials

Officially proscribed acts

Form independent organizations
Participate in dissent (samizdat,
petitions, independent
cultural activities)
Take part in strikes, riots,
acts of violence
Engage in social deviance

the citizens' (often surface) acceptance of the regime.

Research done in the last two decades in both communist and non-communist countries indicated that the dichotomy between citizens' political activism in communist and democratic systems was not as sharp as once thought. Studies of mass political participation in the West, for example, illustrated the symbolic aspects of many kinds of political participation in democratic societies (see Milbrath, 1965; and Edelman, 1971). Studies of mass political activities in the communist world conducted in the 1970s and 1980s highlighted certain activities that had an impact on policies and that therefore should be seen as effective participation (see Hough, 1976, pp. 3-20; Nelson, 1980; DiFranceisco and Gitelman, 1984, pp. 603-21). Developments in the political situation in several of the communist countries in the late 1980s, such as Poland and Hungary, included changes in the activities of certain mass organizations and governmental bodies that made participation in those activities more effective. The proliferation of new, informal, political groups that presaged the end of communist rule also increased the political options available to citizens.

It is possible, then, to view the political activities of citizens in both democratic and communist systems on a continuum ranging from symbolic to effective. One can then judge the extent to which particular activities are symbolic or effective in particular countries; one can also discuss the changes over time that take place in this regard (see Figure 2.1). As Figure 2.1 suggests, there are symbolic and effective dimensions of political activity in all polities. There are also a number of types of actions, both officially sanctioned and proscribed, whose impact varies, depending on the political climate and the concrete case under discussion. However, although such an approach makes it easier to evaluate the impact of change in the political realm, in normal political times, most of the political activities open to citizens in communist countries were clearly symbolic. Ordinary citizens thus had very few avenues to participate effectively in politics, particularly at the policy-making stage.

This pattern was evident in Czechoslovakia. Both the range of possibilities for taking part in politics and the impact of particular political activities varied somewhat with changes in the general political climate during the communist period. The effort by political leaders in 1968 to rebuild public trust and confidence in the socialist system by allowing open political debate and discussion was followed by a resurgence of public interest and involvement in politics, for example. The numerous public opinion polls designed to ascertain popular confidence in particular leaders, the party itself, and the course of the reform and determine citizen preferences in regard to public policy issues that were conducted also conveyed information concerning citizen preferences to political leaders (see Gitelman, 1977; see Piekalkiewicz, 1972, for summaries of many of these polls). The renewal that took place in the official mass organizations, the emergence of new political groups, and the process of change that began to have an impact in the government and in the party apparatus, particularly after the effective end of censorship in March 1968, also created greater opportunities for Czech and Slovak citizens to participate in politics in meaningful ways (see chapter 1; Skilling, 1976, chs. 17-18; and Kusin, 1972). However, the Communist Party's continued dominance of political life, the lack of opposition parties, and the absence of institutional guarantees of political pluralism meant that there were still significant limitations on the political activities of citizens during this period.

With the brief exception of this period in 1968, most of the political activities available to citizens in Czechoslovakia served a symbolic function during the communist period. Most citizen activism also took place because it was mobilized or organized by the elites, rather than as the result of the independent initiatives of individual citizens. Nearly all eligible Czech and Slovak citizens took part in elections, but these involved little choice, as there was a single slate of candidates, all of whom were nominated and approved by the Communist Party. The outcome of the elections also had virtually no impact on policy.

Citizens also were mobilized to take part in a number of other public activities, including demonstrations organized by the leadership, such as celebrations of May Day, and the anniversaries of other important events since 1945, and volunteer labor brigades. As in the case of participation in elections, most citizens took part in these activities largely because it was expected or required, rather than out of conviction (see Slavíková, 1989; and Tomek, 1990, for evidence from surveys conducted during the last years of communist rule). Participation in the activities of the mass organizations and minor parties, although often a more voluntary activity, also was largely symbolic rather than effective political action.

While these activities clearly were at the symbolic end of the continuum, a number of other forms of citizen activism fell somewhere in between. The impact and effectiveness of these activities varied, depending on political circumstances and the individuals involved. Large numbers of citizens were involved in the work of the national legislature and national committees at all levels, either as deputies or as members of the citizens' committees attached to the national committees. In 1988, for example, 196,704 citizens were deputies of the national committees at all levels, and an additional 212,000 were involved in the citizens' committees (Jeneral). Because the national legislature and the national committees at lower levels had almost no role in policy formulation, participation as either a deputy or member of one of the various citizens' committees and commissions was generally a symbolic act.

At the national level, the power of deputies to request information from ministries and the obligation of government officials to provide such information within a specified period of time allowed certain deputies to achieve some of their purposes. Deputies and other members of the governmental apparatus also were in a position to have an impact on policy-making through their activities in the parliamentary and other commissions responsible for formulating public policy proposals. In both of these cases, however, the influence of individual deputies depended largely on factors other than their status as legislators. The impact of these actions was also limited by the slight role that these groups played in determining national policies.

At the local level, the responsibility of district and local national committees for resolving housing disputes, problems with retail store hours and practices, and other local issues meant that deputies and citizen activists had some influence on local affairs, particularly on low-level, individualized issues that did not involve larger questions of state policy or the expenditure of large amounts of money. Although the competence of local governmental organs was severely circumscribed and the ability of deputies to initiate policy limited at all levels, citizens who served in these capacities were also able to have some impact on policy by their actions or inaction in implementing centrally determined directives and regulations (Wolchik and Curry, 1984. See Hough, 1976; and DiFranceisco and Gitelman, 1984, for evidence from the Soviet Union).

The impact of other activities, such as letter writing and contacting public officials also varied, depending on the political climate and individual involved. The letters to the editor that were published in Czechoslovakia during the communist period, as in the Soviet Union and other communist countries, were selected to serve elite purposes. Thus, letters that raised controversial issues or discussed approved issues in ways that were not to the liking of the political leadership had little chance of being published in normal political times. However, given this limitation, such letters sometimes had an impact in rectifying particular abuses or in highlighting poor performance on the part of lower-level public or economic officials. They were also used by other political actors in both the political leadership and the specialist and professional community to raise new issues and argue for particular policy alternatives (see Oliver, 1969; and Shultz and Adams, 1981, for a discussion of the uses of letters to the editor in the Soviet Union. See Scott, 1974; Heitlinger, 1979, pp. 161-4; and Wolchik, 1981a, for discussion of the use of these letters to broaden debate on women's issues in Czechoslovakia).

As in Western societies, citizens in Czechoslovakia also took part in the political process during the communist period by contacting public officials. There is little direct information on the extent of these contacts, which took place through both formal and informal channels, in Czechoslovakia. Judging from studies of citizen behavior in this regard in the Soviet Union (see Oliver, 1969; Hough, 1976; DiFranceisco and Gitelman, 1984; and Bahry and Silver, 1990), these contacts, which generally involved low-level, individual problems, such as those related to housing, social welfare benefits, and access to educational institutions, rather than broader political issues, were probably quite numerous. Information concerning the impact of these acts in the Soviet Union does not give any clear picture concerning their effectiveness. The results of the Soviet Interview Project, which are based on the responses of 2,793 *émigrés*, for example, suggest that these contacts were generally effective in achieving the desired results for the individual (see Bahry and Silver, 1990). DiFranceisco and Gitelman (1984), in their study of 1,161 Soviet *émigrés*, also found that many citizens initiated contacts with party and, particularly, government officials. However, most respondents in their study did not view the outcome of these contacts positively. Unfortunately, we do not have comparable information on either the extent or results of this form of activity in Czechoslovakia during the communist period.

Turning to activities that fall closer to the effective end of the spectrum, citizens could become members of the Communist Party. Although the act of joining the party did not in and of itself mean that an individual would have greater influence on policy-making, it was a clear precondition for having such influence. However, given the concentration of power at the top of the party, most party members had very little influence on policy-making.

Citizens in Czechoslovakia also participated in policy-making as professionals and specialists. Individuals in these categories, who were brought into the policy-making process by the political leadership or took part by virtue of their occupational responsibilities or at their own initiative, played an important role at most stages of policy-making. In addition to bringing new problems to the attention of political decision-makers and thus helping to determine the political agenda, they also articulated and argued for policy alternatives and helped determine the outcome of policies once they were adopted by their actions in implementing policies. Specialists and professionals also evaluated policy measures and proposed new alternatives for consideration.

Specialists and professionals took part in policy-making in the loose, informal coalitions Franklyn Griffiths argued characterized such activity in the Soviet Union (Griffiths, 1971, pp. 335-78). However, in Czechoslovakia, many of these coalitions, particularly in less sensitive policy areas, were of relatively long duration, despite the changes that accompanied the end of the reform period (Wolchik, 1983b; and Wolchik and Curry, 1984). As in the case of Communist Party members, the influence individual specialists and professionals exercised varied considerably according to the resources and contacts of the individuals involved, the nature of the issue under consideration, and the political climate of the time. In general, specialists and professionals appear to have had most influence in areas that were not sensitive ideologically and in which decisions could be presented as largely technical questions. Even in these areas, however, political factors often intervened. The roles of these actors were also circumscribed and controlled to a large degree by the party leadership, and their input was often disregarded (see Skilling, 1976; Korbonski, 1971, pp. 57-79; Kusin, 1971; Wolchik, 1983b; Wolchik and Curry, 1984; and Kaplan, 1987. See Zimmerman, 1973; and Kelley, 1973, for discussions of the impact of these factors on the policy-making process in communist states more generally).

Given the restrictions on effective political participation that existed during the communist period, much citizen input into policy-making occurred indirectly through the mediation of other political actors. Not commonly considered dimensions of political participation in Western societies, these channels of mass-elite linkages nonetheless provided information to political leaders about mass preferences and, at times, resulted in policy change. Two of the more important of these indirect channels of citizen input were public opinion polls and withholding support. In the first area, Czech and Slovak leaders were able to draw on a substantial body of public opinion data to judge citizen reactions and desires in formulating public policies. The tradition of public opinion research, which dates from 1946 in Czechoslovakia, was interrupted as the Stalinist system was consolidated, but revived in the mid-1960s as part of the resurrection of empirical social science (see Gitelman, 1977, pp. 83-103). In the late 1960s, and in particular during the 1968 reform period, the Institute for Research on Public Opinion in Prague conducted numerous surveys on the major political issues of the day. Citizens were polled concerning their opinions on such previously taboo topics as the changes taking place in the country; the performance and competence of particular political leaders and the Communist Party; the role of the mass media in socialist society; and their views of socialism and capitalism (Gitelman, 1977, pp. 95-9; see Piekalkiewicz, 1972, for more detailed discussions of the results of individual polls).

Public opinion surveys on such explicitly political topics ceased after the Institute, along with sociology and other social science departments and institutes, was 'normalized' at the end of the reform period. However, public opinion polls and survey research continued to be conducted on a wide variety of less sensitive issues that nonetheless had political implications and were of relevance to policy-making. Thus, the Institute for Research on Public Opinion in Prague conducted numerous public opinion polls, many at the request of party or government organs or commissioned by the mass organizations, to assess citizen opinion and reactions to contemplated policy measures or policy alternatives. The results of these surveys were supplemented by survey research on a broad variety of topics, ranging from the attitudes of youth and the situation of women to popular evaluations of the social positions of various social groups. Although there were a number of problems with many of these studies, including methodology, the possibility of response bias under the political conditions of the time, and political interference in the conduct and reporting of research results, they provided political leaders with information about mass preferences and values that was sometimes used in policy-making, particularly in non-sensitive areas (see Wolchik, 1983b, for a discussion of the impact of this factor in the area of demographic policy).

Finally, citizens in Czechoslovakia also had an impact on policy-making during the communist period as a result of their actions in opposing particular policy measures adopted by the elite. Although there were limits on its effectiveness, the withholding of support or refusal to behave as the political leadership wished sent a message to the elites concerning citizen reactions to policies or the needs of particular groups of citizens that sometimes resulted in change in public policies. One of the clearest examples of this impact is evident in the area of demographic policy. Through their inaction (in this case, refusal to have more than one child, evident in the declining birthrate), young women and men in Czechoslovakia contributed to a reorientation of demographic policy and the eventual adoption of a package of measures designed to increase the birthrate by improving the situation of young couples and easing the burdens of young working women. These measures, which were controversial in terms of their ultimate impact on women's equality but were extremely popular with the groups involved, came about not as the result of any direct pressure on political leaders by members of these groups, but as a consequence of the impact of the sum of individual actions on desired elite goals. A similar process appears to have been behind the improvement in the social welfare and pension benefits of agricultural workers adopted in the mid-1970s (Wolchik, 1981a, and 1983b).

As both of these cases illustrate, effective citizen input into the political process was most often indirect during the communist period in Czechoslovakia. Mediated by specialists and professionals or bureaucratic officials, this input at times succeeded in getting new problems onto the political agenda or in producing changes in existing policy in particular areas. Given the strictures on the formation of independent organizations to promote the interests of particular groups that existed for much of the communist period, change in policies that affected particular groups typically did not come about as the result of direct political action by members of these groups to pressure political leaders. Rather, it occurred because other actors, including specialists and professionals, or bureaucrats, determined that there was a connection between the situation and concerns of particular groups and a broader policy issue and then translated those concerns to political decision-makers.

In addition to these activities and forms of mass-elite relations, citizens in Czechoslovakia also engaged in political behaviors that were either on the borderline of what was officially sanctioned or were explicitly prohibited during the communist period. These included using private channels to attain one's ends; participating in strikes and unauthorized demonstrations; and dissent. In the first area, citizens in Czechoslovakia used personal contacts, connections, and bribes to influence public officials. As chapter 4 will discuss in greater detail, the use of such methods, as well as participation in illegal economic activities, was widespread. Although these activities were not legally permitted, they were quietly tolerated for the most part, except in those cases the leadership chose to highlight in order to remove particular officials from office or achieve some other purpose.

The political impact of strikes, riots, and other forms of protest in communist countries was illustrated by the Polish experience of the last 30 years and, most graphically, by the fall of communist leaders in Czechoslovakia, East Germany, and Romania in late 1989. Until very recently, however, these forms of open protest were rare in Czechoslovakia. Despite the tradition of working-class organization and the frequency of strikes in the interwar period (see Evanson, 1985), Czech and Slovak workers were reluctant to use this tool during the communist period. With the exception of the workers' unrest in Plzen in 1953, and the strike in the Northern Bohemian region in November 1985, which were soon quelled by the political authorities, workers' discontent generally was expressed not in strikes but in less visible forms. Developments in the late 1980s, including the detonating of a bomb in the atrium between the regional and city national committees in Ustí nad Labém in February 1989, the throwing of a tear gas bomb during the official demonstration commemorating the February 1948 events, and the bomb scares that caused the evacuation of subway stations in Prague in spring 1989, were indications that certain groups and individuals were becoming more willing to use direct action and violent tactics. However, these occurrences were rare, as were organized mass protests, until the end of the communist period. As the section on dissent that follows illustrates, there were important changes in the willingness of citizens to oppose the regime openly in the late 1980s.

During the communist period, then, citizen activism in Czechoslovakia differed markedly from the patterns found in democratic political systems. Most political activities were symbolic, in that they occurred not as the result of individual initiative but because citizens were mobilized by the elites, and had little impact on political decisions. Citizens were forbidden to form autonomous groups and could go beyond established organizations only at great personal risk. Although citizens' actions did at times have an effect on policymaking, they were generally mediated by other political actors. The concentration of all political life in a single party which controlled political recruitment as well as the means of political socialization and the mass media meant that the channels available to citizens to voice grievances and make demands on political leaders were very restricted. This fact and the evident lack of impact of most official political activities led to high levels of apathy in regard to politics and a general lack of interest in political events. The retreat of many citizens to the private sphere and widespread alienation from politics were accompanied by the development of political attitudes that reflected the reality of political life under communist rule. But while most citizens responded to the situation by withdrawing from political life, others, including many of the country's current leaders, emerged as open opponents of the regime.

Dissent and opposition during the communist period

For much of the post-1948 period, citizens in Czechoslovakia, as in most other communist countries, were not able to form independent organizations or interest groups to articulate their policy preferences or pressure political leaders. This channel of influence existed to some extent in 1968, when independent political organizations, such as the *Klub angažovaných nestraníků* (KAN, the Club of Engaged Non-Party Members), Club 231 (the club of former political prisoners, who had been charged under article 231 of the penal code), and others were formed to express views independent of those of the official mass organizations. After the end of the reform period, however, the authorities were quick to punish citizens who took part in almost any independent organization or unauthorized protest. As noted in chapter 1, Charter 77 and other dissident groups challenged the regime in the early 1980s, but the numbers of independent activists remained small until the late 1980s. The last two years of communist rule saw the re-emergence of independent organizations and mass protest in Czechoslovakia on a scale not seen during the rest of the communist period. Independent organizations were still illegal and, in contrast to the situation in the Soviet Union, Poland, and Hungary, participation in their activities still carried substantial risks for most citizens. However, these risks did not stop increasing numbers of Czechs and Slovaks from joining such groups and participating in mass demonstrations and protests.

Open opposition to the system was slow to develop in Czechoslovakia. While dissident intellectuals and youth in Poland and Hungary challenged the policies of the government soon after Stalin's death, and large numbers of citizens in both countries became involved in protest and reform efforts in 1956, there was little open opposition in Czechoslovakia, aside from workers' riots in Plzen in 1953 (see Tökés, 1979; and Curry, 1983, for overviews of dissent in Central and East European countries).

To some extent, the lack of dissent during this period reflected the harshness of the Stalinist system in Czechoslovakia. But it also demonstrated the ways in which Czechoslovakia's earlier history conditioned the actions of intellectuals and ordinary citizens in the post-Second World War period. In contrast to the situation in Hungary and Poland, in Czechoslovakia there was a sizeable core of intellectuals who had joined the party during the interwar period, and who were, therefore, supporters of the new political system. As noted in chapter 1, they were thus less likely to question the system than their counterparts in Poland and Hungary, many of whom were influenced by the strong anti-communist and anti-Russian sentiment prevalent in those countries prior to the Second World War. The lack of a strong anti-Soviet or anti-Russian tradition and the fact that the economy continued to provide a standard of living higher than in most other socialist countries throughout the 1950s also meant that ordinary citizens were less inclined to protest than citizens in Poland and Hungary.

As the 1960s progressed, dissenting voices were increasingly heard among writers and other restive intellectuals. These activists, who tested the limits of nonconformity at the time, were important to later developments. They also pushed the leadership to make more radical changes than planned. However, the primary impetus for the reform effort that came to the fore in the late 1960s came from within the political and intellectual establishment, rather than from outsiders.

The emergence of true dissent, then, occurred only in the wake of the reversal of the 1968 reforms. Although, as noted in chapter 1, there was very little armed resistance to the August 1968 invasion, individuals as well as many of the official groups protested the forced end of the reform effort immediately after the invasion. These public acts of courage, which included the self-immolation of the Czech student Jan Palach in January 1969, soon tapered off, however, and most citizens, disaffected and disillusioned, renounced political involvement and retreated to the private sphere. Non-conformist activities continued at a less visible level throughout the 1970s, particularly among youth, but for the most part, dissatisfaction was not openly voiced (see Kusin, 1978, and 1983, pp. 48-59; Skilling, 1989, chs. 3 and 4; and Curry, 1983, pp. 364, 383).

The founding of Charter 77 in January 1977 marked a new stage in dissident activity in Czechoslovakia. Drawing their inspiration from the Helsinki Agreements, the signatories of the Charter called on Czech and Slovak leaders to observe the pledges they had made to uphold human rights in international documents as well as those contained in Czech and Slovak laws. Insisting that they were not a group, but rather merely individuals who shared a common concern for human rights, the signatories of the Charter maintained that they were acting within the framework of Czech and Slovak laws. The Charter was soon joined by the VONS, or Committee to Defend the Unjustly Persecuted (*Výbor na obranu nespravedlivě stíhaných*), which also sought to focus attention on and rectify human rights abuses.

In the first years of its existence, Charter 77's activities were those typical of other human rights organizations in the region. Charter spokespersons issued documents protesting violations of human rights and called on Czech and Slovak leaders to rectify these abuses. Soon, however, the Charter's activities broadened, and Charter activists came to serve as the nucleus of a second, unofficial, intellectual community in Czechoslovakia. The group began issuing analyses of public issues the regime ignored, such as the gypsy problem and problems with the safety of nuclear power plants in Slovakia. It also prepared independent analyses of other public issues, including environmental deterioration and the economic situation that diverged from those of public officials (see Havel, 1990; Heneka, Janouch *et al.*, 1990; Skilling, 1981, and 1985; and Kusin, 1978, pp. 275-325, and 1979. See Skilling, 1989, for a detailed analysis of dissident writings and samizdat publications). Drawing on information provided in some cases by people in official positions, these documents and analyses served to support and encourage independent thought in Czechoslovakia.

Intellectuals affiliated with the Charter also supported other dissident or independent initiatives, including those in the arts and culture and in the broader scholarly world. These included independent publishing such as the *Edice petlice*, or *Padlocked Editions*, a series of samizdat publications that had published 367 book-length manuscripts by the late 1980s, *Edice expedice,* and a variety of independent sociological, historical, and foreign affairs journals (see Skilling, 1989).

Other segments of the population also expressed their dissatisfaction with the political situation during this period, although generally in less organized ways. Young people adopted unorthodox lifestyles and occasionally took part in more openly political activities, such as signing and circulating petitions against the stationing of new Soviet missiles in Czechoslovakia, for example, or those calling for greater religious freedom. Creative artists who could no longer exhibit or earn their livelihoods as artists due to their support of the 1968 political reforms staged numerous independent art exhibits and organized unauthorized performances of plays and other literary events privately. Rock, jazz, and other musicians also challenged the regime's dictates in the cultural world (see, for example, Samson, 1988, p. 17; and Skilling, 1989, chs. 3 and 4). But for the most part, Czechs and Slovaks expressed their disaffection with the regime by withdrawing from politics and focusing on private concerns (see Musil and Linhart, 1990; Triska, 1975; and Ulč, 1974).

Beginning in the early 1980s, the hierarchy and laity of the Catholic Church became more active forces in Czech and Slovak society. The greater willingness of certain priests and officials of the Church, including Cardinal Tomášek, to challenge regime policies and protest against violations of human rights was coupled with an increase in the number of lay Catholics who participated in pilgrimages or took part in unauthorized masses and other religious observations (M.P., 1986c, p. 5; and Heneka, Janouch *et al.*, 1985).

In Slovakia, there was less open dissent, apart from that based on religious grounds. This difference reflected the different political conditions in the two parts of the country. Thus, many Slovak intellectuals were able to use the somewhat looser political climate to engage in non-conformist activities while ostensibly remaining part of the official world. The activities of individuals like philosopher Miloslav Kusý, who became Rector of Comenius University in 1990, and Ján Čarnogurský, who signed the Charter and were labelled as dissidents by the regime, were supplemented by those of a much larger group of historians, sociologists, writers, and other intellectuals who developed networks of non-conformists, published unauthorized independent journals, and, in the words of Martin Bútora, the sociologist and author who was one of the founders of Public Against Violence, developed 'softwares,' or alternative methods and solutions to problems that went around the system. One of the most important of the groups which engaged in 'constructive deviance' developed in the Guardians of Nature organization, which focused on ecological issues (Szomolányiová, 1990). These individuals, many of whom had links to dissidents in Prague, became the core of Public Against Violence and the new leadership in Slovakia in 1989 (see Bútora, 1990; *Bratislava Nahlas*, 1987; and reports in 'Nahlas o životím,' 1988, p. 7).

The importance of these groups and activities in keeping independent thought alive in Czechoslovakia and in providing a moral reference for young people and others apart from the official value system, was demonstrated by the events of late 1989. However, the activities of the Charter and other dissident groups did not pose a serious threat to the communist regime until close to the end of the communist period. The limited impact of dissident activities in the 1970s and early to mid-1980s reflected several factors. The first of these was the response of the leadership to dissident activities. Despite the fact that they acted within the confines of Czechoslovak law in most cases, the Husák leadership adopted a very hard line toward the dissidents. Interrogation, house arrest, loss of jobs, forced exile, imprisonment, and other forms of harassment kept the price of open identification with the Charter and other dissident groups high and restricted their activities (see Heneka, Janouch *et al.*, 1985; Vladislav and Prečan, 1990; Skilling, 1981, 1985, and 1989; and Kusin, 1978, and 1979).

In addition to the high cost to individuals of participating openly in dissident activities, the social composition of the Charter and other dissident groups also limited their impact. Although the signatories of the Charter included people from a broad variety of occupational groups, most of those who were most actively involved in dissent during the communist period were intellectuals and white-collar workers. This fact, coupled with the near certainty of a harsh response by the authorities, meant that dissident intellectuals were not able to forge strong links to other sectors of the population, such as the workers or collective farmers, as happened in Poland during the 1980-1 period (see Connor, 1980, for an analysis of intellectual-worker links in Poland at that time).

As discussed in greater detail in chapter 1, there were important changes in this respect in 1988 and 1989. The increase in the number of new independent groups and the involvement of larger numbers of people in demonstrations and other unauthorized activities that openly challenged the government were clear indications of the growing alienation of the populace from the regime. As the events of November 1989 demonstrated, the work of long-time dissident activists in preserving independent thought and serving as moral referents contributed to the willingness of the population to demand an end to communist rule. The often decades-long acquaintance of independent activists, and the new links forged between older dissidents and younger people in the last years of communist rule also formed the basis for the organizations that emerged to lead the revolution in both Prague and Bratislava in November 1989. As noted earlier in this chapter, former dissidents also play important roles in the new governments formed after 1989.

Citizen participation in the post-communist period

The repluralization of Czechoslovakia's political life has recreated numerous opportunities for citizens to participate in political life. With the end of the Communist Party's monopoly of power, citizens are now free to express their political preferences openly, organize with others who share their political views to make their preferences known to government leaders, and pressure political leaders to take action on issues of importance to them. They may also join the numerous political parties and voluntary organizations discussed earlier in this chapter. The expansion of the role of the legislature and other governmental bodies, and the greater openness of the policy-making process have also increased the number of channels available to those who wish to take part in policy-making.

In the months immediately after the fall of the communist system, citizens responded to new opportunities to be involved in political life enthusiastically. As noted earlier in this chapter, public opinion polls and survey research found high levels of interest in politics and personal involvement in public affairs. Support for the country's new leaders and optimism about the country's political future were also widespread (see Boguszak, Gabal, and Rak, 1990a).

With the restoration of a multiparty system, elections have once again become one of the most important channels of mass-elite linkages in Czechoslovakia. The results of the parliamentary elections held in June 1990 reflected the impact of the extraordinary circumstances in which they were held. Popular enthusiasm and support of the country's movement toward democracy were evident in the very high (95 percent) turnout rates for the election. They were also reflected in the results of the election, which reaffirmed citizen support for Civic Forum and Public Against Violence. As noted in chapter 1, the June 1990 elections validated the policies of the Government of National Understanding and legitimized the new government created in June. However, because they took place at a time when the electoral laws, party system, and broader political system were themselves still in flux, their results are not necessarily predictive of future political alignments in Czechoslovakia. Voter preferences and identifications remain fluid at present.

As in other political systems in transition (see Barnes *et al.*, 1985; McDonough *et al.*, 1981; O'Donnell, Schmitter, and Whitehead, 1986; and Bruszt, 1988), this fluidity of political preferences and partisan identification was illustrated quite clearly by the results of the local elections held in November 1990. Although Civic Forum once again received the largest share of the vote in the Czech Lands (35.4 percent), the Christian Democratic Movement received more votes than Public Against Violence (27.4 percent of the seats compared to 20.4 percent) in Slovakia. The volatility of voter preferences was also reflected in the fluctuating fortunes of the Slovak National Party, which received only 3.2 percent of the vote, despite public opinion polls conducted in October and November that indicated that it was the strongest political force in Slovakia (Pehe, 1990g, p.3). The results of surveys of voter preferences conducted soon after the November elections found, however, that the poor showing of SNS did not mean a dramatic decline of support for the party. Thus, the election results in part reflected the fact that SNS was not able to field candidates in all areas. A survey conducted just before the vote by the Institute for Public Opinion Research found, for example, that 36 percent of inhabitants of

Slovakia, if they had had ten votes, would have given at least one to the SNS (Janyška, 1990, p. 4).

As was to be expected, levels of interest in politics have declined since the heady days of late 1989 and early 1990. Evident in results of survey research discussed earlier in this chapter, this trend is also reflected in the lower voter turnout for the local elections held in November 1990, when 63 percent of eligible voters in Slovakia and 73.6 percent in the Czech Lands voted ('Definitívne výsledky,' 1990; and Tréglová, 1990c, p. 1). These levels of voter turnout are still higher than usual levels in many Western democracies, including the United States.

To some extent, this decline in interest and political involvement may well be an inevitable reaction to the high levels of political mobilization and intensity of political involvement evident in late 1989 and early 1990. But it may also reflect the impact of communist rule on citizens' perceptions of government and their own roles as citizens. As numerous Czech and Slovak analysts have argued, the political behavior, as well as the political attitudes and values, of Czechs and Slovaks continue to be influenced by the patterns of mass-elite relations that prevailed during communist rule. Conditioned to see themselves as objects of politics rather than independent participants in political life by 40 years of communist rule, many citizens continue to view political affairs as largely the business of government rather than the responsibility of individual citizens (see Petrušek, 1990; Musil and Linhart, 1990; Slejška, 1990; Brokl, 1990a, 1990b). As Jiří Musil and Jiří Linhart note in a recent discussion of the moral aspects of value change, the creation of citizens who see themselves as empowered and responsible will be a long-term process (Musil and Linhart, 1990).

At the same time, survey research and the actions of certain groups of citizens in 1990, demonstrate that the high levels of political mobilization of late 1989 and early 1990 are still present to some extent. As noted earlier in this chapter, large numbers (41 and 66 percent) of citizens interviewed concerning their views of the economic reform in May 1990 indicated that they would be willing to strike if the living standard decreased drastically or if there were radical reductions in social welfare provisions (Boguszak and

Rak, 1990a, p. 36). Several groups, including miners, and groups opposed to the language law eventually passed by the Slovak National Council engaged in strikes to protest government decisions in 1990, and others, including the Czech and Slovak Confederation of Trade Unions, have called strike alerts to pressure public officials (see Nováček, 1990, p. 2).

The potential threat that this readiness to strike poses to political stability is compounded by a further legacy of the communist period, the lack of interest of many citizens in joining a political party. As a survey conducted by the Association for Independent Social Analysis in May 1990 indicated, 10 percent of all citizens were affiliated with a political party. Only 14 percent stated that they would become members of a party (Boguszak and Rak, 1990a, Table 3). By December 1990, only 17 percent of the population aged 15 and over indicated that they would join Civic Forum or Public Against Violence if they were to become political parties. Reluctance to join partisan political groups was stronger in the Czech Republic (79 percent) than in Slovakia (35 percent) ('Kdyby se OF a VPN,' 1990, p. 2).

Conclusion

As this chapter has illustrated, there have been important changes in all aspects of political life since the end of communist rule in Czechoslovakia. These have been reflected in the country's legal system and in the way in which existing political institutions operate. They are also evident in the process of constitutional revision and the redefinition of the relationship between governmental bodies that continues at present and in the development of the party system, as well as in the characteristics of political leaders. There have also been changes in the political values, attitudes, and behavior of citizens. The influence of the past 40 years continues to be evident to a certain degree in all areas, as is the impact of the sudden change of regime in 1989. As a result, patterns of mass-elite relations, as well as the way the political system operates, continue to be in flux. However, although remnants of the past continue to have an influence and the political system itself is still in transition, the end of one-party rule has been followed by a fundamental shift in the nature of the political formula and in the political opportunities available to citizens.

The continued influence of the past 40 years on the political behavior of citizens cannot obscure the changes in the channels of mass-elite relations that have occurred since November 1989. Although many citizens have once again given priority to private concerns, substantial numbers continue to be interested in political affairs. In contrast to the communist period, when the political options of citizens were tightly controlled, there are now numerous avenues for citizens to voice their concerns and participate in politics. As the many new political groups and other associations that have been created since the fall of the communist government, and the public demonstrations and manifestations related to a variety of issues that have taken place illustrate, citizens in Czechoslovakia may once again make use of the opportunities for political participation available to citizens in pluralistic societies when they choose to do so.

3 Social structure and social change

The tasks political leaders faced when they established a communist-dominated system in Czechoslovakia, as well as the resources available to carry out those tasks, were influenced to a large degree by the nature of Czech and Slovak society. The occupational and ethnic structure of the country, as well as cleavages based on other grounds, raised major public policy issues and had an important impact on the way the political system operated during the communist period. Social changes that occurred under communist rule helped to precipitate the fall of the communist system. These factors continue to condition political and economic life in the post-communist period. At the same time, the political and economic changes that have occurred since November 1989 have had important implications for Czechoslovakia's social structure.

The end of communist rule has been followed by the re-emergence of social issues and tensions that could not be dealt with openly under the previous regime. New social problems have also developed. This chapter examines some of the underlying features of Czech and Slovak society, including population developments, educational levels, and the occupational and ethnic structure. It also discusses the system of rewards and the distribution of benefits that predominated in the communist period and the changes that are taking place in this system at present. It then considers other important cleavages, including those based on gender and religion, and the position and attitudes of youth.

Population trends

Czechoslovakia currently has a population of approximately 15,671,000 (1990), including 10,366,000 inhabitants of the Czech Lands and 5,305,000 of Slovakia ('Vzhledém k úbytku,' 1991, p. 3). Beginning in the early 1950s, the birthrate began to decline. As in several other Central and East European countries, the drop in the birthrate in part reflected the impact of modernization. However, in Czechoslovakia, the decrease in the birthrate was greater than one would have expected, given its level of economic development, as a result of the problems in housing and services created by the uneven growth strategy adopted by the political leadership after 1948. It also reflected the high levels of economic activity among women in the prime child-bearing years. The drop in births was particularly evident in the early 1960s, when live births fell to 15.5 per 1,000 population. The birthrate has consistently been somewhat lower in the more developed Czech Lands than in Slovakia, but rates of reproduction also have declined in the latter region. The adoption of aggressive pronatalist policies in the 1970s, which included positive incentives to encourage young families to have more than one child as well as restrictions on the grounds for abortion, led to a short-term increase in births. However, rates of reproduction fell once again in the 1980s, and ranged from 12.9 per 1,000 population in the Czech Lands to 16.8 per 1,000 population in Slovakia in 1986 ('Pohyb obyvatelstva, 1988, p. 162. See Heitlinger, 1976; David and McIntyre, 1981, pp. 22147; and Wolchik, 1981a, and 1981c, for discussions of population trends and population policies in Czechoslovakia). In 1990, the birthrate was expected to drop to 12.2 per 1,000 population in the Czech Lands ('Pomalu nas ubýva,' 1990, p. 2).

Experts foresee a continued decline in the birthrate through the early 1990s, followed by a temporary increase to approximately 15.2 births per 1,000 population by the end of the 1990s. The result of the higher number of births during the 1970s, this increase will be short-lived. Births are expected to decline once again after the year 2000 (Šimek, 1988, p. 21). However, demographers and officials responsible for population policy in the late communist period did not envision any marked expansion of the pronatalist measures adopted in the 1970s. Rather, they shifted emphasis to the need to ensure a highly qualified, healthy, although smaller population. Several also called for reorganization of the economy in order to allow the nation to produce adequately with a smaller labor force (see Kuchař and Pavlík, 1987, 289-98). This orientation also informs policy-making in this area in the post-communist period.

Policy-makers have criticized the pronatalist emphasis of family and social policy and proposed changes that will not link children's allowances and family benefits as closely to the number of children in the family as previously. Paid leave for mothers to care for young children, for example, has been changed to parental leave and extended to groups that were previously ineligible to receive it, such as families with only one child (see ha, 1990).

As in much of the rest of the region, abortion remains the primary means of birth control in Czechoslovakia. In 1988, there were 87.0 abortions for every 100 live births in the country as a whole, 96.4 in the CSR and 70.9 in Slovakia (Federální statistický úřad, 1990, p. 114). Abortion rates are highest in the largest cities and lower in the less developed, more rural areas where fewer women work and the population is more influenced by religion (see Stloukal, 1988, pp. 212-19). Restrictions on women's rights to abortion enacted in the early 1970s proved ineffective in reducing the numbers of abortions and were rescinded in January 1987 (see Grumlík, 1989, p. 4, for discussion of the liberalization of the abortion law and attitudes toward contraception).

Most (approximately 96 percent), citizens of Czechoslovakia eventually marry (Kroupová, 1988, p. 244). Marriages per 1,000 population have ranged from 9.9, in the period between 1945 and 1949, to 7.8 in 1987 (Federální statistický úřad, 1988, p. 99; 'Pohyb obyvatelstva,' 1988, p. 162). However, as in other industrialized countries, family stability has decreased in the recent past. The incidence of divorce increased dramatically from the early post-Second World War period, when there were 9.0 divorces per 100 marriages (1945-9), to the 1980s, when there were 30.8 per 100 marriages (1980-4). Czechoslovakia's divorce rate (2.35 per 1,000 population), was lower than that of the Soviet Union (3.48), East Germany (2.9), and Hungary (2.59), but higher than that of the other Central and East European countries in the late 1980's (see Haderka, 1987). Rates of marriage are approximately the same in the two parts of the country, but divorce rates are substantially higher in the more developed Czech Lands than in Slovakia. In 1988, for example, there were 37.6 divorces per 100 marriages in the Czech Lands, but only 22.1 per 100 marriages in Slovakia (Federální statistický úřad, 1990,

p. 103). In Slovakia divorce rates are above average in the Magyar areas as well as in the larger cities, a reflection of the higher than average rates of employment of women and the rapidity of economic change. Divorce rates are lower than average in the predominantly Ukrainian areas, which are still heavily rural and in which the influence of the church, the larger number of families with three or more children, and lower economic activity rates of women act as deterrents to divorce (Gurán, 1988, p. 203).

Educational levels

As noted in chapter 1, most regions of Czechoslovakia already had very high literacy rates during the interwar period. The annexation of the Subcarpathian Ruthene by the Soviet Union after the Second World War removed many of those who remained illiterate from the Czechoslovak state. There were still elements of the population, mainly Ukrainians or Ruthenians, who were illiterate in 1948, but their numbers were very small. Communist leaders in Czechoslovakia thus did not face the task of creating a literate citizenry that confronted leaders in many other communist states. As in other communist countries, they nonetheless expanded opportunities to obtain education, and the educational levels of the population continued to increase during the communist period. In 1950, 0.7 percent of the total population aged 15 and over had no education, and 77.6 percent had elementary education. Slightly over 4 percent (4.3), had complete secondary education, and 0.7 percent had higher education. By 1970, the proportion of those without any education had decreased to 0.4 percent, and those with only elementary education to 55.9 percent; 13.4 percent of the population aged 15 and older had completed secondary education and 3.3 percent, higher education (Kalínová, 1979, p. 78). Education levels are somewhat higher among the economically active segment of the population. In 1970, for example, 16.4 percent of employed men and 18.3 percent of employed women had completed secondary education; 6.2 percent of employed men and 3.2 percent of employed women had higher education in that year (Kalínová, 1979, p. 80).

As in other countries in the region, the increase in the number of people with secondary and higher education was especially noticeable in the technical area. The proportion of all white-collar workers with higher and secondary education who had technical educations increased from 33.1 percent in 1955 to 45.8 percent in 1966, for example. This increase, which reflected the heavy emphasis placed on vocational and technical education during the communist period, was particularly evident at the secondary level (Krejčí, 1972, pp. 60-2). In 1973, 39.4 percent of all specialists with higher education and 46.4 percent of those with secondary education had technical training (Kalínová, 1979, p. 86).

Despite the country's already high rates of literacy and basic education at the outset of the communist period and the expansion of educational access since that time, Czechoslovakia lags behind many of the other Central and East European states in the extent to which the population has higher or completed secondary education. In 1970, for example, 3.3 percent of the population in Czechoslovakia had higher education, compared to 3.9 percent in Bulgaria in 1965; 5 percent in Hungary in 1969; and 6.5 percent in the Soviet Union in 1970 (Kalínová, 1979, p. 81). This situation in part reflected the heavy emphasis placed on apprenticeship training rather than other kinds of education at the secondary level (see Matějů, 1990). By 1980, Czechoslovakia had fewer specialists with higher education per 1,000 population than the USSR, Hungary, Poland and Yugoslavia (Dohnalová, Roth and Storchová, 1989).

Czech and Slovak experts often decry the lower than desirable qualification levels of workers and employees in the economy. Only seven percent of all workers had secondary or higher education in 1970, for example. Educational levels were substantially higher among younger workers in both the Czech Lands and Slovakia, but in both areas, women workers, including young women, continued to lag behind men considerably in the amount of training received (Charvát, 1980, p. 155; Kalínová, 1979, pp. 79-80. See Matějů, 1990, for an analysis of these (and other) results of the educational policies of the communist period). The relatively small proportion of the total labor force with completed secondary specialized or higher education in Czechoslovakia is reflected in the discrepancy that is often found between the education levels required for non-manual positions and the actual qualifications of employees. In 1971, for example, only 60.3 percent of people in positions requiring higher education actually had attained such levels. Approximately 27 percent of employees in such positions had completed secondary education, 5 percent specialized, 3.7 percent general secondary, and 4 percent elementary education. The situation was similar among those employed in positions that formally required completed secondary education (only 61.4 percent of whom had such an education), and worse among those whose positions required specialized secondary training (34.1 percent of whom had the appropriate educations) (Charvát, 1980, p. 184; see also Kalínová, 1979, pp. 129-32). The negative economic impact of this situation during the communist period was compounded by the fact that many of those who had secondary and higher education were employed in positions that did not utilize their qualifications (Kalínová, 1979, pp. 133-4).

The reform of the educational system that has occurred in Czechoslovakia since the end of communist rule will result in changes both in the balance between technical and other types of education and the educational levels of the population. However, the skill levels and educational patterns that are the product of the communist era will continue to condition economic performance for some time to come. They will also influence the transition to a market economy. Thus, although Czechoslovakia has, in world terms, an educated populace and labor force, there are important differences in the value of these educations in various fields. In certain areas, the skills, techniques, and approaches learned will provide a useful base for further learning and employment. In areas in which Czechoslovakia and its communist neighbors lagged behind other European countries, however, workers and employees will need substantial retraining and updating of their knowledge and skills. In still others, including those most influenced by Marxist-Leninist ideology, entirely new approaches and methods must be learned.

Occupational structure

One of the most developed of the states that became communist after the Second World War, Czechoslovakia's social structure differed considerably from that of its neighbors in the interwar period. As noted in chapter 1, Czechoslovakia was far less agrarian than other states in the region. Only in Czechoslovakia, where approximately 34 percent of the population remained in agriculture in 1930, and in what was to become East Germany, did the occupational structure of the population approximate that found in the more developed West European countries (Wolchik, 1985b, p. 32). These differences, which were also reflected in the literacy and educational levels of the population as well as in the occupational structure of the country, are still evident to some extent today. While sizeable portions of the population in Bulgaria, Albania, Yugoslavia and Romania still earn their living in agriculture at present, in Czechoslovakia most people are employed in either industry or the service sector.

Czechoslovakia's social structure thus changed less in certain respects than that of other Central and East European communist states in the course of the communist period. However, as in the least developed countries in the region, the institution of a communist system and the adoption of ambitious economic growth targets resulted in the further industrialization of the country and a further reduction in the dependence of the population on agriculture. In 1960, 24.2 percent of the economically active population worked in agriculture; 51.6 percent worked in industry; and 24.2 percent in the service sector. By 1970, 16.8 percent were employed in agriculture, 53.4 percent in industry, and 29.8 percent in the service sector (Charvát, 1980, p. 102). The proportion of the labor force engaged in agriculture continued to decrease throughout the 1970s and 1980s, reaching 13.0 percent in 1980, 12.4 percent in 1985, and 11.1 percent in 1987 (Federální statistický úřad, 1985, pp. 191-3; 1986, pp. 184-6; and 1988, p. 185). As the next section will discuss, changes in developmental levels and the shift away from agriculture have been particularly evident in Slovakia.

The proportion of the labor force engaged in the service sector increased substantially during the communist period, but this sector is still underdeveloped (see Deyl and Kerner, 1966, pp. 509-20, for discussion of the impact of nationalization on the service sector). In 1984, for example, 40 percent of the economically active population worked in services. The number of workers in this sector per 1,000

Table 3.1   Social composition of the population, 1930–84

	1930[a]	1946	1950	1961	1970	1981	1984
Workers	57.3	62.8[b]	56.4	56.3	58.0	48.1	48.1
Other employees	6.0		16.3	27.9	30.0	40.9	40.7
Coop. producers	0.0	0.0	0.0	11.8	9.5	9.6	9.7
Agriculture	0.0	0.0	0.0	10.6	8.3	8.8	8.8
Other coop.	0.0	0.0	0.0	1.2	1.2	0.8	0.9
Private sector	36.7	37.2	27.3	4.0	2.5	0.3	0.3
Agriculture	22.2		20.3	3.5	2.0	0.1	0.2
Artisans and craftsmen	8.2		3.6	0.4	0.4	0.1	
Free professionals	0.5		0.2	0.1	0.1	0.1	0.1
Capitalists[c]	5.8	4.2	3.2	0.0	0.0		
Other and no data						1.2	1.2

Notes: [a] In territory that became post–Second World War Czechoslovakia.
[b] Includes workers and employees.
[c] Factory and business owners, owners of large farms, managers.

Sources: Charvát, 1972, p. 30; Krejčí, 1972, p. 43, Table 15; Federální statistický úřad, 1972, p. 103 and 1986, p. 95.

population in Czechoslovakia in that year (197), was higher than in most of the other communist countries, except the GDR (203 per 1,000 population). However, the proportion of the labor force engaged in this area in Czechoslovakia remained considerably lower than in most developed capitalist countries, including the United States (294), Japan (264), Great Britain (265), West Germany (210), and Sweden (378) in the late 1980s (V. Michalová, 1988, p. 615).

In addition to changes due to continued economic development, the structure of society in the Czech Lands and Slovakia was also influenced by the elimination of most forms of private enterprise and by the restrictions on inheritance adopted soon after the communist system was instituted. These measures resulted in a sharp shift in the balance of private and state employees in the economy (see Krejčí, 1972, pp. 12–27, for a summary of these changes).

As Table 3.1 illustrates, the proportion of the population engaged in the private sector in Czechoslovakia dropped sharply to 27.3

Table 3.2 Structure of the economically active population

	1960	1970	1973	1980	1985	1987
Workers and employees	79.6	86.0	87.6	88.8	89.1	88.8
Cooperative producers	16.1	12.1	11.2	10.9	10.7	10.6
Agriculture	14.0	9.7	8.7	8.5	8.3	8.3
Other cooperative	2.1	2.4	2.5	2.4	2.3	2.3
Private sector	4.3	2.2	1.2	0.3	0.3	0.6
Agriculture	4.2	2.1	1.1	0.2	0.1	0.1
Free professionals, artisans and craftsmen	0.1	0.1	0.1			
Others				0.1	0.2	0.5

Sources: Charvát, 1980, pp. 98, 138; Federální statistický úřad, 1986, p. 190, and 1988, p. 191.

percent by 1950, two years after the communist system was established. This proportion continued to decline in the 1960s and 1970s, reaching 4.0 percent in 1961 and 2.5 percent in 1970 (see Table 3.1). The move out of the private sector, particularly in agriculture, proceeded somewhat more slowly in Slovakia than in the already more industrialized Czech Lands. Differences between the two regions in this respect narrowed after 1950, when 21.6 percent of the population in the Czech Lands and 39 percent in Slovakia were in the private sector. However, the proportion of the population employed in the private sector was still approximately three times greater in Slovakia in 1969 (4.8 percent) than in the Czech Lands (1.7 percent), (Charvát, 1972, p. 31). The change in the economic organization of society is further evident in the share of the private sector in the creation of national income. Already small by 1960 (1.5 percent of the total), this share decreased further to 0.8 percent by 1965 and 1970 (Charvát, 1980, p. 101).

The impact of nationalization and the development strategy used by the communist leadership was also reflected in the composition of the labor force. By 1960, for example, individual farmers accounted for only 4.2 percent of the total labor force, and those in the free professions, artisans and craftsmen, an additional 0.1

percent. Most of those who were privately employed were concentrated in Slovakia, where private farmers accounted for 11 percent of the labor force (Charvát, 1980, p. 98). The proportion of private farmers, craftsmen, artisans, and free professionals continued to decrease in the 1960s and early 1970s (see Table 3.2). Measures adopted during the late communist period to encourage small-scale private enterprise resulted in an increase of approximately 15,600 in the numbers of private entrepreneurs in the non-agricultural sectors of the economy between 1985 and 1987 and a corresponding slight increase in their proportion of the labor force. However, the private sector continued to play a small role in the creation of national income.

There was also a large increase in the proportion of the labor force classified as members of the intelligentsia. Defined as those non-manual workers who engage in highly qualified mental work which requires higher education, the share of this social category in the labor force nearly doubled between 1960 (12.9 percent) and 1973 (20.5 percent). Within this category, the increase was especially great in technical areas (Charvát, 1980, pp. 98, 138).

In contrast to the situation in several formerly communist countries in which a sizeable portion of the labor force was employed in the private sector during the communist period, then, in Czechoslovakia the effort to recreate a market economy with a substantial private sector had to begin with an economy that was almost completely in state hands. Changes in the laws governing ownership rights, which equalized all forms of property ownership and provided for certain types of agricultural and other property confiscated by the communist authorities to be restored to their owners, were enacted in 1990. Together with the privatization of the economy now under way, they will result in a marked increase in the numbers of workers and employees who are employed in the private sector of the economy. However, given the very high degree of state ownership, these processes will take some time. Privatization, the reorientation of the country's external economic relations, and other aspects of the move to a market economy, including the end of subsidies to unprofitable enterprises, the end of guaranteed sources of raw materials, energy, and markets, and the resulting need to compete on the world market, will also lead to structural changes in Czechoslovakia's economy (see Brokl, 1990a, 1990b; Večerník, 1990a; and Tuček, 1990, for discussions of likely changes).

Social stratification and social mobility

The change in the structure of Czech and Slovak society that accompanied the establishment of a communist system was paralleled by changes in the position of particular social groups. Efforts to improve the status of previously disadvantaged social groups and the need to use financial incentives to draw workers into branches of the economy, such as heavy industry, mining, and construction, that became high priority sectors after 1948 led to marked changes in the wages of particular categories of workers and employees. These policies also led to a decrease in income differentials and to a substantial levelling of the living standards of the population (see Connor, 1979, pp. 83–6; Krejčí, 1972, pp. 12–20; Parkin, 1971, pp. 141–9; and Lane, 1971, pp. 74–9). As in the other communist countries, there was a fair degree of tension throughout the communist period between those who sought to equalize the income and living conditions of members of different social groups and those who warned of the negative impact of too great a degree of equalization on economic performance (see Lowenthal, 1970, pp. 33–116, for a general discussion). However, until very late in the communist period and with the exception of the period leading up to and during the political reform in the 1960s, the advocates of egalitarianism had the upper hand in Czechoslovakia.

As is the case with studies of social stratification in other socialist countries, there are numerous barriers to determining the extent of inequality in Czechoslovakia during the communist period. Part of the difficulty stems from the fact that the top layer of society, the Communist Party elite, was not included in social science research. We thus have little but anecdotal evidence concerning their incomes and lifestyles. We have similarly little hard information concerning the extent of monetary and other privileges that accrued to lower-level officials and party members as a result of their political positions and activities. The contribution that unofficial economic activities, as well as support from relatives, barter, and exchange among friends made to the living standards of individuals and families also eluded researchers in most cases (see Asselain, 1987, pp. 59-61; Duchêne, 1987; Vítečková, 1985a, pp. 377-8, and 1987, pp. 48-50). The impact of 'normalization' on social science research in Czechoslovakia posed additional difficulties, for many of those social scientists who did innovative research on the social structure and social stratification were removed from their positions after 1968. The range of subjects thought appropriate for investigation by social scientists also narrowed considerably. The need to have even articles in specialized professional journals approved before publication and the tendency to report relatively little hard information regarding research findings made it difficult to judge the results of much social science research (see Otava, 1988, for a discussion of these issues by a Czech sociologist). Certain of these criticisms, particularly the narrow range of research subjects, were echoed in the official sociological journals in Czechoslovakia in the late 1980s).

With these caveats in mind, there is nonetheless a substantial amount of evidence to support the official claims made during the communist period that Czechoslovakia was a highly egalitarian society. Sociological research done on the structure of socialist society in the mid- to late 1960s found that the reward structure in Czech and Slovak society paralleled that found in other advanced industrial states to some degree, except in the area of the relationship between other indicators of status and political power. This research also demonstrated that the three categories generally used in sociological research in Czechoslovakia (workers, agricultural workers, and employees), were too simple to describe the nature of socialist society adequately. Thus, income levels, social prestige, and standard of living tended to vary according to the individual's level of education and the complexity of work performed as well as by general social category (see Machonin, 1966; Connor, 1979, pp. 83-6 and 102; Kende and Strimska, eds, 1987, pp. 177-81; and Lane, 1971, pp. 54-70 and pp. 84-6 for discussions of these studies). However, differences in the incomes of individuals in different categories were very small. Differentials between the incomes of

Table 3.3 Wages of different categories of workers in Czechoslovakia

	1953	1955	1960	1965	1970	1972
Wages of: (Kcs)						
Worker	1155	1272	1406	1529	1902	2048
Engineering-technical worker	1494	1607	1868	2068	2569	2686
Administrative worker	1019	1081	1225	1319	1626	1737
Workers' wages as percentage of:						
Engineering-technical workers'	77.3	79.2	75.3	73.9	74.0	76.2
Administrative workers'	113.3	117.7	114.8	115.9	117.0	117.9

Source: From Večerník, 1985, p. 149.

different social groups, and particularly between manual and non-manual workers, decreased in all of the Central and East European countries after the Second World War, but egalitarianism in this respect went further in Czechoslovakia than elsewhere (see Connor, 1979, pp. 231-2, for a comparison of income differentiation in four Central and East European countries and the Soviet Union. See Asselain, 1987, pp. 21-34; Connor, 1979, ch. 6; Parkin, 1971, pp. 62-80; and Lane, 1971, pp. 71-8, for further information).

More recent studies of social stratification in Czechoslovakia confirm these patterns. They also indicate that wage differentials continued to be lower in Czechoslovakia than in the Soviet Union and the other Central and East European countries (Večerník, 1985, pp. 147-8; Matějů, 1986b, p. 602. See Asselain, 1987, for a comparison of income distribution in Czechoslovakia, Hungary, and Poland). As Table 3.3 illustrates, the relationship between the wages of workers and engineering-technical workers did not change to any degree between 1953 and the 1970s. Workers' wages as a proportion of administrative workers' wages increased only slightly (see Charvát, 1972, pp. 75-81; Večerník, 1985; and Matějů, 1986b for further analysis).

The difference between the wages of the best- and worst-paid groups of the population was also stable from the late 1950s to the late 1970s. In 1979, for example, the highest wage (4,004 Kcs), was only 2.5 times greater than the lowest (1,637 Kcs) (Vitečková, 1987, p. 47).

The reduction of inequalities in the wages of members of different social classes and different categories of workers did not eliminate all inequalities in incomes in Czechoslovakia. Substantial differences continued to exist in the incomes of men and women and in the incomes of individuals who worked in various sectors of the economy. In the first area, women continued to earn approximately one-third less than men, a proportion that remained stable throughout the communist period (Wolchik, 1978, ch. 3, and 1979, pp. 589-90; and Asselain, 1987, p. 51). As the section on gender issues later in this chapter will discuss further, this ratio varies to some extent by the educational levels of women and by the sector of the economy in which they are employed, but women earn less than men in all categories.

Differences are also evident in the incomes of workers and employees in different sectors of the economy. Although there has been some change in this respect since the 1950s, average wages tend to be highest in transport, construction, and industry, and lowest in trade, education and culture, and health (Asselain, 1987, pp. 47-8; see also Charvát, 1972, pp. 74-9; and Vitečková, 1987, p. 47).

Although a sample of 342 Czech and Slovak experts surveyed in 1984 agreed that wages should reflect differences in qualifications and levels of education, in actuality, wages continued to bear little relationship to individuals' educational levels during the communist period (Matějů, 1986b, pp. 600-2, 611). Gender is a far more important factor in explaining variation in wages among both workers and employees (Večerník, 1985, p. 152). Popular attitudes during the communist period reflected an acceptance of the limited relationship between education levels and income. A 1984 survey of attitudes and values based on a sample of 4,000 individuals, for example, found that most respondents gave little weight to education in proposing wages for various kinds of work. There was also widespread support for a further decrease in wage differentials

Table 3.4 Net monthly income per capita by social group (Kcs)

	1956	1970	1980
Worker	501	992	1423
Employee	554	1187	1632
Collective Farmer	397	1087	1529
Pensioner	387	838	1227
Average	461	1019	1467

Source: Večerník, 1984, p. 2.

(Linhart, Tuček, and Vodáková, 1986, pp. 639–41).

Differences in the per capita income of individuals in different social groups decrease further if one considers household units. As Table 3.4 illustrates, per capita income has consistently been higher in employee households than in agricultural families. However, the most important element in explaining per capita income variation is not social group but a demographic factor, i.e. the number of children in the household. The importance of this factor is highlighted by a study of the changing importance of social group, education, and other factors in determining income per capita from 1956 to 1980 that found that the standard indicators followed in studies of income differentiation, such as education and complexity of work, explained only one-fourth of the variance in incomes. Demographic factors explained the rest (see Večerník, 1984, and 1990a).

The relatively narrow differences in the incomes of various social groups were reflected in a levelling of living standards. These trends were especially noticeable in the material conditions of families (Vitečková, 1985a). A 1978 study of the living standards of the families of 3,175 married men found, for example, that differences in age, wage levels, and education explained relatively little (29 percent) of the differences in living standards (Matějů, 1986b, p. 608). Differences in education levels were more important than wage levels in explaining variation in living standards, but the educational level of the head of the household explained only 4 percent of the variance in household living standards (Matějů, 1986b, pp. 609-10). As in the case of differences in per capita income, the number of individuals in the household played a more important role in determining a family's standard of living (Matějů, 1986b, pp. 606, 610; see also Asselain, 1987, pp. 53-5).

Despite the high degree of equalization of wages and material living standards during the communist period, members of different social groups continued to differ in other areas. These differences were evident in the ways in which income and time were used, as well as in the values expressed in families (Vitečková, 1987, p. 42). Thus, although differences in the amount of free time available to members of different social groups decreased after the early 1960s (Vitečková, 1985b, pp. 571-2), workers, employees, and agricultural workers put free time to different uses. Time budget studies conducted in 1980, for example, found that men and women employees spent more time than those in other social groups on educational and recreational artistic activities, as well as on public and political activities. Women employees also spent substantially more time than other women reading (Vitečková, 1985a).

More educated white-collar workers and members of the intelligentsia are also more likely than blue-collar workers with similar incomes to attend concerts and other cultural events; they also own more books and read more (see Lane, 1971, pp. 76-7 and 84-6 and Krejčí, 1972, pp. 93-6 for discussions of studies illustrating these trends). The differences in values and attitudes these patterns reflect are important because they have a significant impact on social mobility. Differences in values and lifestyles were reflected in parents' aspirations for their children as well as in children's success in school during the communist period. As the section to follow on social mobility illustrates, a certain proportion of parents in all social groups wanted their children to go on to secondary and higher education, and some children of manual and agricultural workers did complete such programs. However, far more white-collar parents aspired to such schooling for their offspring, and a higher proportion of those who successfully completed further study at both the secondary and higher level came from white-collar or employee households (see Lane, 1971, pp. 108-16 for a general discussion of these trends).

As chapter 2 illustrated, the political attitudes of the population varied to some extent by social group during the communist period. Approximately two-thirds of the intellectuals surveyed in a study done in the mid 1980s, compared to one-third of agricultural workers, for example, held a 'scientific', or non-religious view of the world. Ten percent of intellectuals, but one-third of agricultural workers, adhered to religious views (Zich, 1986, pp. 445-6). Attitudes toward politics and economic reform also vary by social group in the post-communist period (see chapter 2).

The highly egalitarian nature of Czechoslovak society was one of the recurring concerns of economic reformers in Czechoslovakia during the communist period, for the narrow income differentials between highly skilled, highly demanding work and less demanding activities did not provide sufficient incentives for workers and employees to increase their qualifications or work efficiently. As noted in chapter 2, popular support for egalitarianism, which predates communism to some extent, is one of the factors that will complicate the process of economic transformation now under way. As chapter 4 will discuss in greater detail, public opinion concerning economic reform is divided. Although many citizens support the move to the market, there is widespread fear of the negative consequences of this move on the standard of living and the division of wealth. Large disparities of wealth are likely to provoke resentment and possible political action. The end of state subsidies and the creation of privately owned companies as a consequence of the privatization of large sectors of the economy will result in wages that are determined by market forces rather than by state planners. Wage differentials will thus increase substantially. These differences will also be reflected in different standards of living to a much greater degree than they are at present.

In the near future, several factors may limit these changes. First, popular pressure on political leaders and the willingness to strike if the economic situation deteriorates markedly expressed by a significant portion of the population will be reflected in efforts to provide a safety net for those affected by economic changes. The fact that privatization of large-scale enterprises will take some time to accomplish will delay the full impact of privatization on wage differentials. The decline in economic performance that will accompany the economic transformation may also limit the extent of inequalities at least temporarily. However, the shift to a market economy will lead eventually to greater differentiation in both income and living standards (see Tuček, 1990).

Social mobility

The institution of a communist system and continued industrialization led to a substantial amount of both upward and downward social mobility in the early years of communist rule in Czechoslovakia (see Krejčí, 1972, pp. 152-3; and Connor, 1979, pp. 117-29). In contrast to other Central and East European societies, in which mobility occurred in the context of change from peasant to industrial societies, in Czechoslovakia many of the upwardly mobile were children not of peasants but of industrial workers. A 1967 study, for example, found that over one-fourth of sons of workers became highly trained employees; an additional 10 percent became officials (Charvát, 1972, p. 39). As a result of Czechoslovakia's level of industrialization prior to the communist period, a sizeable portion (over 55 percent in 1967), of the working class came from working class, rather than peasant, origins (Charvát, 1972, pp. 36-7).

As Connor notes in his discussion of a 1967 study of the structure of socialist society in Czechoslovakia, 'Czechoslovakia is a society with a quite developed starting point that maintained a high rate of structural mobility thereafter' (Connor, 1979, p. 118). The extent of social mobility in Czechoslovakia, which as noted earlier was the most egalitarian of the Central and East European communist countries if one looks at wage differentials, was also greater than in other Central and East European countries through the 1970s (Connor, 1979, pp. 142-4). The extent of social mobility was particularly great prior to 1960 (Charvát, 1972, p. 38).

Measures to eliminate the economic base of the large landowners and industrialists in the early years of communist rule were accompanied by steps to limit the access of children of upper and middle class origin to education. Many children of the former economic and political elite did obtain higher educations, but were forced to do so through evening or correspondence classes or to study subjects that were not their original choices. Students from working-class or peasant families, on the other hand, were given preference in admission to secondary and higher education programs.

However, although children of peasants and workers thus had opportunities to enter non-manual and professional positions during the communist period, the sons and daughters of intellectuals and other non-manual employees were still more likely to occupy these positions than those from manual or agricultural backgrounds. The results of a 1967 study of social mobility illustrate this tendency. From 85 to 92 percent of the sons from working-class backgrounds studied in 1967 remained workers, while from 0.4 to 7.5 percent (depending on age and educational level), became non-manual employees with specialized training, and from 0.5 to 9.7 percent became officials. From 89.1 to 91.4 percent of sons of non-manual employees with specialized training kept their father's occupations while from 1.7 to 7.5 percent became officials, and from 0.8 to 6.9 percent became workers (Charvát, 1972, p. 38). Although approximately 60 percent of those non-manual employees with secondary education came from worker or peasant families in 1967, from 47 to 56 percent of those with higher education came from 'other' backgrounds (Charvát, 1972, p. 47).

Similar patterns characterized educational access. Although the expansion of educational opportunities allowed many children of working-class and agricultural families to obtain secondary and higher educations, the educational options and later occupations of young people in different social categories continued to differ substantially. Research on the social and professional orientations of young people conducted in the late 1970s found that 81.8 percent of apprentices, for example, came from working-class or working-class-agricultural families. Approximately 13 percent came from families in which one parent was a white-collar worker or employee. Only 5.6 percent of apprentices came from families in which both parents were employees (Macháček, 1982, p. 195). Differences in the educational options and later occupations of young people of different social categories are also evident in the proportion of all students who come from worker, peasant, or mixed worker-peasant backgrounds. In 1979, for example, 32.3 percent of all students in the general secondary schools that led to university admission (*gymnázia*), came from worker-peasant backgrounds; such students accounted for 63.2 percent of students in secondary trade and trade schools, and 74 percent of those in secondary apprentice training programs (Macháček, 1982, p. 200). Thus, although the fact that approximately a third of students in programs that led to higher education came from worker or peasant families attests to a sizeable degree of social mobility, children of white-collar parents who had higher or secondary education still clearly had an advantage in gaining access to higher education.

The different social composition of the student bodies in different types of educational programs illustrates the continued importance of the family in determining individuals' values and behaviors during the communist period. It also reflects the influence of family values and culture on the aspirations of parents and children as well as on the performance of children from different social strata. As in other societies, children who came from families in which the parents were well-educated were more likely to continue their educations and tended to do better in their studies, even though the material standards of living of families with different educational levels did not differ greatly.

The return to a market economy, as well as the repudiation of communist policies in regard to educational access, will also have an impact on social mobility in Czechoslovakia. Greater wage differentials and the elimination of political considerations as a factor in admissions decisions in higher education will result, in all likelihood, in a decrease in the numbers of students from working-class and agricultural-worker families at that level and a resulting decrease in social mobility. Social mobility will also decline during the transitional period, as economic performance declines. Whether education and political leaders will enact measures to counteract such trends is an open question at this time.

Ethnic composition

Czechoslovakia has been a multi-ethnic state from its foundation as an independent state. As noted in chapter 1, the ethnic composition of the country is less complex now than during the interwar period, when sizeable Jewish, German, Hungarian, and Ukrainian minorities lived within its borders. The expulsion of the Sudeten Germans, the forced repatriation of much of the Hungarian minority in Slovakia, and the annexation of part of the Subcarpathian Ruthene by the Soviet Union removed many members of these groups from the boundaries of the post-Second World War state. The death of most of the country's estimated 250,000 Jews (Nyrop, 1982, p. 82) at the hands of the Nazis further reduced the country's ethnic diversity (see Paul, 1981, pp. 129-30; and Nemec, 1973, pp. 425-6).

Although these measures simplified the ethnic composition of the post-Second World War Czechoslovak state, members of other nationalities continue to exist within its borders. These include the Hungarians, who are concentrated largely in the southern areas of Western Slovakia, and the Ukrainians or Ruthenians who are found primarily in the northern districts of Central and Eastern Slovakia. Many of the 595,000 Hungarians living in Slovakia and the 56,000 Ukrainian/Ruthenians who inhabit what is left of the most backward areas of the interwar Czechoslovak state are agrarian. The Ukrainians, who are heavily concentrated in four districts of Eastern Slovakia and comprise approximately 3 percent of the population in that region (Bajčura, 1975, p. 13), have educational levels that are still substantially below those of other groups in the population (see Magocsi, 1985). However, differences in the occupations and educational levels of members of these groups have decreased in recent decades (see Kusin, 1972, pp. 149-51, for a discussion of variations in the estimates of the numbers of minority nationalities).

The impact of these changes is most evident in Eastern Slovakia, the region which has the highest concentration of Ukrainians and approximately 15 percent of the total Hungarian minority. Until recently, the majority of both Hungarians and Ukrainians were engaged in agriculture. Compared to the Czechs and Slovaks who reside in the region, Hungarians and Ukrainians are still far more likely to work in the agricultural sector. The results of the 1980 census found that 24 percent of Hungarians and 23.1 percent of

Ukrainians, compared to 16.3 percent of Slovaks and 6.5 percent of Czechs in the region of Eastern Slovakia worked in agriculture and forestry in 1980 (Bajčura and Výrost, 1986, p. 262). Similarly, 9.3 percent of all Hungarians and 6.2 percent of all Ukrainians in the area were employed as agricultural workers, compared to 4.6 percent of Slovaks and two percent of Czechs. The proportion of each group who were members of collectives or state farms also exceeded that of Czech and Slovaks considerably (12 percent of Ukrainians and 10.4 percent of Hungarians, compared to 4.3 percent of Czechs and 8.7 percent of Slovaks), (Bajčura and Výrost, 1986, p. 263). However, in contrast to the situation at the beginning of the communist period, by 1980, the majority of both groups were workers (45.1 percent of Hungarians and 33.7 percent of Ukrainians) or employees (35 percent of Hungarians and 47.9 percent of Ukrainians) (Bajčura and Výrost, 1986, p. 263; see Čorný, 1975; Ričalka, 1975; Magosci, 1985; and Sokolová, 1987, for further information).

In addition to these groups, there are approximately 72,000 Poles and 55,000 ethnic Germans who reside in Czechoslovakia at present. Most of the Poles and Germans (69,000 and 52,000, respectively) live in the Czech Lands (Federální statistický úřad, 1988, p. 96). Approximately 51,000 citizens were classified as 'other' or were of unknown nationality in the 1980 census. This number in all probability includes the small number of Jews (estimated to be from 15,000 to 18,000), who survived the Holocaust. It also may include some of the gypsies who live in Czechoslovakia at present.

Although they were not officially regarded as an ethnic group by Czechoslovak authorities during the communist period, gypsies are in fact the largest or second largest minority in the state. Estimates of the number of gypsies who live in Czechoslovakia vary greatly. Because they were not recognized as an ethnic group, gypsies had to identify themselves as members of one of the established nationalities for official purposes. The 1980 census, which estimated that 288,440 gypsies lived in Czechoslovakia (Srb, 1984, p. 161) indicates that most gypsies (approximately three-quarters) identified themselves as Slovak; 15 percent chose to identify themselves as Hungarians; and approximately 10 percent as Czechs (Srb, 1984,

p. 170). This pattern of identification reflects the fact that the large majority of gypsies currently live in Slovakia (73 percent of the total) (Srb, 1984, p. 161). Although gypsies are found throughout the country, most of those in Slovakia live in the Central and Eastern regions. In certain districts of these regions, between 10 and 14 percent of the population are gypsies. The 1970s saw an extensive migration to urban areas on the part of the gypsy population, in part as a result of government measures designed to resettle Slovak gypsies in industrial cities in Northern and Western Bohemia (Ulč, 1988, pp. 313-15). As a result, a majority of gypsies (52.5 percent) are now urban. In the Czech Lands, over 80 percent of gypsies live in urban areas (Srb, 1984, p. 162). In 1990, unofficial data suggested that there are approximately 800,000 gypsies. Gypsy activists argue that there are up to a million (ČTK, 15 November 1990).

During the communist period, Czechoslovak sources pointed to the progress that had been made in improving the living standards and educational levels of the gypsy population. However, they also acknowledged the difficulties that remained in both of these respects. Thus, the proportion of gypsies 15 years of age and older who had no schooling decreased from 12.4 percent of men and 19.5 percent of women in 1970 to 5.1 percent of men and 8.7 percent of women in 1980, while the number of those with elementary education increased from 66.0 percent of men and 62.8 percent of women in 1970 to 81.7 percent of men and 83.3 percent of women by 1980 (Srb, 1984, p. 169). However, illiteracy rates among gypsies (approximately 10 percent) are still much higher, and educational levels much lower than those of other national groups. As Ulč notes, only 4 percent of gypsies continued their education after the eighth grade in 1980; only 0.3 percent of gypsy men and 0.2 percent of gypsy women had higher or university education (Ulč, 1988, pp. 319-20; and Srb, 1984, p. 169; see also Kostelančík, 1987).

Trends in housing are similar. Thus, while both the level of housing and the availability of basic amenities such as hot and cold running water, central heating, etc., increased between 1970 and 1980, most gypsies still live in small houses or apartments with fewer basic conveniences than the rest of the population (Kučera, 1984, p. 175-6). The employment structure of the gypsy population also differs considerably from that of the population as a whole. Approximately 76 percent of employed gypsies are industrial workers (compared to 33.4 percent of the total labor force), and 9.5 percent (compared to 3.3 percent of the total labor force) agricultural workers. Far fewer gypsies (7.2 percent), work as non-manual employees than the population as a whole (54.5 percent). Gypsies have also been far less likely to be members of collective farms (0.5 percent) than the population as a whole (7.5 percent) (Srb, 1984, p. 168).

Gypsies are also distinguished from the rest of the population by their high fertility levels and the lower median age of the gypsy population. Fertility levels among gypsy women dropped by 10 percent between 1970 and 1980, but still are much higher than those among the rest of the population. The average number of live births among gypsy women, for example, exceeded the national average by 166 percent in 1980. Whereas the state-wide average number of children of women at the end of their reproductive lives (aged 45 to 49) was 2.4 children, among gypsy women it was 6.4 (Srb, 1984, p. 171-2).

Gypsies were subjected to assimilationist pressures during much of the communist period. With the exception of a brief time in the late 1960s, when they were allowed to form their own organization and more open discussion of the need for recognition of the cultural and other rights of gypsies was tolerated, the official approach to the gypsy problem during the communist period emphasized settlement and resettlement, coupled with restrictions on fertility. Popular prejudices, fostered by the higher crime rates found among gypsy youth, were reflected in discussions of the gypsy situation and its possible solutions (see Skilling, 1976; Ulč, 1988; and Kostelančík, 1987. See Danáš, 1988, p. 7, for a discussion of gypsy criminality in the late communist period. See the studies in *Slovenský národopis*, 1988; and Bačová, 1988a and 1988b, for more nuanced views).

Members of minority national groups expressed dissatisfaction with their status from time to time during the communist period (see Skilling, 1976, pp. 603-10; and Ulč, 1988). Hungarian activists were the most vocal about perceived injustices in the last years of communist rule and voiced complaints about the cultural, educational, and political opportunities available to the Hungarian population (see Časnochová, 1988, p. 3; and Duray, 1989).

With the end of the communist system, members of these ethnic groups have organized to call attention to their needs and promote their interests. Hungarian activists have focused on language and cultural issues and have argued for the creation of a Hungarian University (see Rod, 1990; Bogdan, 1991; and Šamudovský, 1991). Hungarian activists also opposed the effort by Slovak nationalists to pass a language law that would have made Slovak the only officially recognized language in Slovakia. The law that was passed allows other languages to be used for official purposes in localities which have at least 20 percent minority populations. The inhabitants of Moravia and Silesia have also organized to promote their interests. As noted in chapter 2, Moravian nationalism threatened the dominant coalition in the Czech Republic's legislature in early 1991, as Moravians and Silesians sought a change in constitutional arrangements and budgetary decisions more favorable to their interests. As in 1968, gypsies have also formed a number of organizations, including a political party, that are working to improve the situation of gypsies and pressure the government to deal with the roots of gypsy involvement in crime and delinquency. Certain groups have also raised the issue of negative stereotypes about and discrimination against gypsies (see Rod, 1990; Bogdan, 1991; and Šamudovský, 1991 for recent discussions). The end of communist rule has also been followed by more open expression of ethnic prejudices and hostilities. Attacks by 'skinheads' on Vietnamese guest workers and gypsies in 1990 were the most violent of these. However, the hostile reception given to refugees from Romania in mid-1990 was further evidence that ethnic stereotypes and tensions had been submerged rather than eliminated during communist rule (see 'Kde se v teto zemí vzal rasismus?,' 1990, p. 2; 'Výzvá československé vláde,' 1990, p. 2; and 'Konec mnoha fam,' 1990, pp. 1-2. See also Mrázová and Kučerová, 1990, p. 4).

Issues related to the position and rights of several of these ethnic groups were important politically in Czechoslovakia, particularly in the interwar period, and have re-emerged as political issues in the post-communist period. However, the dominant ethnic cleavage in earlier time periods and at present is that between Czechs and

Table 3.5 Nationality composition of Czechoslovakia (percent of total)

	1950	1961	1970	1980	1985	1987
Czech	68.0	66.0	65.0	64.1	63.2	62.9
Slovak	26.3	27.9	29.3	30.6	31.5	31.8
Hungarian	3.0	3.9	4.0	3.8	3.8	3.8
Polish	0.6	0.5	0.5	0.4	0.5	0.5
German	1.3	1.0	0.6	0.4	0.4	0.3
Ukrainian/Ruthenian	0.6	0.4	0.4	0.4	0.3	0.4
Other	0.3	0.3	0.2	0.4	0.3	0.3

Sources: Zvára, 1988, p. 7; Federální statistický úřad, 1969, p. 87, 1977, p. 97, 1988, p. 96, 1989, p. 98.

Slovaks. As Table 3.5 illustrates, Slovaks now comprise a somewhat higher proportion of the total population than they did 40 years ago. The impact of the slightly higher birthrates evident in Slovakia during this time has been offset to some extent by continuing differences in levels of infant and general mortality in the two parts of the country. However, population projections envision a continued increase in the proportion of Slovaks in the population through at least 2010, when Slovaks will comprise 34 percent of the population, and Czechs 61 percent (Zvára, 1988).

As noted in chapter 1, the status of Czechs and Slovaks was markedly different at the outset of the communist period. Efforts to improve the material situation of Slovaks made little headway during the interwar period, in part due to the impact of the Great Depression (see Pryor, 1973, pp. 212-15). Paradoxically, the one area in which the interwar government's policies produced some real change, educational levels, fueled rising Slovak discontent during this period, because it increased Slovak awareness of the inequities between Czechs and Slovaks and also created an educated community that could be mobilized behind ethnic claims more easily than previously (see O. Johnson, 1985). As chapter 2 discussed, the promises Czechoslovakia's communist leaders made to Slovaks concerning Slovak autonomy and the rights of the Slovak people in the new state immediately after the Second World War were soon forgotten. Slovak desires for institutional recognition of Slovakia's special status in the common state were only realized in the context of the political reform of 1968. However, despite the centralization evident in the formal structure of the state prior to 1969 and in practice after that time, the communist regime in Czechoslovakia was successful in reducing many of the persistent disparities between the two groups. These results contrast sharply with the continuing gap in the living standards and levels of economic development of different national groups in Yugoslavia and the Soviet Union (see Burg, 1983; Singleton, 1976; and Banac, 1984, for analyses of the Yugoslav situation; see Connor, 1984, for a discussion of the policies in regard to the national question in the Soviet Union and other socialist countries). Much of the available information concerns regional differences. It thus does not allow direct comparison of the status of the Czechs and Slovaks only, as other national groups residing in the two regions are included. However, the predominance of Czechs and Slovaks in their regions means that such a comparison is a good estimate of these differences. If anything, use of regional data should underestimate the degree of equalization between Czechs and Slovaks, given the higher proportion of members of other national groups in Slovakia.

The primary tool used to equalize the status of the two regions was a higher level of capital investment per capita in Slovakia than in the Czech Lands. According to official statistics released during the communist period, Slovakia was most favored in this regard in the early post-Second World War period, when the ratio of capital investment per capita in Slovakia to that in the Czech Lands was 1.23 (1950). By 1955-8, this ratio had decreased to 1.09. Official statistics claimed that it remained at approximately this level after that time, and did not change to any degree after 1969 (Wolchik, 1983a, pp. 253-4). However, in 1990, Czech analysts argued that the average rates of investment in Slovakia were much higher (33 percent) than in the Czech Lands (see Kříž, 1990b, p. 1).

The results achieved by this differential investment in Slovakia have been dramatic. The occupational structure of the population in the two parts of the country, for example, which differed substantially in 1948, has become very similar. As Table 3.6 illustrates,

Table 3.6 Percentage of the labor force in industry and construction
(selected years and five-year averages)

	Czecho-slovakia	Czech Lands	Slovakia	Ratio: Slovakia/ Czech Lands
1948	29.6	39.0	21.3	0.55
1950	36.3	40.5	25.2	0.62
1954–58	40.4	45.0	27.5	0.61
1959–63	45.4	49.7	35.8	0.73
1964–68	46.6	49.0	39.4	0.80
1969–73	46.9	48.8	42.0	0.86
1974–78	48.0	49.4	44.5	0.90
1979–83	46.4	47.6	43.6	0.92
1985	45.7	46.9	43.0	0.92
1987	46.3	47.3	44.3	0.94

Note: Including women on maternity leave and extended maternity leave.

Sources: From information in Státní statistický úřad, 1968, pp. 22–3; 44–5; 62–3; Federální statistický úřad, 1969, pp. 22–3; 42–3; 58–9; 1970, pp. 22–3; 42–3; 58–9; 1977, pp. 20–1; 40–1; 56–7; 1981, pp. 22–3; 40–1; 56–7; 1985, pp. 191–3; 1986, pp. 184–6; and 1988, pp. 22–3; 40–1, 56–7.

although more people in the Czech Lands continue to be employed in industry and construction than in Slovakia, differences between the two regions have been minimal during the last decade.

The degree of change in Slovakia's occupational structure is also reflected in the dramatic decrease in the proportion of the labor force engaged in agriculture. Although a larger proportion of the total population is engaged in agriculture in Slovakia than in the Czech Lands, differences between the two regions have decreased markedly from 1948, when almost twice as many people worked in agriculture in Slovakia as in the Czech Lands (see Table 3.7). Thus, approximately 60 percent of the labor force was concentrated in this area in 1948, but 16 percent in 1980 and 13 percent in 1987 (Státní statistický úřad, 1968, pp. 22–3; 44–5; and 62–3; and Federální statistický úřad, 1981, pp. 22–3; 40–1; 56–7; 1986, pp. 191–3; and 1988, p. 190).

Table 3.7 Percentage of the labor force in agriculture, 1948-85

	Czechoslovakia	Czech Lands	Slovakia
1948	40.7	33.1	59.8
1950	37.2	30.8	54.0
1960	24.4	20.3	36.1
1970	17.1	14.6	23.6
1975	14.5	12.9	18.4
1980	13.0	11.6	16.0
1985	12.4	11.1	15.4
1987	11.1	11.0	13.2
1989	10.6	8.4	12.6

Source: From information in Federální statistický úřad, 1986, pp. 24-5; 42-3; 58-9; 1988, pp. 22-3; 40-1; 56-7; and 1989, pp. 198-200.

Changes in the occupational structures of the two regions also have been accompanied by change in the levels of urbanization. However, although differences in the two regions have declined substantially, the Czech Lands are still more urbanized. The 1980 census found that 68.8 percent of the population in the Czech Lands, compared to 50 percent in Slovakia, lived in urban areas (Andrle and Srb, 1988, p. 266).

The gap in educational access, infant mortality, and living standards in the two regions has also narrowed. As Table 3.8 illustrates, access to higher education (as measured by the total number of students in higher education per 1,000 inhabitants 20 to 29 years of age) increased dramatically in both parts of the country during the communist period. Differences in such access in the Czech Lands and in Slovakia decreased substantially by the late 1950s. By the mid-1960s, there were more students per 1,000 population in Slovakia than in the Czech Lands. Slovakia's advantage in this respect was greatest in the five years after 1968 as the result of the more severe purge of the universities in the Czech Lands after the end of the reform period. Decreases in the student population in Slovakia in the mid- to late 1980s resulted in a narrowing of the gap between the two regions. Although the ratio of students to the population 20 to

Table 3.8   Total students in higher education per 1,000 population, 20-29 years of age

	Czecho-slovakia	Czech Lands	Slovakia	Ratio: Slovakia/ Czech Lands
1949[a]	25.2	27.6	19.4	0.70
1955	38.3	39.2	36.3	0.93
1960[b]	53.2	54.4	50.1	0.92
1965	77.4	74.4	83.7	1.13
1970	57.4	51.1	72.0	1.41
1975	61.1	54.6	75.8	1.38
1980	82.1	79.0	87.6	1.10
1985	76.1	78.7	71.9	0.91
1987[c]	77.9	81.8	71.3	0.87

Notes: [a] Based on population figures for late 1949.
[b] Based on population figures for 1961.
[c] Based on population figures for late 1987.

Sources: Based on information in Státní úřad statistický, 1957, p. 232; 1959, pp. 55-8; and 1967, p. 75; Ústřední úřad státní kontroly a statistiky, 1962, p. 67; Federální statistický úřad, 1972, p. 102; 503; 1975, pp. 86; 510; 1976, p. 86; 1981, p. 112; 1987, p. 97; and 1988, pp. 97, 584.

29 years of age is currently somewhat lower in Slovakia than in the Czech Lands, the differences are not great.

There has been a similar decrease in the disparity in living standards in the two regions, as measured by both average per capita income and the equipment of homes with consumer durables. Average monthly wages in the socialized sector of the economy excluding agricultural cooperatives were slightly lower in Slovakia at the beginning of the communist period (764 crowns) than in the Czech Lands (834 crowns). By the mid-1960s, these differences had decreased to the extent that average wages in Slovakia were 0.96 of those in the Czech Lands, and by 1964-8, 0.98 (Wolchik, 1983a, pp. 260-1). Differentials in this area continued to be extremely small throughout the 1970s and 1980s, and had virtually disappeared by 1985 (Federální statistický úřad, 1986, pp. 43 and 59). Average wages of full-time members of agricultural cooperatives in the Czech Lands in Slovakia also were virtually identical by 1985 (Federální statistický úřad, 1986, p. 307).

This picture of near equalization of incomes in the two regions does not take into account the different occupational structures found in each. Because average wages in industry are higher than in agriculture and a somewhat higher proportion of the population in Slovakia is engaged in agriculture, the average incomes of people living in Slovakia are still somewhat lower than those of inhabitants of the Czech Lands. In 1985, for example, members of agricultural cooperatives accounted for 13.4 percent of the total labor force in Slovakia, compared to 9.6 percent in the Czech Lands (Federální statistický úřad, 1986, p. 190). The average wages of cooperative members were 91.4 percent of those of wages in the rest of the socialized economy in that year in the country as a whole, 92.8 percent in the Czech Lands and 89.4 percent in Slovakia (from information in Federální statistický úřad, 1986, pp. 25, 43, 59, 190, and 307).

However, the remaining differences in average incomes that result from these factors are not reflected to any extent in differences in living standards in the Czech Lands and Slovakia. Homes in Slovakia were much less likely to have such items as washing machines, refrigerators, televisions, and radios in the early communist period, but by 1980 differences between Slovakia and the Czech Lands had all but disappeared in many of these areas. Differences in levels of automobile ownership have also decreased markedly (Wolchik, 1983a, pp. 261-3).

The impact of the near equalization of these two regions on nationality relations has been somewhat paradoxical. The progress that has been made in creating equal material conditions for Czechs and Slovaks has not led to any diminution of the strength of ethnic identification or loyalty. Intermarriage among members of different nationalities remains low. Migration from one part of the country to the other is similarly limited and continued to decrease throughout the communist period. Never higher than 1.1 per 1,000 population in the Czech Lands, rates of movement from one region to the other also decreased in Slovakia from 3.6 per 1,000 population in 1960 to

1.1 in 1985 (Federální statistický úřad, 1986, p. 120).

Research on language use in ethnically mixed regions of Czechoslovakia found that a large majority of each ethnic group considers its own language to be its mother tongue. Among the smaller national groups, rates of retention of one's own language vary and are greatest among the Hungarians, only 1.1 percent of whom identified Slovak as their primary language, and Ukrainians, of whom 4.2 percent identified a language other than Ukrainian as their primary language. Czechs living in Slovakia are also more likely to retain Czech as their main language (only 10.5 percent chose another language) than Slovaks living in the Czech Lands (20.6 percent), but the majority of members of both groups continue to regard their own languages as primary (Sokolová, 1985, pp. 214-15).

At the same time, substantial proportions of all nationalities have some knowledge of another language. Approximately 99 percent of Poles, 96 percent of Ukrainians, and 88.3 percent of Hungarians have some knowledge of either Czech or Slovak. Levels of knowledge differ considerably, however, as only 61 percent of the Ukrainians, 50 percent of the Poles, and 41 percent of the Hungarians studied claimed to know either Czech or Slovak well. Younger, better-educated members of these groups are more likely to know one of the two dominant languages (Sokolová, 1985, pp. 215-16). Substantial numbers of Czechs and Slovaks in ethnically mixed regions have some knowledge of minority languages, particularly in Slovakia where minorities comprise a higher proportion of the population (Sokolová, 1985, p. 215; see Silver, 1974a and 1974b, for comparative information on national groups in the Soviet Union).

As noted in chapter 2, ethnicity continued to be one of the most important political cleavages in Czechoslovakia during the communist period. Although the adoption of a federal system in the late 1960s formally recognized Slovak claims to parity, it did not eliminate all tensions between Czechs and Slovaks. Exacerbated during the Husák era by the perception on the part of many Czechs that the Slovaks were benefitting disproportionately from developments in normalized Czechoslovakia, tensions between Czechs and Slovaks continued to grow, although they were seldom given open political expression (see chapter 2; and Leff, 1988). Survey research conducted during the late communist period found that the majority of Czechs and Slovaks felt that they benefitted from the presence of the other national group (Slovaks to a greater extent than Czechs) (see Zvára, 1988). However, as the surveys discussed in chapter 2 illustrated, members of each group have very different frames of reference in terms of their views of important historical events. Members of each group also tend to have somewhat different cultural and political values. These differences were paralleled by different attitudes toward the communist regime and by different expectations regarding the likelihood of success of efforts to restructure the economy in the last years of communist rule (see Linhart, Tuček, and Vodáková, 1986, pp. 637-8).

During the communist period, conflict over ethnic issues was artificially suppressed. Although federalization formally institutionalized ethnicity as an aspect of policy-making, open expression of serious dissatisfaction with the existing arrangements or the position of the Czech Lands or Slovakia within the common framework was not permitted. The fact that communist leaders in Czechoslovakia were more successful than those elsewhere in reducing regional inequalities also helps to explain why ethnic tensions, although still present, did not erupt into the violent confrontations that have occurred sporadically in other multi-ethnic communist states or threatened the political stability of the Czechoslovak state, as they did in the interwar period.

In this area as in many others, the late communist period saw the beginning of more open debate and discussion. Expert discussions of Czech-Slovak relations made public in the late 1980s, for example, drew attention to still unresolved problems, including the continued use of central funds to fund development in Slovakia and controversial aspects of Slovakia's recent history. Slovak intellectuals began to question whether the federation allowed adequate representation of Slovak interests (see Matuška, 1989, for a summary of these discussions).

The re-emergence of such discussions presaged the crystallization of public opinion along ethnic lines and the central role that ethnic issues have once again come to play after November 1989. As noted in chapter 2, important differences have become evident in Czechs' and Slovaks' evaluations of the current government and the performance of public officials. Members of the two groups also differ in the level of their support for economic reform and the continued existence of a federal state.

Although there was a good deal of cooperation between Czechs and Slovaks in late 1989 and in the governing coalition at the federal level, ethnic conflict pervades discussion of most of the critical issues facing the current government. Evident in the prolonged debate over the name of the country, Czech-Slovak conflict increased throughout 1990. In late summer 1990, nine Slovak political parties, led by the nationalist Slovak National Party, issued a call for Slovakia to become an independent state. Support for the Slovak National Party continued to grow in the fall of 1990. Public Against Violence representatives, as well as those of the Christian Democratic Movement, rejected separatism, but most political parties and groupings in Slovakia want to see an increase in Slovakia's autonomy. Although, as noted in chapter 2, the Slovak National Party received a very small share of the votes in the local elections in November 1990, its actions have increased the salience of ethnic issues and pushed other political forces into more nationalistic positions. Certain leaders of the Christian Democratic movement, in particular, began to push more forcefully for Slovak autonomy in the fall of 1990. Differences of opinion on the national question thus strained the coalition between Public Against Violence and the Christian Democratic Movement in Slovakia as well as at the federal level (see Pecháčková, 1990; Liška, 1990; and Zavarský, 1990; Boguszak and Rak, 1990a; and Staněk, 1990). In the first months of 1991, divisions within PAV on this as well as other issues also intensified.

Ethnic tensions have also been reflected in efforts to reform the economy as well as in the process of constitutional revision now under way. Although the federal, Czech and Slovak governments issued a joint plan for economic reform in early September 1990, important differences have emerged in the perspectives of officials of each government concerning the pace of economic change, the priority to be given to environmental issues, and many other aspects of the proposed economic reforms, including structural changes.

Because many of the most inefficient large enterprises are in Slovakia, for example, the scheduled end of government subsidies will be particularly painful there. The plan to end Czechoslovakia's production of arms for export would also have been felt disproportionately in Slovakia, where many of the country's armaments plants are located, and has therefore been modified by Slovak leaders.

Despite the agreement reached in December 1990 concerning the division of power between the federal and republic governments which assigns large powers to the republics, the two sides continue to disagree on several important issues which must be resolved before the new constitutions are adopted. Conflict between Czechs and Slovaks continues to dominate the political agenda. As noted in chapter 1, different perspectives within Public Against Violence on ethnic relations and on Slovakia's position in the federation were among the issues that led to the removal of Vladimír Mečiar as Prime Minister of Slovakia and several other members of the Slovak government in April 1991. As in the interwar period, then, ethnic conflict has once again emerged as a critical political issue and the main threat to political stability in post-communist Czechoslovakia.

Gender issues

Czech and Slovak society is also stratified along gender lines. The situation of women and current pattern of gender relations continue to reflect the impact of the policies adopted during the communist period. As in other communist countries, gender equality was formally guaranteed by the Constitution and other legal measures in Czechoslovakia. The institution of a communist government was followed by changes in women's roles and in gender relations. However, as was common elsewhere in the region, the pattern of change that occurred during the communist period was uneven, and substantial inequalities still exist in the status of men and women (see Jancar, 1978; Heitlinger, 1979; and Wolchik, 1978, 1981a, 1981b, 1990b, 1991d, and 1991e, for previous discussions of gender issues).

Women's roles changed most in the areas of access to education and participation in paid employment outside the home. Girls came to account for approximately 63 percent of all students in secondary

Table 3.9 Women as a percentage of students in higher education

	Czechoslovakia	Czech Lands	Slovakia
1950	22.4	23.1	19.5
1960	37.1	36.3	38.9
1970	40.2	38.1	43.5
1980	43.0	42.6	43.7
1985	44.0	43.1	45.6
1989	44.4	43.8	45.6

Sources: Wolchik, 1979, p. 584; Federální statistický úřad, 1985, p. 580; 1986, p. 566; and 1989, p. 611.

general and specialized education in the late 1980s (from information in Federální statistický úřad, 1988, p. 567). Forty-three percent of all students in higher education were women in 1987 (see Table 3.9).

These percentages, which were relatively stable during the last decade, were among the highest in the communist world. Women's increased access to education over the last 40 years has also been reflected in an increase in women's levels of education. As Table 3.10 indicates, men still have educational levels slightly higher on the average than women. Among younger age groups, however, women have slightly higher levels of completed education (see Krejčí, 1972, p. 60; and Wolchik, 1979, pp. 583-6).

The success evident in equalizing educational opportunities for men and women was paralleled by women's increased participation in paid employment outside the home. As Table 3.11 illustrates, women's share of the total labor force increased from 37.8 percent in 1948 to 45.5 percent in 1980 and 46.1 percent in 1985 and 1987. Although women's labor force participation rates have tended to be somewhat higher in the Czech Lands than in Slovakia, these differences were not large in the early communist period and have decreased further in the last decade.

Despite the positive changes that have occurred in women's educational access and participation in paid employment, substantial inequalities still remain in both of these areas. In the first, women continue to choose and to be channeled into different areas of

Table 3.10 Average number of years of schooling of people 15 and over, according to the censuses of 1950, 1961, 1970, and 1980

	Czechoslovakia		
	Men	Women	Total
1950	9.50	9.22	9.35
1961	9.70	9.39	9.54
1970	10.69	9.94	10.30
1980	11.28	10.54	10.89

	Czech Lands			Slovakia		
	Men	Women	Total	Men	Women	Total
1950	9.60	9.30	9.44	9.22	8.98	9.10
1961	9.80	9.48	9.63	9.47	9.17	9.32
1970	10.79	10.01	10.38	10.45	9.77	10.10
1980	11.34	10.57	10.94	11.10	10.48	10.78

Source: 'Národnost posluchářů,' 1988, p. 267.

education. Although there has been an increase in the number of women in technical studies, most women continue to enter fields of study traditionally thought suitable for women, or medicine, a field of study that became 'feminized' during the communist period. As a result, men and women still enter the labor force with markedly different levels and kinds of qualifications, despite the increase in women's access to education. In 1970, for example, 53.7 percent of working women, compared to 32.9 percent of working men, had elementary education. Only 15.5 percent of women, compared to 38.1 percent of men had been trained as apprentices, and only 3.2 percent of women, but 6.2 percent of men, had higher education (Kalínová, 1979, p. 80-1. See Heitlinger, 1979, pp. 149-52; Jancar, 1978, pp. 208-10; and Wolchik, 1981a, pp. 139-42, for summaries of these trends. See Kuchařová and Kuchař, 1985, pp. 506-7, for information on the skill levels of men and women workers).

Table 3.11   Women as a percentage of the labor force, 1948-88

	Czechoslovakia	Czech Lands	Slovakia
1948	37.8	36.9	40.1
1960	42.8	44.0	39.2
1970	46.7	47.8	44.0
1980	45.5	45.8	44.7
1985	46.1	46.4	45.4
1987	46.1	46.3	45.6
1988	46.0	46.3	45.5

Sources: Wolchik, 1979, p. 586; Federální statistický úřad, 1981, pp. 195-7; 1986, pp. 187-9; 1988, pp. 189-90; and 1989, pp. 198-200.

The impact of these patterns is reflected in the occupational segregation by gender that continues to characterize the Czechoslovak economy and in the continued disparity in the incomes of men and women. Although women now enter a broader range of occupations, including technical occupations, than previously, the majority of working women in Czechoslovakia continue to be employed in fields that are low priority areas of the economy with lower than average wages (see Scott, 1974; Connor, 1979, pp. 239-42; Heitlinger, 1979, pp. 147-55; Jancar, 1978, pp. 19-28; Wolchik, 1978, ch. 3, 1981a, 1985b, and 1991d; Slušná, 1988, pp. 60-7; and Večerník, 1990a). Despite the large numbers of women in the labor force, women are also far less likely than men to hold leadership positions in the economy (Hora, 1972; Bauerová, 1974, pp. 450; Bauerová and Bártová, 1987; Jančovičová, 1974; Slušná, 1988, pp. 68-9).

The persistence of gender inequality in the exercise of power in the labor force has been paralleled by similar inequalities in the realm of politics. During the communist period, there were few differences in the extent to which Czech and Slovak men and women participated in mobilized activities that demonstrated support for the regime. However, there were considerable differences between men's and women's participation in activities that required more individual initiative or carried more potential for influence. Women were less likely than men, for example, to indicate that they paid attention to political news or discussed politics with friends and acquaintances. They also spent less time on public activities and were less likely to be members of the Communist Party (see Jancar, 1978, pp. 88-99; and Wolchik, 1981b, pp. 457-62).

A 1980 study conducted by the Institute for Public Opinion Research of the Federal Statistical Office found that fewer women (16 percent) than men (24 percent) were highly engaged politically. Women were only approximately half as likely as men to be party members. Women also were less involved than men in all other political and social organizations studied, except the Women's Union and the Red Cross (Bártová, 1984, pp. 361-4). In a pattern similar to those found in many other communist states, the women's proportion of Communist Party members declined as the Stalinist system was consolidated in Czechoslovakia and only began to increase again in the mid-1960s. Although the proportion of women party members increased steadily during the last two decades of communist rule, women still accounted for a lower percentage (28.9 percent in 1986) of party members than in the early years of the communist era.

Women were also far less likely than men to hold positions of political influence. Women were well represented in the governmental elites, especially at the lower levels where they comprised from 31 to 35 percent of deputies of local, district, and regional national committees in 1981. Their representation was also substantial among members of the national legislature, 24.3 percent of whom were women in 1986 and 28.3 percent of whom were women in 1988 (from information in 'Poslanci federálního shromáždění,' 1986; and Slušná, 1988, p. 107). They were also well represented in the central committees of several of the mass organizations, including the trade union organizations at both the republic and central levels (see Slušná, 1988, p. 105).

However, there were far fewer women in the more influential and powerful party elites. Thus, while 14 percent of women surveyed in 1980 (compared to 17 percent of men) held trade union functions, only 5 percent of women (compared to 13 percent of men) held responsible offices within the Communist Party (Bártová, 1984,

p. 364). As discussed in greater detail in chapter 2, women accounted for a small proportion of Central Committee members throughout the communist period. Although a woman was frequently one of the top officials of the National Assembly, few women served in the highest bodies of the party, the Presidium or the Secretariat.

Women were also underrepresented on the central committees and in the leadership of the minor political parties which served largely to mobilize their members to support the initiatives of the Communist Party during the communist period. Women accounted for 15.7 percent of members of the Central Committee of the Czechoslovak Socialist Party in the late 1980s, for example, when one woman was a member of the Presidium. Approximately 11 percent of the members of the Slovak Revival Party were women in 1988, when there were no women in the top leadership (from information in 'Ustavující schůze,' 1987; 'Členové ÚV strany,' 1987; and 'Novozvolené ústredné,' 1988).

Women members of both the governmental and party elites often differed from their male colleagues in terms of social background characteristics and previous political experience. Differences in these areas were reflected in the fact that women leaders in both groups tended to have lower tenure and higher rates of turnover than men. The few women who served in the Presidium or were members of the Secretariat of the Communist Party during the communist period differed from their male colleagues in these respects as well as in their routes to the top (see chapter 2). The occupations of male and female members of the governmental elites also differed during the communist period. In 1986, for example, 67.4 percent of all women deputies were workers (compared to 20.0 percent of all male deputies), and an additional 7 percent were agricultural workers (compared to 5 percent of men). Not one woman deputy was a Communist Party or government official, a category that accounted for 28.7 percent of all male deputies (from information in 'Poslanci federálního shromáždění,' 1986).

There were fewer gender differences among opposition activists. Although men outnumbered women as signatories of Charter 77, the largest and oldest dissident grouping, women accounted for a substantial proportion of those who signed the Charter. In contrast to the situation among most dissidents in other communist countries, women also played a large role in the leadership of the Charter, as one of the three designated Charter spokespersons was generally a woman. Although women's issues were not a high priority in the activities of the Charter, those Charter documents that dealt with women and the family reaffirmed women's right to work and other aspects of women's equality (Jancar, 1985, p. 177). A number of young women also emerged as leading activists of the new independent groups that formed in Czechoslovakia during 1988 and 1989. Young women also played a prominent role in organizing and leading the mass demonstrations in late 1989.

Differences in men's and women's public roles are paralleled by and to some degree reflect gender inequalities within the home. The results of survey research conducted during the communist period found that most Czechs and Slovaks accepted the notion of women's equality at a theoretical level; they also accepted, in theory, the notion that there must be equality in the family if men and women are to achieve equal status and have equal opportunity outside the home (see Bártová, 1973). However, substantial differences remained in the division of labor within the home between men and women on a daily basis. As the numerous studies of the 'double burden' done in Czechoslovakia illustrate, women continued to bear major responsibility for the organization and functioning of the household as well as for childcare. They also had far less free time than men. These differences in turn had an impact on women's roles in other areas. Thus, women expressed less interest than men in increasing their qualifications or accepting promotions to leading positions. Domestic responsibilities were also one of the factors that contributed to women's reluctance to become more involved in political activities (see Wolchik, 1978, ch. 6, and 1979, pp. 591-8; Heitlinger, 1979, pp. 160-1; and Jancar, 1978, pp. 161-6; Navarová, 1990; and Šiklová, 1990).

Although Czech and Slovak officials admitted that the lack of change in gender roles within the home hampered the achievement of gender equality elsewhere, there were few efforts to encourage a redistribution of duties and burdens within the home. In the more open discussion of women's actual situation and the continued barriers to gender equality that occurred after the mid-1960s, social scientists occasionally pointed out the need for such changes (Charvát, 1980; Slušná, 1988). Most analyses of gender issues, however, as well as government policies, called instead for improvements in services and consumer durables to ease the burdens women faced.

The pronatalist approach adopted by the government in the early 1970s emphasized the social importance of women's maternal roles. The policy measures adopted to increase the birthrate, including extensions of maternity leave and the creation of a mother's allowance for women who stay home to care for infants, are popular with most groups of women and help alleviate the strain young women face in combining childbearing and careers in the short run. However, they do not bode well for gender equality, for they appear to have reinforced the traditional division of labor within the home. The negative impact on women's careers of interrupting employment for from three to six years was not counteracted by programs to help women keep their expertise and skills current, although such measures were originally discussed (see Heitlinger, 1979; Wolchik 1981a, and 1981c; and Slušná, 1988).

Despite official acceptance as a goal, issues related to gender equality were subordinated to other, higher-priority policy concerns throughout the communist period. Thus, while the greater openness in discussing remaining gender inequalities and women's situation that began in the late 1960s was reflected among specialists and in the pages of the mass women's magazines in the last two decades of communist rule (see, for example, reports of a 1985 symposium on women's issues in Plávková, 1985, pp. 337-9; and Šolcová, 1984), gender equality received little direct attention from the leadership. The pronatalist emphasis on women's maternal roles also continued to inform policy toward women.

This orientation was not challenged to any great extent by the population prior to the end of communist rule. The June 1989 congress of the official women's organization saw the more open airing of complaints about women's problems, including their lack of representation in decision-making positions in trade unions and elsewhere, but the organization did not call for any radical changes in the overall approach to women's issues (see Neoveský, 1989).

Although there was ample evidence that Czech and Slovak women were dissatisfied with many aspects of their situation, this dissatisfaction was not translated into political action during the communist period. No discernible feminist movement in Czechoslovakia similar to the small movements of this type that developed in the Soviet Union, Poland, and Yugoslavia in the last decade emerged in Czechoslovakia prior to the end of communist rule. The barriers to autonomous organization, the perception of gender equality as a goal, which, though shared to some extent, was nonetheless imposed from above rather than chosen from below, and the tendency to subordinate women's issues to broader economic and political concerns were reflected in a lack of interest in pushing for greater gender equality on the part of the population (see Wolchik, 1989b; Siemiéňska, 1986; Navarová, 1990; Šiklová, 1990, for more detailed discussions of the impact of these factors. See mf, 1988, p. 5; and Šulcová, 1988, p. 9, for independent analyses during the communist period).

The somewhat greater tolerance for non-conformist views evident in the official media as well as the discussion that accompanied the call for economic reform were reflected in greater attention to women's roles in the media in Czechoslovakia in the late 1980s. However, as in the mid-1960s, when discussion of economic reform led many political leaders, economists and managers to question the efficiency of women's economic labor and call for women, especially those with young children, to return to the home (see Scott, 1974; Heitlinger, 1979, pp. 159-64), the more open climate also allowed the expression of more traditional views on gender relations.

The end of the communist era has had an important impact on women and on discussion of gender roles. The end of the Communist Party's monopoly of power and the repluralization of political life have created new of opportunities for women as well as men to participate in politics in meaningful ways. Changes in the policy-making process have increased the channels available to women as well as men to express political preferences and have an impact on policy-making. Women can also organize independently to pressure political leaders and defend their interests.

However, debate and discussion about women's situation and

gender roles continue to be influenced by the legacy of the communist period. Although the formal commitment to gender equality has not been repudiated, women activists and policy-makers alike are questioning the previous approach to women's issues. In reaction to the difficulties women faced in trying to work outside the home, and manage their families and households with very little help from the state or their husbands, many women appear to have rejected the goal of gender equality. Discussion of gender roles and policies toward women thus have been influenced by what appears to be a widespread backlash against the uneven pattern of role change achieved during communist rule. The impact of these attitudes is evident in the political realm as well as in the economy. It is also reflected in the social policies adopted by the new government.

The very high degree of citizen turnout for the June parliamentary elections indicated that women, as well as men, were eager to use their new opportunity to vote in democratic elections. However, the political marginalization of women evident during the communist period continues. Young women activists were among the leaders who organized the demonstrations that provided the catalyst for the fall of the communist system and women played an important role in the mass demonstrations that followed. However, as discussed in chapter 2, women hold very few positions of leadership in the new political parties and the democratically elected governments at any level. The low levels of women's representation among political leaders do not bode well for gender equality, for they appear to coincide with the view that women should concern themselves primarily with their domestic roles.

Similar attitudes have come to the fore concerning women's employment outside the home. Many political leaders and economic experts, as well as ordinary citizens, feel that levels of women's employment were too high during the communist period. The end of subsidies and the sectoral adjustments that will accompany the move to a market economy will in all likelihood increase levels of unemployment among women more than among men. As a result, and coupled with the attitudes discussed above, the numbers of women in the labor force will decrease somewhat. However, given the increases in the prices of food, rent, services, and other necessities that are accompanying the shift to the market, most households will continue to need two incomes. It is thus unlikely that levels of women's employment will decline dramatically in the near future (see Wolchik, 1991d). Most women will thus experience the changes that economic transformation will bring in the workplace as well as in the home.

Many activists also call for a re-emphasis of women's maternal roles. The call for public policy measures that will allow young women to remain at home with their children for longer periods of time has been followed by changes in the regulations governing mothers' allowances. Men who care for small children are now eligible for such allowances, which have also been made available to broader groups of parents (see Wolchik, 1991d, 1991e).

A similar orientation informs the work of many of the new independent women's groups that have formed since the end of communist rule. Although there are groups and individuals that openly identify themselves as advocates of gender equality, most of the newly formed groups call for greater attention to women's roles as mothers and homemakers (see Wolchik, 1990b). There is as yet no discernable feminist movement in Czechoslovakia. However, the increased burden that the dislocations that accompany economic transformation will mean for women in the home and continued experience with inequality in the workplace in a market economy may eventually find political expression. Challenges to women's reproductive rights may also radicalize some women in the new political conditions. By providing women with a forum and a meeting place to discuss and define their own needs, several of the independent women's groups may contribute to this process (see Navarová, 1990; Šiklová, 1990; Wolchik, 1990b).

Youth

In contrast to the general lack of attention given to women's issues, young people and their political attitudes and behavior were often the subject of commentary by political leaders and experts during the communist period. This concern reflected the role which students have played traditionally in Central and East European politics and the extent to which students and other young people supported the reform effort of the 1960s (see Ulč, 1974, pp. 108-18 and 126-8; Skilling, 1976, pp. 72-80, 200-2, and 596-9; and Kusin, 1972, pp. 123-42). The communist leadership also attempted to foster correct political attitudes and values among young people.

Until late 1989, Czech and Slovak young people were often depicted by analysts in Czechoslovakia and abroad as disillusioned, apathetic individuals with little or no interest in public affairs who had withdrawn into the private sphere to focus on their own gain and enjoyment. Many commentators also emphasized the attachment of youth to Western culture and lifestyles, including music, clothing, and other consumer goods. The relative scarcity of public opinion polls on the attitudes of youth after the late 1960s (see Piekalkiewicz, 1972, for information concerning the attitudes of young people in the 1960s) makes it difficult to assess the accuracy of this picture. However, the results of those attitude surveys that were made public, as well as public commentary on the problems and behavior of young people during the late communist period, suggest that it was accurate in many respects. Although there are problems with many of the surveys conducted during the communist period, the results of several studies of young people conducted in the last decade and a half of communist rule foreshadowed the events of 1989 and the attitudes and values expressed since that time. These sources document the alienation of many young people from the communist political system and give hints of the attitudes that young people expressed so vividly in late 1989. At the same time, these sources indicate that the attitudes of young people, like those of their elders, varied to some degree by social position, occupation, educational level, and gender.

Several of the available surveys provide glimpses of the sources and extent of dissatisfaction among young people under communist rule. One of the primary concerns of young people in Czechoslovakia as elsewhere is their future or current occupation. Several studies conducted during the late communist period document a high degree of dissatisfaction on the part of apprentices and students with their options in this area. During the communist era, most Czech and Slovak young people did not go on to higher education.

Instead, the majority of young people who continued their educations beyond elementary school entered secondary trade schools or apprentice training programs (see Matějů, 1990 for a critical analysis of these trends). Despite the effort made to increase the prestige of manual labor and the fact that the incomes of skilled blue-collar workers often exceeded or equalled those of individuals with higher education during the communist period, many of those who entered workers' occupations did so unwillingly. The results of surveys of students about to complete basic education in Slovakia in 1980 and the country as a whole in 1982 illustrate the gap in student aspirations and government plans. Thus, while the 1981-2 plan called for 15.2 percent of all students to continue their studies in general secondary schools, 23.2 percent to attend secondary trade schools, and the balance (58.7 percent) to enter secondary apprentice training programs, more students than planned (20.4 percent in Slovakia and 24.3 percent in the country as a whole) preferred to enter general secondary schools and secondary trade schools (29.3 percent in 1980 and 33.8 percent in 1982). Far fewer students than the plan called for wished to enter apprentice training (38.6 percent of those surveyed in Slovakia in 1980 and 36.4 percent of those surveyed in the country as a whole in 1982) (Macháček, 1985, p. 493). Problems in achieving the desired distribution of students were particularly great among women students (see Macháček, 1985, pp. 495-7).

A survey of apprentices conducted in Slovakia in 1983 found that many were very dissatisfied with their future occupations. Although 65 percent of those surveyed had generally positive attitudes toward their occupation's earning power, 53 percent indicated that they would have liked a different occupation, and 45 percent stated that they would like to change their occupations. Over 50 percent felt that they would like their future occupations, but 35 percent disagreed totally or partially with that statement (Lovaš and Jurečková, 1986, pp. 164-5). Attitudes were more positive among those who had chosen their occupations voluntarily, as well as among those whose parents worked in the same or similar areas (Lovaš and Jurečková, 1986, pp. 167 and 172).

As in other countries, there were important differences in the attitudes and values of young people and those of their elders in Czechoslovakia in the communist period. A study of youth conducted in the early 1970s, for example, found that young people tended to be more liberal in their attitudes than a group of 140 older scientific workers in Bratislava (Jurovský, 1974, p. 207). Differences were greatest among the youngest group surveyed and tended to decrease with age. Responses also varied by educational levels, type of employment, and gender (see Jurovský, 1974, pp. 213-15).

As one would expect, summaries of surveys of the attitudes of young people conducted in the 1970s claimed that the majority of young people were convinced of the superiority of socialism over capitalism. However, the variation in responses reported is interesting. Thus, young men and women were said to see socialism as preferable to capitalism particularly in the areas of ensuring peace, social measures to safeguard and care for children, ensuring job opportunities for young people, providing social security for the aged, creating equality among nationalities, and producing opportunities for citizens to take part in leadership. Young people were more critical of socialism and believed that capitalist systems do a better job in the areas of developing science and technology and in making good use of the ideas and talents of people (Macháček, 1988, p. 136).

Research on the world views of various groups of the population conducted in 1979 provided further evidence of the disaffection on the part of young people that came into the open so dramatically in 1989. Thus, only approximately one-half of all youth studied had attitudes that reflected the approved Marxist-Leninist world view. The rest had perspectives that were labelled 'opportunistic' or 'liberal', or were not a coherent set of views. Although they did not provide data on factors associated with different attitudes, the researchers noted that religious attitudes were marked in approximately a tenth of young people (Tomek, 1985).

Studies conducted in the 1970s and 1980s indicate that most young people in Czechoslovakia as elsewhere valued personal relationships and personal fulfilment more highly than service to society or political involvement. Thus, a survey of young people conducted in Southern Moravia in the late 1970s found that the majority felt that finding a partner and establishing a family were high-priority goals; over half of the sample also identified satisfying work as an important concern. The low priority given to political activism and work for the good of society is evident in the fact that relatively few young people (6 percent) ranked being socially active as a priority, a proportion equal to those who valued gardening and raising one's own animals highly (Osecká and Maček, 1987, pp. 92-8). The goals of young men and women were generally similar, although women tended to give more emphasis to establishing a satisfactory family life; they also emphasized the social aspects of work, while young men were more likely to value work as a source of income. The study indicates that the values of students and working young people also differed to some extent, as the former gave more importance to self-improvement, study, and intellectual pursuits, while the latter emphasized material interests to a greater extent (Osecká and Macek, 1987, pp. 98-9).

The same emphasis on private concerns and the lack of interest in official political activities evident above were also reflected in the way young people used their time. Time budget studies conducted in 1979-80 by the Federal Statistical Office found that young people spent very little time on public activity. Although time use in this as in other areas varied to some degree by gender, age, and social group, the time spent per day on public activity ranged from a low of zero minutes among women apprentices and working women aged 15 to 19 to a high of six minutes per day among working men aged 20 to 29 (Vítečková, 1985b, p. 570). The lack of interest young workers and collective farmers displayed in public activity, self-education, attending the theatre, concerts, etc. (Ošmerová and Blaho, 1982, p. 205), was paralleled by the general lack of interest in these activities by young people in other groups (Vítečková, 1985b, pp. 570-4).

The political passivity of youth, which persisted despite the fact that from 60 percent of students in vocational schools to 90 percent of students in higher educational institutions were nominally members of the official youth organization (Obrman, 1988a, p. 10), and the prevalence of unorthodox or undesired attitudes and behaviors among young people concerned communist leaders, who frequently urged greater attention to the proper education and socialist upbringing of youth (see Kohák and Muff, 1988, pp. 28-30, for example). Educators and youth organization officials often discussed methods of encouraging young people to use their free time more usefully and creatively (see, for example, Švirloch and Ševčík, 1988, pp. 232-4; 'Náměty jsou-teď',' 1988, pp. 1-3; 'Program SSM, 1988, p. 3; and 'Život není jen práce,' 1988, p. 3).

Discussions of young people during the late 1980s also addressed some of the other concerns of youth more openly, including the poor living conditions and lack of housing for university students; the difficulties graduates had in finding appropriate work; the difficulties of obtaining admission to one's chosen faculty or area of specialization; the quality of education; and the health problems of young apprentices (Hatina, 1988, p. 2; Hlavica, 1988, pp. 11-13; Šimonovičová, 1988, p. 2; 'Přijímací řízení,' 1988, p. 2; Kalous, 1988, p. 3; Žiarska, 1988, p. 14; Poliaková, 1988, p. 14). Authorities and experts also discussed criminality, and alcohol and substance abuse among youth more openly in the late 1980s than previously (see Labudová and Wlater, 1986, p. 3; Hudáková and Števušková, 1988, pp. 245-52; and Fazík, 1982, pp. 163-71). However, measures to invigorate the official youth organizations and encourage young people to take a more active role in approved political activities had little success. The increase in the number of party members under 35 in the late communist period may have indicated a greater willingness on the part of young people to go through the motions of being politically active. However, as the events of 1989 indicated, it clearly did not reflect higher levels of desired political consciousness among young people.

The role of young people in organizing public demonstrations and in founding new unofficial groups in Czechoslovakia in 1988 and 1989 demonstrated the extent to which certain groups of young people were alienated from the current regime. These activities, and the leading role that students played in organizing and participating in the demonstrations that brought down communist rule in late November 1989, indicate that the lack of interest in politics of the current generation evident in both casual conversations with young people and the survey research discussed above was not as pervasive as previously thought. The willingness of many young people to take significant personal risks to speak out and the search for ideals untainted by the experiences of the communist period indicated that there was a reservoir of youth who would be willing to be active in politics, provided the nature of political life and discourse changed. In contrast to the situation in the mid- and late 1960s, when dissatisfied students supported the reform initiatives of the reform intellectuals within the party, young activists found support primarily among the dissident community prior to November 1989. Had the leadership of the Communist Party made a serious effort to initiate political change prior to 1989, some of these young people might have supported their policies. However, the demands and actions of young people involved in independent activities and the mass demonstrations of 1988 and the first half of 1989 suggested that such change would have had to have been substantial to enlist their support. As such changes did not occur, the radicalization of those young people, primarily students but also manual workers, who participated in the demonstrations of 1988 and 1989 served to replenish the ranks of independent activists rather than reinvigorate existing political organizations.

Fearing a spread of dissident activities and ideas among young people, youth organization leaders and political officials made sporadic efforts to begin a limited dialogue with disaffected but activist young people in late 1988 and early 1989. They also attempted to coopt the activities of independent youth groups by sanctioning activities previously outlawed. In the wake of the mass protests in November 1989, the communist leadership moved to initiate discussions with young people and other protesters. However, these actions had little impact.

The critical role that students played in November 1989 was acknowledged in the early days after the fall of the communist government by older leaders. Student representatives took part in the deliberations of Civic Forum and Public Against Violence, and several were named to the national legislature to replace discredited communist deputies in early 1990. As the movement to restore a multiparty democracy moved from the streets into the political arena, the direct political role of students decreased. Although certain student activists decried this situation, many appeared to view the return to a more usual form of politics as an inevitable occurrence. Most young people are once again focusing primarily on private concerns, such as their studies and occupations. However, although the high levels of mobilization and political involvement of late 1989 and early 1990 have decreased, public opinion research documents a large degree of support for the new political order among young people. Young people are also more likely than their elders to support privatization and other aspects of the economic reform program (see Boguszak and Rak, 1990a). Students and other young people, then, will be an important source of democratic political activists and future reformist leaders.

As in other areas, the end of censorship has led to greater openness in discussing the problems of young people. Students and other young people have also formed a large variety of independent groups to represent their interests. These groups, which range from Christian to Social Democratic groups and also include traditional Czechoslovak organizations for young people such as the Boy Scouts, have replaced the official youth organization (see Obrman, 1990b, pp. 6–10).

Religious cleavages

It is difficult to determine the extent to which religious belief persisted in Czechoslovakia during the communist period, as communist leaders did not keep official records of the numbers of believers after the 1950 census. Survey research on religious belief and practice was rare and subject to bias, due to the reluctance of respondents to answer questions on this topic honestly. Nonetheless, a number of types of information indicate that although religious practice declined from the early communist period, when approximately 95 percent of the total population and 99.6 percent in Slovakia identified themselves as affiliated with a religion (Ramet, 1989, p. 275), religious belief and practice continued to be important to sizeable portions of the population throughout the communist period. Surveys conducted in Northern Moravia in 1963 and in Slovakia in 1964 found 30 percent and 71 percent, respectively, of all adults to be practicing believers or to consider themselves religious (Ramet, 1989, p. 275). Officials estimated that 36 percent of the total population 15 years of age and over, including 30 percent in Bohemia and Moravia and 51 percent in Slovakia, were believers in 1984 (Ramet, 1989, p. 275). In 1986 Karel Hrůza, the former head of the Secretariat of Church Affairs, stated that approximately four to five million of Czechoslovakia's roughly 15 million people were believers. Ivan Hodovský, Director of the Research Institute of Social Consciousness and Scientific Atheism of the Czechoslovak Academy of Sciences, provided a similar estimate when he stated that 30 percent of the population were believers in 1989.

Statistics on the numbers of baptisms, church weddings, and church funerals shed further light on the extent to which people continued to rely on religion to guide them or mark important events in their lives during the communist period. In a 1988 article that appears to have been based on research conducted by the Institute for Public Opinion Research in Prague in 1980, researchers at the Institute for Research on Social Consciousness and Scientific Atheism in Brno noted that 44.8 percent of all children in the CSSR were baptized. Approximately 30 percent of all marriages and 62.5 percent of all burials were religious (Scheuch, 1989, p. 97).

Religious belief and practice are much more widespread in Slovakia than in the Czech Lands, particularly in Bohemia. In 1984, 71.6 percent of children in Slovakia and 31.2 percent of those in the Czech Lands were baptized; approximately 81 percent of all funerals in Slovakia and 50.6 percent of those in the Czech Lands were held in churches. Fifty-three percent of all weddings in Slovakia, compared to 15.8 percent in the Czech Lands, were religious. The higher developmental levels and more secular culture of the Czech Lands (particularly Bohemia), and the differing role of Catholicism in the national movements and histories of the Czech Lands and Slovakia were also reflected in the results of the studies discussed above. Thus, 43.4 percent of all districts in Bohemia and Moravia were markedly less religious than average (based on the proportions of baptisms and church weddings and funerals), and 32.9 percent, moderately below average. Fourteen districts were somewhat above average, and four districts were markedly above average. None were 'maximally' religious. In Slovakia, on the other hand, there were no districts that fell into the 'markedly lower than average' category and only two of 38 that were less than average. Sixteen of thirty-eight (42.1 percent) were markedly above average, and fourteen, or 36.8 percent, were 'maximally' religious (based on information in Scheuch, 1989, pp. 97-8). Reliance on the church to mark these life events was found to be higher in districts with higher fertility levels, which also had lower levels of divorce and abortion (Scheuch, 1989, p. 97).

The 1980 Institute for the Study of Public Opinion survey found that religiosity was higher among women, individuals with elementary education, agricultural workers, housewives, people over age 70, Slovaks or those living in Slovakia, and widows. Non-believers were more likely to be men, individuals with higher education, students and apprentices, those 20 years of age or younger, Czechs or those living in the Czech Lands, and unmarried individuals (Foret, 1986, pp. 69-70).

In addition to the Catholic Church, which officials estimated accounts for 70 percent of all practicing believers in Czechoslovakia, there were an estimated 1,300,000 members of other churches in Czechoslovakia in the mid-1980s. The largest portion of these were members of Protestant denominations, including the Slovak Evangelical Church of the Augsburg Confession, the Evangelical Church of Czech Brethren, the Silesian Evangelical Church of the Augsburg Confession, and the Reformed (Christian) Church in Slovakia. There are also an estimated 150,000 members of the Orthodox Church, primarily Ukrainians living in Eastern Slovakia (M.P., 1986d, pp. 4-5). An estimated 15,000 Jews actively participated in religious services in the late communist period (*The Europa Yearbook*, 1988).

Official policies toward organized religion generally were harsh during the communist period. The confiscation of church property and the restrictions placed on the activities of Catholic and other religious leaders in the early communist period were accompanied by campaigns to spread scientific atheism and discourage people from relying on the church, particularly in Slovakia. The ability of churches to conduct religious education and train new priests or ministers continued to be very restricted. The consequences of being identified as a practising believer were often severe (see Ramet, 1989, pp. 279–81). Relations between the Vatican and Czechoslovak officials improved somewhat in the late 1980s, but the impact of decades of poor relations was evident in the large numbers of parishes without priests and dioceses without bishops (see Ramet, 1989, pp. 280–1; and Martin, 1989c, pp. 7–11).

There was a revival of interest in religious observation in Czechoslovakia in the late 1980s. The leadership and laity of the Catholic Church in particular became far more outspoken in challenging the regime and pressing for religious freedom. Cardinal Tomášek emerged as a more visible leader who spoke out on controversial issues. Catholic activists signed and circulated petitions that called on the government and party to change certain policies, including the stationing of missiles in Czechoslovakia in the early 1980s and the planned liberalization of the abortion law in 1987, as well as a petition that called for religious freedom which gained over 600,000 signatures. These developments were paralleled by the emergence of mass religious processions and the development of religious dissident groups. Pilgrimages to holy shrines in Moravia and Slovakia grew from approximately 100,000 per year in the early 1980s to an estimated 800,000 by 1988. Catholic and other activists also demonstrated in favor of religious freedom in Bratislava in March 1988 and in Levoča in July 1988. Although its influence was not great, particularly compared to that of the Catholic Church in Poland, the Catholic Church in Czechoslovakia thus emerged in the late 1980s in a new, more political role as a focus of opposition to the communist regime. The numbers of citizens who adhered to other, less established religious groups, such as Jehovah's Witnesses and evangelical Christian movements, also grew in the late communist period (see Martin, 1988; Wilson, 1988).

With the end of communist rule, many of the restrictions on organized religion have been removed. Symbolized by the *Te Deum* on the occasion of Václav Havel's installation as President of Czechoslovakia in December 1989, the new policy in regard to religion was soon evident in many areas. Certain church properties have been returned, and penalties for openly practising one's religion have ended. Relations with the Vatican and world religious organizations have been restored. The 13 vacant Catholic bishoprics were filled prior to John Paul II's April 1990 visit to Czechoslovakia (see 'Poselství dobré vůle,' 1990). Religious orders are now free to recruit and train priests and ministers, and churches once again openly organize religious education for young people (see Martin, 1990a). Many individuals who previously practised their religion in private now do so openly.

Paradoxically, the return of religion to a private rather than political matter may decrease religious observation among certain groups. Now that there are other avenues of political expression and participation, organized religion has lost its role as a focus of political dissent, a role that gained it a certain degree of support during the communist period, particularly among young people.

Conclusion

As the preceding pages have illustrated, the establishment of a communist system in Czechoslovakia and continued economic development had a differential impact on various aspects of the country's social structure. In certain areas, there was marked change in the 40 years of communist rule. In others, there was greater continuity with the pre-communist situation. In both cases, the diversity and cleavages in Czech and Slovak society had implications for political discussion and policy-making. As chapter 4 will demonstrate, Czechoslovakia's social structure and the social changes that occurred during the communist period also had an influence on the functioning of the economy.

The end of communist rule has led to important changes in the opportunities available to members of different social groups. The move to a market economy, the repudiation of policies adopted in the communist period in many areas, and the greater openness of the policy-making process will undoubtedly be reflected in further changes in the country's social structure. Changes in the political and economic realm will also lead to the further growth of new social problems such as drug abuse, and the re-emergence of others that were suppressed under communist rule, such as increased crime and prostitution. However, economic and political life will continue to be conditioned in significant ways by both the intended and unintended changes in the social structure that occurred during the communist period.

4 Economics

In addition to recreating the institutions and values of a democratic political system, Czechoslovakia's new, non-communist leaders have also had to deal with the economic repercussions of 40 years of communist rule. As in other formerly communist countries they are transforming the country's highly centralized, inefficient command economy into a market economy, reorienting its external economic relations, and dealing with the ecological destruction created by past economic policies. As Václav Havel noted in his 1991 New Year's Day address, the magnitude of these tasks has proved to be greater than the country's new leaders anticipated when they came to power. The difficulty of the economic transformation now under way, as well as current economic developments, reflect the impact of the organization of the economy and economic performance during the communist period.

As discussed in chapter 3, Czechoslovakia's economy was dramatically reorganized once the Communist Party gained power. The increase in the role of the state in economic life that began after 1945 continued after 1948. Rapid nationalization and the forcible collectivization of agriculture resulted in an economic structure that paralleled that of the Soviet Union and other communist countries. The creation of a central planning apparatus and emulation of the Soviet strategy of economic development that prevailed under Stalin transformed Czechoslovakia's industry and redirected the economy from its traditional strengths in light industry to heavy industry. There were also major changes in the country's external economic relations.

Although there were several efforts to change the organization and functioning of the Czechoslovak economy, it remained one of the more centralized of the centrally planned economies in the region throughout the communist period. It also continued to be firmly integrated in economic relations with the Soviet Union and other communist countries and relatively little involved in trade or other economic transactions with the West. Both of these features had a negative impact on economic performance. They also have conditioned the effort to recreate a market economy that has accompanied the transition to democracy in Czechoslovakia.

Economic organization and enterprise management

Control of economic decision-making rested to a large degree with central authorities throughout the communist period in Czechoslovakia. In contrast to the situation in some of the country's neighbors, the private sector was virtually eliminated and private ownership of all but small amounts of land and family homes restricted (see chapter 3).

As the section to follow on economic reforms illustrates, there were several efforts to decrease the role of central authorities and allow enterprises more autonomy during the communist period. However, the attempt to decentralize that was a key element of the economic reforms of the 1960s was not successful, and the economic changes introduced in the early 1980s did not aim to give greater autonomy to lower levels. Economic planning and decision-making thus remained highly concentrated in the hands of the State Planning Commission and the ministries responsible for various branches of the economy. This situation persisted despite the adoption of a federal system in 1968, as amendments enacted in 1971 reduced the economic powers granted to the republics. As in other areas of life, party organizations at each level also played an important role in economic decision-making throughout the communist period.

Policies introduced in 1988 and 1989 as part of the program for economic change adopted in January 1987 were designed to give greater authority to enterprises, but in fact did little to reduce the role of the central economic authorities in economic decision-making. According to the provisions of this program, which prior to the overthrow of the communist system was scheduled to encompass the economy as a whole by January 1990, the central institutions, which included the economic ministries of the federal and republic governments as well as the State Planning Commission, would no longer issue binding annual plans to set production targets, prices, etc. Nevertheless, they were to continue to engage in medium- and long-range planning. The staff of the central planning apparatus was reduced somewhat in 1988 and 1989, and further reductions were planned. However, there were still substantial numbers of state and party bureaucrats with vested interests in maintaining a sizeable role for central bodies. The continuation of the *nomenklatura* system, which allowed the Communist Party to determine who would hold the most important positions in the economy, was another tool that preserved the influence of central authorities. The new economic measures also allowed central authorities to intervene in a number of special areas. Thus, although lower-level units were to play a greater role in economic decision-making, the economy was still subject to a high degree of central control.

As a result of measures adopted in the 1970s, basic enterprises were consolidated into larger production units. These units, which in many cases amounted to virtual monopolies, were designed to improve the efficiency of planning and facilitate central oversight. The law on state enterprises adopted in the late 1980s aimed to reduce the size of enterprises by removing this middle level of organization. However, the enterprises created according to the provisions of this law were in many cases as large as those they replaced.

Several groups played a role in the day-to-day management of Czechoslovakia's enterprises during the communist period. These included the enterprise director and other members of the management team; and officials of the Communist Party and the trade unions.

Although they theoretically were to play a role in enterprise management as well as in representing the interests of workers, the role of the trade unions in actuality was modest in both respects. Subordinate to the Communist Party at both the national and plant level, unions did little to represent workers' preferences or express their grievances *vis-à-vis* management during the communist period. The official unions had relatively little authority with either the workers or management. Strikes were illegal throughout the communist period, and workers played very little role in enterprise management.

In theory, the enterprise director and his or her subordinates held primary responsibility for the efficient functioning of economic enterprises. In practice, however, the ability of managers to manage effectively was limited during much of the post-Second World War period by the subordination of enterprises to the binding central plan and the authority of the central planning bodies and ministries. The autonomy of managers also was circumscribed by the need for consultation with plant and local Communist Party authorities.

The management of Czechoslovakia's enterprises underwent a number of changes in the late communist period as part of the overall economic reform program adopted in January 1987. As will be discussed later in this chapter, the new measures envisioned an increase in the discretion and authority of managers as enterprises shifted to full self-accounting and the role of central planning authorities decreased. Had the planned move away from binding economic indicators and increase in enterprise autonomy occurred, they would have put new and different demands on managers, many of whom appeared to have few of the skills necessary to do well in less controlled circumstances. If implemented, the economic changes would also have increased the influence of specialists and professionals working at the enterprise level, as more technical skills would have been needed to manage factories successfully in the new economic conditions.

The economic measures adopted in January 1987 also called for workers to play a greater role in decision-making at the enterprise level. Thus, workers' councils consisting of elected representatives were to be set up in all enterprises. Workers and employees were also to participate in selecting managers and enterprise directors. First started on an experimental basis in 1988, such councils were scheduled to be established more broadly as the economic reform was implemented (see 'První rady,' 1988). To some extent these councils were reminiscent of those first established in Czechoslovakia as part of the economic reform of the 1960s (see Skilling, 1976, pp. 433-42). However, the authorities asserted that the new councils, in contrast to those established at that time, were to act with restraint and serve as 'responsible partners' of management rather than as adversaries. It is not clear how many of these bodies actually were established prior to the end of communist rule or what their role in decision-making at the enterprise level was. This effort was suspended along with other aspects of the 1987 reform program after the end of communist rule. A similar fate met the 'brigade system,' which was introduced in Czech and Slovak enterprises in the mid-1980s. As in the Soviet Union where it was first adopted, the brigade method was designed to improve labor productivity by creating more cohesive work collectives and giving individual workers a greater say in production decisions. In Czechoslovakia, it was also seen as a way to remedy the high degree of egalitarianism in wages, as each work collective, rather than the foreman alone, was to categorize different areas and types of work and thus determine the level and range of compensation for particular jobs. Perhaps due to this aspect of the brigades' activities, the brigade system met a good deal of resistance in Czechoslovakia. Although the program of economic changes adopted in January 1987 envisioned the gradual extension of the brigade system to other areas of the economy, relatively small numbers of workers were organized in brigades (approximately 10 percent by mid-1987) (Pohl, 1988a, p. 20, 1988b, p. 21).

The political changes that occurred after November 1989 have been accompanied by corresponding changes in the organization of the economy and enterprise management. Private property has once again been recognized as a legal form of ownership, and citizens' rights to form economic corporations, joint stock companies, and economic ventures with foreign investors have been restored. The non-communist government took steps in its first year to reduce the power of the central planning apparatus dramatically by eliminating many of the central economic ministries that controlled economic life. The State Planning Commission became the Ministry of the Economy, and its functions were redefined. Further changes in economic organization and decision-making will follow as the program of economic reforms adopted in September 1990 leads to the recreation of a sizeable private sector, the elimination of central control, and structural changes.

The process by which economic decisions are made has also changed markedly since November 1989. The end of the

Communist Party's monopoly of political power has allowed broader groups of actors to play a greater role in the process at all levels. The elimination of the *nomenklatura* system and workplace party units reduced the Communist Party's ability to control the day-to-day implementation of economic policy at the enterprise level.

However, throughout 1990, many communist managers remained at their positions. This situation, which was the subject of increasing dissatisfaction in mid-1990, was acknowledged by President Havel in August 1990, when he called for a second revolution, which he identified as a rapid move to privatize the economy to reduce the influence of communist managers (see Pehe, 1990c, pp. 6-10). Concern about the continued influence of these individuals has been tempered by a reluctance to use political criteria as a basis for personnel decisions as well as by the fact that it is not practical to replace large numbers of them quickly.

The developing private sector and increased number of joint ventures have also begun to diversify management methods at the enterprise level. The ability of managers of both private and state-owned enterprises to run their enterprises effectively was hampered in 1990 by the lack of clarity and rapid changes in regulations governing enterprises and other aspects of economic policy as well as by difficulties in obtaining supplies and energy. Regulations issued in late 1990 and early 1991 were aimed at clarifying certain of these issues, but ongoing reforms in many sectors of the economy will continue to create uncertainties in this as well as other areas of economic life in the near future (dk, 1990a, p. 1).

The changes currently under way ultimately will result in an economic system and economic policies that differ radically from those that prevailed during the period of Communist Party dominance. However, economic performance and economic policies, as well as the course of the economic reform, will continue to be influenced in important ways by the structures and policies that characterized that period for some time to come.

Economic performance

Czechoslovakia's economy did not experience the serious crises that occurred in many other Central and East European countries during the communist period. The country's standard of living also continued to be higher than that in most other Central and East European states. However, the Czechoslovak economy also suffered from the distortions caused by central planning and communist economic policies. Although the revolution of 1989 was not based primarily on economic grievances, poor economic performance helped to erode popular support for or toleration of the communist system during the last years of communist rule.

As in the Soviet Union and other communist states, central planning led to a number of chronic economic problems in Czechoslovakia. These included many of those difficulties, such as low labor productivity, poor quality goods, poor labor morale, lack of ability to determine the true costs of production, lack of incentives for both workers and management, structural imbalances, difficulties in innovating and resulting inability to compete on the world market that plagued other centrally planned economies. In Czechoslovakia, these difficulties were compounded by others, including labor shortages and the aging of the industrial plant, that reflected the country's particular history and conditions prior to the establishment of a communist system (see Dyba and Ježek, 1989; Levcik, 1981, pp. 377–424; Brada, King, and Schlagenhauf, 1981, pp. 425–82; Kusin, 1982b, pp. 31–5; Levcik, 1986, pp. 85–108; Dyba, 1989b; Brada, 1989; and Wolchik, 1987, pp. 36–42).

The impact of these chronic economic problems was exacerbated in the late 1970s by external factors, including the delayed but significant effects of the energy crisis and economic recession in the West, and difficulties in obtaining raw materials and other supplies. Czechoslovakia was originally shielded to some extent from such disruptions by its low level of trade and other economic links to the West, as well as by its dependence on the Soviet Union for much of its energy and important raw materials. However, by the late 1970s, Czechoslovakia also began to experience energy shortages and difficulties in obtaining needed supplies of raw materials. The

Soviet Union continued to supply the bulk of the country's oil, as it had in earlier periods, but the price of energy increased in reaction to the increase in the world market price and its reflection in the Soviet pricing formula. The expiration of a special agreement made in 1966, which guaranteed the delivery of a certain amount of oil at fixed prices between 1971 and 1984, in return for Czechoslovak loans of machinery and consumer goods between 1966 and 1974 also contributed to higher prices for Soviet oil. In addition, Soviet deliveries of oil, which accounted for approximately 90 percent of Czechoslovakia's oil and 35 percent of the country's total energy supplies in the late 1970s, declined in the early 1980s (see Hardt, 1981, pp. 189-220; Vaňous, 1981, pp. 541-60; Kramer, 1981, pp. 459-75; Vaňous, 1982, pp. 1-19; Kramer, 1985, pp. 32-47; Wolchik, 1987, pp. 36-8; Bornstein, 1981a, pp. 31-61, and 1981b, pp. 105-24; and Zimmerman, 1981, pp. 87-104; see Gitelman, 1981, pp. 127-61, for a discussion of the political repercussions of these patterns).

As the section to follow illustrates, difficulties in the industrial sphere were compounded in the late 1970s and early 1980s by problems in agriculture, where harsh weather and poor harvests depressed output (Levcik, 1981, pp. 390-5). As a result, Czechoslovakia experienced chronic, although not acute, economic crises throughout the 1980s. In contrast to the improvement in material conditions that occurred in the early and mid-1970s, the standard of living stagnated.

The negative repercussions of these domestic and external factors on economic performance were particularly evident in the early 1980s, when national income and average wages virtually stagnated, and industrial output increased very little. According to official figures released during the communist period, industrial production in the productive sphere as a whole increased 3.7 percent from 1976 to 1980, but an average of 1.6 percent from 1981 to 1984. Results were particularly poor in 1981 and 1982, when industrial production increased by 0.3 percent and 0.9 percent (Jezdík, 1986).

Economic performance improved somewhat in the mid-1980s in both the agricultural and industrial sectors. Official Czechoslovak sources claim that national income grew by 2.2 percent in 1983 and by 3.2 percent in 1984 (gross national income). Direct comparison of the results of 1984 with those of previous years is hampered, however, by the fact that gross figures were used in that year rather than the net figures used in previous years. Western estimates of the net growth in national income in that year (2.7 percent) suggest that the economy continued to recover, although at a somewhat slower rate than officials claimed (see Levcik, 1986, pp. 91–5). Thus, the national product produced in 1984 exceeded that of 1980 by only 5 percent; average real wages in 1984 were 2 percent below those of 1978 (Levcik, 1986, p. 96).

Gross national income also increased in 1985 (by 3.3 percent), as did industrial production (3.4 percent), and gross agricultural production (5.4 percent). Personal earnings increased by 3.1 percent and wages by 2.5 percent. Real wages, however, remained at 1984 levels ('Zpráva federálního statistického úřadu,' 1986, pp. 1–3). Economic performance continued at approximately the same level in 1986, when gross national income increased by 3.4 percent compared to a 3.5 percent planned increase, and industrial production increased by 3.1 percent, compared to a 2.6 percent planned increase. The planned target in gross agricultural production (0.5 percent) was barely met in that year, in contrast to the positive results in this area in 1985. The planned increases for food products and livestock were exceeded slightly, but grain production targets were generally not met ('Statistics Office Issues 1986 Economic Report,' 1987).

Similar trends continued in the late 1980s. Nominal wages rose by 2.7 percent, and real incomes by 3.2 percent in 1987. The plan for agriculture was also fulfilled in that year. Czech and Slovak leaders also claimed positive results in the area of foreign trade and provision of foodstuffs. Industrial output rose by 2.3 percent in 1987, and labor productivity rose somewhat more than planned (2.3 percent compared to 1.2 percent). However, in both areas the planned targets had been lowered the previous year ('Statistics Office Releases Economic Report,' 1988, pp. 13–14).

According to official statistics released during the communist period, economic performance remained at about the same level in 1988. National income rose by approximately 3 percent, a figure somewhat higher than the planned increase. Personal consumption also rose more than planned (4.5 percent), as did incomes from wages (3 percent), and average monthly wages (2.3 percent). Industrial output targets were also met in terms of volume, although qualitative indicators were not fulfilled completely. Gross agricultural production increased 2.2 percent, as planned ('Přírůstek národního důchodu,' 1989, pp. 1, 3; see Myant, 1989, pp. 220-40; and Brada, 1989, for overviews of economic performance in the 1980s). As noted in analyses by leading economic officials after November 1989, measures of economic performance during the communist period did not take into account hidden inflation, estimated at from 2 to 2.5 percent a year. Actual economic performance as reflected in the worsening of Czechoslovakia's international position thus was considerably lower than many of these figures appear to indicate (see 'Analýza vývoje,' 1990, pp. 1-15).

Economic and political leaders continued to view economic performance as unsatisfactory in the late 1980s. As in the early and mid-1980s, officials identified the poor results of efforts to improve the effectiveness of foreign trade, difficulties in applying scientific-technical progress in practice, and problems with efficient use of investments and capital construction as major problems. They also highlighted continued difficulties in ensuring high quality products and sporadic shortages of foodstuffs and consumer durables ('Přírůstek národního důchodu,' 1989, pp. 1, 3). Planned targets for the 1985-90 period were not ambitious and were reduced further after their adoption. The annual growth rate set by the 1985-90 five-year plan (3.5 percent), for example, was not met in the first three years of the plan, and targets for the last two years of the plan were lowered (Martin, 1989a, pp. 7-10. See also Čechlovský and Marek, 1988).

Economic planners and officials envisioned continued austerity and modest growth in the last years of communist rule. The 1989 plan, for example, called for a 2.2 percent increase in gross national income. This rate was considerably lower than the 3.5 percent annual increase called for in the original plan for 1985-1990; it was also lower than the 2.7 percent increase in national income achieved in the first three years of the plan (B. Urban, 1988, pp. 1, 5). Even these modest targets were not met in the last years of communist rule. Growth in the gross domestic product decreased from 2.8 percent in 1988 to 1.7 percent in 1989. Nominal cash incomes rose by 3.3 percent and personal real cash incomes by 1.8 percent. However, as the report of the Federal Statistical Office issued in February 1990 noted, with hidden inflation, real incomes probably stagnated (zr, 1990b; and 'Report of the Federal Statistical Office,' 1990, pp. 178-84). Prices in a number of areas, including food products and consumer durables also increased substantially.

Economic performance continued to decline in several areas in the first year of non-communist rule as a result of political change, the disruptions that legal changes produced in many areas of economic life, and uncertainty concerning future economic policies. External economic trends and developments, including the Soviet Union's unilateral reduction in oil supplies to Czechoslovakia in August 1990; the abrogation of the former GDR's trade agreements with Czechoslovakia; economic crises in Czechoslovakia's other Central and East European trading partners; and the war in the Persian Gulf also had a negative impact on economic performance. The crisis in the Gulf, which disrupted plans to import oil from Iraq and prevented exports to that country, was estimated to have cost Czechoslovakia a total of $1.4 billion in increased oil prices and loss of exports (J. Franěk, 1990, p. 1). The impact of the oil shock on the population is clearly reflected in the increases in the price of coal and coke (44 to 50 percent), heat (74 percent), electricity (53 percent), and natural and manufactured gas (65 percent), in December 1990 (ČTK, November 30, 1990).

The decline in economic performance was particularly great in the first months of 1990, when gross industrial production decreased by 3.7 percent and labor productivity per worker by 1.1 percent. According to the Chair of the Federal Statistical Office, gross national income in 1990 was estimated to be 3.5 percent lower than in 1989, and gross national product 4 percent lower. Industrial production declined by 3.3 percent, agriculture by 3.4 percent, and the construction industry by 10 percent (vl, 1990c, p. 2). Czechoslovak officials note that the overall figures mask certain developments that were in fact positive from the perspective of future economic development. Thus, the decline in industrial output was particularly great in branches of the economy that are to be de-emphasized as the country moves to a market economy or have been affected most by changes in the international arena and Czechoslovakia's trading patterns, such as coal mining, the uranium industry, metallurgy and machine building, and the chemical and crude oil processing industries. Production of consumer goods decreased very little (0.9 percent), and production in several branches of light industry increased (1.5 to 7.1 percent) (see vl, 1990a, p. 2, and 1990b, p. 2; see 'Czechoslovak Economic Performance' for an overview of the economy's performance in the first half of 1990).

Unemployment also increased in 1990, although levels remained considerably below those in many developed capitalist countries. By the end of 1990, an estimated 75,000 people were unemployed, a figure equivalent to less than 1 percent of the work-capable population (Červenková, 1991, p. 7). In Slovakia, unemployment was substantially greater in East Slovakia (15,000 of a total 38,000) than in the rest of the country (Jánku, 1991, p. 2). An estimated 10,000 graduates of secondary schools and universities were unemployed as of September 1990 (ČTK, November 11, 1990). By the end of January 1991, unemployment in Slovakia had nearly doubled to encompass 65,000 individuals, or 2.2 percent of the labor force ('Nezaměstnanost' narasta,' 1991, p. 1). Inflation averaged 10 percent, while labor productivity recovered somewhat in the latter half of 1990 and was equivalent to that achieved in 1989. Average wages increased somewhat in both the Czech Lands and Slovakia, despite the stagnation of labor productivity (Červenková, 1991, p. 7).

The impact of these developments and the oil shock was reflected in a 14.1 percent increase in the cost of living between July and September 1990. Real incomes dropped by 1 percent during this period. As the result of price increases enacted in July 1990, food prices increased by 20 percent, industrial goods by 11 percent, and services by 9.9 percent (ČTK, October 18, 1990). The magnitude of these increases in the service sector is evident in the fact that nursery fees, for example, increased 36.5 percent and kindergarten fees 86.3 percent in the third quarter of 1990 (min, 1990, p. 37).

Agriculture

The performance and organization of the agricultural sector reflect the changes that took place in the early communist period as well as the reluctance of the communist leadership to allow expansion of the private sector in the last years of communist rule. As noted in chapter 3, collectivization proceeded rapidly in Czechoslovakia and, by 1960, all but approximately 10 percent of agricultural land was incorporated in state or collective farms (Korbel, 1977, p. 261; Wadekin, 1982, pp. 85-6). The extent of private agriculture diminished further after that time, declining to 5 percent of all arable land in 1975 and 3 percent in 1985. Czechoslovakia thus had a smaller private sector than most of the other Central and East European countries (Wadekin, 1982, p.85; Cochrane, 1988, p.48).

Despite its small size, the private sector played an important part in agricultural production in Czechoslovakia particularly in the early communist period. In the 1960s, for example, private agriculture produced approximately 28 percent of gross agricultural output. By 1977, this proportion had declined to 13.5 percent, a figure lower than that in most other communist states aside from the GDR (Wadekin, 1982, p. 97). By 1985, 10 percent of agricultural output came from private farms (Cochrane, 1988, p. 48). Nonetheless, the private sector continued to play a key role in supplementing the output of state and collective farms, particularly in the production of certain foods, such as fruit, in which private plots produced 60 percent of all production, poultry (25 percent), vegetables (40 percent), and eggs (40 percent) in 1985 (Cochrane, 1988, p. 48).

These figures reflect the poor record of collectivized agriculture in Czechoslovakia for much of the communist period. Growth rates incorporated into the early five-year plans were not met, and production of many agricultural products remained at or below pre-Second World War levels as late as 1960 (see Taborsky, 1961, pp. 409-23). As a result, Czechoslovakia, which in the pre-communist period had a system of small- to medium-size farms that produced efficiently enough to assure near self-sufficiency in food supplies (Koenig, 1957, pp. 246-7), had to import many categories of foodstuffs (Taborsky, 1961, p. 416).

The performance of the agricultural sector improved substantially in the early to mid-1970s, when production of crops and animals grew rapidly. This expansion reflected both the continuation of certain of the economic reforms enacted in the agricultural sector in the 1960s after the invasion as well as the increased investment in agriculture during the 1971-5 five-year plan period. In the early 1970s, for example, investments in the agricultural sector increased 11.3 percent per year (Lukas, 1989, pp. 38-42. See also Brada and King, 1983).

However, these positive trends did not persist into the 1980s. By the late 1970s, growth rates in both animal and crop production decreased substantially. Declining performance in these areas reflected the increased discrepancy between the rising demands of the expansion of the meat production sector initiated in the early 1970s and the country's grain supplies, unreliable harvests due to severe weather, and the reorganization of agriculture, which reduced the number of farms and increased the size and area of those which remained. The diminishing returns of further investments of technology and capital in agriculture also played a role (Brada and King, 1983, pp. 345-7 and Lukas, 1989, p. 38).

Measures enacted in response to the agricultural crisis of the late 1970s led to renewed growth in the early and mid-1980s. Increased investments in agriculture (an average of 6.8 percent per year at a time when total investments declined by 1.1 percent per year), and the encouragement of private farming on a limited scale after 1979 were reflected in better performance throughout the agricultural sector. Gains were particularly noticeable in grain production. Czechoslovakia had a record harvest in 1984, and was nearly self-sufficient in grain in 1987 and 1988 (Lukas, 1989, p. 38).

The extension of the economic experiment begun in the late 1980s to agriculture occurred in early 1989. As a result, state farms gained a certain degree of autonomy *vis-à-vis* the central planning authorities. In contrast to past practice, investments were to be financed primarily by the state farms' own resources or through loans. Higher prices and 'free prices' of an increasing group of farm goods were expected to provide further incentives for efficient production in the agricultural area. As in other areas of the economy, the role of the state plan was reduced substantially in theory. Farms were to be subject to only one mandatory indicator, the sale of grain to the state, although central officials were still permitted to authorize emergency measures if severe shortages of meat or other agricultural products were to develop. The authorities expected changes in the agricultural tax code enacted in January 1989, including a uniform tax rate on profits, to stimulate greater productivity (Sourek, 1989, pp. 14-15). Agricultural enterprises were authorized to engage in trade with the West directly except in those cases in which the amounts involved exceeded certain specified limits. They also were permitted to enter into joint ventures with Western businesses as the result of the joint venture law enacted in November 1988. In contrast to Soviet experiments in this area in the late 1980s, the *de facto* expansion of the private sector by the use of long-term leases did not play a large role in government plans to improve agricultural performance articulated prior to November 1989 (Lukaš, 1989, pp. 40-1). The measures enacted in the late communist period also preserved certain types of subsidies for the 25 percent of all agricultural enterprises that were subsidized to one degree or another by the state ('Agriculture Under the New Economic Conditions,' 1989, p. 28; 'O novém hospodářském mechanismu,' 1989). As in other areas of economic policy, agricultural performance increased somewhat in most areas in 1989; monthly wages in agriculture also increased sharply by 4.7 percent ('Report of the Federal Statistical Office,' 1990, p. 26). However, as critics would note in 1990, the relative 'successes' of agriculture during the communist period were purchased at the cost not only of state subsidies but of the degradation and contamination of large areas of farmland (Kabátek, 1991, p. 8).

The second economy

During the communist period, a good deal of economic activity took place outside the framework of the official economy. The extent and openness of the second, or unofficial economy varied somewhat within the Central and East European states, but it was an important aspect of economic life in all of them. Although the economic policies adopted by the new non-communist governments in the region have legalized certain activities previously prohibited, illegal economic activities continue in a variety of areas.

The existence of the second or 'shadow' economy, as it was often termed in Czechoslovakia, was admitted openly by economic officials and analysts only in the last years of communist rule. In the course of 1989, several remarkable analyses of unofficial economic activities appeared in economic journals. Taken together, these analyses shed considerable light on the functioning of this area of the economy. They also illustrate shortcomings of the official economic system during the communist period.

Basing his estimate in part on official findings and in part on other published estimates, which relied on statistical data concerning the numbers of family homes and cottages of workers in particular branches of the economy, the volume and structure of retail trade, and service payments, Martin Fassmann, an official of the State Planning Commission, suggested that the minimum amount of unofficial economic activity equaled 18 to 20 billion Czechoslovak crowns (1.19 to 1.32 billion US dollars at the official exchange rate of the time in the late 1980s). He further estimated that the minimum growth of this activity in the decade between 1979 and 1989 was from 6 to 8 billion crowns.

Average citizens were estimated to spend between 1 and 10 percent of their work earnings in the shadow economy. In addition to highlighting the large number of people who engaged in moonlighting, the author noted that dishonest or illegal activities in the retail sector were also widespread. Thus, honesty checks conducted in commercial and public eating establishments in 1985 revealed that cheating of customers accounted for approximately 3 percent of the total turnover of these establishments. The estimated 3 percent of all employed persons who profited from these transactions were thought to have increased their incomes by anywhere from 20 to over 200 percent in this manner (Fassmann, 1988, p. 3).

Experts from the Economic Research Institute in Prague arrived at similar estimates. Thus, in accounts published in mid-1989 they estimated that the second economy (defined as all economic activities that were not, even partially, recorded in official statistics),

Table 4.1 Proportion of respondents who used bribery (gifts, additional payments, reciprocal services) by area, 1988 (%)

Purchasing retail goods	75.0
Health care	49.5
Repair and other tradesmen's work	44.5
Purchase and repair of automobiles	37.5
Services (hairdressing, restaurants, cleaning services, etc.)	19.0
Activities connected with construction	18.5
Obtaining official actions and permits	18.5
Allocation and exchange of apartments	13.5
Education	13.0
Transportation	9.0
Tourism	7.5
Obtaining scarce books and magazines	6.5
Obtaining tickets to cultural programs	3.0
Purchase of cottages and plots	2.5
Getting favors at work or a better job	1.5

Source: From information in Hanzl, Ševberová, Štěpová, and Žůrek, 1989, pp. 8–9

accounted for approximately 11.8 billion crowns in 1985 in the area of productive activities performed by members of a household for other people for payment (see Table 4.1). 'Non-productive' activities, such as cheating customers and overcharging by the estimated 140,000 people working in the retail and public catering sectors, amounted to 2.5 to a further 3 billion crowns a year. The authors also discussed another area of non-productive activity: activities designed to obtain goods or services in short supply for payment. These activities, which ranged from importing goods from abroad for speculation to providing health care services and medication, also included exchanging foreign currency; arranging for services not easily available or attractive work assignments; and ensuring acceptance at higher educational institutions. Although they pointed out the difficulties involved, the authors nonetheless provided rough estimates of certain of these activities. They estimated, for example, that the approximately 500,000 people who travelled to capitalist countries in 1988 imported privately goods worth approximately 2.5 billion crowns (equivalent to 170 million US dollars at the official exchange rate at that time). The authors note that this estimate, which was based on the assumption that each traveller brought back goods equal to the legal limit of duty-free imports (5,000 crowns), was in all likelihood conservative, as it did not capture goods smuggled into the country. They estimated that the total amount of private imports, including those from the socialist world, especially Hungary, the GDR, and Yugoslavia, amounted to a figure equivalent to 20 percent of all imports.

The results of an April 1988 survey of a group of 200 households conducted by the Economic Research Institute provide further information on the nature of the second economy in the late communist period. Noting that the response rate was 100 percent, the authors suggest that such a high degree of willingness to discuss these activities illustrates the extent to which such activities were 'all so widespread that they have come to be considered an ordinary part of life' (Hanzl, Ševberová, Štěpová, and Žůrek, 1989, pp. 8-9). Only six of 200 respondents stated that they had never used a bribe of one sort or another to get what they needed in some area. As Table 4.1 illustrates, the use of such methods appears to have been especially great in the retail sector and medicine, as well as in services and in the purchase and service of automobiles.

The amount and frequency of bribes varied to some degree in different areas. In the area of retail trade, for example, in which bribery was used at least once by all but 45 of the 200 respondents, monetary bribes, generally in the range of 100 to 500 crowns (6.6 to 33.1 US dollars at the time), predominated. Monetary bribes were also prevalent in health care, where such means were used most often in cases of surgery, especially for childbirth and abortions, generally in somewhat larger amounts (between 500 to 5,000 crowns, approximately 33 to 330 US dollars, per treatment). Bribery also was used frequently to obtain dental services and special examinations. In the area of services, bribes fluctuated from 20 to 50 crowns for routine repair of household electrical and gas appliances (the most frequent area), to from 100 to 500 crowns for the issuing of certificates or expert opinions from craftsmen for bureaucratic or insurance purposes. Extra payments connected to obtaining or servicing automobiles ranged from 500 to 5,000 crowns to purchase automobiles without being on the waiting list, or to obtain special options to the use of rewards in kind or reciprocal services in the area of service or spare parts.

The authors also discussed the use of bribes to obtain official permits or actions. Monetary bribes used in this area ranged from 500 crowns for matters related to building materials and construction work to much higher amounts for preferential access to an apartment (from 2,000 to 3,000 crowns). The results of the survey indicate that small gifts in kind (such as boxes of chocolates, coffee, flowers, etc.) were generally used to secure a place or better care in preschool facilities. However, monetary bribes worth far more (from 500 to 10,000 crowns) were used to ensure places for children in high schools and higher educational institutions.

Further information on the second economy and a sign of the change in the official approach to these issues in the last years of communist rule appeared in an interview with an official of the Presidium of the federal government, Petr Krejčí, published in mid-1989. Noting that only part of the second economy consisted of illegal activity, Krejčí argued that even certain illegal economic activities, as well as those forms of activity that were not illegal *per se* but simply not counted in official statistics, such as do-it-yourself activities and home repairs, had a positive function for the economy as they provided the population with services that could not be obtained legally. Noting that consumers often turned to the second economy because the services or materials they needed were 'absolutely unavailable' through official channels, he estimated that a minimum of one-quarter of all materials used in building family homes came from 'unidentifiable sources,' i.e., the second economy (Reboun, 1988, p. 3).

These analyses provide empirical support for the widespread view that bribery, extra payment for access to services supposedly guaranteed by the state, and other forms of unofficial economic activity were ubiquitous in Czechoslovakia by the late 1980s. In certain areas, such as trade and medicine, extra compensation for providers of services had come to be commonplace. Large proportions of the population also evidently routinely engaged in other illegal or semi-legal economic acts in order to supplement their regular incomes or obtain goods and services that were unavailable through official channels.

The articles discussed above also illustrate the debate that took place among economic experts in the late 1980s concerning the best way to deal with unauthorized economic activity. Opinions on this issue were linked to views on the extent and kind of economic reform needed in Czechoslovakia. Thus, Mr Fassmann of the State Planning Commission and the authors from the Economic Research Institute all agreed that only economic change and the elimination of the conditions of scarcity in many areas would resolve the problem of the second economy. However, their views differed considerably concerning the most appropriate and effective solution in the interim. Mr Fassmann advocated a tightening of tax regulations and the enactment of property taxes designed to provide indirect measurements of gains obtained through illegal or semi-legal economic activity. The model he proposed was the system used in Romania at the time, where property taxes required the individual to prove that acquired objects did not exceed his/her means, and taxes of 80 percent of an object's value were levied on property that could not be justified in this way. He also called for greater criminal prosecution of those who engaged in illegal economic acts. The researchers at the Economics Institute, on the other hand, urged the adoption of very different policies. These included the legalization and privatization of many activities currently in the second economy in health care, services, the retail sector, and the food sector, and changes in price policy to reflect supply and demand to a greater extent. Thus, they advocated using foreign currency to make emergency imports before shortages created a profitable item for the black market and the development of a comprehensive system for allocating foreign currency. They also urged a reconsideration of policy toward the hard currency stores and other measures designed to make speculation and illegal trading of currency less attractive. Finally, they called for a 'renewal' of ethical and moral standards on the part of those who provide services or work in the retail sector, and argued that greater emphasis on the legal rights of citizens and consumers would help alleviate illegal payments and the expectation of such payments on the part of public officials (Hanzl, Ševberová, Štěpová, and Žůrek, 1989, pp. 8-9).

A similar approach was evident in the proposals set forth by Mr Krejčí, who also advocated legalizing many illegal activities in both the service and productive sector, in order to allow private initiative to provide badly needed services and goods. He also called for making the prerogatives and preferential access to materials, tools, transport, etc. available to certain citizens by virtue of their positions or connections less lucrative by making such items and services available to ordinary citizens for use in the their homes through expanded and well-supplied rental and do-it-yourself shops (Reboun, 1988, p. 3).

Many of the illegal economic activities that were prevalent during the communist period have continued after the end of communist rule. Certain of these, such as speculating with currency, increased in 1990 along with the numbers of foreign visitors and the abolition of the requirement that tourists exchange a fixed amount of hard currency per day in the country. The activities of the 'vekslaci,' or unofficial money changers, have become increasingly open and profitable. Measures to reduce these activities, including changes in the exchange rate of the crown, the legalization of registered private exchange operations, and regulations linking the amount of goods tourists can take out of the country to the amount of hard currency officially exchanged were supplemented in February 1991 by harsher penalties for speculators. Elimination of restrictions on the amount of hard currency Czechoslovak citizens can obtain legally, scheduled for 1991, may also reduce the demand for illegal exchanges (see dk, 1990a, p. 1). The early post-communist period has also seen the development of new types of illegal economic activities. These include financial transactions related to the sale and use of illegal drugs, and organized crime, both of which are estimated to have increased significantly in the recent past.

In the near future, the dislocations and economic disruptions that will occur as part of the move to a market economy may enhance the importance of certain elements of the unofficial, or second economy. In the long run, however, the expansion of the private sector in services and other areas, and the legalization of many previously illegal economic activities should help to alleviate the problems associated with the second economy.

Efforts at reform and the transition to the market

Czechoslovakia experienced several attempts at economic change or reform during the communist period. These included the effort to implement modest economic changes in 1958; the economic reforms of the mid- to late 1960s; a package of economic changes adopted in the early 1980s; and the program of economic changes designed to promote *přestavba*, or restructuring, which was approved by the Party in January 1987. Although all four attempts were designed to improve economic performance, each effort was influenced by the political climate in which it occurred. The principles of each attempt, as well as the analyses on which they were based and remedies proposed to improve the economy, thus differed (see Korbonski, 1989, for an overview of the political dimensions of economic reform in Central and Eastern Europe). The economic measures outlined and advocated by Ota Šik and other reform economists in the 1960s were the most far-reaching and potentially significant of these during the communist period.

Discussions of the economic situation by political leaders and experts as well as members of the opposition in the late 1980s reflected an awareness of the seriousness of the economic problems Czechoslovakia faced in the last years of communist rule. After several years of discussion, the Party officially approved a program of economic reform in January 1987. However, there were significant differences both within the leadership of the Communist Party and between the leadership and expert communities concerning the nature and extent of economic change needed. In this as in the political realm, the attitudes and actions of both groups of actors were conditioned to some degree by the country's previous experiences with economic change. They were also constrained by the need to confine changes to modifications within the framework of a socialist economy. These experiences form the background of the more radical move toward a market economy that is being enacted by the current government. In contrast to previous efforts, the present strategy of economic reform is based on a clear rejection of the institutions and policies of a centralized economy.

Economic reform in the 1960s

Although there is some dispute as to whether it merits the term reform, Czechoslovakia's first effort to change the centralized economy set up after 1948 occurred in the late 1950s. Adopted in the wake of the discussion of economic problems that occurred at the elite level after the Twentieth Party Congress of the CPSU, these changes were confined solely to the economic realm; they were also very limited in scope. The mechanical application of Soviet experience and institutions was criticized in this context, but the proposed changes at this time in fact did not depart in any major way from existing practice. Thus, an effort was made to rationalize the planning system, but long-term central planning was intended to remain. Similarly, there was no real change in fixed prices. As would be the case with the package of economic changes adopted in 1981, these changes had little impact on economic performance because they left the main elements of the system untouched (Myant, 1989, pp. 79-85; see also Dyba and Ježek, 1989).

Czechoslovakia's next reform attempt followed soon after. By the early 1960s, Czechoslovakia's economy, which had maintained a high rate of growth throughout the 1950s, began to experience the negative effects of the Stalinist pattern of centralized economic planning and imbalanced investment. These effects, which were evident in the performance of the Hungarian and Polish economy somewhat earlier, were particularly noticeable in 1961 and 1962 in Czechoslovakia. Changes in the international realm, including developing trade problems, also contributed to poor performance in some sectors. The serious consumer shortages that developed and a virtual stagnation in the rate of economic growth in 1963 signalled the need for concerted action to improve economic performance (see Myant, 1989, pp. 97-109).

Alarmed by the economy's poor performance, Communist Party leaders established a commission of experts to propose reforms. As noted in chapter 1, the proposals put forth by this group in the mid-to late 1960s were Czechoslovakia's first serious attempt at economic reform. One of the catalysts that led to the political reforms of the Prague Spring, the economic changes proposed at the time were conditioned both by the failure of the previous effort to improve economic performance by very limited decentralization in 1958-9 and by the growing momentum of forces for change in other areas of life (see Myant, 1989, pp. 79-89; and Dyba and Ježek, 1989. See also Batt, 1988).

The recommendations of the commission, headed by Ota Šik of the Institute of Economics, formed the basis for the program of reforms adopted in principle by the party in the mid-1960s. Although the reforms as adopted did not go as far as Šik and certain other members of the commission wished in rejecting the command economy, they went considerably farther than reform efforts in the Soviet Union and elsewhere in the region. Thus, the influence of the plan was to decrease, with a corresponding increase in the authority and decision-making power of the enterprise. Elements of the market, in the form of profit, competition, and greater use of wage differentiation as incentives, were to be introduced to complement the general influence of the overall, long-range economic plan. In addition to proposals designed to introduce a limited market mechanism, economic reformers also called for the establishment of workers' councils to increase worker participation in decision-making at the enterprise level (see Šik, 1967. See also Holešovský, 1973, pp. 313-46; Skilling, 1976, pp. 57-62 and pp. 412-50; Stevens, 1985, chs. 3-5; Kusin, 1971, pp. 83-96; Myant, 1989, chs. 5 and 6; and Dyba and Kouba, 1989).

Frustrated by bureaucratic opposition to the implementation of the reforms in the mid-1960s, economic reformers came to view political reform as the precondition for successful economic change (see chapter 1). When the reform movement for which they and other intellectuals had helped to create the theoretical foundation moved into the political realm and gained a larger base, they supported it and used the opportunity to elaborate more far-reaching proposals for economic change (see Myant, 1989, ch. 7). The program for economic reform elaborated during this time met the same fate as the political reforms of the period. Šik and many other advocates of reform were removed from public life, and orthodoxy came to govern economic as well as political life (see Stevens, 1985, ch. 6; Batt, 1988; and Myant, 1989, pp. 176–85).

The set of measures

The forcible end of the reform period and the implementation of so-called 'normalization' discredited the ideas of the economic reformers of the 1960s. They also handicapped Czech and Slovak leaders in dealing with the economic crises of the late 1970s and early 1980s. In responding to that crisis, the leadership adopted a two-pronged approach. In the area of energy, leaders urged conservation and attempted to develop new domestic and foreign supplies. The Soviet Union still remained Czechoslovakia's primary energy supplier, but greater efforts were made after the early 1980s to develop domestic supplies of energy, including soft coal and nuclear energy. Czechoslovakia also agreed to participate in CMEA projects to provide additional sources of energy (see Levcik, 1981, pp. 405–9; Kramer, 1981, and 1985; Hardt, 1981; Vaňous, 1982; Hannigan and McMillan, 1981, pp. 259–96; and Wolchik, 1987, p. 40).

In addition to measures designed to deal with the energy problem, the leadership also increased retail prices several times in the 1980s. The first of these increases, which involved many foodstuffs, consumer durables, and services, was enacted in January 1981. It was followed by a series of graduated increases in wholesale prices designed to bring prices into line with production costs and better reflect the cost of energy in finished products (Boura, 1983, p. 1; Spani, 1989, p. 5; and Wolchik, 1987, pp. 41–2).

The leadership's approach to other economic problems during this period is best reflected by the package of economic changes adopted in the early 1980s. Titled the 'Set of Measures to Improve the System of Planned Management of the National Economy,' these measures were adopted in 1980 and scheduled to go into effect throughout the economy in January 1981. Designed in theory to ensure more rational use of scarce resources and improve the quality of goods, the Set of Measures called for change in several areas of economic practice. Chief among these were greater emphasis on qualitative rather than quantitative indicators of plan fulfilment and greater use of material incentives to improve the quality of production and stimulate more rational use of energy and raw materials. The guidelines also discussed the need to increase the influence of science and technology in economic production and set out procedures to evaluate the efficiency of future investments. However, as was the case with Soviet efforts at economic reform prior to Gorbachev's rise to power, as well as with the approach to economic reform in East Germany and Bulgaria during most of the communist period (see Bornstein, 1973, and 1979), the Set of Measures did not envision any real departure from centralized planning. In contrast to the reforms attempted in Czechoslovakia in the 1960s, those proposed in the early 1980s were in fact designed to make central planning more efficient rather than to reduce its scope or role in economic decision-making. Thus, the Set of Measures reaffirmed the usefulness of binding plans in setting production targets and guiding economic development and in fact called for a strengthening of the influence of the central plan to counter what were termed poor management practices. This aspect of the proposed measures contrasted sharply with the move toward decentralization taking place in the Hungarian economy during this period.

In contrast to the efforts of the Poles, Hungarians, and Yugoslavs to improve economic performance by borrowing capital and importing technologies from the West, Czech and Slovak leaders planned to modernize their industrial plant and increase productivity by relying on domestic resources and Czechoslovakia's existing trading patterns. In line with this approach, the Set of Measures, as well as the economic plans adopted during this period, envisioned continued reliance on economic ties with the Soviet Union and other CMEA countries, with very little increase in economic links to the West (see 'Usnesení předsednictva ÚV KSČ a vlády ČSSR;' 'Soubor opatření,' 1980; and 'Hlávní směri dalšího rozvíjění,' 1984).

The utility of this approach in resolving Czechoslovakia's long-standing economic problems was questionable from the start. Certain of the proposed policies, including those designed to link reward to performance and penalize producers of substandard goods, were unpopular with workers and ran the risk of increasing popular discontent with the regime. Reports from the enterprise level indicate that efforts to implement the new measures met a good deal of resistance from managers and workers alike ('Problems in Economic Transition,' 1980, pp. 5-8).

There were also more fundamental problems. Experts within and outside of Czechoslovakia soon questioned the value of the whole approach, based as it was on continued reliance on centralized planning without any introduction of market elements. In the event, the usefulness of the proposed changes was not really tested, as most of the measures were never fully implemented. The leadership attempted to salvage the program in 1983 and 1984 by amending it, but the resistance of bureaucrats, managers, and workers eventually caused it to be quietly abandoned (see Myant, 1989, pp. 209-13; and Wolchik, 1985b).

Debates in the economic weeklies in the early and mid-1980s about the value of the Set of Measures and issues such as the role of profit and world market prices in socialist economies indicate that there was considerable division of opinion among economic experts in Czechoslovakia during this period (see Kusin, 1982a, pp. 1-4; and Wolchik, 1987, pp. 41-2). The fact that these debates were published suggests that there were also divisions within the party leadership on these issues.

Challenges to the approach to economic change embodied in the Set of Measures intensified in Czechoslovakia in the late 1980s. Emboldened by economic debates and changes in the Soviet Union, Czech and Slovak economists began discussing the need to rethink previous positions concerning the role of the market, private property, and incentives, as well as the role of the central planning authorities. These changes in economic thinking, which were initially evident primarily in the specialized, limited-circulation economics journals, and the impact of discussions of economic reform in the Soviet Union eventually were reflected in part in the program of economic reform adopted by the party leadership in January 1987 (see Myant, 1989, pp. 246-53; and Wolchik, 1987, pp. 41-2). They also informed the work of the increasing number of economists who came to believe in the necessity for radical economic changes, including a number of the experts centered in the Institute for Forecasting of the Academy of Sciences after 1987 who have come to determine Czechoslovakia's economic policies since the fall of the communist system.

Přestavba: perestroika in Czechoslovakia

In response to continued economic crisis at home and Gorbachev's policies in the Soviet Union, the Czechoslovak Communist Party leadership adopted a new plan for economic reform in January 1987. Foreshadowed by former Premier L'ubomir Štrougal's speech at the 16th Congress of the Communist Party in March 1986, the principles adopted were very general. The timetable for adoption of concrete laws to implement the reforms was also a very gradual one. However, the reform measures differed in important ways from previous efforts at economic change under Husák. The changes proposed in 1987 departed from the principles of centralization and self-sufficiency that marked economic discussions in Czechoslovakia from 1969 and were similar in many respects to the economic reforms outlined in the 1960s (see 'Usnesení ústředního výboru,' 1987, p. 3; and 'Konkretizace zásad,' 1987, pp. 1-16). In contrast to the period from 1969 to 1987, officials as well as economists once again began talking openly of the need for fundamental change in the organization and functioning of the Czechoslovak economy after 1987.

The package of reforms adopted in January 1987 envisioned marked decentralization of economic decision-making and the gradual introduction of certain market elements into the economy. The role of central economic authorities was to decrease, while the authority and discretion of enterprises increased. Measures to increase the influence of profit on economic decision-making and make the remuneration of both workers and managers more dependent on performance, and to ensure greater worker input in the selection of managers were also included. The program also called for price reform and change in the organization of foreign trade.

By late 1989, it was not clear how successful the new approach would be. The general nature of the measures adopted in 1987 and the gradual timetable for their implementation raised the possibility that this program would meet the same fate as the Set of Measures adopted in 1981. Opportunities for sabotage through inaction and misimplementation were increased by the evident divisions within the leadership of the Communist Party concerning the speed and kind of economic reform desired.

Certain aspects of the 1987 program were implemented prior to the end of communist rule. First introduced only in a few industries that produced largely for export, the economic experiment, which freed enterprises from most centrally determined indicators, was extended to enterprises in other sectors of the economy, including agriculture, in 1989. The new principles of operation were originally planned to be introduced throughout the economy by 1991. In 1988, this date was moved up to January 1, 1990 ('Akční program urýchleného rozvoje,' 1988, p. 1). The adoption, although delayed, of a new law on state enterprises and the reductions in staff that took place at central ministries were signs that certain aspects of the reform were being implemented. A number of changes were also made in the agricultural sector. Changes in the law on agricultural enterprises enacted in 1988, for example, created possibilities for individuals to use agricultural land unsuited for large-scale production, along with, in certain instances, buildings and plots formerly used by the cooperatives (kd, 1988, p. 4).

However, in many areas the results of the new provisions were not those envisioned. The continued concentration of workers in very large enterprises despite the intent of the law on state enterprises illustrates these problems. As of July 1988, 1,546 state enterprises had been created in Czechoslovakia, with an average of 2,200 workers (Matejka, 1989, p. 10). Data compiled by the Institute for Forecasting of the Academy of Sciences indicate that the average number of employees of Czechoslovak industrial enterprises was 3,500, compared to 50 in the United States, 200 in Hungary, and 750 in the Soviet Union in the late 1980s (Valach, 1989, p. 13). Similarly, although it appears that provisions designed to create workers' councils and increase the role of workers in decision-making at the enterprise level were carried out in certain enterprises, it is not clear how widely these policies were implemented. Implementation of the new regulations governing wages, which in theory were to increase differentiation and make higher rewards contingent on superior performance, was also problematic (Menke, 1989, pp. 33-7). In this area as in others, centrally enacted policies were subject to being modified substantially as they were implemented by lower-level administrators and professionals.

But the real problem with the reform effort of the late 1980s in the eyes of many of its critics lay not so much in the bureaucratic and other obstacles to its implementation as in its original conceptualization. According to this view, the 1987 program of change was unlikely to succeed because it was not radical enough. Criticism in this regard focused on two related but distinct issues. First, critics charged that the 1987 program did not go far enough in rejecting administrative control of the economy and introducing elements of the market. The plan to reform prices administratively rather than allowing them to be set by the market is a case in point. The ability of the State Planning Commission to intervene in economic decision-making in certain key areas was another illustration of this limitation. The continued rejection of any significant degree of privatization in agriculture, services, or small-scale production was still another problematic element (see Dyba, 1989b; and Dyba and Kouba, 1989. See also Myant, 1989, pp. 250-2). The potentially negative impact of these aspects of the approach to economic change was compounded by a second major limitation, the fact that in contrast to the economic reforms put forward in the 1960s, the reform effort in the late 1980s was not coupled with significant political reform. Despite the lip-service given by Czech and Slovak leaders to the need to link *přestavba* to democratization, the economic reform enacted in 1987 did not address political impediments to economic efficiency. Nor did its provisions challenge the dominance of the Communist Party in the economic sphere.

In the somewhat more open intellectual climate of the late 1980s, increasing criticism of the 1987 reforms was voiced by economic experts such as Valtr Komárek and others at the Institute for Forecasting of the Czechoslovak Academy of Sciences (see Komárek, 1989). Arguing that the approach adopted in 1987 did not go far enough in rejecting centralized control of the economy, several economists argued that the economy should be reorganized on market principles and that Czechoslovakia should be reintegrated into the world economy (see Dyba, 1989b). As in the 1960s, a number of economists called for political changes as well (see Komárek, 1988a, 1988b, 1989; Turek, 1988; and Dyba, 1989b. See also es, 1989; and 'Notes on the Margin', 1989). Debate concerning the 1987 approach to reform also continued in the economics journals (see Martin, 1989b; Myant, 1989, pp. 254-6). Despite the increasing challenges raised by economists and other specialists, these arguments did not gain the support of Jakeš or other leaders of the Communist Party, who continued to be committed to implementing the reform as originally conceived.

Valtr Komárek's elevation to the position of Deputy Prime Minister and the presence in the cabinet of the non-communist coalition government formed in December 1989 of two other members of the Institute for Forecasting, Václav Klaus and Vladimír Dlouhý, were clear signals that many of the criticisms voiced by radical economists in the last half of the 1980s would be reflected in the economic policies of the non-communist government formed in 1989. There was a good deal of consensus among the experts concerning the need to move to a market economy and integrate Czechoslovakia's economy more closely into the world economy. However, aside from agreement on these general principles, divergent views emerged within the expert community concerning how best to improve Czechoslovakia's economic performance.

In the early months of 1990, efforts to reform Czechoslovakia's economy were hampered by divisions among President Havel's top economic advisors concerning the nature and pace of economic change needed in Czechoslovakia. The main poles in the debate were reflected in the positions of Valtr Komárek and Václav Klaus. The divergences between Komárek and Klaus were particularly evident in their views concerning the speed with which to abandon the centralized system. Economic experts also held differing opinions about how and to what extent to protect the population from the temporary, but significant decline in economic performance and the standard of living expected to accompany the move to the market. Despite these divisions, the Federal Assembly enacted a series of laws that legalized private ownership and changed policies regarding state enterprises, land use, joint ventures, foreign exchange, joint stock companies, and foreign trade in April 1990 ('Právní předpisy pro podníkatele,' 1990; 'Zákon o státním podníku,' 1990; 'Zákon o akciových společnostéch,' 1990; 'Novela Hospodářského zákoníku,' 1990; and 'Zákon o bytovém, 1990). The devaluations of the crown in 1990 were further steps toward economic reform.

As noted in chapter 1, the proposal for economic reform approved by the Federal Assembly in early September 1990 reaffirmed the basic tenets of the plan for rapid economic change adopted in principle prior to the June election. Its key elements, which have begun to be implemented, include privatization of the economy by use of domestic and foreign capital, liberalization of prices and reduction of government subsidies to enterprises, and internal convertibility of the crown. Other important measures of the government program include the continuation of restrictive monetary policies and a reorientation of the country's foreign economic relations ('Scenář pro ekonomické a sociální reformy, 1990' and ha, st, 1990).

Despite continued controversy and fears of the hardships likely to accompany reform in late 1990, the government remains committed to the more rapid variant of economic reform articulated by Klaus and adopted in September 1990. This reform plan is based on a continuation of the stabilization policies evident in the government's macroeconomic policies, which involve measures, such as a restrictive monetary policy, designed to prevent a rapid rise in inflation and growth in foreign debt. Czechoslovak officials argue that anti-inflationary measures are central to this aspect of the program and will take precedence over other goals, such as full employment and growth. Tax reform is also scheduled (Martin, 1990b, pp. 5-8; 'Scenář pro ekonomické a socialní reformy,' 1990; js, 1990, p. 1; 'Kto najviac doplatí?', 1990, p. 5; Klaus, 1990a, pp. 1, 4; Jiři Pehe, 1991a, pp. 11-16; and Móricová, 1990a, p. 3). Although the reform program is currently being implemented, it remains controversial (see Špáni, 1990, pp. 4-5; and Šulc, 1990, pp. 8-9).

Privatization of industrial enterprises and agricultural property is another key element of the reform. The legalization of private property and other laws passed in April 1990 were followed by the development of a small private sector in 1990. A new law on taxes passed in September 1990 lowered tax rates and removed some of the impediments to the development of private businesses by putting private business on an equal basis with state enterprises (ČTK, September 18, 1990). However, private entrepreneurs still face many obstacles. By June 30, there were 163,952 private entrepreneurs in the country ('Kdy nabere hospodářství dech?' 1990, pp. 1,4; and 'Semiannual Czech Statistical Report,' 1990, pp. 36-8). By November 1990, 500,000 private businesses, many of them very small, had been established (os, 1990, p. 8). The largest portion of the 94,353 private entrepreneurs registered by the end of October 1990 in Slovakia (almost one thousand), had been established in agriculture. Seven hundred and forty-seven were in industry and 362 in domestic trade (min, 1990, p. 2). Of the estimated 20 percent of all private entrepreneurs registered with the state statistical office by late November 1990, one-quarter were in repairs and other construction work. Most were independent artisans, with a maximum of a five co-workers. Retail trade and public catering accounted for approximately 10 percent of entrepreneurs, and services were third, particularly in non-traditional areas, such as consulting, etc., as well as hairdressing and photo shops (os, 1990, p. 8).

As part of 'small' privatization, approximately 130,000 state-owned small businesses are to be auctioned to private individuals. In the first round of auctions, only Czechoslovak citizens may participate; foreigners are to be allowed to bid on unsold properties in a second round. 'Large' privatization, which will encompass some 3,000 large enterprises, is to be governed by a transformation law passed in January 1991 and is scheduled to take several years to complete ('Malá privatizace začne,' 1990, p. 4; and ha jop, 1990a, pp. 1, 4). The privatization of agricultural concerns is to be governed by a separate law adopted in January 1991 (see 'zn,' 1991, p. 1; and 'Návrh zákona,' 1991, p. 7).

Determination of which enterprises should be privatized rests in the hands of newly established privatization commissions at the district level. The first auction of small-scale enterprises was held in Prague on January 26 and 27, 1990. Individuals were required to have a balance of not less than 10,000 crowns, or 10 percent of the price to participate (see 'Aukční seznamy dostupné,' 1991, p. 1). Auctions in Slovakia began in early March 1991 (Móricová, 1990b, p. 4). Despite strikes in September and October by retail trade employees, employees of enterprises were not given preferential access at the auctions (vl, hm *et al.*, 1990). However, employees of enterprises being auctioned may pay for their purchases over a five-year period, while others must make payment within 30 days (ČTK, September 27, 1990. See also Móricová, 1990b, p. 1).

Large-scale privatization is also planned. Officials regard this process, which will depend in part on the creation of favorable conditions for foreign investors, as a long-term effort that will take place over a period of several years. Privatization plans for each sale are to be drawn up and must be approved by the federal and republican governments or their finance ministries (Martin, 1991, p. 10). As in plans for small privatization, the role that foreign investors are to play in this process is not clear. The dominant view at present is that, in contrast to the situation in Poland and Hungary, Czechoslovakia will rely primarily on domestic sources to privatize large industries. In order to prevent too great a role for foreign investment, a controversial 'voucher' system, advocated by Finance Minister Václav Klaus will by used as one of the mechanisms for the privatization of large-scale enterprises. Thus, coupons that may later be redeemed for shares or sold will be distributed to the population at nominal cost. According to this plan, from 40 to 80 percent of the capital of enterprises will be sold as non-transferable securities to Czechoslovak citizens, which may then be exchanged for shares or traded on a stock market which is expected to be established in 1991 (Martin, 1991, p. 10; and Dolečková, 1990, p. 2). Such a scheme is also designed to allow broader groups of people to participate in privatization and thus avoid the experiences of Hungary and Poland, in which many former officials of the communist apparatus have been able to use the assets they amassed while in office to buy newly privatized enterprises. Although economic officials continue to be divided concerning how large a role foreign investors should play in privatization, certain enterprises will be made available for purchase by foreign companies (see Klaus, 1990b, p. 1; Skalková and Denemark, 1990, pp. 1,4; and Haba, 1990, p. 5). A number of economic officials and experts continue to argue that a larger role for foreign investment is needed if privatization is to succeed (see Hvížďala, 1990a, pp. 1,2).

Provisions have also been made to create a private sector in agriculture. Changes in the laws on land use and agricultural cooperatives enacted in the spring of 1990 created the possibility of returning land that was marginal to agricultural production or not being used by cooperatives to its previous owners or private owners, but most land remained under the control of the agricultural cooperatives. The public appears to be divided concerning ownership of agricultural land. Most of those interviewed by the Institute for Public Opinion Research in October 1990 concerning the disposition of agricultural land (38 percent), wanted to see such land returned to those who owned it prior to collectivization. However, an additional 36 percent felt that such land should be owned by agricultural cooperatives, and 19 percent thought that cooperatives should be allowed to sell or lease the land ('Veřejné mínění o půdě,' 1991). Interest in private farming appears to be relatively low in Czechoslovakia, although many individuals have applied for the return of small parcels of land, many on the size of private plots (see zn, 1990, pp. 1,3). New regulations under consideration in late February 1991 also included provisions for returning land to those who lost it because of criminal trials and collectivization. Land banks and offices are to administer this process (Chalupová, 1990, p. 7. See also Burda, 1990, p.7). A further change in the law concerning agricultural cooperatives is expected to provide a mechanism for converting existing cooperatives into genuinely voluntary cooperatives of land owners (see Šindelařová, 1991, p. 8).

Price liberalization and the introduction of internal convertibility for the crown are other key parts of the reform program. As of January 1, 1991 some 85 percent of prices were freed. A maximum price has been determined for the remaining 15 percent which include staple foods, certain raw materials, and fuels (see Kříž, 1990a, pp. 1,3; 'Ptáčník,' 1990, pp. 1,2; do, 1990b, p. 1; zc, 1990a; ma, 1990, p. 1; 'Ceny v novém roce,' 1990, pp. 1,4; 'Návrh cenového stropu,' 1990, p. 1; and Pehe, 1991a, p. 12).

These policies have been coupled with measures designed to

introduce internal convertibility of the crown. Thus, all registered enterprises can buy foreign currency at the official rate of exchange, a step that facilitates the repatriation of profits of foreign partners in joint ventures. Individuals may purchase foreign currency equivalent to 5,000 crowns. In an effort to curb speculation in hard currency, the government announced in early February 1991 that all limitations on the purchase of hard currency would be abolished in 1991 (Colitt, 1991, p. 4; ms, 1990a, pp. 1,16; and jop, 1990, pp. 1,8).

Although most of the top economic policy-makers in Czechoslovakia continue to be supportive of further implementation of the reform now under way, controversy continues over a number of issues. Projections concerning the impact of the reform also differ substantially.

Forecasts by the Federal Ministry of Finance envision a continued decline in many areas in 1991 as further economic reforms are inaugurated. Thus, officials anticipate that economic growth will decrease by 5 percent. Prices are expected to rise by 30 percent, most in the early part of 1991. Slovak economic officials have estimated that price liberalization will result in increases of from 35 to 40 percent in the first half of 1991 (Móricová, 1991, p. 3). Projections concerning likely levels of unemployment in the near future differ considerably. Václav Klaus in early February 1991 indicated that he felt the government's estimate made to the IMF of 4 to 6 percent was still accurate. However, other top economic officials, including Minister of the Economy Vladimír Dlouhý and Prime Minister Čalfa, anticipate that unemployment will reach between 8 and 10 percent (Colitt, 1991, p. 4; and Chorherr, 1990, p. 18). Officials from the Federal Statistical Office predicted in early December 1990 that unemployment would rise to between 2.4 and 3.4 percent of the labor force (190 to 350,000 people) by the end of 1991 and to between 3.6 to 7.5 percent by 1995 (John, 1990, pp. 1-2). Estimates of inflation, which reached 30 percent in January 1991, also vary and range from 30 to 50 percent (see Colitt, 1991, p.4; Chorherr, 1990, p. 18; and vc, 1990, p. 2).

The risks of the reform currently under way, then, include a sizeable increase in hardship in day-to-day life for much of the population. One official estimated that up to 60 percent of the population could need some type of social welfare assistance (aa, 1991, p. 2). Although several steps have been taken, such as new pension regulations, to minimize the impact of the reforms on the people in the lowest income sector of society, all social groups will be affected to one extent or another (see Gabrielová, 1991b, p. 4). Changes in the workplace, ranging from increased unemployment to new demands for better performance and adaptation to new expectations, will also exact a psychological cost, particularly when coupled with the impact of the rapid changes in other areas of life and uncertainty concerning the future that the events since 1990 have engendered.

Popular attitudes toward economic reform reflect these sentiments. As noted in chapter 2, 1990 saw a major increase in the numbers of Czechs and Slovaks who favored the creation of a market economy as well as an increase in those who wanted to see a rapid move to recreate the market, even at the cost of a decline in the standard of living. A survey conducted by the Institute for Public Opinion Research in November 1990 found that 32 percent of the population was considering entering the private sector. Forty-one percent of these wanted to do so as their main form of employment and the remaining 10 percent as a supplement ('Soukromé podnikání,' 1990, p. 1). However, a survey conducted by the Institute for Public Opinion Research in January 1991 just prior to the first auctions of small businesses found that relatively few citizens planned to participate. Only 1 percent of respondents, for example, were very eager to become entrepreneurs, and another 3 percent were considering the possibility ('O podnikání není zájem?' 1991, p. 3).

Survey research conducted in 1990 indicated that many citizens were ambivalent about the reform. Many also do not support the measures taken to begin economic reform in 1990 and 1991. As one would anticipate, the price increases that occurred in 1990 were unpopular with large groups of citizens. One-half of a group surveyed by the Institute for Public Opinion Research in September 1990, for example, thought that the price increases that had occurred prior to that time were incorrect; 23 percent were opposed to price liberalization (ČTK, October 2, 1990). Many Czechs and Slovaks also expressed fears about the impact of the reforms on their living standards and employment prior to their adoption.

A November 1990 study conducted by the Association for Independent Social Analysis provides a more comprehensive view of citizen attitudes toward reform and expectations of the future. According to the results of this survey, the population falls into several groups that differ in terms of their attitudes toward the reforms. The authors label the first, which comprises 16 percent of the population, 'theoretically liberal.' Individuals in this category are happy with the political developments of 1990 and prepared to support the reform, but primarily theoretically. The second group, which the authors labelled 'entrepreneurs,' encompassed 7 percent of the population. This group views the establishment of private property as a guarantee of the country's future and is willing actively to support the economic reform personally by becoming entrepreneurs, not only of small businesses but also of larger industrial enterprises. Members of this group, who are generally better educated and in the middle and younger age categories, are the core of support for the economic reform effort. The largest group, however, 24 percent, are opponents of the reform. Individuals in this category are characterized by extremely high fears of the future and by their low levels of support of not only economic reform but also of current political developments. At the same time, many are willing to defend their views (including an unwillingness to change employment or begin to work hard), by strikes if necessary. An additional 10 percent of the population were termed 'handicapped businessmen' by the authors of the study. Although they have much in common with opponents of the reform, these individuals planned to improve their situation by entering into private business. In contrast to those the authors labelled entrepreneurs, however, they have very few of the qualifications needed to succeed at such endeavors. The authors anticipate that many of this group will not succeed in the private sphere and will thus join the opponents of the reforms. Respondents who fell into the category labelled 'employees,' which encompasses 12 percent of the population, also have high levels of fears concerning the results of the reform. However, they are not firmly against it. Although they do not express an interest in private entrepreneurship, they are willing to consider working harder and improving

Table 4.2   Popular reactions to reforms (%)

Reactions to the reforms	CSFR	CR	SR
Theoretically liberal	16	19	12
Entrepreneurs	7	8	6
Opponents of change	24	21	31
Handicapped entrepreneurs	10	9	12
Employees	12	11	12
Entrepreneurial pensioners	8	8	7
Passive individuals	23	24	20

Source: Boguszak and Mejkal, 1990, p. 10.

their qualifications in order to obtain top positions at work. Thus, their reactions to the economic reform are likely to depend on the degree to which they are successful. Individuals in Group Six, 'entrepreneurial pensioners,' which included 8 percent of the population are supportive of the reform and private enterprise. Although many feel they do not have the objective means to become entrepreneurs, primarily because of their age, they will continue to support the economic and political changes. The final group, which the authors termed 'passive individuals,' encompasses 23 percent of the population. These individuals are primarily passive and display a defensive orientation toward the future. The authors of the study note that this passivity, which extends to their lack of willingness to strike, despite fears of the future, makes individuals in this category ideal candidates to be manipulated by other political forces (Boguszak and Mejkal, 1990, p. 10. See also Boguszak, Gabal, and Rak, 1990d).

Thus, large groups of citizens either actively oppose the economic changes under way or are uncommitted. The authors conclude that the positions of four of these groups are fixed and are unlikely to change, irrespective of the course of the reform. The positions of the other groups, however, point in opposite directions. To satisfy the more fearful, passive groups in the population, a strong social safety net must be maintained. To satisfy the others, which include the entrepreneurial and employee categories, as well as the 'handicapped entrepreneurs,' a more active policy of stimulating individual initiative and removing barriers to its exercise must be undertaken (Boguszak and Mejkal, 1990, p. 10. See also Boguszak, Gabal, and Rak, 1990c, p. 4. See Table 4.2).

As noted in chapter 3, fear of the consequences of economic reform is also coupled in many cases with what many experts consider to be overly optimistic views concerning the duration of the economic downturn and unrealistic expectations of what the state can continue to provide citizens. The government has attempted to address some of these concerns by increasing the amount of the budget devoted to social welfare and taking other steps, such as increasing pensions, to cushion the impact of the reforms on the elderly and lowest-income groups of the population. However, as the results of the reform to date on retail prices and employment indicate, the decline in the standard of living that will accompany the economic reform in all likelihood will increase popular dissatisfaction with the government and may provide support for political groups that want to follow other policies.

External economic relations

Trade

Czechoslovakia's levels of foreign trade lagged considerably behind those of non-communist countries at comparable levels of development during the communist period. The country's trade was also highly concentrated in the communist world. There have been important changes in both the regulations governing foreign trade and the distribution of the country's trade since November 1989. Changes in government regulations reflect the effort to reduce state control and monopolies and the introduction of market elements evident throughout the economy. Changes in the distribution of trade have resulted in part from the desire of the country's new leaders to expand economic links to the West and integrate the country more closely into the world economy. They also reflect the disruption of Czechoslovakia's economic relations with the Soviet Union and its other formerly communist neighbors and the impact of economic and political developments elsewhere in the world. At the same time, developments in this as in other areas continue to be shaped by the patterns established during communist rule.

During much of the communist period, the right to engage in foreign trade was held only by government foreign trading companies. Steps were taken to liberalize trade somewhat in the last years of communist rule, but most of the country's trade was channelled through central institutions. This situation began to change in 1990, when 45 joint-stock companies controlled 85 percent of foreign trade. An additional 2,700 private businessmen and enterprises accounted for 15 percent (ČTK, January 18, 1991b). A further relaxation of restrictions on foreign trade occurred in February 1991. All concerns that are registered as enterprises that are not dealing with a product of strategic importance now have the right to engage in foreign trade.

The geographic concentration of Czechoslovakia's trade also changed substantially in 1990 and early 1991. However, the country's trade also reflects patterns established under communist rule. The reorientation of Czechoslovakia's trading patterns that occurred after 1948 had a lasting impact on the country's foreign economic relations. In the immediate post-Second World War period, traditional links to West European countries that had been disrupted by the Second World War were re-established to some degree. Thus, in 1948, advanced Western countries accounted for approximately 45 percent of Czechoslovakia's total trade. The countries that would eventually join the Council for Mutual Economic Assistance (CMEA), which had accounted for a relatively small proportion of the total trade of the interwar Czechoslovak state (approximately 16 percent), accounted for approximately 40 percent in that year.

As the communist system was consolidated in Czechoslovakia, the country's trade with the developed West decreased dramatically. Czechoslovakia was integrated into the system of economic relationships that developed among the CMEA countries, and the country's foreign trade followed suit. By 1953, trade with the developed Western countries had declined to under 15 percent of total trade, with a corresponding increase in the extent of economic transactions with the other CMEA countries. Trade declined most steeply with the United States, which in 1937 was the country's second most important trading partner (Busek and Spulber, 1957, p. 361). This decrease, which was particularly sharp after 1950, in part reflected the adoption of export licensing systems in the United States and other Western countries after 1948 (Busek and Spulber, 1957, p. 361). However, it also reflected the overall shift in focus from West to East in Czechoslovakia's economic as well as political life. Trade also declined substantially with the country's other main Western trading partners, including Sweden, Austria, West Germany, Switzerland, and the United Kingdom.

Trade with other CMEA countries increased to approximately 55 percent of Czechoslovakia's total trade turnover by 1950 and to 78 percent by 1953 (Busek and Spulber, 1957, p. 356). The Soviet Union became and remained Czechoslovakia's primary trading partner. In 1947, 7 percent of Czechoslovakia's imports came from the Soviet Union, and 5 percent of the country's exports went to the Soviet Union. By 1950, the Soviet Union accounted for 29.7 percent of Czechoslovakia's imports and 25 percent of its exports. In 1953, 38 percent of the country's imports came from the Soviet Union and 27.4 percent of its exports went to the Soviet Union (Busek and Spulber, 1957, p. 356).

Change in the regional focus of Czechoslovakia's trading patterns was accompanied by marked shifts in the composition of its trade. Heavy industrial products replaced light industrial goods, including textiles and glass, as the country's main exports. This orientation was particularly noticeable in the vastly expanded trade with the Soviet Union and other communist countries. Czechoslovak exports of metallurgical products, equipment and machinery were coupled with imports of raw materials needed for industry and grains (Busek and Spulber, 1957, pp. 355–6).

Czechoslovakia's trade with the socialist world, which accounted for 71.3 percent of the country's imports and 72.3 percent of its exports in 1960, continued to increase during the 1960s. The concentration of the country's trade with socialist partners remained at approximately the same level in the 1970s. In 1970, 69.4 percent of imports and 70.6 percent of exports involved these countries. Seventy percent of imports in 1975 and 70.2 in 1980, and 71.6

260 *Czechoslovakia in transition*

Table 4.3   Czechoslovakia's trade by region (%)

Exports	1974	1984	1987
CMEA	62.0	70.8	75.4
of this: USSR	29.7	43.4	43.3
Other socialist countries	5.4	5.2	4.1
Developed capitalist countries	24.0	16.2	15.6
Third World	8.6	7.8	5.1

Imports	1974	1984	1987
CMEA	60.1	76.3	75.4
of this: USSR	27.3	46.8	43.6
Other socialist countries	4.9	4.3	3.5
Developed capitalist countries	27.7	15.1	17.6
Third World	7.3	4.3	3.5

Sources: Stránský, 1985, pp. 8–9; Federální statistický úřad, 1988, p. 452.

percent of exports in 1975 and 69.6 percent of exports in 1980 involved the socialist world (Teichová, 1988, p. 146).

This pattern persisted throughout the rest of the communist period. In contrast to the expansion of trade with the West that occurred in Hungary and Poland in the 1970s, and in Yugoslavia and Romania earlier, the proportion of Czechoslovakia's trade with the Soviet Union and other CMEA countries increased sharply in the 1970s and 1980s. In 1974 and 1975, trade with the socialist countries accounted for 70 percent of Czechoslovakia's foreign trade. By 1982, this proportion had reached 75.2 percent and by 1985, 78.8 percent. Trade with the other CMEA countries accounted for the vast proportion of this trade (Altmann, 1986, p. 3; and Federální statistický úřad, 1988, p. 5. See Table 4.3).

Trade with CMEA as a whole and with the Soviet Union in particular grew very rapidly in the 1980s. From 1980 to 1986, trade with all CMEA countries grew by approximately 74 percent; trade with the Soviet Union grew 89 percent during the same period (see Table 4.4). Trade with the Soviet Union accounted for 35.7 percent

Table 4.2 USSR's share in Czechoslovakia's trade (%)

USSR share in Czechoslovakia's total exports						
1948	1960	1970	1980	1984	1986	1987
16.0	34.1	32.5	34.4	42.0	43.5	43.3

USSR share in Czechoslovakia's total imports						
1948	1960	1970	1980	1984	1986	1987
16.8	34.1	32.3	36.0	46.8	45.3	43.6

Source: from Císař, 1985, pp. 16-17; Federální statistický úřad, 1988, p. 5.

of the country's exports and 36.0 percent of its imports in 1980 (Wallace and Clarke, 1986, p. 113). By 1985 trade with the Soviet Union accounted for 44.8 percent of Czechoslovakia's total foreign trade turnover.

These patterns had begun to change prior to the end of communist rule. The 1986-90 economic plan called for a modest reorientation of Czechoslovakia's trading patterns. Thus, trade with socialist countries during the 1986-90 plan was scheduled to increase only half as rapidly as in the previous five years (Altmann, 1986, p. 4). Czechoslovak exports to socialist countries were to increase by 22 to 25 percent by 1990 and exports to non-socialist trading partners by 15 percent (ČTK, June 25, 1986). In addition to the 15 percent increase in exports to capitalist countries, the 1986-90 economic plan also called for a modest increase in imports from the developed Western countries. The Soviet Union's share of Czechoslovakia's total trade decreased for the first time in 1988, when total trade between the two countries dropped by approximately 800 million roubles. Trade with the Soviet Union accounted for approximately 42 percent of total trade turnover in that year. Trade with the Soviet Union was scheduled to decrease by another 7 percent in 1989 (Lacko, 1989; Bautzová, 1989. See also 'Struktura obratu', 1990).

Plans to limit the growth of Soviet-Czechoslovak trade in the late communist period were accompanied by discussion of the need to change the structure of this trade. In the past, machinery and equipment comprised a large share of total Czechoslovak exports to the Soviet Union; consumer goods, including clothing, woven materials, and other textiles accounted for the second largest group of products exported. Czechoslovak imports from the Soviet Union consisted largely of energy supplies and raw materials (Císař, 1985, p. 3). In 1984, for example, machinery and installations accounted for approximately 68 percent of Czechoslovakia's exports to the Soviet Union; raw materials and fuels comprised 78 percent of imports from the Soviet Union. The 1986-90 plan projected continued reliance on the Soviet Union in the area of energy and raw materials. Imports from the Soviet Union were scheduled to provide 100 percent of Czechoslovakia's crude oil, natural gas, ammonia and methanol; 85 percent of its iron ore; 79 percent of its aluminum; 66 percent of its cotton; 62 percent of its copper; and 58 percent of its manganese during this period, for example (Černý, 1986, p. 17). However, in contrast to previous plans, Czechoslovak deliveries of machinery were to be more limited than in the past, and the share of non-engineering products, including consumer goods and food products, was scheduled to increase.

Czechoslovakia's trade with the Soviet Union and other communist or formerly communist countries dropped sharply in 1989 and 1990 but still remains high. In 1989, the share of the communist countries in Czechoslovakia's overall foreign trade turnover was 61.6 percent. Czechoslovak-Soviet trade also declined, but the Soviet Union still accounted for 30 percent of all trade in 1989 and 25 percent in 1990, and remains Czechoslovakia's most important trading partner ('Report of the Federal Statistical Office,' 1990, p. 29; and ČTK, January 18, 1991b). The Soviet Union provided over half of Czechoslovakia's energy supplies and raw materials in 1989 and remained an important market for Czechoslovak goods. Eighty-two percent of Czechoslovakia's exports of machinery and equipment went to the communist countries in 1989, 43 percent to the USSR alone ('Report of the Federal Statistical Office,' 1990, p. 29). Although it is clearly the intention of Czechoslovakia's leaders to increase the country's trade with developed capitalist countries, Czechoslovakia thus remains dependent at present on trade with the Soviet Union and other formerly communist countries (see 'Czechoslovak Foreign Trade Performance,' 1990, for an overview of the first half of 1990).

In June 1990, problems arose with several aspects of these relationships. The most important of these were the dislocations caused by the unilateral Soviet decision to decrease deliveries of oil to Czechoslovakia by 30 percent in the summer of 1990 and the decision reached in 1990 to shift to hard currency trading within CMEA as of January 1991.

Czech and Slovak officials dealt with the crisis caused by the decrease in oil deliveries in 1990 by increasing the price of gasoline 50 percent in July 1990, which cut consumption by 20 percent, and another 33 percent in October for purchases beyond a 25-liter limit (vej, 1990), and by taking other measures to reduce demand. They also reduced petrochemical production to 65 percent of its capacities in late 1990 and began negotiations to obtain oil directly from several Soviet republics in exchange for industrial products and consumer goods (see Truncová, 1990a, p. 1, 1990b, p. 1; and Prague Television Service, October 4, 1990. See also Husák, 1990, pp. 1,3). Negotiations to import close to US$1 billion of oil from Iraq to offset the US$800 million trade surplus with Iraq were halted by Czechoslovakia's support of the international coalition against Saddam Hussein in late 1990 and early 1991.

According to the terms of an agreement negotiated with the Soviet government in December 1990, the Soviet Union agreed to supply Czechoslovakia with 7.5 million tons of oil in 1991, an amount substantially less than the 13 million tons the Soviets tentatively agreed to supply in October. Payment is to be partly in equipment for the Soviet oil industry and partly in hard currency. The agreement also allows the purchase of additional oil from the Soviet republics, although Czechoslovak officials do not anticipate that this source will be very helpful in the near future (Petránek, 1990; and jd, 1991, pp. 1,4). Instead, they are turning to other sources of oil. In 1990, for example, officials made use of the developing steps toward cooperation within the Pentagonal group to secure agreements to use the Adria pipeline to obtain Arab crude oil and agreed with the Austrian government to construct a pipeline between an Austrian refinery near Vienna and the Slovak refinery in Bratislava (Tománek, 1990b, pp. 1,2). They also opened negotiations with a number of developing countries, including Iran, Mexico, Venezuela, and Algeria to provide oil in the future (Truncová, 1990a and b). The financial difficulties of using hard currency to pay for substitutes for Soviet oil were compounded by technical problems, including the fact that new pipelines, which will take two to three years to complete, will be necessary to transport oil from the south and west of the country.

Difficulties also arose in other aspects of Czechoslovak-Soviet economic relations. Some of the most serious of these arose from the fact that the Soviet Union was also Czechoslovakia's largest debtor in late 1990. According to the terms of an agreement reached in December 1990, the two countries agreed to value the amount due at the rate of one rouble for one dollar, rather than the 1.3 dollars per rouble rate proposed by the Czechoslovak government (jd, 1991, pp. 1,4). Of the US$2.8 billion due Czechoslovakia, US$2 billion consists of a bridging credit made by the communist government, whose terms the new Czechoslovak government has been forced to agree to honor ('Maximum možného,' 1990).

Difficulties also arose as the result of economic and political changes in other CMEA states. The impact of broader economic and political changes within the region was reflected in a dramatic drop in mutual trade among members of CMEA. Total turnover among CMEA members in 1990 declined to 40 to 50 percent of the previous year's level when expressed in convertible currencies (Filkus, 1990, pp. 30-1). In the case of Czechoslovakia, problems were particularly acute in 1990 with respect to the GDR, which was Czechoslovakia's second largest trading partner. In anticipation of unification, the GDR did not honor contracts for exports of Czechoslovak goods worth 175 million roubles by July 1990. East German enterprises canceled a further 230 million roubles of orders for Czechoslovak goods and did not draw on a large sum of financial resources for tourism, against which Czechoslovakia had already obtained German products (ČTK, July 19, 1990). Exports to Poland also decreased substantially, resulting in a sizeable trade deficit with that country (see 'Czechoslovak Foreign Trade,' 1990, pp. 1-3). In anticipation of the impending shift to hard currency trading with countries that were members of CMEA and the end of state monopolies of foreign trade, Czechoslovakia's leaders began negotiating new bilateral trade agreements with many of its trading partners, including Bulgaria and Poland (Prague Television Service, December 16, 1990; and sc, 1990, p. 5). However, economic experts predict a further decline in trade with these countries in the near future. In 1991, exports to the Soviet Union are expected to be only 28 percent and imports 40 percent of those in 1990 (Prague Domestic Service, January 4, 1991).

The January 1991 decision to dissolve the Council for Mutual Economic Assistance in February 1991 and replace it with a new organization for international economic cooperation was postponed at the Soviet Union's insistence. When it occurs this step will formalize the changing nature of the economic relationships among the members of CMEA. Czech and Slovak officials describe the new organization that is to replace CMEA, the Organization for International Economic Cooperation, whose seat will be in Moscow, as necessary at present to help resolve the many questions that arise from the large number of economic ties that still exist between the former members of CMEA. In contrast to the agreements used in CMEA, trade among members is to be voluntary and on a market basis (Štětina, 1991, pp. 1,2; Špak, 1991, p. 10; Sobell, 1990a, pp. 40-3, and 1990b, pp. 39-42). Controversy continues over the inclusion of the non-European members of CMEA (Mongolia, Vietnam, and Cuba) in the new organization. Despite the general shift to hard-currency-based trading as of January 1, 1991, Czech officials concluded an agreement in March 1991 with officials of the RSFSR to continue certain forms of trade on an exchange basis.

There have also been changes in Czechoslovakia's trade with the developing world, which was heavily influenced by political factors until late in the communist period. As Table 4.3 illustrates, trade with the developing countries accounted for a relatively small proportion of Czechoslovakia's trade in recent years. However, Czechoslovakia's ties to the developing world predate the communist period. In the 1920s and 1930s, numerous Czech corporations, including Bat'a Shoe Manufacturing, Škoda, and others, established factories or retail outlets in Asia, Latin America, and Africa. These ties were resumed at the close of the Second World War and expanded in the early years of communist rule (Pechota, 1981, pp. 78-9). Trade with the developing world decreased in the early 1950s, as Czechoslovakia's trade became increasingly concentrated in the socialist bloc. In the wake of decolonialization, Czechoslovakia's economic relations with the new countries came to be determined by ideological as well as economic considerations, and Czechoslovakia soon became one of the communist world's largest suppliers of economic aid to the Third World. It also became one of the region's main arms suppliers (see Pechota, 1981, pp. 84-5).

Czechoslovakia continued to play a large role in the developing world until the late 1960s, when internal economic difficulties and the increased role of the Soviet Union and the GDR in providing aid were reflected in a decrease in Czechoslovakia's activities in this area (see Pechota, 1981, pp. 79-92). In 1970, the developing countries accounted for 9 percent of Czechoslovakia's exports and 6.1 percent of its imports. Trade and other economic links to this region continued to increase during the 1970s and 1980s, but more slowly than the overall increase in trade or trade with other parts of the world. Trade with the developing world as a share of total trade thus decreased from 8.6 percent in 1965 to 6.6 percent in 1978 (Pechota, 1981, p. 93). Exports to this part of the world remained fairly stable throughout the 1970s and 1980s but imports decreased to 5.6 percent of Czechoslovakia's total in 1975 and 4.1 percent by 1983 (Wallace and Clarke, 1986, p. 113). Although trade increased by 14.3 percent between 1980 and 1986 ('The Territorial Structure,' 1988, p.38), it still accounted for a relatively small portion of Czechoslovakia's total trade (5.6 percent in 1986) ('The Territorial Structure,' p. 38). Czechoslovakia's main partners in the developing world in the late 1980s were Libya, Egypt, Syria, India, Iraq, Iran, Argentina, Afghanistan, Mexico, and Brazil. Although ideological considerations continued to play some role in Czechoslovakia's economic links with developing countries, economic concerns, including the need to find

other sources of energy and raw materials, were of greater importance in determining these relations after the late 1970s. The impact
of these considerations was evident, among other things, in the
resumption of Czechoslovakia's delivery of arms to the developing
countries in the late 1970s and the increase of these deliveries to
several oil-rich Middle Eastern and African countries (see Kaminski
and Janes, 1988). The debt of developing countries to Czechoslovakia also continued to grow. By mid-1990, for example,
Czechoslovakia had more than a billion dollars' worth of outstanding debts with the Arab world alone (Borovička, 1990, p. 1).

There were also important changes in Czechoslovakia's trade with
the developing world after November 1989. Trade with developing
countries accounted for 7.3 percent of total trade turnover in 1989.
Much of this trade continued to consist of the exchange of
machinery and equipment (58.5 percent of Czechoslovakia's exports
to this region) for raw materials (68.5 percent of imports) and the
granting of long-term credits to finance machinery imports ('Report
of the Federal Statistical Office,' 1990, p. 25). The Gulf crisis of
1990 and 1991 disrupted Czechoslovakia's trade with Iraq, as well
as plans to obtain oil from that country.

As noted earlier in this chapter, problems with the oil supply as
the result of this crisis and the shortfalls in Soviet deliveries led to
renewed efforts to expand ties with a number of oil-rich developing
countries (see no and st, 1990, p. 1). Iran agreed to provide from
three to five million tons of oil a year as well as natural gas to
Czechoslovakia in return for Czechoslovak exports of plants in the
power, metallurgical, textile, leather, ceramic, and other industries,
as well as consumer products (ČTK, December 20, 1990). An
agreement was also reached with Algeria, Czechoslovakia's third
largest trading partner in Africa, to supply natural gas to
Czechoslovakia, as well as payment of Czechoslovakia's outstanding
claims in Algeria at the rate of approximately US$30 million per
year until 2004 in return for engineering products, agricultural
machinery, and aviation technology (Truncová, 1990c, p. 7). Czech
and Slovak officials expressed eagerness to see ties between Czech
and Slovak businesses and Saudi Arabia, as well as Saudi investment
in Czechoslovakia, increase in 1990 ('Dveře jsou otevřený,' 1990,

pp. 1,2). Trade agreements have been signed with North Korea, South Korea, and several other Asian countries, as well as with India and Mongolia (ČTK, November 1, 1990a, and 1990b).

The political and economic changes that occurred in Czechoslovakia and its trade with other CMEA countries in 1989 and 1990 were also reflected in changes in economic relations with developed capitalist countries. In an effort to reintegrate Czechoslovakia into the world economy, Czech and Slovak leaders have attempted to increase trade and other economic ties to West European countries and the United States. They have also rejoined world economic organizations and looked to these groups for assistance to support the economic transformation now under way.

Efforts to increase trade with industrialized capitalist countries began from a lower starting point in Czechoslovakia than in many other formerly communist countries. Trade with the industrialized West remained at modest levels through the 1960s and decreased further in the 1970s and 1980s. Thus, these countries accounted for 22.4 percent of Czechoslovakia's total trade turnover in 1970 and 1975 but only 16 percent in 1984 (Altmann, 1986, p. 3; see also Stránský, 1985, pp. 32-3). A reflection in part of political factors, including the Communist Party leadership's determination not to follow the Polish road in terms of greater integration into the world market, the low level of Czechoslovakia's trade with advanced industrial countries during the communist period also resulted from the inability of Czechoslovak exports to be competitive on the world market, particularly in the areas of machinery and equipment (Altmann, 1986, pp. 5-7). The largest portion of Czechoslovakia's trade with developed Western countries during the communist period took place with West Germany, Austria, Switzerland, Great Britain, Italy, France, the Netherlands, Belgium, Sweden, and Finland, which in 1986 accounted for approximately 85 percent of Czechoslovakia's trade with such countries ('The Territorial Structure,' 1988, p. 38).

Economic experts and officials began discussing the need for a modest increase in such economic contacts in the 1980s. Trade with developed capitalist countries increased somewhat more during the period from 1980 to 1986 (6.6 percent) than in the decade between

1974 and 1984 ('The Territorial Structure', 1988). The 1985 and 1986 plans called for modest increases in Western imports (Altmann, 1986, p. 33), which had been reduced substantially in the 1970s in order to conserve scarce supplies of foreign currency and as a result of the inability of Czech and Slovak goods to compete in Western markets. Imports of machinery and equipment for capital investment, which were scheduled to increase by 45 percent from socialist countries, were to double from capitalist countries during this period ('TV Interview of State Planning Official,' 1986, p. D4).

Czechoslovak officials have been particularly interested in expanding trade links with the EC countries, which comprise the bulk of the country's trading partners among the developed Western countries. This interest pre-dated the end of the communist era. The agreement signed between the EC and Czechoslovakia in January 1989 which exempted half of Czechoslovak industrial products previously subject to quotas was seen as the basis for further expansion in Czechoslovak trade with EC countries ('Základ pro širší', 1989, pp. 11-12; but see Alster, 1988, p. 1, and 1989, p. 16, for criticisms of EC 'interference' in the internal affairs of CMEA countries by promises to support the positive changes occurring in certain communist states). In 1989, EC countries accounted for 18 percent of Czechoslovakia's total trade turnover ('Report of the Federal Statistical Office,' 1990, p. 29).

Trade with Western countries increased rapidly after November 1989. By 1990, the FRG was second among Czechoslovakia's trading partners and accounted for 19.2 percent of total trade, after the USSR, which accounted for 25 percent (ČTK, January 18, 1991b). In the first half of 1990, 39 percent of Czechoslovakia's imports and 40 percent of exports involved developed Western countries ('Czechoslovak Foreign Trade,' 1990, p. 5). Exports to developed countries continued to consist largely of raw materials, semi-finished goods, consumer goods, and food. Machinery and equipment were the dominant imports ('Report of the Federal Statistical Office,' 1990, p. 25). Imports of consumer goods also increased ('Czechoslovak Foreign Trade,' 1990, pp. 3,5).

As in other areas of foreign policy (see chapter 5), it is Europe that is at the center of Czechoslovakia's efforts to rejoin the world economic community. Czech and Slovak officials clearly want to see Czechoslovakia become a member of the European Community. A new trade and cooperation agreement with the EC was signed in early May 1990. Czechoslovakia's application to become an associate member of the EC was under discussion in early 1991. Czech and Slovak officials anticipate that it will be approved by the first half of 1991 and go into effect in January 1992 ('Vykročení do Evropy,' 1991, p. 2; and Jírů, 1991, p. 7). The EC is providing substantial aid to Czechoslovakia through the PHARE-2 program designed to provide aid to help with economic restructuring in formerly communist countries (approximately $120 million), including approximately 30 million ECU, or $40 million for environmental projects (ČTK, January 18, 1991b). EC officials also provided a guarantee for the European Investment Bank's measure to cover 400 million ECUs of investments in Czechoslovakia in the early 1990s (Janík, 1990, p. 1). The European Bank for Reconstruction and Development founded in 1989 will support the economic transformation now under way. Czechoslovakia also signed numerous trade and investment treaties with West European countries in 1990.

Czech and Slovak officials also took steps in 1990 to increase economic relations with the United States. The easing of COCOM restrictions on exports to Czechoslovakia and other formerly communist countries in 1990, and the granting of MFN status to Czechoslovakia as part of a trade agreement with the United States approved in November 1990 are expected to result in a tripling of US-Czechoslovak trade in the near future. This trade, which decreased from $55.2 million in 1988 to $53.7 million in 1989, increased slightly in 1990, but still comprises a very small proportion (less than 1 percent) of Czechoslovakia's total trade (see Kramer, 1990). The Overseas Private Investment Corporation has been authorized to support US businesses in Czechoslovakia. A Czechoslovak-American Enterprise Fund has also been established to encourage US investment in and trade with Czechoslovakia (see 'Czechoslovakia on the Road to Reform,' 1991, for an overview of US programs).

The effort to reintegrate Czechoslovakia into the world economy was also evident in Czechoslovakia's relationships with international economic organizations and in changes in the attitudes of its leaders toward borrowing from the West. Czechoslovakia was readmitted to the International Monetary Fund and the World Bank in September 1990. Czech and Slovak leaders counted on loans from these organizations and other Western sources to stabilize the currency in the early stages of the economic reform, help defray the increased price of oil, and help deal with other changes in international economic relations. Czechoslovakia received a $1.78 billion loan in early January 1991, the largest loan to date to any Central or East European country (Farnsworth, 1991; 'Kolík si půjčujeme,' 1991, pp. 1,2). This loan is expected to be followed by additional help from the European Community and the World Bank. The latter organization has indicated that it is willing to lend from $300 to $500 million to Czechoslovakia to aid in privatizing and improve the banking and telecommunications systems (ČTK, September 23, 1990). The World Bank also agreed to make a loan from one-half to two-thirds of $1 million to Czechoslovakia to aid with energy and environmental problems ('Světová banka nám věří,' 1990, p. 1).

Although the economic policies of the Czechoslovak government are designed to minimize the growth of the country's foreign debt, Czechoslovakia's leaders anticipate that further loans from other sources will be needed in the early 1990s. This attitude reflects a major change in Czechoslovakia's policies toward external borrowing. Throughout the 1970s and most of the 1980s, Czechoslovakia's communist leaders were very cautious about borrowing from the West. In contrast to the Polish, Hungarian, Romanian, and Yugoslav turn to the West for capital in the 1970s, Czechoslovakia kept its foreign debt relatively low. The country's leaders also embarked on a program of repayment in the early 1980s that reduced the debt further. Thus, the country's hard currency debt, which amounted to approximately $3.5 billion in 1981, decreased to $3.0 billion in late 1983 and to $2.3 billion in 1985 (Sobell, 1986b, p. 9; *East European Economic Handbook*, 1985, p. 30; and Clapp and Shapiro, 1986).

Political leaders sanctioned a modest increase in borrowing from the West in the mid-1980s. Czechoslovakia borrowed approximately $350 million in 1985 and $500 million in 1986 in order to finance imports of Western machinery and equipment needed to modernize the economy and improve economic performance ('Focus on Financing,' 1986, p. 392). The 1986-90 economic plan called for a further cautious increase in borrowing from the West. Nonetheless, Czechoslovakia's net hard currency debt was still one of the lowest in Central and Eastern Europe at the end of the communist period. In mid-1989, the Finance Minister reaffirmed the leadership's intention to rely on foreign borrowing to a somewhat greater degree than in the early 1980s. Noting that the country's gross bank indebtedness amounted to $3.8 billion at the end of December 1988, a slight increase from its $3.7 billion debt as measured in that way in 1987, he also cited a number of disquieting trends in the area of foreign currency transactions in the recent past. Thus, exports needed to repay the additional loans failed to increase as quickly as planned, and certain of Czechoslovakia's claims against countries with high foreign debts were not repaid as agreed. Overall indebtedness was thus not reduced as much as planned.

Czechoslovakia's hard currency debt totalled $7.1 billion in mid-1990 (st, 1990, pp. 1,8; and c, 1990a, p. 1). Increased borrowing resulted in a gross foreign debt in convertible currency of between $7.5 and $7.9 billion at the end of 1990 (Bratislava Domestic Service, January 28, 1991). Economic officials anticipate that a 40 percent increase in debt from 1990 levels to $11.8 billion will be needed to pay for goods imported from former CMEA countries and increased oil bills in 1991 (Filkus, 1990, p. 31; Kříž and Kotrbá, 1991, p. 1; and Pehe, 1991a, pp. 11-16).

Joint ventures and cooperation agreements

Czechoslovakia's new leaders also took steps to increase opportunities for joint ventures with Western companies and other forms of direct foreign investment in 1990. However, in contrast to the situation in Hungary and Poland, Czech and Slovak leaders continued to be cautious concerning the role that foreign investment is to play in privatization and other aspects of the economic transformation in Czechoslovakia. Important changes in the regulations governing foreign investment were made in 1990, but impediments to such investment still remain. Many of the country's leaders, including Finance Minister Václav Klaus, see substantial foreign investment in Czechoslovakia as something to be encouraged only after the economic transformation has proceeded further. These reservations, which, as chapter 3 discussed, are shared by the population to a large degree, are reflected in the fact that foreigners are not able to purchase land as well as in a number of other restrictions on foreign investment and acquisition. However, other economic officials and experts view a greater role for foreign investment as critical to the success of the economic transformation now under way and argue that it will be impossible to privatize large industry without foreign capital, which should be sought during the first stages of privatization (see Klusoň, 1990, p. 4; 'Czechoslovakia Mounts Campaign,' 1991, pp. A-5-6; and Hvížďala, 1990a, pp. 1,2). Several governmental as well as private bodies have been created to facilitate such investment.

Attitudes toward direct foreign investment by Western firms had begun to change in the late communist period. Permitted since 1986, joint ventures were originally subject to numerous regulations that made them unattractive to most foreign investors. Thus, foreign partners were limited to owning no more than 49 percent of the joint venture, and the director of the enterprise was required to be a Czechoslovak citizen. Joint ventures were also subject to cumbersome regulations governing access to and use of hard currency and the repatriation of profits. Foreign investors also faced a maze of amended regulations governing the establishment and operation of joint enterprises (see *Joint Ventures in Czechoslovakia*, 1986).

The first joint venture agreements with Western countries were signed with Danish and Japanese companies to produce biotechnology equipment and processes, and consumer video equipment in 1986 ('Now Official,' 1986, p. 316). However, given the restrictions noted above, there was little interest on the part of other Western companies in establishing such ventures.

A new law on joint ventures, adopted in November 1988, included provisions designed to increase foreign interest. It also simplified the regulations governing joint enterprises to some extent. The most important changes involved ownership limits and tax regulations. Foreign partners were allowed to own controlling interest in such enterprises. They also received a tax break. Joint ventures were allowed to make the same contributions to social welfare funds as state-owned enterprises, but were allowed to give only 40 percent of profits to the state rather than the 75 percent required of state enterprises. Joint ventures also had the right to manage their own foreign currency accounts free of the regulations that applied to other enterprises (Smrčka, 1989, pp. 19-21). In contrast to the earlier regulations, which limited joint ventures to the sphere of industrial production, the 1988 law permitted such firms in all areas aside from those important to defense and security.

Western interest in establishing joint ventures in Czechoslovakia increased after the passage of the new law, but the number of such ventures that were established prior to the end of the communist period was still modest, particularly in the industrial area. By mid-1989, there were 20 joint ventures with Western firms. Numerous other agreements were in the negotiating stage. Many of the joint ventures with Western companies (11 of 20 in June 1989) were in tourism, an area closed to Western investment prior to the adoption of the November 1988 law. Joint ventures in this area served primarily customers with hard currency. In the industrial sphere, joint enterprises were established to produce and market polyethylene gas piping, metallurgical products, and textiles, as well as to conduct research in the food industry. Industrial joint ventures in particular encountered numerous problems including difficulties with the bureaucracy, consumer dissatisfaction with the quality of products produced, and erratic performance on the part of suppliers. Austrian firms predominated in the tourist sector, but French, British, and, in one instance, Yugoslav firms were also involved. Foreign partners in the industrial sphere came from the Netherlands, Denmark, West Germany, and the United Kingdom ('Number of CSSR JV's Up,' 1989, pp. 204-5).

Czech and Slovak officials also sought to gain greater access to Western technology and industrial production knowledge by expanding other forms of economic cooperation in the late 1980s. Cooperation agreements and licensing arrangements with Western firms increased substantially in the last years of communist rule. Such agreements, which were allowed long before the possibility of direct foreign investment, increased from 100 in 1984 to 120 at the beginning of 1986 and 220 in February 1989 ('The Business Outlook', *Business Eastern Europe*, February 6, 1989, p. 44). The number of Western companies that established offices in Czechoslovakia in order to pursue trade and other economic links more effectively also increased substantially in the late 1980s ('More Companies', 1989, pp. 243-4).

Both Czechoslovak receptivity to foreign investment and Western interest in investing in Czechoslovakia have increased dramatically since 1989. Changes in the regulations governing joint ventures and other steps taken to lay the foundations for the recreation of a market economy in 1990 have resulted in a substantial increase in the numbers of joint ventures and enterprises wholly owned by foreign investors. Companies from the Federal Republic of Germany, which accounted for more than 50 percent of the 1,000 joint ventures that had been established by the end of 1990, predominate (ČTK, January 18, 1991b). Although these numbers represent a major increase from 1989, when there were 60 joint ventures in Czechoslovakia, most of them involve limited amounts of capital. Most joint ventures have been established with private entrepreneurs or cooperatives; in some cases they involve agreements between *émigrés* and their Czech and Slovak relatives. Only 10 percent of the joint ventures established in 1990 were with state enterprises. Approximately 270, primarily in the service sector, were wholly owned by foreigners. Austrian and Swiss firms have also set up numerous joint ventures. Most joint ventures continue to be concentrated in the tourist and service sectors, but several agreements were signed in 1990 in the building industry, metallurgy, telecommunications, transportation, the glass industry, and banking. The Ministry of the Economy of the federal government has identified a number of areas in telecommunications, transportation, the environment, light and food industry, energy, metallurgy, tourism and services as priority areas of investment. Most joint ventures (over three-quarters by mid-July 1990), are in the Czech Lands (Kobýlka, 1990, p. 243).

The establishment of a joint venture between Škoda and Volkswagen in late December 1990 was an exception to the tendency for most joint ventures to be small-scale. Volkswagen's ownership share of 25 percent will rise to 70 percent in the mid-1990s as a result of further capital investment. The Czech government will continue to have influence on the company's production program, employment, and sale of property once Volkswagen controls a majority share of the company (ČTK, December 29, 1990).

Despite the increase in numbers of joint ventures, impediments still remain to significant foreign investment in Czechoslovakia. Thus, the May 1990 law on joint ventures and foreign investment still included a number of features that were objectionable to many Western businessmen, including the requirement to offer to sell 30 percent of hard currency profits to the state bank, the continued need to receive permission from the Ministry of Finance, and lack of clarity regarding repatriation of profits. Investment protection agreements negotiated with numerous West European governments were used to resolve the latter issue prior to January 1991 ('CSFR Reform Legislation,' 1990, pp. 161–2; Mojžíšková, 1990, p. 4; and Kadaně, 1990, p. 4), but other impediments, including lack of clarity concerning ownership rights and uncertainty concerning the impact of likely further changes in laws governing economic activities, continued to pose problems (Dolečková, 1991, p. 1). Despite the impediments that remained, joint ventures were the best route for foreign acquisitions prior to the passage of the large privatization law in early 1991. However, the process was tightly controlled by the requirement that any joint venture that involved a contribution from a state enterprise of more than $17 million be approved by the Federal Assembly. The law governing large-scale privatization, which was passed in 1991, requires managers of state-owned assets to receive approval of a privatization plan by the government prior to disposing of those assets ('Rules in Poland,' 1990, pp. 393–4).

The move to internal convertibility of the crown has been followed by a number of further measures to make foreign investment in Czechoslovakia more attractive to Western companies, including a reversal of the earlier prohibition of foreign currency accounts in Czechoslovak banks and the elimination in early 1991 of most of the restrictions on exports adopted in July 1990 to protect the domestic market ('CSFR License Scheme,' 1990, pp. 227-8). The requirement that joint ventures receive a license from the Finance Ministry was eliminated in April 1991. Other steps to encourage greater foreign investment are likely to be incorporated in the revisions to the law on joint ventures to be adopted in 1991 (Tománek, 1990a, p. 1).

Conclusion

The strategy of economic development adopted after 1948 as well as the organization and orientation of Czechoslovakia's economy resulted in an economic system that did not correspond to the country's potential. The extent of unofficial economic activity as well as official indicators of economic performance during the communist period reflected the impact of the imbalances and chronic problems that also characterized economic performance in other communist countries. They also highlighted the need for significant change in both the organization and the operation of the domestic economy as well as in Czechoslovakia's external economic relations. At various points during the Communist period, efforts to reform the economy were made, but did not succeed in large part due to political reasons.

The dramatic political changes that took place in the last months of 1989 removed many of these impediments to successful economic reform. Numerous laws have been passed to facilitate the recreation of a market economy and a reorientation of the country's external economic relations. The first stages of a fundamental reform program designed to recreate a market economy were introduced in January 1991. The difficulties inherent in such changes were compounded by the oil shock the country experienced due to a decrease in Soviet oil deliveries and the impact of the Persian Gulf crisis as well as the disruption of economic links with other formerly communist states. Despite international assistance and an anticipated increase in foreign investment, Czech and Slovak officials anticipate that economic performance in the near future is likely to decline substantially.

As chapter 5 will discuss in greater detail, conditions for a transfer to a market economy are in some respects more favorable in Czechoslovakia than in other countries in the region. But political leaders and economic officials face many of the same problems that Polish and Hungarian leaders are encountering in their efforts to move to a market economy and reorient their countries' external economic relations. The degree to which political leaders and economic experts are successful in meeting these challenges in turn will have a major impact on the success of the transition to democracy. Economic issues, then, will continue to dominate the political agenda in Czechoslovakia for some time to come.

5 Policies

As discussed in earlier chapters, the end of communist rule has been accompanied by important changes in Czechoslovakia's polity, society, and economy. It has also been reflected in fundamental changes in public policies. This chapter examines these changes in four important public policy areas: environmental policy, educational policy, cultural policy, and foreign policy. These areas were chosen as the focus of this discussion because the results of policy-making in these areas are particularly significant for the process of transformation now under way in Czechoslovakia. However, the process of coming to terms with the legacy of 40 years of communist rule and radically reorienting public policies is a more general one that is occurring in other areas as well. New public policy issues and issues that were not recognized as legitimate subjects of public discussion or debate have also emerged as political issues since late 1989.

Environmental policy

The degradation of the environment that has occurred elsewhere in Central and Eastern Europe during communist rule has also affected Czechoslovakia. Evident in the dying forests of Northern and Western Bohemia, the polluted air and water of much of the country, and the deterioration in the quality of agricultural land, serious environmental problems arose as the result of the developmental strategy used during the communist period (see Albrecht, 1987, pp. 291–302; Zvosec, 1984, pp. 117–20; Černá and Tošovská, 1990, pp. 1281–90; and Zima, 1988a, p. 7. See Ministerstvo pro životních přostedéch, 1990, for a recent analysis by the Czech government's Ministry of the Environment).

Czechoslovak authorities passed an environmental law in 1966 and several other laws dealing with specific aspects of the environment in the 1970s. However, little information concerning the extent of environmental damage was available to the general population during most of the communist period. Environmental problems became legitimate subjects of public discussion only in the late 1970s. At that time, pushed by the costs of environmental damage in terms of economic development and the health of the population, Czech and Slovak leaders permitted somewhat more open discussion by experts of the extent and seriousness of Czechoslovakia's environmental problems. They also produced a long range environmental plan (Albrecht, 1987, pp. 297-9). Natural scientists in particular continued to compile data on environmental problems, but little effective action was taken to deal with these issues (see, for example, Kulčarová and Gomboš, 1989; Kozová and Bedrná, 1989; and Procházková, Krčmery, *et al.*, 1989).

The policies adopted during the communist period in the wake of expert discussions reflected a two-pronged approach to environmental problems. First, Czech and Slovak authorities emphasized conservation and attempted to eliminate easily controlled sources of pollution through modification of individual behavior. Thus, education campaigns were mounted through film and the mass media to convince Czechs and Slovaks to conserve energy, keep their automobiles in top running condition, and take other steps to improve their environment. Such measures had a very limited impact, due to the unavailability of pollution control devices for automobiles, the voluntary nature of the measures advocated, and the fact that they did not address the main sources of pollution.

In addition to these efforts, the leadership also adopted a more comprehensive set of policies designed to influence major industrial polluters. Central bodies responsible for monitoring environmental pollution were created and laws were adopted that required government officials, planners, and industrial managers to take environmental considerations into account in their decision-making. However, these steps had little impact (see 'Ted'už opravdu činy,' 1990). Efforts to deal with the ecological crisis were hampered by both economic and political factors during this period.

As in other communist countries, political leaders in Czechoslovakia were reluctant to use scarce reserves of hard currency to purchase necessary equipment and technologies abroad. Poor economic performance also contributed to neglect of environmental issues, as political leaders and industrial managers sought to increase agricultural and industrial output at all costs. Environmental concerns thus continued to be superseded by economic considerations. At the central level, officials of the environmental councils carried far less weight than those in the economic planning bodies and ministries. The organs of regional and local governments that were charged with assessing the environmental impact of proposed development at the local level were poorly staffed, had few employees with the necessary expertise, and had less authority than regional and local political leaders and economic officials. In many instances, the commissions required by law were not established or staffed (see Wolchik and Curry, 1984; see also Mašek and Strapec, 1989; and Klapáč, 1989).

The impact of these economic hindrances was compounded by political factors that impeded the formulation and implementation of effective environmental protection policies. Given the central control of the media and the restrictions on independent activity by citizens during the communist period, ordinary citizens had very little input into decision-making in this as in other areas. Nonetheless, public concern over issues such as the safety of the food and water supply, and the visible effects of air pollution grew during the 1970s and 1980s. Environmental studies produced by scientists and experts in the official world found their way to activists of Charter 77, for example, (Albrecht, 1987, pp. 290-1), and small groups of concerned citizens formed in both Prague and Bratislava around environmental issues (see analysis by Zima, 1988b, p. 11). As noted in chapter 2, in Slovakia, activists used the officially sanctioned Club of the Guardians of Nature as a basis for organizing around environmental concerns. The publications of this group, many of whose members emerged as leaders in Public Against Violence in 1989, were circulated among broad groups of interested citizens. Similar groups of concerned scientists and interested lay people were active in Prague (see Budaj, *et al.*, 1987; and 'Nahlas o životním prostředí,' 1988, p. 7). Due to the strict controls on political life, a mass movement of independent environmental activists did not emerge during the communist period in Czechoslovakia. However, as public meetings held in Northern Bohemia in the late 1980s to protest widespread industrial pollution illustrated, public concern with environmental issues increased in the last years of communist rule.

With the removal of restrictions on the press and public debate after the fall of communism in Czechoslovakia, new information has been made public concerning the extent and seriousness of the country's environmental problems. Revelations of the environmental damage done by Soviet troops have accompanied their withdrawal from many regions of the country (see la, 1990, p. 2; and Kurková, 1990, p. 3). The press has also informed the public openly for the first time about problems with heavy metals; radioactive and bacterial contamination of the food and water supply; the extent and consequences of air and water pollution throughout the country; the devastation created in the country's forests; and the impact of these problems on human health and longevity (see Merhaut, 1990, p. 6; Bauer, 1990, p. 1; Pospišilová, 1990, pp. 1,2; Chomcová and Kolová, 1990, p. 5; and vt, 1990, p. 5).

There has also been a proliferation of environmental groups. Several green movements and groups were formed in late 1989 and early 1990 to foster environmental awareness and push for solutions to the country's environmental problems. The Green Alternative; the Green Circle, composed of a number of environmental groups that were formed in the late communist period, including Brontosaurus, the Ecology Section of the Czechoslovak Biological Society under the Czechoslovak Academy of Sciences, the Czech and Slovak Union of Nature Conservationists, the Ecological Society, and others; the Trend of the Third Millennium, a Slovak group with roots in the Slovak academy of Sciences; and a Green Party were among the most important of these. In December 1989, several of these organizations united to form the Czechoslovak Green Party, which in turn joined with the Slovak Green Party in February 1990 and ran candidates in the June 1990 elections (see 'Politická platforma strany zelených,' 1990, p. 6). Although public opinion polls indicated that the Green Party had substantial support in early 1990, it received only slightly over 3 percent of the vote in the June 1990 elections and did not seat any deputies in the Federal Assembly. Six deputies from the Green coalition were elected to the Slovak National Council.

However, many of the other political parties also emphasized environmental concerns in their electoral platforms, and environmental issues remain an important topic of political discussion and debate in Czechoslovakia. The Havel government took a number of steps immediately after coming to power to deal with pressing environmental concerns. Czechoslovak participation in the controversial Gabčikovo-Nagymaros dam project is being reevaluated, for example, and a number of mines that produced highly polluting soft coal were closed (see 'Ide zrejme', 1990; Růžička, 1990; Sibl, 1990; and Parížek and Kamenický, 1990). The post-Communist period has also seen the adoption of a more aggressive and comprehensive approach to environmental issues by public authorities. Ministries for the environment were created in both the Czech Lands and Slovakia. Led by experts who were long-term environmental activists, ministry officials prepared draft laws on several aspects of the environment due to go into effect in January 1991. A new, comprehensive law is being prepared on the federal level (Růžičková, 1990, p. 3). Expert commissions have identified the most pressing ecological problems, and plans are currently being drafted to address these issues, despite the anticipated negative impact of the move toward a market economy on the resources available for this effort. A Federal Committee for the Environment was established in June 1990 to coordinate cooperation between state institutions, legislative organs, and other interested groups.

As part of their strategy to clean up Czechoslovakia's environment, Czech and Slovak leaders have turned to Western countries and international organizations for advice and aid. Czech and Slovak officials received pledges of 30 million ECUs to support environmental programs in 1990 ('Společně o životních prostředéch,' 1990, p. 2. See also H. French, 1991). Ministry officials anticipate that they will continue to turn to the country's neighbors for aid in solving problems that also have an adverse impact on surrounding countries (Mežrický, 1990). Czech and Slovak authorities have also established links to official and private environmental agencies and groups in the United States.

Public protests and petitions centered around environmental issues have become frequent occurrences in Czechoslovakia. Numerous groups of citizens have protested against the environmental damage Soviet troops have left behind (see iba, 1990, p. 2). Others have organized around other environmental issues. A group of young Prague mothers, for example, staged a march with baby carriages to protest what they regarded as the poisoning of the food supply in April 1990. Protestors have also organized demonstrations against nuclear power plants and mines (see Lohmeyer, 1990, p. 4; 'Against the Nuclear Plant,' 1990, p. 2).

Despite the general commitment to clean up the country's environment, there are a number of issues that continue to be controversial. One of the most important of these is nuclear power. Officials appear to be divided in their views on the future of nuclear power in Czechoslovakia. At present, nuclear power accounts for 28 percent of the country's energy. Former Czech Minister of the Environment Bedřich Moldan advocated a gradual phasing out of nuclear energy (Moldan, 1990, pp. 74-8; Lohmeyer, 1990, p. 4). Expressing what appears to be a dominant view, Prime Minister Marián Čalfa argued in September 1990, however, that Czechoslovakia would remain dependent on nuclear energy in the future (see Martin, 1990c). Controversy also continues between environmental activists and groups, such as coal miners, who will lose their livelihoods when more stringent controls are implemented (see Šporer, 1990, p. 5). The primary constraints facing policy-makers in this area at present, however, are economic. Public opinion polls indicate that most citizens rank ecological concerns as secondary at present to economic reform (see Boguszak and Rak, 1990a). The budget for 1991 devotes relatively few resources to this area. However, most leaders and citizens recognize the urgency of actions to deal with the environmental crises.

Cultural policy

In culture as in politics, Czechs and Slovaks see themselves as part of Europe. In earlier periods, Prague was a leading center of European civilization and culture, and numerous Czech and Slovak writers, musicians, playwrights, composers, and artists have made major contributions to the development of European culture. During the communist period, political leaders made efforts to reorient Czechoslovakia's culture to the East. They also attempted to subordinate culture to political ends.

The links between cultural and political figures and the influence of political factors on Czech and Slovak culture pre-dated the communist period. Writers and other creative intellectuals were central to the development of the national movements in the Czech Lands and in Slovakia and, as in other countries in the region, cultural leaders played important roles in the country's political life in the interwar republic (see Wellek, 1963d, pp. 17-31, and 1963c, 32-45; Paul, 1981, pp. 149-60; A. French, 1982, pp. 1-22; and A. Novak, 1976).

The connections between politics and culture became much closer after the institution of a communist system in 1948. In the early communist period, political leaders followed the Soviet example and adopted socialist realism as the reigning principle in the cultural world. According to this doctrine, which continued to govern official art and literature throughout the communist period, all artistic and literary endeavors were to serve political purposes. Similarly, all cultural products were to be judged primarily by their value in inculcating the correct political values or inspiring approved political and social behavior.

The subordination of culture to politics had predictable results. Those artists, musicians, and writers who were suspect politically or proved unwilling to subordinate their work to the aims of the Communist Party were removed from their positions and prevented from working. Cultural life came to be dominated by individuals who were willing to be the servants of the party, either because they believed in the cause or because they viewed such actions as necessary to remain in their professions. Actors, writers, and other creative intellectuals were also cut off from links to the rest of Western culture. Under these conditions the vitality of cultural life declined dramatically. Officially sanctioned cultural activities served largely to glorify the new order. David Paul's comment, in his discussion of Central and East European film, that 'it cannot be said that *no* good films were made under the Stalinists' (Paul, 1983,

p. 16), applies to the cultural arena as a whole. But while individual writers and other artists were able to rise above the strictures imposed by the system, much of what was produced by those who were members of the official cultural establishment was of little value. Independent cultural work continued, but it took place largely outside the realm of the official world except in periods of political crisis or liberalization (see Heneka, Janouch, *et al.*, 1985; Busek and Spulber, 1957, pp. 186-97; Paul, 1981, pp. 161-2; A. French, 1982, pp. 22-84; and Trensky, 1978, pp. 1-12).

However, the success of the leadership in harnessing culture to political ends was largely illusory. As in other communist countries, many intellectuals in Czechoslovakia remained alienated from the political system. Many of those who formed part of the official cultural world tried to increase their autonomy and gain greater freedom of action whenever political circumstances allowed. These actions, which were evident in drama and literature in the mid-1950s, became particularly noticeable in the early 1960s, when the relaxation of ideological pressure in the Soviet Union that followed the 22nd Congress of the CPSU led to a similar brief relaxation in Czechoslovakia. In the more open intellectual climate that developed as a result, writers, playwrights, film-makers, and other artists took the lead in challenging the permissible limits on expression and in pressing political leaders to allow greater autonomy in the cultural world. As noted in chapter 2, the Fourth Congress of the Czechoslovak Writers' Union, held in late June, 1967, was one of the pivotal events in the process of theoretical awakening that preceded the political reforms of 1968, and writers were in the forefront of the movement for political change once it came into the open (see Hamšík, 1971; Trensky, 1978, pp. 7-24; Kusin, 1971, pp. 55-8 and pp. 73-5; Skilling, 1976, pp. 563-79; A. French, 1982, pp. 97-342; and Harkins, 1989).

The party's policies toward literature changed somewhat in the period after the death of Stalin. The thaw that followed Khrushchev's denunciation of Stalin in 1956 also had an impact in Czechoslovakia. The demands for change in the party's approach to culture and for the release and rehabilitation of jailed and purged writers articulated at the 1956 Writers' Congress bore little direct fruit. However, poets and other writers whose writings did not conform to the dictates of socialist realism began to appear (see A. French, 1982, pp. 93-160). These trends accelerated in the 1960s when works by Josef Škvorecký, Ivan Klíma, Ladislav Fuks, Ludvík Vaculík, Vladimír Paral, and Bohumil Hrabal were published (see A. French, 1982, pp. 194-243; Harkins, 1980a, and 1980b; Liehm, 1980a, and 1980b; and Kussi, 1980). Innovative literature continued to appear throughout the late 1960s. In 1968, many authors turned their energies to political issues and to political themes (see A. French, 1982, pp. 364-79).

This period saw a good deal of experimentation in both technique and content. Josef Topol, Pavel Kohout, and Milan and Ludvík Kundera were among the first writers to explore unconventional themes. Czech playwrights also used this period to develop a Czech version of the theater of the absurd. Václav Havel was the best known of these dramatists, but others, including Milan Uhde, Alena Vostia, and Ladislav Smoček also contributed to the vitality of the theater of the absurd in Czechoslovakia at this time (see Trensky, 1978, chs. 3-4; 1980a, and 1980b; and A. French, 1982, pp. 182-92).

The resurgence of creative activity in the literary world in the mid-1960s was paralleled by developments in the cinema. As in literature, the burst of creativity that emerged as the New Wave in the film world in the 1960s was preceded by more tentative experimentation during the thaw that followed Stalin's death (Liehm, 1974, pp. 93-4 and 104-5). Although the political authorities under Novotný's leadership tried to stop this experimentation, it re-emerged in the early 1960s, as the political climate changed once again. Encouraged by the fact that certain films that did not conform to the political strictures of the Stalinist period were allowed to be shown, young film directors and cinematographers began to make films that broke out of the socialist-realist mold.

The new trends in the cinema in Czechoslovakia were the subject of great interest in Western Europe and the United States, and certain films, including those by Miloš Forman, Ivan Passer, Jaroslav Papoušek, Věra Chytilová, Jan Němec, Ester Krumbachová, Jiří Menzel, Elmar Klos, Jan Kadár, and Evald Schorm, achieved world acclaim during this period. The effective end of censorship after March 1968 contributed to the resurgence of creativity and experimentation in this as in other areas of culture (see Škvorecký, 1971; Daniel, 1983, pp. 49-65; Paul, 1983, pp. 1-27; Holloway, 1983, pp. 225-35; and Liehm, 1983. See Liehm, 1974, for brief interviews with leading film figures).

At the same time, many members of the cultural bureaucracies, including central governmental officials, those responsible for censorship, leaders of the official artistic unions, and certain prominent cultural figures who owed their prominence more to political factors than talent, resisted the new currents. The late 1960s were thus a time of conflict within the cultural world, as well as in the more directly political world.

The high level of involvement of Czechoslovakia's creative intellectuals in the reform process of 1968 had far-reaching consequences after the reform was ended by force. As in other areas of life, those writers, playwrights, artists, musicians, directors, actors, and dancers who had supported the reform lost their positions, as well as, in most cases, the opportunity to work in their professions (see Heneka, Janouch, *et al.*, 1985; A. French, 1982, pp. 335-64 and 379-97; Kusin, 1978, pp. 102-6 and 210-15). Many of the most talented either left the country voluntarily or were forced into exile. Those who remained were forced to earn their livelihoods by working at menial jobs. Employed as unskilled laborers or dependent on work from abroad, such as translating, they had little time to practice their real professions. Many nonetheless continued to work in their spare time writing 'for the drawer' or for *samizdat* or independent publications or, in the case of artists, playwrights, and actors, participating in illegal shows and performances.

The vitality of the country's culture and the fortitude of its creative intellectuals was reflected in the quality and quantity of the *samizdat*, publications produced in the post-1968 period, as well as in the continued efforts of film-makers, actors and actresses, and graphic artists to preserve some links with each other and with their former professions by private showings and unofficial performances. In the literary field monographs, including works by Václav Havel, Eda Kriseová, Lenka Procházková, and other members of the opposition were published independently in series such as the *Edice petlice*, or Padlocked Editions, or the *Edice expedice*. Although these works, typed in a limited number of copies each, circulated clandestinely among friends, many were widely read and well known beyond opposition circles (see Kusin, 1978, pp. 214-15). These and numerous other writers, including Ludvík Vaculík, Ivan Klíma, Eva Kantůrková, and Milan Šimečka also were involved in other dissident activities (see Heneka, Janouch, *et al.*, 1985; Pastier, 1990, p. 1; and Pehe, 1989b).

The efforts of dissident intellectuals to keep Czech and Slovak culture alive during the period of 'normalization' were supplemented by the activities of the numerous intellectuals who fled or were forced to leave after 1968. Exiled writers, film-makers, artists, and playwrights living in Toronto, Paris, Philadelphia, and other West European and North American cities continued their work in new surroundings. Many, such as Milan Kundera, Joseph Škvorecký, Antonín Liehm, Miloš Forman, Arnošt Lustig, and Jiří Gruša, gained recognition and distinction in their new countries. The publishing houses, newsletters, and periodicals of these and other *émigrés* supplemented and encouraged the efforts of independent intellectuals living in Czechoslovakia. Many *émigrés* also helped to support opposition cultural figures materially, by arranging to have their works published in the West, finding translating work for them, and staging art exhibits and performances in Western Europe and the United States.

Creative intellectuals also formed the core of the dissident community that emerged in Czechoslovakia in the late 1970s. As noted in the discussion of the Charter earlier in this volume, writers and playwrights, such as Václav Havel, Ludvík Vaculík, and Pavel Kohout, were instrumental in forming the Charter and played a key role in its activities during the communist period. Cut off from their publics within the country, many found in the dissident community an alternative society that provided few material rewards but allowed them to remain true to their moral values and forge links with others in similar situations (see Havel, 1990).

Glasnost in the Soviet Union and its grudging adoption by the Czechoslovak leadership after 1987 were reflected in a slight loosening of the limits in the cultural world in Czechoslovakia in the late

1980s. Although the leadership under Husák and Jakeš clearly was not enthusiastic about Gorbachev's policies, it allowed somewhat greater room for unorthodoxy and new developments in art and culture than previously. A number of cultural figures, including Bohumil Hrabal, who had been on the fringes of the official world, were rehabilitated and allowed back into the official unions.

As in the mid-1960s, the attitudes and activities of certain leaders and members of the official writers' and artists' unions began to change in the late 1980s. Literary magazines such as *Kmen* began to carry open debates on issues such as those of the writers whose works were banned after 1968 (Pehe, 1989e and f). They also published articles in 1989 that discussed other previously taboo subjects, such as the need to heal the schism between Czech and Slovak culture produced within the country and abroad. The Czech Writers' Union decided to re-evaluate banned writers in October 1988 and discussed the issue again in March 1989 (Pehe, 1989e). Slovak cultural journals published the obituary of dissident writer Dominik Tatarka and several of his stories (Pehe and Obrman, 1989a). The discussions of the possibility of publishing works by Havel and Kundera by an official of Odeon publishing house (Pehe, 1989b) and the ability of banned artists and writers to travel abroad once travel regulations were changed in early 1987 were further indications of change in this area. In perhaps the most important step prior to November 1989, the Czech Ministry of Culture announced plans to allow the work of approximately 100 banned writers to be returned to libraries. The legalization of an independent cultural organization, the Art Forum, whose leaders included activists of the banned Jazz Section of the Musicians' Union, in July 1989, was a further sign of the changing official attitude (Obrman, 1989). At the same time, the trial and sentencing of an independent publisher in late June 1989 and the attempt to prevent the newly recreated PEN Club, disbanded in 1971, from meeting in August 1989 showed the limits and inconsistency of these new cultural policies (see Pehe, 1989a).

The late 1980s also saw the beginning of a revival in the film and theatrical worlds. Film-makers began dealing with previously forbidden issues and pressed authorities to allow many of the banned films from the 1960s to be shown. Changes in the leadership of the Theater Section of the Artists' Union in 1989 were followed by calls for greater openness in the theater, and several plays of banned or dissident playwrights were staged in the summer and autumn of 1989. Similar signs of change were evident in September and October 1989 in popular music (see Pehe, 1989b).

For most of the post-1968 period, dissident intellectuals worked in isolation from those in official positions. This separation began to break down in the late 1980s. Emboldened by the changes in the Soviet Union and repelled by the repressive tactics the Jakeš leadership used against dissidents and protesters, establishment intellectuals began to speak out in support of jailed dissidents. As noted in chapter 1, when Václav Havel was jailed after his participation in the January 1989 protests commemorating the suicide 20 years earlier of Czech student Jan Palach, numerous leading intellectuals and cultural figures from the official world joined dissidents and figures outside the country in publicly calling for his release. In the months that followed, many prominent cultural figures signed 'A Few Sentences,' a document that called for democratization and freedom of expression in Czechoslovakia.

The previous experiences of members of the dissident community and the developing links between cultural figures in the opposition and in the official world came into play in November 1989. Together with dissident journalists, economists, social scientists, historians, and other intellectuals, opposition playwrights, actors, writers, and musicians provided the leadership for the newly formed Civic Forum and helped to organize the movement for change. They were soon joined by large numbers of actors, writers, artists and other intellectuals from the official cultural world. In addition to their participation in highly visible leadership roles, creative intellectuals also helped to explain the movement's goals to citizens in Prague and elsewhere. Declaring themselves on strike to support the students, members of the Prague Philharmonic Orchestra and all the major theaters led discussion groups in theaters and concert halls in November 1989, for example.

As in the political and economic realms, the end of the Communist Party's monopoly of power had an immediate impact in the cultural world. One of the more visible of these was the sudden reappearance of cultural figures, such as the singer Marta Kubišová, who had been banned from the stage for two decades. Some of Czechoslovakia's most talented actors and actresses, directors, musicians, and graphic artists also reclaimed their places in the mainstream of the nation's cultural life. The return to Czechoslovakia of Jiří Gruša, Pavel Kohout, Pavel Landovský, and others of the many writers and creative intellectuals who had emigrated or been forced to leave the country and the ability of those who left to play an active role in the cultural life of their country from abroad promised to diversify and enrich Czech and Slovak culture.

The end of the Communist Party's dominance of the mass media and all aspects of cultural life also has been reflected in a repluralization of the country's cultural life. As in other areas of life, a variety of new cultural organizations were formed in late 1989 and 1990. These included, among others, a Civic Forum of Czech Writers, a new organization of Czech film and television artists FITES, an independent union of Slovak artists, and an association of theater workers in Slovakia (Likařová, 1990, p. 4; Melichařková, 1990, p. 5; and Gallo, 1990, p. 5). Other organizations which were set up, such as the Slovak Parliament of Culture, are independent groups of representatives of the new cultural unions and associations established to represent the interests of creative intellectuals and serve as lobbying groups to protect culture from the pressure of commercialization ('Deklarácia o ústanovení,' 1990, p. 2).

The end of the Communist Party's monopoly of culture has also been followed by a radical change in the style and content of many of the country's cultural publications. The public, long used to the products of official culture, was offered a feast of previously unavailable material in 1990. Approximately 500 books by banned writers previously available only in *samizdat* versions or abroad were published in 1990. Many journals that were previously *samizdat* publications have become regular publications, including some, such as *Listy*, that were published abroad (see em, 1990, p. 3; see also *Fragment K*). There has also been a proliferation of new, independent publishing houses (Matějů and Šulcová, 1990, p. 4; and 'Sršňová,' 1990, p. 14).

Similar developments occurred in the areas of theater, film, and music. Plays by Václav Havel, including *The Garden Party*, *Audience*, *Asanace*, and *Largo desolato*, were performed in numerous theaters in 1990, as were those of Klíma, Landovský, and Kundera (see da, 1990, p. 5. See Dvořak, 1990, p. 1, for a view emphasizing the costs of such performances to contemporary playwrights). Banned films from the 1960s and other periods have been released as well (Pilátová, 1990a, p. 5; Míšková, 1990, p. 4; and Taussig, 1990, p. 5). Czech and Slovak musicians previously unable to play in public, as well as those who emigrated, now have the opportunity to perform openly in their homeland (see jan, tič, aš, 1990, pp. 1 and 2; and Tomiček, 1990, p. 6). Musicians from abroad who previously were not welcome in Czechoslovakia, including Joan Baez, the Rolling Stones, and Paul Simon, also have given concerts.

Although the changes since November 1989 have allowed a revitalization of Czech and Slovak culture, they have also raised a number of new issues. The first of these is the changed function of culture. During the communist period, culture was to some extent a substitute for politics. Although the range of permissible topics and interpretations dealt with by official artists was limited, readers of dissident literature and those who attended clandestine performances of plays or concerts were engaging in acts that had political as well as cultural meanings. Similarly, audiences and playwrights, filmgoers and film-makers all understood the political subtexts that suffused cultural productions during periods of liberalization. Now that opportunities for open participation in political activities abound, culture does not need to serve as a surrogate for politics to the same extent. In the early post-communist period, the drama of real politics in fact led to a decrease in attendance at theaters and cinemas, as the population paid attention to the political drama being enacted daily and reported in the nightly news. The ebbing of intense public interest in political developments as political developments stabilized has removed this competition to some degree. But, in the pluralistic political system that now exists in Czechoslovakia, the differentiation in purpose between political and cultural activities can be expected to continue (see Pavelka, 1990, pp. 16, 17; and Pehe, 1990d).

The financing of culture has emerged as an important problem in the post-communist period. Although the Ministers of Culture of both the Czech and Slovak Republics reaffirmed the need for some state role in subsidizing culture, it is clear that the state will not subsidize artists to the same extent as under the communist regime (see Kovač, 1990, pp. 1, 2; Lesná, 1990, p. 7; 'Kultura na přetřesu,' 1991, p. 1; Pilátová, 1990b; and Keltošová, 1991, p. 5). Fear of the commercialization of culture, as well as of personal financial hardship, has led many artists and cultural figures to disagree with new taxes on artists and increased charges for studio space for graphic artists.

A number of other problems have also appeared in particular areas of culture. Established publishing houses, for example, have run into difficulties due to the previous practice of publishing vast quantities of books and the new reluctance of booksellers to place large orders. The proliferation of books by highly respected writers, together with the large numbers of books still typically printed by the large publishing houses, have led to greater differentiation in buying patterns among consumers. Changes in the financing of culture have also created problems for previously subsidized publishers. New private publishers appear to be adapting better to the changed market for books, but many of these also face financial difficulties (see Čierná, 1990, p. 17; 'Sršňová,' 1990, p. 14; and orf, 1990, p. 6). The high level of proposed taxes on books also provoked controversy in early 1991.

Educational policy

As in other communist countries, the educational system in Czechoslovakia was highly politicized during the communist period. Political influences were evident in the organization of the educational system; they were also reflected in the content of education throughout the educational system.

Educational opportunities were expanded at all levels. However, as noted in chapter 3, despite the increase in the number of places at existing universities and the creation of new universities and technical schools, Czechoslovakia lagged behind many other

European communist countries in the extent to which its population and labor force had completed secondary and higher education. The structure and content of education changed dramatically once the Communist Party consolidated its power in Czechoslovakia. Religious schools were abolished and all levels of education came under the control of a central ministry. Changes were made in the organization of primary and secondary schooling, as well as at the level of higher education (see Duchacek, 1957, pp. 161-72; Taborsky, 1961, pp. 506-50; and Lihocký, 1989, pp. 13-20, for overviews of these changes).

There were also numerous changes in the content of education. Thus, the emphasis on humanistic education evident in the interwar period gave way to education designed to prepare citizens to contribute to the building of socialism economically and politically. In practice, these goals were reflected in two primary features that characterized the educational system of the country after 1948. First, much greater emphasis was given than in the interwar period to technical education. The establishment of a new political regime also resulted in changes in the curriculum of educational institutions of all types.

Increased emphasis on technical training began soon after the establishment of a communist system. At the level of higher education, resources were diverted from the humanities and social sciences to technical fields, and new schools of technical studies were created apart from the traditional faculties of the universities. The emphasis on technical education was also evident at lower levels of the educational system. In the 1950s and 1960s, apprentice training programs increased dramatically, as did the numbers of secondary technical or trade schools (see Lihocký, 1989; Kalínová, 1979; and Charvát, 1972). Although secondary general schools continued to prepare students for university education, the majority of students who completed compulsory eight-year schools either went into technical secondary programs or into apprentice training programs. Similar trends were evident in higher education (see Čermáková and Režková, 1990; and Matějů, 1990, for critical analyses).

Education was also politicized at all levels. This aspect of educational policy had several consequences. First, it led to the suppression of certain fields of inquiry and the removal of several departments from the universities. Sociology and other so-called 'bourgeois pseudosciences' were among the first subjects to be eliminated, but other areas also suffered from political interference. As in the Soviet Union, even biology fell prey to political distortions for a period. New, politically relevant, subjects were also added to the curriculum. These courses, which ranged from efforts to inculcate positive attitudes toward Lenin on the part of preschoolers to formal courses in historical materialism and the history of socialism at the secondary and university levels, were designed to socialize the country's young people to the approved value system. As in the Soviet Union and other communist countries, compulsory courses devoted to some aspect of Marxism-Leninism accounted for a substantial share of total coursework in all fields of study. As discussed in chapter 3, political considerations also influenced access to the educational system for much of the post-Second World War period.

Both of these aspects of educational policy were questioned during the reform period of the 1960s. Students and faculty alike raised issues related to freedom of academic inquiry and sought to depoliticize the educational system (see Skilling, 1976, pp. 75-82; and Kusin, 1972, pp. 113-22 and 131-42). These efforts were suppressed along with the broader reform of which they were a part after the August 1968 Warsaw Pact invasion. In the 1970s, the universities and institutes of higher education were among the institutions hardest hit by so-called 'normalization.' The purge of the most vocal advocates of reform that followed Husák's ascent to power in April 1969 was followed in the 1970s by the progressive elimination of non-party people from many areas of the universities and institutes. Some educators forced from their positions in Prague and Bratislava were allowed to teach at regional universities. Other scholars and teachers were not permitted to teach, but were allowed to conduct research as members of research institutes. Many, however, were forced to find other occupations (see Kusin, 1978, pp. 95-9; and Skilling, 1981, pp. 127-30).

Given these developments, it is not surprising that students and faculty at Czechoslovakia's universities and other institutions of higher education took the lead in organizing the protests that toppled the communist regime in Czechoslovakia. As discussed more fully in chapter 1, young people from all walks of life joined the massive protests that developed in November 1989. Students, particularly those in Prague, also played a pivotal role in organizing the smaller protests that led up to the November events, as well as in raising public support and organizing the ongoing protests that developed in Prague and other cities at that time (see Singer, 1990). In late 1989 and early 1990, students demanded change in educational policy as well as broader political changes.

The months since November 1989 have seen major changes in many aspects of educational policy and university life. The changes in part reflect the demands of the students. They also reflect the importance the country's new leaders assign to education as a guarantee of democracy in Czechoslovakia. Students gradually returned to classes in the early months of 1990, as educators and lawmakers revised the laws governing education. One of the chief demands articulated by students in November 1989, the elimination of compulsory Marxism-Leninism at all levels, was granted very quickly. Other demands, including the elimination of favoritism based on political grounds or class origin in admission to higher education, the elimination of political criteria in determining who should teach and hold administrative positions in the educational realm, and a greater role for students and faculty in university governance were also met by the new government.

The selection of new rectors to head the country's main universities in early 1990 presaged larger personnel changes, particularly in higher education (see 'Jmenovací dekrety,' 1990, pp. 1,2). As in other areas of life, the elimination of the Communist Party's control over personnel and appointment decisions increased the diversity of opinions represented at all levels of the educational system. Many of the educators who were forced to leave their positions in the late 1960s and early 1970s have returned to the universities. Many departments, particularly in the social sciences, instituted competitions to determine which of their members had sufficient expertise to remain. Czech and Slovak educators and policy-makers are currently debating the merits of a major reorientation of higher education. Discussion centers around the issue of whether to move to a system closer to the model of general undergraduate and specialized graduate training used in American institutions or retain Czechoslovakia's current system of specialized education from the outset of university study.

The new laws on educational institutions adopted in May 1990 introduced a number of additional changes. Mandatory school attendance was reduced from ten to nine years, and changes were made in the organization of the *gymnázia*, which provide general secondary education. Although most *gymnázia* will continue to provide four years of education, several new eight-year *gymnázia* will be established for especially gifted students (see kf, 1990, p. 1; Hejný, 1990, p. 7; and Hoppanová, 1990, p. 2). The May 1990 law also opened the way for the establishment of religious schools (Zábojníková, 1990a, p. 1). In part because of these changes in the law, small rural schools closed in the 1970s, and religious schools are being re-established (see 'Ministr přípomina bibli,' 1990, p. 1; and Zábojníková, 1990a, p. 1).

Changes have also been made in the organization and financing of vocational training programs formerly run by state-owned factories and local national committees. These programs, which enrolled a majority of all students of secondary school age during the communist period, were not popular with apprentices or their parents. They also gave rise to high levels of dissatisfaction among those officials in the factories responsible for their training and work (see chapter 3). Although the government has adopted measures designed to increase incentives for factories to invest funds in these programs and encourage private craftsmen to pay for the training of students in return for their work, interest in apprenticeship programs and vocational schools is expected to continue to drop. Applications to other secondary schools, by way of contrast, have increased greatly (see Yazdgerdi, 1990, pp. 14–15).

As in other areas of life, controversial aspects of education that could not be openly discussed during the communist period have once again become topics of public debate. A May 1990 survey of educators at the elementary and secondary level, for example, documented their views on problems related to the prestige of their occupations, wages, and working conditions (Ondrejkovič, Ondrašíková, Slaný, and Ivaničková, 1990, p. 7). Measures have also been discussed to deal with the current difficulties of graduates of universities and secondary schools who are unable to find employment in their specializations and the anticipated increase in such cases as the economy privatizes (see 'Potiže středoškoláků,' 1990, p. 4. See Macháček and Macela, 1990, for a critical analysis).

The depoliticization of education will allow Czechoslovakia's educational system to return to its earlier traditions. Banned approaches and subjects in fields ranging from language and literature to philosophy have once again become permissible areas of teaching and research. The social sciences and economics are among the areas which have seen the most radical changes in approach and content. Legal studies have also seen a shift in orientation, as the country returns to a rule of law. Thus, in place of required courses in Marxist-Leninist philosophy, students may now choose from courses in philosophy and the social sciences that present a variety of non-Marxist viewpoints. In place of required Russian language classes, many now study English, French, German, or other Western languages.

Research and teaching methods in many other areas are also changing substantially as the result of greater contact with Western colleagues and greater access to Western technology and equipment. Many of Czechoslovakia's universities have signed agreements with Western universities to promote exchanges of students and faculty and establish other forms of cooperation. Several new educational institutions, including a Central European University with Czech and Slovak branches, have also been founded with the participation of West European universities. West European institutions, including the Higher School of Social Sciences in France, for example, have also sent faculty to help redesign the curriculum of higher educational institutes, such as the Higher Schools of Economics in Prague and Bratislava. Numerous exchanges that involve educators from Western Europe and the United States are now under way in other areas, including management education and international relations (see Hala, 1990, p. 3). Students and faculty from West European and North American universities have also participated in the numerous programs to teach English or other Western languages set up since late 1989.

Certain aspects of the educational policies of the last four decades are likely to remain. These include first of all the principle of low-cost education. The emphasis on technical education is also likely to persist, at least in the short run, as the country attempts to deal with its pressing economic problems. Most educational institutions will also remain in state hands, although the number of private schools will continue to increase.

As in other areas, the end of the communist period has also created a number of new problems in the area of education. Student interest in higher education has increased greatly. Approximately 63,000 applicants vied for the 23,000 places available for the 1990-1 school year, for example, a sizeable increase from the 41,000 applicants the previous year (Valík, 1991, p. 9; and Yazdgerdi, 1990, p. 17). Controversy has arisen over the appropriate strategy for dealing with those who were expelled from higher educational institutions or not allowed to study for political reasons. Charter 77, for example, called for a program to give such students priority in university admissions (see 'Odčiňme křivdy na dětech,' 1990). Others, including Radim Palouš, Rector of Charles University, have argued that such students must meet the same criteria as other applicants (Yazdgerdi, 1990, p. 17).

Conflict has also occurred at all levels of education due to scarce resources. As the 1990 school year opened, shortages of textbooks, seats, and teachers beset many lower-level schools (see Schuster, 1990, pp. 1,2). Discussion also continues over teachers' salaries, student stipends, and the problems students are experiencing in finding appropriate employment after finishing their schooling (see Števulová, 1990, p. 3).

Foreign policy

Czechoslovakia's foreign policy from 1948 to 1989 was determined to a great extent by the country's relationship to the Soviet Union. The need for a special relationship with the Soviet Union was recognized by many non-communist politicians at the close of the

Second World War, including Edvard Beneš. However, this view was balanced in the early postwar period by efforts to retain Czechoslovakia's traditional links to the West. Thus, although most political leaders acknowledged the need for ties to the Soviet Union, and many shared popular disillusionment with the West for allowing Hitler to occupy Czechoslovakia after the Munich Agreement in 1938, Czechoslovakia took part in many of the international institutions such as the IMF, the World Bank, and the United Nations, that emerged after the end of the Second World War. Certain Czechoslovak leaders also wanted the country to participate in the Marshall Plan before Stalin's objections foreclosed this possibility. With the assumption of power by the Communist Party after February 1948, Soviet interests came to dominate policy-making in these as in other areas. As a result, Czechoslovakia's foreign policy came to parallel Soviet policy very closely.

In the early communist period, Soviet influence was evident in the decrease in ties to Western countries and the growing importance of diplomatic as well as economic links with the other countries of Central and Eastern Europe. Formal, although minimal, diplomatic relations were maintained with Western countries, but Czechoslovakia's leaders attempted to limit contact with the West as much as possible. As the Stalinist system was consolidated, any contact with the non-communist world became cause for suspicion. The cooling of official relations was accompanied by the creation of barriers to travel and an attempt, through jamming of West European and American radio broadcasts and bans on Western media, to insulate the population from possible contagion by Western, non-communist ideas.

Soviet policies also determined Czechoslovakia's relations to the developing world to a large degree during this time. As noted in chapter 4, Czechoslovakia played an important role in supplying arms to the developing countries and national liberation movements that the Soviets supported in the early communist period. The country also devoted considerable resources to training and aid programs for countries friendly to Soviet interests during this time (see Pechota, 1981, pp. 83-96).

Czechoslovakia's reputation as one of the Soviet Union's most loyal allies in the international realm persisted with only a slight interruption until the end of the Communist period. In the context of the reform period of the late 1960s, Czech and Slovak leaders diverged briefly from Soviet policy in regard to Israel. They also made overtures to West Germany in 1968 that were unwelcome to the Soviets (see J. Valenta, 1979, pp. 85-92; and Skilling, 1976, pp. 626-50). However, these brief experiences in developing a more independent foreign policy line were soon stamped out along with the broader political reform of which they were a part, and Czechoslovakia once again reverted to its former subservient position in international relations.

This pattern was evident throughout the 1970s and 1980s, when other Central and East European states, such as Poland and Hungary, joined Romania and Yugoslavia, which had diverged earlier, in developing stronger trade and other economic links to the West. Czechoslovakia's foreign economic relationships, on the other hand, remained largely confined to the communist world (see chapter 4). Czechoslovakia also continued to have antagonistic relationships with many Western countries, including the United States. Although one of the major impediments to a warming of US-Czechoslovak relations, the gold-claims issue, was removed in 1974, relations remained cool due to US displeasure with Czechoslovakia's human rights violations. The late 1980s saw some movement toward more cordial relations, but this process had not progressed very far prior to the November 1989 revolution.

Czechoslovakia's foreign policy has changed dramatically since the end of the communist period. President Havel and Foreign Minister Jiří Dienstbier have undertaken a number of initiatives to assert Czechoslovakia's independence in international relations and increase the country's visibility abroad. Evident in the large number of state visits by the President, these efforts have been accompanied by major changes in the orientation of the country's foreign policy (see Hoda and Hokeová, 1990, pp. 1,3; and Jírů, 1991, p. 7, for overviews).

Under the direction of Havel and Dienstbier, Czechoslovakia's relationship with the Soviet Union has changed markedly. Asserting the sovereignty and independence of Czechoslovakia, the country's new leaders negotiated the withdrawal of Soviet troops. The first stage of the withdrawal according to the terms of the February 26, 1990 agreement signed in Moscow was completed by May 31, 1990; all Soviet troops are to be withdrawn by the end of 1991 (see 'Dohoda ČSSR a SSSR o odchodu vojsk,' 1990, p. 14). As the basis of a new relationship, the Soviet leadership also condemned the 1968 invasion. Czechoslovakia remained a member of both CMEA and the Warsaw Treaty Organization throughout 1990. However, its representatives led the effort to change and effectively dissolve both.

Soon after taking office, Finance Minister Václav Klaus and other top economic officials argued that CMEA was a 'dead' organization that should eventually be superseded by bilateral business relationships. As discussed in chapter 4, the political and economic changes in the region, including economic and political events in the Soviet Union, steps to reintroduce the market and rejoin Europe within individual countries, and the unification of Germany led to a marked decrease in trade within CMEA in 1990. The decision to move to hard currency for all transactions within CMEA as of January 1991 further decreased the utility of the organization to the Central and East European states. Czech and Slovak officials took the lead in the process that led to the decision made in early 1991 to disband CMEA and replace it with a voluntary organization for international economic cooperation, which will operate on a market basis (see Hardt, 1991; and Špak, 1991, p. 10). As discussed in chapter 4, Czechoslovakia's economic relationships to individual communist countries also changed in 1989 and 1990.

Czechoslovakia continued to be a member of the Warsaw Treaty Organization in 1990. Arguing that unilateral withdrawal would not be useful because it would not contribute to the neutralization of Europe as a whole, President Havel and Foreign Minister Dienstbier took the lead in working to change the structure and function of the organization. Both viewed the WTO as a transitional body that was to serve a different purpose than it had in the past. Czechoslovak proposals, which were also supported by the Hungarian and Polish governments, provided the basis for the decision taken in February 1991 to abolish the military structures of the Warsaw Pact (see Clarke, 1990a, pp. 34-7, and 1990b, pp. 37-9;

Sadykiewicz, 1990, pp. 47-8; and Petránek, 1991). As the result of this decision, which went into effect March 31, 1991, the WTO no longer functions as a military alliance although its political structures remain intact. This step was to a large extent a formal recognition of the changes that have already occurred. Thus, in 1990 effective control of the national armies had been removed from the Joint Command of the Warsaw Treaty Organization and subordinated to national commands, and several countries, including Czechoslovakia, no longer participated in large-scale Pact exercises (Petráček, 1991, p. 2; ČTK, February 25, 1991; and ga, 1991, p. 1). The primary purpose of the Warsaw Treaty Organization has thus come to be that of a temporary negotiating partner to NATO for arms negotiations and troop reduction talks. Although Czech and Slovak officials described the WTO as a way to prevent the Soviet Union from being isolated and draw it into the all-European security process for much of 1990, they have called for the complete dissolution of the Pact by the end of 1991 ('Ministři v Budapešti,' 1990, pp. 1,2).

Despite the progress that the effective break-up of these Soviet-dominated organizations represents there are numerous unresolved issues in Czechoslovakia's relationship with the Soviet Union. In addition to the economic issues discussed in chapter 4, these include the issue of whether Soviet troops will cross Czechoslovakia as they return to the USSR from Germany. Relations with the Soviet Union were also complicated in early 1991 by Czechoslovakia's condemnation of the Soviet crackdown in the Baltic states (see Slezáková and Pokorný, 1991, pp. 1,2; ga, 1991, pp. 1,2; and Adamičková, 1991a, pp. 1,2).

Czechoslovakia's relationships to the United States and other Western democracies have also changed significantly. Supported from its inception by the United States, the new government of Czechoslovakia moved very quickly to normalize its relationship with the United States. President Havel's early visit to the United States symbolized the importance his government attached to reinstituting the traditionally warm ties between Czechoslovakia and the United States that date to the founding of the Czechoslovak state. On the diplomatic front, the new warmth in US-Czechoslovak relations was evident in plans to reopen the US Consulate in Bratislava, a step which years of fruitless negotiations with the communist authorities had failed to achieve. The Havel government also acknowledged the role, long ignored by the communist regime, that American forces played in liberating part of Czechoslovakia at the close of the Second World War (see Janková, 1990, pp. 1,2).

Increased cultural, scientific, and technical links also attest to the new relationship between the two countries, as do changes in the economic ties between the United States and Czechoslovakia. Radio Free Europe and other American media organizations have opened bureaus in Czechoslovakia, and Czechs and Slovaks now have access to American, as well as other Western media (see Soukup, 1990, p. 3). Czechoslovakia's call for more favorable treatment in the economic area was answered by the granting of most-favored nation status and by a trade agreement between Czechoslovakia and the United States in the latter months of 1990, as well as by the pledge of $90 million in aid made in the context of President Bush's visit to Czechoslovakia on the first anniversary of the November 1989 revolution. Numerous other government and private sector initiatives to aid the transformation now under way have also been introduced in the United States (see 'Czechoslovakia on the Road to Reform,' 1991, for a concise summary of these). The changed relationship between the two countries is also evident in the elimination of visa requirements for US citizens who visit Czechoslovakia and in the increase in tourism and travel by Americans ('Místo na Javaj do Prahy,' 1990). It also is reflected in the new attitude toward Americans of Czech and Slovak origin (see Minar, 1990 p. 20; and 'Jesenné predsednictvo SKS bude v Bratislava?' 1990, p. 1).

Important as changes in Czechoslovakia's relationships with the Soviet Union and the United States are, the primary focus of the new government's foreign policy has been Europe. This emphasis was evident in President Havel's earliest state visits, which were to West and East Germany, Poland, and Hungary, as well as in the campaign slogans of Civic Forum and Public Against Violence, which called for Czechoslovakia's return to Europe. Pointing to the traditional links between Czechoslovakia and the other European states, Havel and other Czechoslovak leaders have repeatedly reaffirmed their desire to see Czechoslovakia take its place as an equal, independent actor on the European stage. They have also made clear their desire to see their country included in European institutions (see Havel, 1990; 'Vykročení do Evropy,' 1991). As noted in chapter 4, a new association agreement between Czechoslovakia and the EC that gives Czechoslovakia access to Western markets and envisions further cooperation in the areas of science, technology, and banking was signed on May 7, 1990 ('Program odstránenia obmedzení,' 1990, p. 8), and a new, special type of association agreement that would also involve political consultations is now under consideration. Czechoslovakia has also been admitted to the Council of Europe (see Čech, 1991, pp. 1,8; and Prague Domestic Service, February 21, 1991).

President Havel and Foreign Minister Dienstbier also took the lead in articulating a new vision of Europe without military blocs. Their central proposal in this respect is the call for the CSCE process to become the foundation for a new security system in Europe. Articulated soon after the collapse of the communist regime, the proposal for an upgrading and expansion of the function of the CSCE has become a cornerstone of Czechoslovakia's foreign policy. Arguing that both NATO and the Warsaw Pact eventually must be dissolved, Havel and Dienstbier called for the elaboration of a new security structure, based on the CSCE framework, to replace them. Czech and Slovak leaders proposed the establishment of a permanent CSCE organ to be headquartered in Prague to institutionalize the CSCE process (see Horský, 1990, p. 7; and ČTK, April 6, 1990). As articulated by Dienstbier, the Czechoslovak proposal envisions three stages: the formation of a European security commission; the establishment of an organization of European states, including the United States and Canada; and the creation of a confederated Europe (ČTK, April 6, 1990).

However, the position of Czechoslovakia's leaders in regard to NATO changed somewhat as the result of the negative developments in the Soviet Union in late 1990. Although the expectation that NATO should be dissolved eventually continues to be voiced by many Czechoslovak officials, the government has established regular contacts with NATO (see 'Sen o Evropě,' 1990, pp. 3-4;

Blech and Rottenberg, 1990, p. 4; ČTK, September 6, 1990, and December 6, 1990a). Czechoslovak officials, including Foreign Minister Dienstbier, reiterated in late October 1990 and early February 1991 that Czechoslovakia does not want to join NATO. However, they now argue that NATO should not be dissolved but rather integrated into a comprehensive European security system that would lean on NATO as the best functioning security organization in Europe (Martinek, 1991, p. 6). President Havel, who addressed the North Atlantic Council in Brussels in March 1991, has urged that NATO create a form of 'associate membership' for Central and East European countries (Colitt, 1991, p. 4). NATO's offer of association status was approved by the Czechoslovak Federal Assembly on April 10, 1991 (ČTK, April 10, 1991). Thus, although the emphasis on European institutions and the CSCE as the core of new security arrangements in Europe continues to color Czechoslovak initiatives in this area, NATO has come to be seen as a guarantee of European security at present (ČTK, February 5, 1991).

The Czechoslovak government has also become involved in several new forms of regional cooperation. The first of these, a grouping of Adriatic-Danubian countries, including Yugoslavia, Austria, Italy, Czechoslovakia, and Hungary, termed the Pentagonal Group, or Pentagonale, grew from a proposal articulated at an April 9, 1990 meeting in Bratislava. This proposal called for an effort to elaborate a common position on ten questions including the face of Europe of the future, the efforts of the Central and East European countries to enter Europe, the Soviet Union, China, and the developing world, as well as for cooperation on regional issues (see Parížek, 1990, p. 1). A number of concrete initiatives developed within this framework in late 1990, including creation of a series of working groups. Czechoslovakia is focusing primarily on transport and energy issues within the working groups and will give particular attention to steps to link the Adria pipeline to refineries in Bratislava (ČTK, September 20, 1990). Agreements have also been reached to cooperate in other areas including trade union affairs ('Význam generálnej dohody,' 1990, p. 1) and joint actions to obtain natural gas (Truncová, 1990b, p. 1; and Bym, 1990, pp. 1,3).

In early 1991, a summit between Czechoslovakia, Poland, and Hungary held in Visegrad resulted in an agreement to increase consultations and cooperation between the three countries on a variety of issues. These included coordination of the positions of the three countries concerning the dissolution of the Warsaw Pact and CMEA and the establishment of bilateral treaties to guarantee the security of each state (Petráček, 1991, p. 2; and Jírů, 1991, p. 7).

The country's new leaders have also undertaken numerous diplomatic initiatives to normalize relations with individual European countries. Steps to open the country's borders were among the first acts of the new government, which also attempted to resolve issues that had created problems in relationships with a number of Czechoslovakia's neighbors in the past. President Havel's apology for the expulsion of the Sudeten Germans, which was criticized in many quarters in Czechoslovakia, was an early signal of his willingness to deal with controversial issues in the foreign as well as domestic realm. The new government also began to address issues related to minority groups and nuclear power. Discussions were opened with Hungary, for example, to address the Hungarian government's concern about the treatment of the Hungarian minority in Slovakia. Czech and Slovak officials also met with Hungarian representatives to discuss their dispute about the Gabčíkovo-Nagymaros Dam project. In anticipation of the dissolution of the Warsaw Pact as a military organization, Czechoslovakia's leaders signed military and defense cooperation agreements with Hungary in January 1991 and Poland in February 1991.

Relations with Austria were also given a good deal of attention soon after the change of regime. The opening of the Czechoslovak-Austrian border was followed by extended discussions in 1990 concerning the safety of nuclear power plants near the Austrian border, as well as possible avenues for cooperation on environmental issues and an increase in economic ties between the two countries (see 'Spor o Bohunice,' 1990, pp. 1-2). New issues, such as the influx of Austrian and other Western tourists to buy cheap Czechoslovak goods once the borders were opened and resulting Czechoslovak regulations on exports by tourists in early March 1990, also complicated relations with Austria again in early 1990.

However, leaders on both sides remain committed to maintaining cordial relations (see kc, 1990, p. 6; trg, 1990, pp. 1,2; Koubská, 1990; and Ferko, 1991, p. 5).

Relations with Poland were strained during much of 1990 by the closing of the border to prevent short shopping trips by Poles from disrupting the Czechoslovak market. Negotiations in late October led to an agreement to open the border for weekends and holidays and set a strict limit on the value of gifts citizens may import form each state ('Omezený pohraniční styk,' 1990). The border between the two states was reopened in March 1991 after the signing of an agreement that limits the export of items from Czechoslovakia to 50 crowns and from Poland to 100,00 zlotys ('Briefly From Home,' 1991, p. 2). Travel by Czechoslovak citizens to Poland, as well as to Romania, Bulgaria, and the Soviet Union, has been complicated by the decision of those governments to accept only convertible currency for tourism after January 1991 (Matějovský, 1991, p. 1). However, as noted earlier, leaders of Czechoslovakia and Poland agreed at the Visegrad summit to consult and coordinate their actions *vis-à-vis* CMEA and the Warsaw Pact, as well as in a number of other areas. Czechoslovakia's leaders also supported Poland's desire to be involved in the talks concerning German unification (see Vlček, 1990, p. 2).

Relations with Germany occupy a special position in Czechoslovakia's foreign policy. The new Czechoslovak government was an early supporter of German reunification within the framework of an overall European security system, despite evidence that many Czechs and Slovaks wanted unification to happen more slowly or had other reservations about it. Long Czechoslovakia's primary Western trading partner, West Germany has taken the lead among Western countries in exploring investment opportunities in Czechoslovakia. While Czech and Slovak leaders welcome German interest, they clearly hope to see other Western investment as a counterbalance. Negotiations on a security treaty with Germany also began in early 1991 ('Koncepce bezpečností,' 1991, p. 1).

Czechoslovakia's relationships with other countries have also changed. President Havel made a state visit to Israel, and diplomatic relations were restored in 1990 (see Vodička, 1990, p. 5). The Havel government recognized South Korea and has taken steps to improve diplomatic and economic relations with Japan and China. The new spirit in foreign relations has also been reflected in the country's relationship to the Vatican. As noted in chapter 3, Pope John Paul II visited Czechoslovakia in April 1990. Improved relations between the Vatican and Czechoslovakia have led to the resolution of a number of outstanding issues.

There have also been changes in Czechoslovakia's relationships to developing countries. Czech and Slovak leaders pledged to fulfil the commitments of aid and training that were made by the old regime. However, many of these agreements will not be extended once their terms expire. Trade commitments are also undergoing review, as the effort to change the basis of these relationships from political criteria and ideological considerations to mutual economic benefit begun during the last years of the communist regime continues (see Lavička, 1990, p. 1. See also chapter 4).

As part of the effort to change the country's international role, the Havel leadership suspended Czechoslovakia's sales of Semtex explosive abroad. However, an early pledge to end the export of arms, despite the economic dislocations this step would cause, particularly in Slovakia, has been repudiated (see Fučík, 1991, p. 4). The state monopoly on arms exports was abolished in March 1991. A new law on arms sales is scheduled to be passed in 1991. In the meantime enterprises that engage in such sales must abide by certain restrictions (Kroulik, 1991).

Conclusion

As the preceding discussion has illustrated, the current government is engaged in a far-reaching effort to reorient government policies. The effort to eliminate the distortions caused by 40 years of communist rule has led to radical shifts in all four of the policy areas examined in this chapter. This process, which has its parallels in other areas of policy-making, is still under way and can be expected to take some time to complete. In contrast to the situation during the communist period, when participation in the formulation of public policies was limited to small numbers of political officials and experts, the country's pluralistic political system allows far larger groups of people to have some input into the policy-making process. The orientation of public policies in these and other areas, then, is likely to reflect shifts in public opinion to a greater extent than in the past. In the near future, however, choices in these as well as other policy areas are likely to be constrained by economic considerations.

6 Conclusion

As the preceding chapters illustrate, Czechoslovakia is currently in the midst of a far-reaching process of political, economic, and social transformation. Although the traces of 40 years of communism are still evident, few areas of life have been left untouched by the changes that have occurred since November 1989.

The events of 1989 were sparked in part by outside forces, but they had their roots in the contradictions and distortions produced during four decades of communist rule. The tasks that the country's new leaders and citizens face at present also reflect the impact of policies adopted during the communist period.

In the political realm, the imposition of one-party rule led to a marked simplification of the country's political and associational life and the monopolization of such political processes as political socialization, recruitment, policy-making, and implementation, by the Communist Party. It also led to a break with the country's pre-communist political traditions and the effort to eliminate Czechoslovakia's connections with the rest of European culture. Political life also was characterized by a large gap between political elites and ordinary citizens, as well as by high levels of alienation from politics and lack of interest in public affairs. Although the use of coercion decreased after the death of Stalin, force continued to be used against citizens, including those in the growing dissident movement, who challenged the regime.

Communist rule also had far-reaching consequences for Czechoslovakia's social structure. Nationalization of property, the adoption of ambitious industrialization plans, and collectivization reordered the stratification hierarchy and changed the position of social groups. Changes were most noticeable in the material positions of members of different social classes and ethnic groups. Women's roles also changed in certain respects. Elite efforts were less successful in changing more subjective aspects of social life, such as values and attitudes toward members of other ethnic groups and social classes, relations between men and women in the home, and the attitudes and interests of young people. Similarly, although they were able to influence the extent to which people openly practised their religions, elite efforts did not succeed in persuading all citizens to abandon their religious beliefs.

In the economic sphere, policies adopted during the communist period resulted in a pattern of economic organization and economic policies that differed in fundamental ways not only from Czechoslovakia's previous economic traditions, but also from those of other European countries at comparable levels of development. The focus on heavy industry to the neglect of light industry and the service sector, reorientation of the country's trade to the socialist world, and divorce of the economy from links with non-communist countries produced negative results similar to those brought about in other communist countries. In addition to negative effects on work morale and initiative, labor productivity, and the ability of the country to compete on the world market, the model of development used during the communist period also resulted in a marked degradation of the environment.

The impact of communist rule was also evident in the policy areas examined in chapter 5. Party control of culture and the attempt to link all cultural products to political ends resulted in a stagnation of officially approved culture. During most of the communist period, much of what was vital in the country's cultural life occurred in the unofficial world or abroad. In the area of education, the expansion of educational opportunities led to increased access for many groups of people. However, the population's overall level of education failed to keep up with that of other European countries at comparable levels of development. The politicization of education also led to serious distortions in the content and orientation of education at all levels. Environmental devastation was a further consequence of communist rule, despite efforts in the 1970s and 1980s to take steps to protect the environment. Finally, Czechoslovakia's foreign policy during communist rule reflected the subordination of Czechoslovakia's national interests to those of the Soviet Union.

As the brief summary above illustrates, the legacy of 40 years of communist rule inherited by Czechoslovakia's new leaders is not an enviable one. The preceding chapters have outlined some of the most important changes that have been adopted to deal with these issues as part of the overall effort to recreate democracy, reinstitute a market economy, and reorient the country's foreign policy.

The sudden demise of communist systems in much of Central and Eastern Europe in 1989 and the rapid pace of change in political developments within the region since that time are ample warning, if such be needed, of the folly of attempting to predict the outcome of the complex process of transformation under way in Czechoslovakia at present. Many areas of life continue to be in flux. Given the magnitude of the changes now set in motion and the impact of the communist period in suppressing conflict in many areas, further crises and shifts in political alignments and policies are to be expected. Social unrest is also likely to increase as the result of the economic reform and the continued existence in Czechoslovakia of forces, such as the Communist Party and nationalist parties, that will seek to exploit popular dissatisfaction. Nonetheless, despite these uncertainties, the experiences of the early post-communist period provide some ground for assessing the prospects for continued progress toward the creation of a stable democratic system and a prosperous market economy.

As the preceding chapters indicate, 1990 and early 1991 saw progress toward these goals in a number of areas. In the political realm, the rapid repluralization of political life was followed by free elections of both national and local leaders and a rejuvenation of many government institutions, including the federal and republic legislatures. Despite the fact that few are experienced as legislators or administrators, the country's new leaders have enacted a sizeable body of the basic legislation needed to pave the way for the recreation of a market economy and overcome the distortions of the communist period. The government has also been able to withstand several serious crises related to ethnic issues.

In the economic area, the adoption of a series of laws to legalize private enterprise and the elaboration of an economic reform designed to move quickly to the market in 1990 have been followed by the first steps to implement this plan in 1991. The ability of Czechoslovakia's leaders to win the confidence of international institutions, such as the IMF and World Bank, as well as of the numerous governments and private institutions that have made loans and set up programs to assist with the economic transformation now under way, and the interest foreign companies have displayed in investing in Czechoslovakia are further indications of the progress achieved to date. Czechoslovakia's leaders have also succeeded in defining a new role for the country in international affairs. The agreement concerning the withdrawal of Soviet troops, Czechoslovakia's acceptance as a member of the Council of Europe, the discussions concerning a new, enlarged associational agreement with the EC, and the responsiveness of foreign leaders to Czechoslovakia's initiatives in regard to European security all attest to the progress made in articulating an independent foreign policy.

At the same time, as developments in 1990 and 1991 also illustrate, the effort needed to overcome the legacy of 40 years of communist rule has proved to be much greater than the country's leaders originally anticipated. This legacy is perhaps most evident in the economic arena. But it also pervades most other areas of life and requires change in the way most social, political, and economic institutions operate.

As in the interwar period, when democracy survived in Czechoslovakia while it failed elsewhere in the region in part because the conditions for establishing and maintaining democracy were better in Czechoslovakia than elsewhere, so today the country has many of the prerequisites for sustaining a democratic political system (see Bunce, 1990, for an analysis of the requirements of stable democracy). Its position at the heart of Europe, the deep roots of the country's culture in European values, and the legacy of a democratic system that was ended by outside force rather than internal actors all create a good basis for a successful transition to democracy. The developmental level of the country, and the fact that it has a differentiated social structure and highly educated population are further factors that may contribute to a successful outcome. Nonetheless, there are a number of problems in both the political and economic realm that counterbalance these advantages.

In the political realm, the dominant democratic political culture of the interwar period provides a better starting point for efforts to change the values and attitudes of the population and create citizens who will actively participate in and support democratic institutions than exists in many formerly communist countries. In contrast to the situation in many of these countries, in Czechoslovakia there are relatively few elements of the pre-communist value system and political culture that threaten democracy. As noted earlier in this volume, there were certain anti-democratic elements in political life in Czechoslovakia, as in other countries in the region, during the interwar period, particularly in Slovakia. The strong support in the interwar period for the Communist Party also indicates that although the country's dominant political culture at the time was democratic, there were also non-democratic, authoritarian sub-cultures. A number of the actions of the government immediately after the Second World War, such as the expulsion of the Sudeten Germans and of the Hungarians in Slovakia, also provide grounds for questioning the extent to which democratic values such as tolerance were widespread in the population. However, the dominant political culture and traditions in Czechoslovakia prior to the imposition of communist rule were supportive of democracy. The country's 20 year experience with a functioning democracy, then, at the very least provides a better basis for reconstructing democracy in Czechoslovakia than exists in many other countries in the region. The country has also benefitted in the post-communist period from the clear commitment of President Havel to democratic ideals and his ability to serve as a symbol of the country's hopes.

Nonetheless, there are several unresolved issues here as well. The first of these is how widespread and deep the attachment to democracy and democratic procedures is in the population at present. In Czechoslovakia, as elsewhere in the region, there has been a high degree of consensus on the major outlines of the post-communist order: pluralistic political life and an economic system that will have more elements of the market. However, it is unclear how the population will respond to the need for day-to-day involvement as the political situation normalizes.

As noted in chapter 2, a large sector of the population appears to have become extremely cynical about political affairs, as well as apathetic and alienated from politics. The enthusiastic support for the protests that brought down the communist system, the interest in politics demonstrated by respondents in survey research done in the early part of 1990, and the high levels of voter turnout in the June 1990 elections indicate that this legacy can be overcome. However, certain attitudes towards politics fostered during the communist period may prove more difficult to eradicate. The early post-communist period has also seen the growth of other attitudes, including racial intolerance, and, more importantly, nationalist sentiments, that also have the potential to threaten the stability of the democratic political system. The task of creating a political culture that is based on a view of oneself as a political subject and actor rather than an object of politics will be a lengthy one in Czecho-slovakia as well as elsewhere in the region.

The split in Civic Forum and disarray evident in the ranks of Public Against Violence further illustrate the lack of stability in the political situation at present. At one level, the breaking up of the original coalitions as political opinions become more differentiated may be a positive step on the way to the formation of a stable party system. But, given the continued existence of the Communist Party and the growth of nationalist pressures, the disruptions within the ranks of the forces most committed to continued cooperation across ethnic lines in both the Czech Lands and Slovakia are cause for concern.

The intensification of ethnic conflict in the course of 1990 and early 1991 is also troublesome. Evident in the prolonged negotia-tions over the nature of the federation in 1990 and early 1991, ethnic tensions pervaded discussion of most of the central issues of the day, including economic reform and constitutional revision, and reached a crisis point once again in February and March 1991. Separatist sentiments are pronounced. The upsurge of nationalism in Moravia in early 1991 has its counterpart in Slovakia where the split in the ranks of PAV that former Prime Minister Mečiar provoked in early 1991 weakened the main political force that supported the federa-tion. Although the feared declaration of Slovak independence on the anniversary of the founding of the Slovak state in March 1991 did not materialize, ethnic tensions clearly will continue to complicate the process of consolidating democracy and implementing economic reform. They also pose the most significant threat to political stability in Czechoslovakia at present.

Equally serious problems exist in the economic sphere. As in the political realm, Czechoslovakia has a number of advantages over some of its Central and East European neighbors that may make the transition to a market economy less painful than it will be elsewhere. These include the country's level of development, a skilled labor force, with high levels of technical training, and a strong industrial tradition that pre-dates the communist period. In addition, the country had very low levels of external debt at the end of the communist period, and the standard of living was among the highest in the region.

Although these factors may cushion the impact of measures to reintroduce a market economy, they may pose liabilities as well. Thus, the fact that Czechoslovakia was one of the most developed countries to become communist means that it also has one of the most outdated physical plants, particularly in Bohemia and Moravia. The low foreign debt that resulted from administrative limitations on imports also meant that the country had to forgo the modernization that the import of Western technologies and processes might have provided. Similarly, although the standard of living provides a buffer that many of the other countries in the region do not have at present, it may also foster resistance to economic change.

There are also other impediments to successful economic reform. As in other countries in the region, Czechoslovakia's economy is in need of major structural changes as the result of the pattern of development pursued in the communist period. Lack of domestic capital will hamper plans to privatize the economy, particularly large industrial enterprises. The lagging interest of Western investors evident in the second half of 1990 also suggests that foreign capital, even if sought more aggressively than to date, may prove insufficient to modernize and restructure Czechoslovakia's major industrial enterprises. The heavy dependence of Czechoslovakia's economy on external sources of energy and raw materials and the extent to which the country remains linked to its former communist trading partners are further impediments to successful economic reform.

Changing public attitudes and values will also be complex in the economic sphere. As in the political realm, although the population clearly rejected much of the official value system, certain aspects appear to have been internalized in the economic sphere. For the most part, these do not bode well for the prospects of economic reform and efficiency. Thus, poor worker morale, the lack of individual responsibility in the workplace, and the deep-seated egalitarianism fostered by the experiences of the last 40 years will create barriers to efforts to reform the economy and improve economic performance. As noted in chapter 4, popular attitudes toward reform are divided, and much of the population appears willing to strike if the reforms depress the standard of living too greatly or cut too deeply into social welfare programs. The success of the government's efforts to reform the economy and deal with the impact of changes in the country's external economic relations without producing a prolonged decline in the standard of living in turn will have important implications for the success of the transition to democracy.

Although primary responsibility for dealing with these issues rests in the hands of Czechoslovakia's citizens and leaders, developments in the international realm will also have an important influence. As noted in chapter 1, although the roots of the developments that led to the overthrow of the communist system in 1989 must be sought in political and economic developments within Czechoslovakia, outside factors played an important role in facilitating these changes. In addition to the demonstration effect of events in Hungary, Poland, and the former GDR, Soviet policies toward the region and the general climate of US–Soviet relations were also significant. These factors in turn reflected the changes set in motion within the Soviet Union by Mikhail Gorbachev.

The responses of outside actors and developments in the broader international arena will continue to be important to the success of the transformation in progress in Czechoslovakia. The impact of the Gulf Crisis in 1990 and 1991, and changes in the country's trade relations with the Soviet Union and other members of CMEA since the end of 1989 illustrate the vulnerability of Czechoslovakia to disruptions arising from external sources. Given Czechoslovakia's continued dependence on the Soviet Union for energy supplies, and

320 Czechoslovakia in transition

the presence of Soviet troops in Czechoslovakia and in neighboring
countries, developments in the Soviet Union are particularly critical.
The impact of economic dislocations within the Soviet Union has
already made itself felt in respect to Czechoslovakia's oil supplies. As
the change in the position of Czechoslovakia's leaders concerning
NATO in late 1990 and early 1991 indicates, the turn to more
conservative policies within the Soviet Union is also of obvious
concern to Czechoslovakia's leaders. Most Czech and Slovak
officials discount the possibility that remaining Soviet troops or
other armed forces would be used to interfere directly in Czechoslovakia's internal affairs. However, a continued conservative turn in
the Soviet Union may endanger progress toward the consolidation
of Czechoslovakia's democratic political system and threaten political
stability by encouraging political forces within Czechoslovakia to
exploit the social tensions created by economic change or ethnic
resentments.

Given this possibility, the response of Czechoslovakia's West
European neighbors, the United States, and international organizations is particularly important. The positive response of other
Western countries to the policies of Czechoslovakia's new government has been evident in the high levels of interest and multifaceted
programs that the IMF, World Bank, European Community, West
European and American governments, and many organizations in
the private sector have established to aid the process of transformation. In addition to direct aid, loans, and foreign investment, the
interest of other Western governments is also evident in the technical
assistance Czechoslovakia has received in dealing with problems as
diverse as the environment and rewriting the country's constitution.
Czechoslovakia's acceptance as a member of the Council of Europe
and the new association agreement under negotiation with the European Community reflect the extent to which the country's leaders
have achieved their goal of rejoining Europe. The diplomatic and
political support for the Czechoslovak government's initiatives in
foreign policy provided by the governments of the United States and
many West European countries have also been important. At the
same time, however, the actions of other democratic governments,
although beneficial, may have unanticipated and at times negative

consequences. The concerns about foreign domination, albeit indirect, that are evident in the unwillingness to allow foreign capital too large a role in the privatization process also extend to concern that the country's educational system and culture will be influenced to too great an extent by foreign approaches. Problems may also arise from the limited resources most Western governments are willing or able to commit to Czechoslovakia and from the tendency for public attention and interest to shift fairly rapidly to other issues in Western Europe and the United States. The willingness of foreign investors to deal with the uncertainties and problems still inherent in operating private businesses in Czechoslovakia is another open question at this time.

In sum, although Czechoslovakia is well on the way toward recreating a stable democratic system and a market economy, the process is far from over. Efforts to deal with the many issues that the country faces have proceeded without major disruptions to date. Although there have been a number of political crises, the political leaders and institutions of the newly recreated democratic state have proved able to contain the conflicts and reach acceptable compromises. However, as the ongoing controversy over the constitutional arrangements of the state and the high level of ethnic tensions in early 1991 illustrate, the outcome of the process is not certain. Although Czechoslovakia has many of the preconditions needed to succeed in creating a functioning democracy and market economy, developments since November 1989 demonstrate the complexity of the process of transition to post-communist rule even in the most favorable case.

Bibliography

'1. KDH, 2. VPN, 3. KSS-SDL.' *Lidové noviny*, November 26, 1990, pp. 1, 2.

aa. 'Šedesát procent občanů v sociální síti?' *Hospodářské noviny*, February 7, 1991, p. 2.

'Accord.' *Pravda*. October 31, 1990, p. 2. As reported in 'Slovak Economic, Social Council Established.' FBIS-EEU-90-216 (November 7, 1990): 30.

ada and nig. 'Klub Poslanců-Komunistů.' *Rudé právo*, June 27, 1990 (a), p. 2.

—— 'Majetek KSČS vyvlastnit.' *Rudé právo*, October 12, 1990 (b), pp. 1, 2.

Adam, Jan, ed. *Employment Policies in the Soviet Union and Eastern Europe*. Second Edition. London: The Macmillan Press, Ltd., 1987.

Adamičková, Naďa. 'Jak vystoupit z Varšavské smlouvy.' *Rudé právo*, January 17, 1991 (a), pp. 1, 2.

—— 'Prezident a vláda ČSFR žádají mimořádné pravomoci.' *Rudé právo*, January 25, 1991 (b), pp. 1, 2.

Adamičková, Naďa, and Königová, Marie. 'Penize pro policii.' *Rudé právo*, September 20, 1990, pp. 1, 2.

'Against the Nuclear Plant.' *Pravda*, February 21, 1990, p. 2. In 'Demonstrators Protest Kecerovce Nuclear Plant.' Foreign Broadcast Information Service, *Daily Report, East Europe*, FBIS-EEU-90-040 (February 28, 1990): 25.

Agnew, Hugh LeCaine. 'Enlightenment and National Consciousness: Three Czech "Popular Awakeners".' In *Nation and Ideology: Essays in Honor of Wayne S. Vucinich*, edited by Ivo Banac, John G. Ackerman, and Roman Szporluk. Boulder, CO: East European Monographs, 1981, pp. 201-26.

—— 'Josephinism and the Patriotic Intelligentsia in Bohemia.' *Harvard Ukrainian Studies* 10:3/4 (October–December, 1986): 577-97.

—— 'Czechs, Slovaks and the Slovak Linguistic Separatism of the 19th Century.' In *The Czech and Slovak Experience*. London: Macmillan, 1991 (a), forthcoming.

—— 'Noble "Natio" and Modern Nation: The Czech Case.' *Austrian History Yearbook* 1991 (b), forthcoming.

'Agriculture Under the New Economic Conditions.' *Zivot strany*, April 1989, pp. 8-9. As reported in 'Agriculture Under New Economic Conditions Viewed.' FBIS, *JPRS Report, East Europe*, JPRS-EER-89-067 (June 12, 1989): 28-30.

'Akční program urýchleného rozvoje.' *Rudé právo,* November 10, 1988, p. 1.

'Ako je zaistený národný a kultúrny život mad'arskej a ukrajinskej národnosti na Slovensku.' *Naše snahy* 3 (1988): 9-12.

'Aktivní přístup k světu.' *Lidové noviny,* December 19, 1990, pp. 1, 2.

Albrecht, Catherine. 'Environmental Policies and Politics in Contemporary Czechoslovakia.' *Studies in Comparative Communism* 20:3/4 (Autumn/Winter 1987): 291-302.

Alster, Ladislav. 'Základní kámen normalizace.' *Rudé právo,* December 27, 1988, p. 1.

—— 'Kostky byly vrženy.' *Rudé právo,* June 29, 1989, p. 7.

Altmann, Franz-Lothar. 'Economic Relations Between the Soviet Union and Czechoslovakia in the 1980's.' Occasional Paper #207, Kennan Institute for Advanced Russian Studies, Washington, February 1986.

—— 'Employment Policies in Czechoslovakia.' In *Employment Policies in the Soviet Union and Eastern Europe,* edited by Jan Adam. Second Edition. London: The Macmillan Press, Ltd., 1987.

am. 'Chci uzavřít rozumný kompromis.' *Česke noviny,* January 30, 1991, p. 1.

'Analýza vývoje čs. národního hospodářství v roce 1989 a v prvních měsících roku 1990.' *Příloha Hospodářských novin,* June 13, 1990, pp. 1-15.

Anderle, Josef. 'The First Republic, 1918-1938.' In *Czechoslovakia, the Heritage of Ages Past,* edited by Hans Brisch and Ivan Volgyes. New York: Columbia University Press, 1979.

Andrle, Alois and Srb, Vladimír. 'Nová klasifikace "měst" a "venkova."' *Demografie* 30:3 (1988): 265-7.

Ash, Timothy Garton. 'The Revolution of the Magic Lantern.' *The New York Review of Books,* January 18, 1990, pp. 42-51.

Asselain, Jean-Charles. 'The Distribution of Incomes in East-Central Europe.' In *Equality and Inequality in Eastern Europe,* edited by Pierre Kende and Zdeněk Strmiska. New York: St. Martin's Press, 1987, pp. 21-63.

'Aukční seznamy dostupné.' *Svobodné slovo,* January 12, 1991, p. 1.

b. 'Česká národní rada ustavena.' *Lidová demokracie,* June 27, 1990 (a), pp. 1, 3.

b. 'Diskuse o platech poslanců ČNR.' *Lidová demokracie.* August 22, 1990 (b), p. 1.

Bačová, Viera. 'Seminár k problémom výskumu cigánskych obyvatelov a cigánskych rodín.' *Sociológia* 20:5 (1988 (a)): 595-7.

—— 'Spoločenská integrácia cigánskych obyvatel'ov a cigánska rodina.'

Slovenský národopis 36:1 (1988 (b)): 22-34.

Bahry, Donna, and Silver, Brian D. 'Public Perceptions and the Dilemmas of Party Reform in the USSR,' in *Comparative Political Studies* 23:3 (July 1990): 171-209.

Bajčura, Ivan. 'Vývoj a riešenie ukrajinskej otázky v ČSSR.' In *Socialistickou cestou k národnostnej rovnoprávnosti*, edited by Michal Čorný. Bratislava: Pravda, 1975, pp. 11-32.

Bajčura, Ivan and Výrost, Jozej. 'Výsledky riešenia národnostnej otázky v podmienkach Východoslovenského kraja.' *Sociológia* 18:3 (1986).

Banac, Ivo. *The National Question in Yugoslavia: Origins, History, Politics.* Ithaca: Cornell University Press, 1984.

Barnes, Samuel H., McDonough, Peter, and Lopez Pina, Antonio. 'The Development of Partisanship in New Democracies: The Case of Spain.' *American Journal of Political Science* 29:4 (November 1985): 695-720.

Bártová, Eva. 'Žena a rodina v zrcadle společenských výzkumů v ČSSR.' *Sociologický časopis* 9:2 (1973): 206-16.

—— 'Společenská a politická aktivita v—reflexi veřejného mínění.' *Sociologický časopis* 20:4 (1984): 358-75.

Batt, Judy. *Economic Reform and Political Change in Eastern Europe: A Comparison of the Czechoslovak and Hungarian Experiences.* New York: St. Martin's Press, 1988.

Bauer, Jan. 'Černobyl v Českem krasu.' *Zemědělské noviny*, December 4, 1990, p. 1.

Bauerová, Jaroslava. 'Rodinná problematika vedoucích pracovníc.' *Sociologický časopis* 5:5 (1970): 449-62.

—— *Zamestnaná žena a rodina.* Prague: Práce, 1974.

Bauerová, Jaroslava and Bártová, Eva. *Proměny ženy v rodině, práci a veřejném životě.* Prague: Svoboda, 1987.

Bautzová, Libuše. 'Vnést nové aspekty do vztahů ČSSR-SSSR.' *Svět hospodářství*, April 4, 1989, p. 2.

bč and nig. 'Iniciativa KSČS v parlamentu.' *Rudé právo*, November 9, 1990, p. 5.

Beck, Carl. 'Career Characteristics of East European Leadership.' In *Political Leadership in Eastern Europe and the Soviet Union*, edited by R. Barry Farrell. Chicago: Aldine Publishing Company, 1970.

Beneš, Ladislav. 'Daňová reforma-ale kdy?' *Hospodářské noviny*, August 29, 1990, p. 1.

Beneš, Václav L. 'Czechoslovak Democracy and Its Problems.' In *A History of the Czechoslovak Republic, 1918-1948*, edited by Victor S. Mamatey and Radomir Luza. Princeton, NJ: Princeton University Press, 1973.

'Bez obav z nepřítele.' *Lidové noviny*, November 1, 1990, p. 2.

Bialer, Seweryn. *Stalin's Successors: Leadership, Stability, and Change in the Soviet Union*. Cambridge: Cambridge University Press, 1980.

Bielasiak, Jack. 'Modernization and Elite Cooptation in Eastern Europe, 1954-1971,' *East European Quarterly* 14:3 (Summer 1980): 345-69.

Birgus, Vladimir. *Československo '89*. Prague: Panorama, 1990.

Blackwell, Robert E., Jr. 'Elite Recruitment and Functional Change: An Analysis of the Soviet *Obkom* Elite, 1950-1968.' *Journal of Politics* (February, 1972): 124-52.

Blaha, Jiří. 'Český Klondike, nebo špinavá pena?' *Lidové noviny*, May 30, 1990, p. 4.

Blech, Anet, and Rottenberg, Hella. 'Everyone Is Afraid of a Neutralized Germany.' *De Volkskrant*, March 2, 1990, p. 4. As reported in 'Dienstbier Cited on European Unification.' FBIS-EEU-90-047 (March 9, 1990), pp. 27-9.

Blondel, Jean. *Comparative Legislatures*. Englewood Cliffs, NJ: Prentice-Hall, 1973.

Bogdan, Ivan. 'Možnosti sučasností.' *Učitelské noviny*, January 10, 1991, pp. 6-7.

Boguszak, Marek. 'Je to málo!' *Lidové noviny*, December 5, 1990 (a), p. 3.

Boguszak, Marek, Gabal, Ivan, and Rak, Vladimír. 'Československo—leden 1990. Prague: Skupina pro nezávislou socialní analyzu, 1990 (a).

—— 'Kde jsou skutečna sociální rizika reformy.' *Lidové noviny*, September 17, 1990 (b), p. 4.

—— 'Nezaměstnanost u nas.' *Mladá fronta*, March 21, 1990 (c), p. 3.

—— 'Československo—Listopad 1990.' Prague: Skupina pro nezávislou sociální analýzu, November 1990 (d).

Boguszak, Marek, and Mejkal, Ales. 'Kostky jsou vrženy.' *Lidové noviny*, December 21, 1990, p. 10.

Boguszak, Marek, and Rak, Vladimír. 'Czechoslovakia—May 1990 Survey Report.' Prague: Association for Independent Social Analysis, 1990 (a).

—— 'Společně, ale každý jinak.' *Lidové noviny*, June 28, 1990 (b), p. 4.

Bornstein, Morris. 'Introduction.' In *Plan and Market: Economic Reform in Eastern Europe*, edited by Morris Bornstein. New Haven: Yale University Press, 1973, pp. 313-46.

—— 'Economic Reform in Eastern Europe.' In *Comparative Economic Systems: Models and Cases*, edited by Morris Bornstein. Fourth Edition. Homewood, IL: Richard D. Irwin, Inc., 1979, pp. 279-315.

—— 'Issues in East-West Economic Relations.' In *East-West Relations and the*

326   *Bibliography*

Future of Eastern Europe: Political and Economic, edited by Morris Bornstein, Zvi Gitelman, and William Zimmerman. Boston: Allen and Unwin, 1981 (a), pp. 31-61.

—— 'Soviet-East European Economic Relations.' In *East-West Relations and the Future of Eastern Europe: Political and Economic*, edited by Morris Bornstein, Zvi Gitelman, and William Zimmerman. Boston: Allen and Unwin, 1981 (b), pp. 105-24.

Borovička, Michael. 'Příliš drazí přátele?' *Práce*, March 17, 1990, p. 1.

Boura, Vlastimil. 'Ceny v Souboru opatření.' *Hospodářské noviny*, October 14, 1983, p. 1.

Brabic, Vladimír. 'Dostatečný manévrovací prostor.' *Hospodářské noviny*, November 23, 1990, p. 2.

Brada, Josef C. 'Czechoslovak Economic Performance in the 1980's.' In *Pressures for Reform in the East European Economies*. Joint Economic Committee, Congress of the United States. Washington, DC: United States Government Printing Office, 1989, pp. 215-29.

Brada, Josef C., Hey, Jeanne C., and King, Arthur E. 'Inter-regional and Inter-organizational Differences in Agricultural Efficiency in Czechoslovakia.' In *Socialist Agriculture in Transition*, edited by Josef C. Brada and Karl-Eugen Wadekin. Boulder, CO: Westview Press, 1988, pp. 334-43.

Brada, Josef C. and King, Arthur E. 'Czechoslovak Agriculture: Policies, Performance and Prospects.' *East European Quarterly* 17:3 (September 1983): 343-59.

Brada, Josef C., King, Arthur E., and Schlagenhauf, Don E. 'Policymaking and Plan Construction in the Czechoslovak Fifth and Sixth Five-Year Plans.' In *East European Economic Assessment*, Part 1. Joint Economic Committee, Congress of the United States. Washington, DC: Government Printing Office, 1981, pp. 425-82.

Bradáč, Vlastimil, Krýl, Pavel, and Pergl, Václav. 'KSČS je federací.' *Rudé právo*, November 5, 1990 (a), pp. 1, 2.

—— 'L. Adamec odstoupil.' *Rudé právo*, September 3, 1990 (b), p. 1.

Bradáč, Vlastimil, Pergl, Václav and Růžička, Jiří. 'Předsedou KSČM Jiří Svoboda.' *Rudé právo*, October 15, 1990, pp. 1, 2.

Bradley, J.F.N. *Czechoslovakia: A Short History*. Edinburgh: Edinburgh University Press, 1971.

Bratislava Domestic Service. December 19, 1990. 'Defense Ministry Briefing on Military Policies.' FBIS-EEU-90-246 (December 21, 1990): 16.

—— January 28, 1991. As reported in '1990 Gross Foreign Debt Figures Given.' FBIS-EEU-91-019 (January 29, 1991): 21.

Bratislava Nahlas. Mimeograph. Bratislava, 1987.

'Briefly From Home.' *Pravda*, March 1, 1991, p. 2. As reported in 'Small Contacts with Poland reestablished.' FBIS-EEU-91-045 (March 7, 1991): 21.

Brisch, Hans and Ivan Volgyes, eds. *Czechoslovakia, the Heritage of Ages Past: Essays in Memory of Josef Korbel.* New York, NY: Columbia University Press, 1979.

Brock, Peter. *The Slovak National Awakening.* Toronto: University of Toronto Press, 1976.

Brock, Peter and Skilling, H. Gordon, eds. *The Czech Renascence of the Nineteenth Century.* Toronto: University of Toronto Press, 1970.

Brokl, Lubomír. 'Překonáváni byrokratického charakteru správy společnosti.' *Sociologický časopis* 26:4 (1990 (a)): 262-8.

—— 'Problémy přechodu k pluralitní demokracii.' *Sociologický časopis* 26:4 (1990 (b)): 249-61.

Broun, Janice and Sikorska, Grazyna. *Conscience and Captivity: Religion in Eastern Europe.* Washington, DC: Ethics and Public Policy Center, 1988.

Brown, Archie and Gray, Jack, eds. *Political Culture and Political Change in Communist States.* Second Edition. London and New York: Holmes and Meier Publishers, 1979.

Brown, Archie and Wightman, Gordon. 'Czechoslovakia: Revival and Retreat.' In *Political Culture and Political Change in Communist States*, edited by Archie Brown and Jack Grey. New York: Holmes and Meier Publishers, 1979.

Bruegel, J.W. *Czechoslovakia Before Munich: The German Minority Problem and British Appeasement Policy.* Cambridge: Cambridge University Press, 1973.

Bruszt, Laszlo. 'Without Us but For Us: Political Orientation in Hungary in the Period of Later Paternalism.' *Social Research* 55 (Spring/Summer 1988): 43-76.

Brychnáč, Vlastimil and Čechák, Vladimír. 'Socialistické společenské vědomí, jeho výzkum a formování.' *Sociologický časopis* 22:5 (1986): 450-8.

Brzezinski, Zbigniew K. *The Soviet Bloc: Unity and Conflict.* Cambridge, MA: Harvard University Press, 1967.

Bucha, Tibor. 'Dnes je to už jasne—vědu na Slovensku bude riadit' vláda Slovenskej republiky.' *Smena,* September 5, 1990, p. 4.

Budaj, Ján *et al. Bratislava nahlas.* Bratislava: Slovensky zväz ochrancov prirody a krajiny, 1987.

Bukowski, Charles J. and Cichock, Mark A., eds. *Prospects for Change in Socialist Systems: Challenges and Responses.* New York, NY: Praeger Publishers, 1987.

Bunce, Valerie. *Do New Leaders Make a Difference? Executive Succession and Public Policy under Capitalism and Socialism.* Princeton, NJ: University Press, 1981.

—— 'Rising Above the Past: The Struggle for Liberal Democracy in Eastern Europe.' *World Policy Journal* 7 (Summer 1990): 395-430.

Burda, Karel. 'Návrh privatizace zemědělských družstev.' *Zemědělské noviny*, September 22, 1990, p. 7.

Burg, Steven L. *Conflict and Cohesion in Socialist Yugoslavia: Political Decision Making since 1966.* Princeton, NJ: University Press, 1983.

Burks, Richard Voyles. *The Dynamics of Communism in Eastern Europe.* Westport, CT: Greenwood Press, 1976.

Busek, Vratislav. *Czechoslovakia.* New York, NY: Praeger Publishers, 1957.

Busek, Vratislav and Nicolas Spulber, eds. *Czechoslovakia.* New York, NY: Frederick A. Praeger, 1957.

'The Business Outlook: Czechoslovakia.' *Business Eastern Europe* (February 6, 1989): 44.

Bútora, Martin. Bratislava. Interview, June 14, 1990.

Bým, Petr. 'Perspektiva je Pentagonála.' *Lidové noviny*, September 25, 1990, pp. 1, 3.

c. 'Reforma na obrazovce.' *Svobodné slovo*. September 6, 1990 (a), p. 1.

c. 'Šance a očekávání.' *Zemědělské noviny*, May 21, 1990 (b), p. 7.

Campbell, F. Gregory. *Confrontation in Central Europe: Weimar Germany and Czechoslovakia.* Chicago, IL: University of Chicago Press, 1975.

Čapko, Gustáv, Pavol Minárik and Eduard Drábik. 'Noční rozpůlení VPN.' *Rudé právo*, March 7, 1991, pp. 1, 2.

Časnochová, Jana. 'Looking for What Unites Us.' *Rudé právo*, July 25, 1988, p. 3. As reported in 'Official Says Hungarians Have Problems in CSSR.' *RFE/RL Daily Background Reports*, July 29, 1988, p. 211.

Čech, Stanislav. 'Vizitka, která zavazuje.' *Zemědělské noviny*, January 31, 1991, pp. 1, 8.

Čechlovský, Vladimír. 'Jaké výsledky, takové možnosti.' *Rudé právo*, May 19, 1989, p. 3.

Čechlovský, Vladimír and Marek, Václav. 'O plánu roku 1989.' *Rudé právo*, September 28, 1988, p. 3.

Centrum pre výskum spoločenských problémov pri KC VPN. 'Slovensko pred vol'bami.' Bratislava, April 11, 1990 (a).

—— 'Slovensko pred vol'bami II.' Bratislava, May 11, 1990 (b).

—— 'Slovensko pred vol'bami III.' Bratislava. May 24, 1990 (c).

—— 'Slovensko pred vol'bami IV.' Bratislava. June 2, 1990 (d).

'Ceny v novém roce.' *Svobodné slovo*, December 28, 1990, pp. 1, 4.

Čermáková, Marie, and Navarová, Hana. 'Women and Elections '90.' 1990, MS.

Čermáková, Marie, and Režková, Miluše. 'Sociologický výzkum a školství.' *Sociologický časopis* 26:5 (1990): 449-55.

Černá, Alena, and Tošovská, Eva. 'Vazby ekologické a hospodářské politiky.' *Politická ekonomie* 11 (November 1990): 1281-90.

Černý, Miroslav. 'National Economic Plan Coordination between CSSR and SSSR for 1986-1990.' *Planované hospodářství* 2 (1986): 43-8. As reported in 'Plan Coordination with USSR for 1986-1990 Summarized.' JPRS-EER-86-079 (May 29, 1986): 17-24.

Červenka, Ivan. 'Podraz místo dohody.' *Práce*, November 6, 1990, pp. 1, 2.

Červenková, Anna. 'Ekononomové sněmovali.' *Lidové noviny*, January 1, 1991, p. 7.

Čerovský, Zbyněk. 'Raport vrchnímu veliteli.' *Občanský deník*, October 18, 1990, pp. 1, 2.

Chalupová, Eva. 'Vlastník před uživatelem.' *Zemědělské noviny*, September 15, 1990, p. 7.

Charvát, František. *Sociální struktura ČSSR a její vývoj v 60. letech*. Prague: Academia, 1972.

—— *Sociální struktura socialistické společnosti a její vývoj v Československu*. Prague: Academia, 1980.

Chomcová, Ivana, and Kolová, L'uba. 'Prestava homo sapiens mysliet?' *Praca*, January 5, 1990, p. 5.

Chorherr, Thomas. 'CSFR Fears Social Unrest, Price Hikes, Unemployment, Strikes.' *Die Presse*, November 26, 1990, pp. 1, 2. As reported in 'Calfa Discusses Economic Development Problems.' FBIS-EEU-90-228 (November 27, 1990): 18-19.

Chovanec, Jaroslav. *Zastupitelská soustava Československé socialistické republiky*. Prague: Mladá fronta, 1974.

Chronc, Oldřich. 'Dopiňkový zdroj v reformované ekonomicé.' *Hospodářské noviny*, April 17, 1989, p. 11.

Čierná, Miroslav. 'Bude kniha luxus?' *Nové slovo* 11 (March 15, 1990): 17.

Císař, Jan. 'Czechoslovak-Soviet Trade: A Linkage Important to Life.' *Hospodářské noviny*, May 31, 1985, p. 3. As reported in 'Trade with USSR Our Lifeline Says Ministry Official.' JPRS-EER-85-062 (July 29, 1985): 16-21.

cka and zr. 'Hrozí generální stávka?' *Práce*, November 28, 1990, pp. 1, 2.

čl. 'Volební výsledky o den dříve.' *Hospodářské noviny*, November 28, 1990, p. 1.

Clapp, Allen E. and Shapiro, Harvey. 'Financial Crisis in Eastern Europe.'

In *East European Economies: Slow Growth in the 1980's,* volume 2. Joint Economic Committee, Congress of the United States. Washington, DC: US Government Printing Office, 1986, pp. 242-57.

Clarke, Douglas L. 'Warsaw Pact: The Transformation Begins.' *Radio Free Europe Report on Eastern Europe* 1:25 (June 22, 1990 [a]): 34-7.

'Členové ÚV strany.' *Svobodné slovo,* February 23, 1987, p. 2

—— 'What Future for the Warsaw Pact?' *Radio Free Europe Report on Eastern Europe* 1:3 (January 19, 1990 [b]): 37-9.

'Členové a Kandidátí přdsednictva ÚV KSČ členové sekretariátu ustřední kontrolní a revizní komise KSČ.' *Rudé právo,* March 29, 1986, p. 3.

Cochrane, Nancy J. 'The Private Sector in East European Agriculture'. *Problems of Communism* 37:2 (March/April 1988): pp. 47-53.

Colitt, Leslie. 'Prague minister warns of large job losses on path to economic reform.' *Financial Times,* February 6, 1991, p. 4.

Connor, Walker. *The National Question in Marxist-Leninist Theory and Strategy.* Princeton, NJ: University Press, 1984.

Connor, Walter D. *Public Opinion in European Socialist Systems.* New York: Praeger Publishers, 1977.

—— *Socialism, Politics, and Equality.* New York: Columbia University Press, 1979.

—— 'Dissent in Eastern Europe: A New Coalition?' *Problems of Communism* 29 (January/February 1980): 1-17.

Čorný, Ivan. 'Úspešné riešenie sociálno-ekonomických problémov a životnej úrovne obyvateľstva ukrajinskej národnosti v ČSSR.' In *Socialistickou cestou k národnostnej rovnoprávnosti.* Bratislava: Pravda, 1975.

'CSFR License Scheme to Restrict Exports.' *Business Eastern Europe* (July 9, 1990): 227-8.

'CSFR Reform Legislation: Not as Liberal as Hoped.' *Business Eastern Europe* (May 14, 1990): 161-2.

'ČSSR Expands Plans for Cooperation Deals.' *Business Eastern Europe* 18:6 (January 18, 1986): 20.

'ČSSR Government Held Meeting.' *Rudé právo,* May 12, 1989, pp. 1,2. As reported in 'Government Session on Economic Development.' FBIS-EEU-89-094 (May 17, 1989): 12-13.

ČTK. June 25, 1986. As reported in 'Foreign Trade Minister Urban Speaks on Exports.' FBIS-EEU-86-128 (July 3, 1986): D2-D3.

ČTK. *Dokumentační přehled,* no. 321, 1987.

ČTK. August 5, 1988. As reported in 'Foreign Debts to be Paid, Credits Rejected.' FBIS-EEU-88-151 (August 5, 1988): 9.

ČTK. February 16, 1990. As reported in 'Trade Union Confederation to

Replace RoH.' FBIS-EEU-90-036 (February 22, 1990): 17.

ČTK. April 6, 1990. As reported in 'Dienstbier Proposes European Security Commission.' FBIS-EEU-90-068 (April 9, 1990): 13.

ČTK. July 19, 1990. As reported in 'Unification Negative Influence on GDR Trade.' FBIS-EEU-90-140 (July 20, 1990): 14.

ČTK. July 30, 1990. Reported as 'Environmentalists Meet in Prague 29 July.' FBIS-EEU-90-149 (August 2, 1990): 18.

ČTK. September 5, 1990. As reported in 'Deputy Minister on Cutting Army by 1/3.' FBIS-EEU-90-175 (September 10, 1990): 23.

ČTK. September 6, 1990. As reported in 'Agrees with Dienstbier on Main Issues.' FBIS-EEU-90-177 (September 12, 1990): 11.

ČTK. September 14, 1990. As reported in 'New Secret Service Established: No Police Powers.' FBIS-EEU-90-182 (September 19, 1990): 27.

ČTK. September 18, 1990. As reported in 'Parliament Passes Law Supporting Private Business.' FBIS-EEU-90-183 (September 20, 1990): 12.

ČTK. September 20, 1990. As reported in 'Government 'Line' on Pentagonal Issues Approved.' FBIS-EEU-90-185 (September 24, 1990): 33-4.

ČTK. September 23, 1990. As reported in 'World Bank Official on Nation's Credit Limit.' FBIS-EEU-90-187 (September 27, 1990): 9-l0.

ČTK. September 26, 1990. As reported in 'General Council Elects New Trade Union President.' FBIS-EEU-90-188 (September 27, 1990): 32.

ČTK. September 27, 1990. As reported in 'Pithart Outlines Tripartite Talks.' FBIS-EEU-90-189 (September 28, 1990): 10-11.

ČTK. October 1, 1990. As reported in 'First Border Police Post Put into Operation.' FBIS-EEU-90-195 (October 9, 1990): 17.

ČTK. October 2, 1990. As reported in 'Poll Taken on Growth of Prices, Privatization.' FBIS-EEU-90-195 (October 9, 1990): 27.

ČTK. October 11, 1990. As reported in 'Bilateral Customs Agreement Signed with US' FBIS-EEU-90-200 (October 16, 1990): 39.

ČTK. October 15, 1990. As reported in 'Klaus, Austria's Lacina Sign Investment Agreement.' FBIS-EEU-90-200 (October 16, 1990): 39.

ČTK. October 17, 1990. As reported in 'No Reason Given for Firing of Defense Minister.' FBIS-EEU-90-202 (October 18, 1990): 7.

ČTK. October 18, 1990. As reported in 'National Cost of Living up 14.1 percent.' FBIS-EEU-90-204 (October 22, 1990): 13.

ČTK. October 29, 1990. As reported in 'Military Counterintelligence Service Dissolved.' FBIS-EEU-90-210 (October 30, 1990): 14.

ČTK. October 30, 1990. As reported in 'Border Guards Redesignated to Reinforce Police.' FBIS-EEU-90-211 (October 31, 1991): 24-5.

ČTK. November 1, 1990 (a). As reported in 'Dienstbier Discusses Results of Asian Tour.' FBIS-EEU-90-213 (November 2, 1990): 28.

ČTK. November 1, 1990 (b). As reported in 'Trade Agreement with North Korea Signed.' FBIS-EEU-90-216 (November 7, 1990): 17.

ČTK. November 3, 1990 (a). As reported in 'Carnogursky, Christian Democrats Meet in Kosice.' FBIS-EEU-90-216 (November 7, 1990): 28-9.

ČTK. November 3, 1990 (b). As reported in 'Nationalist Socialist Party Views Noted.' FBIS-EEU-90-215 (November 6, 1990): 10.

ČTK. November 7, 1990 (a). As reported in 'Poll Shows Drop in VPN Popularity Stops.' FBIS-EEU-90-219 (November 13, 1990): 32.

ČTK. November 7, 1990 (b). As reported in 'Professional Army Expected by Year 2000.' FBIS-EEU-90-218 (November 9, 1990): 10.

ČTK. November 11, 1990. As reported in 'More than 10,000 Students Jobless.' FBIS-EEU-90-221 (November 15, 1990): 25.

ČTK. November 14, 1990. As reported in 'Poll Shows Popularity of OF, VPN Declines.' FBIS-EEU-90-223 (November 19, 1990): 33.

ČTK. November 15, 1990. As reported in 'Romanies in CSFR Seek Status as Nationality.' FBIS-EEU-90-223 (November 19, 1990): 36.

ČTK. November 17, 1990. As reported in 'Communists Protest Property Expropriation Law.' FBIS-EEU-90-223 (November 19, 1990): 33.

ČTK. November 19, 1990. As reported in 'USSR Seen as Complicating Foreign Trade.' FBIS-EEU-90-227 (November 26, 1990): 30-1.

ČTK. November 25, 1990. As reported in 'Christian Democrats Gain 27.4 Percent.' FBIS-EEU-90-227 (November 26, 1990): 25.

ČTK. November 30, 1990. As reported in 'Power, Fuel Prices to Increase.' FBIS-EEU-90-232 (December 3, 1990): 19.

ČTK. December 3, 1990. As reported in 'Spokesman Says no KGB, Ministry Cooperation.' FBIS-EEU-90-235 (December 6, 1990): 12-13.

ČTK. December 5, 1990. As reported in 'Director Outlines Security Office's Problems.' FBIS-EEU-90-235 (December 6, 1990): 13.

ČTK. December 6, 1990 (a). As reported in 'Delegation Head Addresses Vienna Disarmament Talks.' FBIS-EEU-90-239 (December 12, 1990): 28.

ČTK. December 6, 1990 (b). As reported in 'Federal Assembly Creates Armed Forces Inspector.' FBIS-EEU-90-238 (December 11, 1990): 16.

ČTK. December 6, 1990 (c). As reported in 'Trade Agreement Signed with Bulgaria.' FBIS-EEU-90-238 (December 11, 1990): 17.

ČTK. December 6, 1990 (d). As reported in 'Trade Unions Complain of Curtailed Rights.' FBIS-EEU-90-239 (December 12, 1990): 26.

ČTK. December 10, 1990. As reported in 'Assembly Debates Bill on

Federation Powers.' FBIS-EEU-90-237 (December 10, 1990): 29-30.

ČTK. December 11, 1990. As reported in 'Slovak Confidence in Federal Bodies Drop.' FBIS-EEU-90-242 (December 17, 1990): 32.

ČTK. December 20, 1990. As reported in 'Trade, Economic Agreement Signed with Iran.' FBIS-EEU-90-246 (December 20, 1990): 16-17.

ČTK. December 22, 1990. As reported in 'Last Soviet Unit Withdraws From Slovakia.' FBIS-EEU-90-247 (December 24, 1990): 23.

ČTK. December 28, 1990. As reported in 'Finance Ministry Issues 1991 Economic Forecast.' FBIS-EEU-90-251 (December 31, 1990): 15.

ČTK. December 29, 1990. As reported in 'Government Approves Skoda-Volkswagen Agreement.' FBIS-EEU-91-002 (January 3, 1991): 29.

ČTK. January 10, 1991. As reported in 'ČTK Summarizes Federal Government Session.' FBIS-EEU-91-008 (January 11, 1991): 16-17.

ČTK. January 18, 1991 (a). As reported in 'EC Provides Funds for Environmental Projects.' FBIS-EEU-91-014 (January 22, 1991): 19.

ČTK. January 18, 1991 (b). As reported in 'Government Officials on Foreign Trade in 1990.' FBIS-EEU-91-016 (January 24, 1991): 23.

ČTK. January 21, 1991. As reported in 'Poll: Czechs Trust President, Slovaks Government.' FBIS-EEU-91-018 (January 28, 1991): 18-19.

ČTK. February 5, 1991. As reported in 'Desire for Closer NATO Ties Expressed.' FBIS-EEU-91-025 (February 6, 1991): 21.

ČTK. February 25, 1991. As reported in 'Dobrovsky on Abolition of Warsaw Pact.' FBIS-EEU-91-040 (February 28, 1991): 10.

ČTK. April 10, 1991. As reported in 'Assembly Accepts NATO Association Status.' FBIS-EEU-91-070 (April 11, 1991): 6.

Curry, Jane Leftwich (ed). *Dissent in Eastern Europe.* New York, NY: Praeger, 1983.

Czafik, Jozef and Virsík, Anton. *Normotvorba vo federatívnej ČSSR 1969-1979.* (Bratislava: Obzor, 1980).

'Czechoslovak Economic Performance During the First Half of 1990.' *PlanEcon Report* 6:36-37 (September 14, 1990): 1-32.

'Czechoslovak Economy in 1986—Office of Statistics Report.' As reported in FBIS-EEU-87-020 (January 30, 1987): D3-D5.

'Czechoslovak Foreign Trade Performance Through the First Half of 1990 and Survey of External Finances During 1980-90.' *PlanEcon Report* 6:34-35 (August 31, 1990): 1-34.

'Czechoslovakia Mounts Campaign to Attract More Foreign Investment.' *The Bureau of National Affairs* 33 (February 19, 1991): A-5-6.

'Czechoslovakia Parliamentary Elections on June 8th-9th 1990,' *Daily News and Press Survey Bulletin.* Prague: Czechoslovak News Agency, n.d.

'Czechoslovakia on the Road to Reform: Challenges and Opportunities for US Policy.' Washington, DC: The Atlantic Council of the United States, February 1991.

Czerwinski, E.J. and Piekalkiewicz, Jaroslaw A., eds. *The Soviet Invasion of Czechoslovakia: Its Effects on Eastern Europe.* New York, NY: Praeger Publishers, 1972.

da. 'Divadelní premiéry v březnu.' *Rudé právo,* March 5, 1990, p. 5.

'Dálnopisem, poštou, telefonem.' *Rudé právo,* August 23, 1990, p. 2.

Danáš, Kornel. 'Polemický názor čitateľa na riešenia cigánskej otázky.' *Nedeľná pravda,* August 5, 1988, pp. 7-8.

Daniel, František. 'The Czech Difference.' In *Politics, Art, and Commitment in East European Cinema.* London: Macmillan, 1983, pp. 290-6.

David, Henry P. and McIntyre, Robert J. *Reproductive Behavior: Central and Eastern European Experience.* New York: Springer, 1981.

Dean, Robert W. *Nationalism and Political Change in Eastern Europe: The Slovak Question and Czechoslovak Reform Movement.* Denver, CO: Denver University, 1973.

'Definitívne počty mandátov politických strán vo voľbách do SNR.' *Práca,* June 14, 1990, p. 1.

'Definitívne výsledky až v stredu.' *Národná obrana,* November 26, 1990, p. 1.

'Deklarácia o ústanovení Slovenského parlamentu kultury.' *Dialog 90,* July 3, 1990, p. 2.

Demeková, Adela. 'Eter v štyroch okruhoch.' *Smena,* September 4, 1990 (a), p. 5.

—— 'Prvá nezávisla studentska.' *Smena,* June 14, 1990 (b), p. 1.

'A Destabilizing Nervous Influence on the Public.' *Národná obroda,* March 4, 1991, p. 2. As reported in 'VPN Reacts to Mečiar's Allegations.' FBIS-EEU-91-045 (March 7, 1991): 14.

Deyl, Zdeněk and Kerner, Antonín. 'Postavení pracovníků městských služeb v ČSSR.' In *Sociální struktura socialistické společnosti,* edited by Pavel Machonin. Prague: Nakladatelství Svoboda, 1966, pp. 509-26.

DiFranceisco, Wayne and Gitelman, Zvi. 'Soviet Political Culture and 'Covert Participation' in Policy Implementation.' *American Political Science Review* 78:3 (September 1984): 603-21.

'Diferenciácia názorov a stanovy.' *Národná obroda,* November 7, 1990, p. 3.

'Dialog suverénních partnerů.' *Zemědělské noviny,* January 30, 1991, p. 1.

dk. 'Jak v příštím roce.' *Svobodné slovo,* October 5, 1990 (a), p. 1.

dk. 'KSČ vrátí majetek.' *Svobodné slovo,* October 16, 1990 (b), p. 1.

Dlouhý, Vladimír. *Mladá fronta.* Interviews, April 6, 1990, p. 3, and June 21, 1990.

do. 'Cenu už neurčuje státní úředník.' *Hospodářské noviny*, December 28, 1990 (a), p. 1.

do. 'Strategie čs. ekonomiky do roku 1992.' *Hospodářské noviny*, November 23, 1990 (b), pp. 1, 16.

Dohnalová N., Roth, O., and Storchová, M. 'Naše školství v mezinárodním srovnání.' 1989, MS.

'Dohoda ČSSR a SSSR o odchodu vojsk.' *Mladá fronta*, November 28, 1990, p. 5.

Dolečková, Marcela. 'Capital Market in the CSFR About To Be Opened: Which Czechoslovak Enterprise Will Deserve to Be Listed on the Stock Exchange?' *Hospodářské noviny*, October 12, 1990, p. 2. As reported in 'Bank Official on Capital Market Legislation.' FBIS-EEU-90-201 (October 17, 1990): 10-11.

—— 'Proč váhají zahraniční investoři?' *Hospodářské noviny*, February 4, 1991, p. 1.

Doležalová, Sylva. 'Muž a žena bez předsudku.' *Tvorba* 21 (December 1988): 12.

Drábek, Ivan. 'List, ktorý rozvíril vášne.' *Smena*, May 12, 1990, p. 1.

Drabek, Zdeněk. 'Czechoslovak Economic Reform: The Search for Minimum Market Approach.' In *Pressures for Reform in the East European Economies*. Joint Economic Committee, Congress of the United States. Washington, DC: United States Government Printing Office, 1989, pp. 215-29.

Drábik, Eduard. 'Peter Weiss předsedou KSS-Strany demokratické levice.' *Rudé právo*, October 22, 1990, pp. 1, 2.

'Draft Document on Labor Brigades Introduced.' FBIS-EEU-88-174 (September 8, 1988): 14.

ds. 'Rodí se Levicový Klub OF.' *Rudé právo*, December 15, 1990, pp. 1, 2.

Dubský, Josef. 'Co si lidé myslí o KSČ.' *Informace*. Prague: Institut pro výzkum veřejného mínění, 1990.

Duchacek, Ivo. 'Education.' In Vratislav Busek and Nicolas Spulber, eds. *Czechoslovakia* (New York: Praeger, 1957), pp. 154-72.

Duchêne, Gérard. 'The Parallel Economy and Income Inequality.' In *Equality and Inequality in Eastern Europe*, edited by Pierre Kende and Zdenek Strmiska. New York: St. Martin's Press, 1987, pp. 63-8.

Duray, Miklos. *Political Problems of the Hungarian Minority in Czechoslovakia*. Indiana, PA: The Graduate School of Indiana University of Pennsylvania, 1989.

'Dveře jsou oteveřený.' *Svobodné slovo*, January 4, 1990, pp. 1, 2.

Dvořák, Jan. 'Nejdříve veřejnou diskusi!' *Scéna* 9 (May 2, 1990): 1.

Dyba, Karel. 'Růst, strukturální změny a otevřenost ekonomiky.' *Politická ekonomie* 37:5 (1989 [a]): 559-69.

—— 'Reforming the Czechoslovak Economy: Past Experience and Present Dilemmas.' Paper presented at Woodrow Wilson International Center for Scholars, Washington, DC, 1989 (b).

Dyba, Karel, and Ježek, Tomáš. 'Czechoslovak Experience with Central Planning.' Paper prepared for the Conference 'Socio-Economic Development and Planning,' Budapest, 1989.

Dyba, Karel, and Kouba, Karel. 'Czechoslovak Attempts at Systemic Changes.' *Communist Economies* 1:3 (1989): 313-25.

dz. 'Den voleb: 24. listopad.' *Zemědělské noviny*, September 6, 1990 (a), p. 1.

dz. 'Obce jsou schváleny!' *Zemědělské noviny*, September 5, 1990 (b), p. 1.

East European Economic Handbook. London: Euromonitor Publications, 1985.

Edelman, Murray. *Politics as Symbolic Action: Mass Arousal and Quiescence.* Chicago: Markham, 1971.

Eidlin, Fred H. *The Logic of 'Normalization': The Soviet Intervention in Czechoslovakia of 21 August 1968 and the Czechoslovak Response.* New York, NY: Columbia University Press, 1980.

em. 'Listy se vracejí domů.' *Svobodné slovo*, March 14, 1990, p. 3.

es. 'Matejka vs. Matejka.' *Lidové noviny*, January 1989, p. 11. As reported in 'Economic Reform Controversy Viewed.' JPRS-EER-89-038 (April 6, 1989): 38-40.

es. 'Rodinka je tady.' *Práce* (July 2, 1990), p. 2.

The Europa Year Book 1989. London: Europa Publications, Ltd., 1989.

Evanson, Robert K. 'Regime and Working Class in Czechoslovakia 1948-1968.' *Soviet Studies* 37 (April 1985): 248-68.

—— 'The Czechoslovak Road to Socialism in 1948.' *East European Quarterly* 19:4 (January 1986): 469-92.

Farnsworth, Clyde H. 'Czechoslovakia Gets $1.8 Billion IMF Loan.' *New York Times*, January 8, 1991.

Fassmann, Martin. 'The Shadow Economy's Funds: From Where Are Drawn the Grey Billions on the Market and in Services?' *Hospodářské noviny*, December 9, 1988, p. 3. As reported in 'Solutions to 'Shadow Economy' Problems Proposed,' JPRS-EER-89-035 (March 31, 1989): 40-3.

Fazik, Alexander. 'Delikvence a mládež. Příspěvek k řešení jevů v životě mládeže.' *Sociologický časopis* 18:2 (1982): 163-71.

Federální statistický úřad, Česky statistický úřad, Slovenský statistický úřad. *Statistická ročenka ČSSR.* Prague: SNTL 1969-89.

—— *Statistické přehledy.* 1989.

Federální statistický úřad, Česky statistický úřad, Slovenský statistický úřad. *Statistická ročenka České a Slovenské Federativní Republiky.* Republiky. Prague: SNTL, 1990.

Ferko, Tibor. 'Táto cesta nie je na preteky.' *Národná obroda*, January 23, 1991, p. 5.

Fiala, Zbyněk. 'Nereálné mzdy.' *Mladá fronta*, January 30, 1991, p. 2.

Filip, Miroslav. 'Otázek víc než času.' *Občanský deník*, December 15, 1990, p. 1.

Filkus, Rudolf. 'Ohniská krízového stavu ekonomiky.' *Verejnost'*, November 8, 1990, p. 3.

Fillo, Anton. 'Armáda týchto dní.' *Národná obroda*, October 3, 1990, pp. 1, 3.

'First Labor Councils Are Stepping Into Life.' *Rudé právo,* April 26, 1988, p. 1. As reported in 'Initial Experience With Self-Management.' FBIS-EEU-88-083 (April 29, 1988): 16–17.

Fleron, Frederic J., Jr. *Communist Studies and the Social Sciences: Essays on Methodology and Empirical Theory.* Chicago: Rand McNally, 1969.

—— 'Career Types in the Soviet Political Leadership.' In *Political Leadership in Eastern Europe and the Soviet Union*, edited by R. Barry Farrell. Chicago: Aldine, 1970, pp. 108–39.

'Focus on Financing.' *Business Eastern Europe* (December 8, 1986): 392.

Foret, Miroslav. 'Specifika sociologického zkoumání náboženské víry.' *Sociologický časopis* 22:1 (1986): 62–73.

Fragment K 4:2 (1990).

Franěk, Jiří. 'Souvislosti ropných šoků.' *Lidové noviny*, October 17, 1990, p. 8.

Franěk, Rudolf. 'Výzkum absolventů vysokých škol.' *Sociologický časopis* 18:2 (1982): 211–17.

—— 'Aktuální problémy formování socioprofesionálního profilu studentů a absolventů vysokých škol v ČSSR.' *Sociologický časopis* 21:5 (1985): 529–38.

Freeze, Karen J. 'The Young Progressives: The Czech Student Movement, 1887–1897.' Unpublished Ph.D. Dissertation, Columbia University, 1974.

French, A. *Czech Writers and Politics, 1945-1969.* Boulder, CO: East European Monographs, 1982.

French, Hilary F. *Green Revolutions: Environmental Reconstruction in Eastern Europe and the Soviet Union.* Washington, DC: Worldwatch Inc., 1991.

Frič, Pavol. 'Rodí sa nová politická kultúra.' *Verejnost'*, August 18, 1990, p. 1.

Frič, Pavol, Gál, Fedor, and Dianiška, Ivan. 'Profesiová orientácia sociológa vo svetle spoločenských očakávaní.' *Sociologia* 20:1 (1988): 71-83.

Friedgut, Theodore H. *Political Participation in the USSR*. Princeton, NJ: Princeton University Press, 1979.

Fučík, Josef. 'Jak vyzrát na zbraně.' *Hospodářské noviny*, January 31, 1991, p. 4.

Fuele, Jan. 'Právomoci — pomoc k moci.' *Národná obroda*, December 15, 1990, p. 3.

fuk. 'První aukce za měsíc.' *Svobodné slovo*, December 19, 1990, p. 1.

Fuk, Martin. 'Župy, kraje, okresy.' *Svobodné slovo*, October 9, 1990, p. 3.

ga. 'Varšavská smlouva bez nás?' *Zemědělské noviny*, January 17, 1991, pp. 1, 2.

Gabrielová, Marie. 'Již letos lze očekavat zvýšení ńajemného.' *Svobodné slovo*, February 4, 1991 (a), p. 4.

—— 'Vláda trvá na svém.' *Svobodné slovo*, February 21, 1991 (b), p. 1.

Gallo, Igor. 'Spolky-čertove volky?' *Čas*, March 19, 1990, p. 5.

Garver, Bruce M. *The Young Czech Party, 1874-1901, and the Emergence of a Multi-Party System*. New Haven, CT: Yale University Press, 1978.

gc. 'Převažuje mírná skepse.' *Lidové noviny*, January 3, 1991, pp. 1, 8, 9.

'Generalní dohoda na rok 1991 uzavřená v Bratislavě 28. ledna 1991.' *Hospodářské noviny*, January 30, 1991, p. 3.

Gibian, George. ''The Haircutting and I Waited on the King of England'': Two Recent Works by Bohumil Hrabal.' In *Czech Literature Since 1956: A Symposium*, edited by William E. Harkins and Paul I. Trensky. New York: Bohemica, 1980.

Gitelman, Zvi. 'Power and Authority in Eastern Europe.' In *Change in Communist Systems*, edited by Chalmers Johnson. Stanford, CA: Stanford University Press, 1970.

—— 'Public Opinion in Czechoslovakia.' In *Public Opinion in European Socialist Systems*, edited by Walter D. Connor and Zvi Gitelman. New York: Praeger, 1977(a).

—— 'Soviet Political Culture: Insights from Jewish Emigrés.' *Soviet Studies* 29:4 (October 1977[b]): 543-64.

—— 'The World Economy and Elite Political Strategies in Czechoslovakia, Hungary, and Poland.' In *East-West Relations and the Future of Eastern Europe: Politics and Economics*, edited by Morris Bornstein, Zvi Gitelman, and William Zimmerman. Boston: Allen and Unwin, 1981, pp. 127-61.

'God in Gorbachev's Backyard.' *The Economist*, April 12, 1986, pp. 53-4.

Golan, Golia. *The Czechoslovak Reform Movement: Communism in Crisis, 1962-1968*. Cambridge: Cambridge University Press, 1971.

—— *Reform Rule in Czechoslovakia: The Dubcek Era, 1968-1969.* Cambridge: Cambridge University Press, 1973.

Griffiths, Franklyn. 'A Tendency Analysis of Soviet Policy-Making.' In *Interest Groups in Soviet Politics*, edited by H. Gordon Skilling and Franklyn Griffiths. Princeton, NJ: Princeton University Press, 1971.

Grumlík, Josef. 'Potraty místo antikoncepce?' *Svobodné slovo*, February 17, 1989, pp. 4-6.

Guráň, Peter. 'Priestorová a regionálna diferenciácia rozvodovosti na Slovensku.' *Sociológia* 20:2 (1988): 199-206.

ha. 'Ne materský, ale rodičovský příspevek.' *Hospodářské noviny*, September 21, 1990, 2.

ha and jop. 'První osnovy sociální sítě.' *Hospodářské noviny*, December 5, 1990 (a), pp. 1, 4.

—— 'Zákon o tzv. malé privatizaci schválen.' *Hospodářské noviny*, October 26, 1990 (b), pp. 1, 16.

ha and st. 'Scénář ekonomické reformy příjat.' *Hospodářské noviny*, August 31, 1990, pp. 1, 8.

Haba, Zdeněk. 'Vlastnictví-levicová alternativa.' *Hospodářské noviny*, August 22, 1990, p. 5.

Haderka, Jiří. 'Právně sociologické problémy rozvodovosti v evropských socialistických státech.' *Sociologický časopis* 23:1 (1987): 55-65.

Hajek, Jiří. 'Třikrát Václav Havel.' *Rudé právo*, May 15, 1990, p. 4.

Hala, Jan. 'Francie a my.' *Lidové noviny*, August 6, 1990, p. 3.

Halada, Jan, and Ryvola, Mirko. *Něžná revoluce v pražských ulicích*. Prague: Lidové nakladatelství, 1990.

Hamšík, Dušan. *Writers Against Rulers*. New York, NY: Random House, 1971.

Hannigan, John and McMillan, Carl. 'Joint Investment in Resources Development: Sectoral Approaches to Socialist Integration.' In *East European Economic Assessment*, Part 2. Joint Economic Committee, Congress of the United States. Washington, DC: US Government Printing Office, 1981, pp. 259-96.

Hanzl, Vladimír, Ševerová, Marie, Štěpová, Vlasta, and Žůrek, Jan. 'Problém nejen morální, ale i ekonomický.' *Hospodářské noviny*, January 20, 1989, pp. 8-9.

Hardt, John P. 'Soviet Energy Policy in Eastern Europe' in *East European Economic Assessment*, Part 2. Joint Economic Committee, Congress of the United States. Washington, DC: US Government Printing Office, 1981, pp. 189-220.

—— 'East-West Policies Toward East European Commerce in the 1990s.'

In *United States–East European Relations in the 1990s*, edited by Richard F. Staar. New York: Taylor and Francis, Inc., 1989.

—— 'European Regional Market: A Forgotten Key to Success of European Economics in Transition.' *CRS Report for Congress* 91-113 RCO (January 25, 1991).

Harkins, William E. 'The Czech Novel Since 1956: At Home and Abroad.' In *Czech Literature Since 1956: A Symposium*, edited by William E. Harkins and Paul I. Trensky. New York: Bohemica, 1980 (a).

—— 'Vladimír Paral's Novel Catapult.' In *Czech Literature Since 1956: A Symposium*, edited by William E. Harkins and Paul I. Trensky. New York: Bohemica, 1980 (b).

—— 'Five Works on Contemporary Czech Literature: A Review Article.' In *Cross Currents: A Yearbook of Central European Culture*, volume 8. Edited by Ladislav Matejka. Ann Arbor, MI: Michigan Slavic Materials, 1989, pp. 233-42.

Harkins, William E. and Trensky, Paul I, eds. *Czech Literature Since 1956: A Symposium*. New York: Bohemica, 1980.

Hartl, Jan, and Večerník, Jiří. 'Sociálně třídní diferenciace v subjektivní reflexi.' *Sociologický časopis* 22:5 (1986): 526-36.

Hatina, Bohuslav. 'Jak si kdo ustele.' *Večerní Praha*, August 31, 1988, p. 2.

Häufler, Vlatislav. *Národnostní poměry České socialistické republiky*. Prague: Academia.

Havel, Václav. *Disturbing the Peace*. New York: Alfred A. Knopf, 1990.

—— January 1, 1991. As reported in Jiří Pehe, 'The Agenda for 1991.' *Radio Free Europe Report on Eastern Europe* 2:3 (January 18, 1991): 13.

Havlik, Peter and Levcik, Friedrich. *The Gross Domestic Product of Czechoslovakia, 1970-1980*. World Bank Staff Working Paper #772, Washington DC, 1985.

Heitlinger, Alena. 'Pro-natalist Population Policies in Czechoslovakia.' *Population Studies* 30:1 (March 1976): 122-36.

—— *Women and State Socialism: Sex Inequality in the Soviet Union and Czechoslovakia*. Montreal: McGill-Queen's University Press, 1979.

Hejný, Milan. 'Novela zákona o "malých školách."' *Nové slovo* 21 (May 24, 1990): 7.

Heneka, A., Janouch, František, Prečan, Vilem, and Vladislav, Jan. *A Besieged Culture*. Stockholm-Vienna: The Charter 77 Foundation, 1985.

Herzmann, Jan. 'Zpráva z operativního výzkumu č. 89-14.' Prague: Ústav pro výzkum veřejného mínění při Federálním statistickém úřadu, December 1989.

'Hlas nezavislých spisovatelů.' *Lidové demokracie*, November 25, 1989, p. 5.

Hlaváček, Jiří. 'K ekonomické subjektivitě plánovacího centra.' *Politická ekonomie* 36:10 (1988): 1039-52.

Hlaváček, Jiří, Kysilka, Pavel, and Zieleniec, Józef. 'Plánování a averze k měřeni.' *Politická ekonomie* 36:6 (1988): 593-605.

Hlaváček, Jiří, and Tříska, Dušan. 'Funkce plánového žadání a její vlastnosti.' *Politická ekonomie* 35:4 (1987): 389-99.

Hlavatý, Egon. 'Rozhovor s predsedom Slovenskej ekonomickej spoločnosti pri SAV'. *Ekonomický časopis* 36:8 (1988): 707-15.

Hlavica, Marek. 'Ještě jednou: Uplatnění.' *Mladý svet* 12 (March 14, 1988): 11-13.

'Hlávní směří dalšího rozvíjění souboru opatření ke zdokonalění soustavy plánovítého řízení národního hospodářství.' *Příloha Hospodářských novin* 42 (October 19, 1984) and 43 (October 26, 1984).

Hlavní směry hospodářského a sociálního rozvoje ČSSR na léta 1986-1990 a výhled do roku 2000. Prague, 1986.

Hoda, Jindřich, and Hokeová, Veronika. 'Československo v roce jedna.' *Občanský deník*, December 29, 1990, pp. 1, 3.

Hodnett, Gray and Potichnyj, P.J. *The Ukraine and the Czechoslovak Crisis.* Canberra: Australian National University, 1970.

Hoensch, Jörg K. 'The Slovak Republic, 1939-1945.' In *A History of the Czechoslovak Republic, 1918-1948*, edited by Victor S. Mamatey and Radomír Luža. Princeton, NJ: Princeton University Press, 1973.

Holešovský, Václav. 'Planning and the Market in the Czechoslovak Reform.' In *Plan and Market: Economic Reform in Eastern Europe*, edited by Morris Bornstein. New Haven: Yale University Press, 1973, pp. 313-46.

Holloway, Ronald. 'The Short Film in Eastern Europe: Art and Politics of Cartoons and Puppets.' In *Politics, Art and Commitment in the East European Cinema*, edited by David Paul. London: The Macmillan Press Ltd, 1983, pp. 225-51.

Holubec, Petr. *Kronika sametové revoluce.* Prague: ČTK, 1989.

Hoppanová, I. 'V 'malom' školstve očakávame závažne zmeny.' *Práca,* May 11, 1990, p. 2.

Hora, Štefan. *Za vyššiu účast zamestnaných žien v riadiacej činnosti.* Bratislava: ÚV SSŽ, 1972.

Horčic. Luboš. 'Otevřený kanál 3.' *Mladá fronta*, April 29, 1990, p. 3.

Horský, Ivan. 'Nikto neprehral—zvít'azil rozum!' *Národná obroda*, July 10, 1990, p. 6.

Host'ovečká, Adriana. 'Nepripustíme segregáciu.' *Verejnost'*, May 8, 1990, p. 3.

Hough, Jerry. 'Political Participation in the Soviet Union.' *Soviet Studies* 28:1 (January 1976): 3-20.

—— *The Soviet Union and Social Science Theory.* Cambridge, MA: Harvard University Press, 1977.

Hough, Jerry and Fainsod, Merle. *How the Soviet Union is Governed.* Cambridge, MA: Harvard University Press, 1979.

'Hovoříme o přestavbé.' *HV 1200*, September 5, 1988, pp. 15-17.

Hrbková, Renata. 'Situace na trhu pracovních sil.' *Hospodářské noviny*, September 12, 1990, p. 2.

Hrčka, Štefan. 'Is it like this, or like that?' *Pravda*, December 12, 1990, 3. As reported in 'Press Reacts to Havel's 10 Dec. Proposals.' FBIS-EEU-90-244 (December 19, 1990): 13-14.

—— 'Čaka nás výnimočný stav?' *Pravda*, January 30, 1991 (a), p. 5.

—— 'Demokracie už bolo dost'?' *Pravda*, February 6, 1991 (b), p. 5.

Hríb, Štefan. 'Definitívne rozdelené.' *Lidové noviny*, March 7, 1991, pp. 1, 2.

Hrončeková, Judita. 'Rozdiely v úrovni miezd mužov a žien vo vybraných odvetviách národného hospodárstva.' *Práce a mzda* 2 (1988): 10-16.

Huba, Maňo. 'Prvý raz v historii.' *Smena*, June 16, 1990, p. 3.

Hudáková, G. and Števušková, S. 'Problematika alkoholizmu a závislosti od drog vo svetle štatistických ukazovateľ'ov.' *Protialkoholický obzor* 4 (1988): 245-52.

Husák, Petr. 'Budeme mít na ropu?' *Svobodné slovo*, October 19, 1990, p. 3.

Hvížďala, Karel. 'Bez cizího kapitálu přijde nutná krize.' *Mladá fronta*, October 20, 1990 (a), pp. 1, 2.

—— 'Za šestatřicet měsíců nová armáda.' *Mladá fronta dnes*, December 13, 1990 (b), p. 3.

Hvížďala, Karel, and Vajnerová, Trana. 'Zloděj křiči: chyťte zloděje.' *Mladá fronta*, October 12, 1990, pp. 1, 2.

iba. 'Zabránit' d'alším škodám.' *Rol'nícke noviny*, January 29, 1990, p. 2.

'Ide zrejme o Gabčíkovo.' *Smena*, December 11, 1990, p. 2.

ij. 'Moravská krize.' *Lidové noviny*, February 20, 1991, pp. 1, 2.

Illner, Michal, Linhart, Jiří, Tuček, Milan, and Vodáková, Alena. 'Metodické pojetí výzkumu' Třídní a sociální struktura obyvatelstva ČSSR v roce 1984' a zkušenosti z etapy sběru dat.' *Sociologický časopis* 21:4 (1985): 403-18.

'Importance of Expedient Self-Management.' *Rudé právo*, April 25, 1989, p. 1. As reported in 'Doubts About New Self-Management Viewed.' FBIS-EEU-89-081 (April 28, 1989): 15-16.

'Infighting Apparent in Slovak National Party.' *Národná obroda*, October 31, 1990, p. 13. As reported in FBIS-EEU-90-216 (November 7, 1990): 27.

Institut pro výzkum veřejného mínění. 'Chances and Expectations: Results of the Survey-Czechoslovakia, May, 1990 (a),' p. 7. As reported in 'Growing Dissatisfaction With Political Situation.' FBIS-EEU-90-104 (May 30, 1990 (a)): 17-18.

—— 'Informace pro ČTK.' *Informace*, 1990 (b)

—— 'Informace pro novináře-názory na federální vládu.' *Informace*, 1990 (c).

—— 'Informace pro secretariát prezidenta republiky.' *Informace*, 1990 (d).

—— 'Kdy začít s hospodářskými reformámi?' *Informace*, 1990 (e).

ivvm. 'Vracení majetku.' *Hospodářské noviny*, November 23, 1990, p. 1.

JaD. 'Propuštěno 600 příslušníků.' *Lidové noviny*, October 20, 1990, p. 3.

'Jak jsme volili.' *Lidové noviny*, June 11, 1990, p. 1.

Jak a koho volit? Prague: Spektrum, 1990.

Jakeš, Miloš. 'Plnění programu XVI. sjezdu KSČ.' *Hospodářské noviny*, September 28, 1984, pp. 1, 8-9.

jan, tič, and aš. 'Má vlast v novém hávu.' *Mladá fronta*, May 14, 1990, p. 1, 2.

Jancar, Barbara Wolfe. *Czechoslovakia and the Absolute Monopoly of Power: A Study of Political Power in a Communist System*. New York, NY: Praeger Publishers, 1971.

—— 'Women Under Communism.' In *Women in Politics*, edited by Jane Jaquette. New York: John Wiley, 1974.

—— *Women Under Communism*. Baltimore, MD: Johns Hopkins University Press, 1978.

—— 'Women in the Opposition in Poland and Czechoslovakia in the 1970s' in *Women, State, and Party in Eastern Europe*, edited by Sharon L. Wolchik and Alfred G. Meyer. Durham, NC: Duke University Press, 1985, pp. 168-85.

Jančovičová, Jolana. 'Problematiky ženy v lekarském povolání na Slovensku.' *Sociólogia* 6:5 (1974): 451-9.

Janík, Branislav. 'The CSFR Does Not Need Charity, It Needs Active Trade.' *Národná obroda*, July 28, 1990, p. 1. As reported in 'EC Official Holds Talks, Offers Financial Aid.' FBIS-EEU-90-148 (August 1, 1990): 14-15.

Janková, Kateřína. 'Opožděné díky osvoboditelům.' *Práce*, March 13, 1990, pp. 1, 2.

Janků, Jana. 'Málo dobrých správ.' *Národná obroda*, January 21, 1991, p. 2.

Janos, Andrew. 'The One-Party State and Social Mobilization: East Europe Between the Wars.' In *Authoritarian Politics in Modern Society*, edited by Samuel P. Huntington and Clement Moore. New York, NY: Basic Books, 1979.

Janyška, Petr. 'Co řekly volby.' *Respekt* 39 (December 11, 1990): 4, 5.
—— 'Čistý řez.' *Respekt* 9 (February 25–March 3, 1991 (a)): 2.
—— 'Strana bez rozkolu.' *Respekt* 3 (January 14–20, 1991 (b)): 2.
jaš and jvs. 'Změna vládu neohrozí.' *Lidové noviny*, February 25, 1991, p. 2.
jb. 'Účet armádního generála.' *Občanský deník*, October 4, 1990, p. 1.
jd. 'Mrazíky místo ropy.' *Svobodné slovo*, January 5, 1991, pp. 1, 4.
'Jedna otázka místopředsedovi federální vlády P. Rychetskému.' *Svobodné slovo*, February 2, 1991, p. 2.
Jelínek, Jan. 'Sám v ekologickém poli.' *Mladá fronta dnes*, December 6, 1990, p. 3.
Jelinek, Yeshayahu. *The Parish Republic: Hlinka's Slovak People's Party.* Boulder, CO: East European Monographs, 1976.
—— *The Lust for Power: Nationalism, Slovakia, and the Communists, 1918-1948.* Boulder, CO: East European Monographs, 1983.
Jeneral, Jaroslav. 'Komunisté v národních výborech pří rozvojí socialistické demokracie a přestavbě společností.'
'Jesenné predsednictvo SKS bude v Bratislava?' *Pravda*, February 14, 1990, p. 1.
'Ještě jednou: uplatnění.' *Mladý svět* 12 (March 14, 1988): 11-13.
jet. 'Osudným mu byl listopad 1989.' *Mladá fronta dnes*, October 19, 1990 (a), pp. 1, 2.
jet. 'Policie nemá lidi.' *Hospodářské noviny*, August 24, 1990 (b), p. 8.
Jezdík, Vaclav. 'The First Quarter of 1986.' *Hospodářské noviny* 17 (1986): 2.
Jičínský, Zdeněk. 'Československo—právní stat.' *Lidové noviny*, December 1988, p.7.
Jírů, Jaroslav. 'Vstupujeme do dramatického období.' *Lidové noviny*, January 4, 1991, p. 7.
'Jmenovací dekrety.' *Práce*, March 15, 1990, pp. 1, 2.
John, Zdeněk. 'Jaká bude nezaměstnanost.' *Mladá fronta*, December 8, 1990, pp. 1, 2.
—— 'Dohodnou se?' *Mladá fronta dnes.* January 4, 1991, p. 3.
John, Zdeněk, and Leschtina, Jiří. 'The Oil Puzzle Continues.' *Mladá fronta dnes*, October 10, 1990, pp. 1,2. As reported in 'Economics Minister: Gas Rationing to Stop 1 November.' FBIS-EEU-90-200 (October 16, 1990): 23.
Johnson, Chalmers, ed. *Change in Communist Systems.* Stanford, CA: Stanford University Press, 1970.
Johnson, Owen V. *Slovakia, 1918-1938: Education and the Making of a Nation.* New York, NY: Columbia University Press, 1985.

Joint Ventures in Czechoslovakia. Prague: Czechoslovak Chamber of Commerce and Industry, 1986.

jop. 'Devizový zákon schválen.' *Hospodářské noviny*, November 29, 1990, pp. 1, 8.

Josko, Anna. 'The Slovak Resistance Movement.' In *A History of the Czechoslovak Republic, 1918-1948,* edited by Victor S. Mamatey and Radomir Luza. Princeton, NJ: Princeton University Press, 1973, pp. 362-86.

Jowitt, Kenneth. 'An Organizational Approach to the Study of Political Culture in Marxist-Leninist Systems.' *American Political Science Review* 68:3 (September 1974): 1171-91.

js. 'Scénáře reforem připraveny pro parlament.' *Hospodářské noviny*, September 4, 1990, p. 1.

Jurovský, Anton. *Mladež a špolocnost'.* Bratislava: Veda, 1974.

'K otázkám přestavby hospodářského mechanismu.' *Rudé právo*, January 29, 1987, pp. 3-5.

'K perestroike khoziaistvennogo mekhanizma v ChSSR.' *Voprosy ekonomiki* 6 (June 1988): 114-20.

Kabátek, Zdeněk. 'Úspěchy čs. zemědělství.' *Respekt*, February 18-24, 1991, p. 8.

Kadaně, Lubomír. 'Zákon o podniku.' *Hospodářské noviny*, May 11, 1990, p. 4.

Kalínová, Lenka. *Máme nedostatek pracovních sil?* Prague: Nakladatelství Svoboda, 1979.

Kalous, Jaroslav. 'Druhá půlka žebříčku.' *Mladá fronta*, November 23, 1988, p. 3.

Kaminski, Bartlomiej and Janes, Robert W. 'Economic Rationale for Eastern Europe's Third World Policy.' *Problems of Communism* 37:2 (March/April, 1988): 15-27.

Kandidat Občanského Fóra. Prague: Koordinační centrum OF, 1990.

Kaplan, Karel. *The Communist Party in Power: A Profile of Party Politics in Czechoslovakia,* Translated and edited by Fred Eidlen. Boulder, CO: Westview Press, 1987.

Kavka, Jiří. 'Politická platforma strany želených.' *Zelení*, May 24, 1990, p. 6.

kc. 'Hranice otevrené nebo zavrené.' *Svět hospodářství*, March 3, 1990, p. 6.

kčr. 'Armádu jen k obraně.' *Lidová demokracie*, November 9, 1990, p. 7.

kd. 'Recommendation with Suggestions for Extra Provisions.' *Zěmědelské noviny*, May 25, 1988, p. 4. As reported in 'Amendment to Permit

Reprivatization of Land.' FBIS-EEU-88-l07 (June 3, 1988): 22.

'Kde se v této zemi vzal rasismus?' *Fórum* 31 (August 29-September 4, 1990): 2.

'Kdy nabere hospodářství dech?' *Hospodářské noviny*, August 15, 1990, p. 1, 4.

'Kdyby se OF a VPN staly stranámi.' *Hospodářské noviny*, November 11, 1990, p. 2.

Kelley, Donald. 'Toward a Model of Soviet Decision-Making: A Research Note.' *American Political Science Review* LXCII:4 (1973).

Keltošová, Olga. 'Konečne peniaze aj pre kultúru.' *Čas*, January 4, 1991, p. 5.

Kende, Pierre. 'The Division of Resources in the Area of Consumption.' In *Equality and Inequality in Eastern Europe*, edited by Pierre Kende and Zdeněk Strmiska. New York: St. Martin's Press, 1987, pp. 72-110.

Kende, Pierre and Strmiska, Zdeněk. *Equality and Inequality in Eastern Europe*. Translated by Frančoise Read. New York: St. Martin's, 1987.

Kerner, Robert J. *Bohemia in the Eighteenth Century*. New York: Macmillan, 1932.

—— *Czechoslovakia*. Berkeley, CA: University of California Press, 1949.

kf. 'Prispeje kompromis k zlepšeniu školstva?' *Smena*, April 19, 1990, p. 1.

Kis, Pavol. 'Skvalitňovat' dozor nad dodržiavaním zákonnosti.' *Pravda*, November 10, 1988, p. 4.

kk. 'Joint-Ventures v Československu.' *Lidové noviny*, January 10, 1991, p. 7.

kl. 'Dražobný bonbón v Bratislave.' *Hospodářské noviny*, February 2, 1991, pp. 1, 2.

Klapáč, Jozef. 'Právo životného postredia v územnom plánovaní a stavebnóm konámi.' *Životné postredie* 23:6 (1989): 323-4.

Klaus, Václav. 'Cíle a postupy finančni politiky v roce 1991.' *Hospodářské noviny*, December 19, 1990 (a), pp. 1, 4.

—— 'Proč privatizace.' *Občanský deník*. August 17, 1990 (b), p. 1.

Klaus, Václav, and Tříska, Dušan. 'Ekonomické centrum, přestavba a rovnováha.' *Politická ekonomie* 36:8 (1988): 817-29.

Klein, George. 'The Role of Ethnic Politics in the Czechoslovak Crisis of 1968 and the Yugoslav Crisis of 1971.' *Studies in Comparative Communism* 7:4 (Winter 1975): 339-69.

Klevisová, Nada. 'Kudy? Kam?' *Tvorba*, December 21, 1988, pp. 1, 2.

'Klidný průběh voleb.' *Lidové noviny*, November 26, 1990, pp. 1, 2.

Klusoň, Václav. 'K přestavbě hospodářského mechanismu.' *Politická ekonomie* 36:11 (1988): 1-16.

—— 'Peníze neznají hranice.' *Hospodářské noviny*, November 21, 1990, p. 4.

Klusoň, Václav, Hrnčíř, Miroslav, and Seják, Josef. 'Směry vývoje hospodářského mechanismu intenzívního typu.' *Politická ekonomie* 35:5 (1987): 477-88.

Koenig, Ernest. 'Agriculture.' In *Czechoslovakia*, edited by Vratislav Busek and Nicholas Spulber. New York: Frederick A. Praeger, 1957, pp. 245-67.

Kobýlka, Jari. 'Westerners Discover CSFR JVs: 220 in Three Months.' *Business Eastern Europe* (July 23, 1990): 243.

Kohák, Jaroslav, and Muff, František. 'Prvoradý úkol: pozornost mládeži.' *Život strany* 4 (1988): 28-30.

'Kolik si půjčujeme.' *Lidové noviny*, February 22, 1991, pp. 1, 2.

Komárek, Martin. 'Odvolán s plnou důvěrou.' *Mladá fronta dnes*, October 19, 1990, p. 2.

Komárek, Valtr. 'Quality and Convertibility, Not Quantity. Conditions and Constraints on CSSR Social Development.' *Hospodářské noviny*, October 21, 1988 (a), pp. 8-9. As reported in 'Quality, Convertibility Most Important, Says Komarek.' JPRS-EER-89-015 (February 15, 1989): 42-8.

—— 'Restructuring: Theory and Practice; Open Economic Issues of the Future.' *Nová mysl*, October 5, 1988 (b), pp. 69-80. As reported in 'Komarek Views Problems of Economic Future.' JPRS-EER-89-015 (February 15, 1989): 36-42.

—— 'Prognostická sebereflexe čs. společnosti.' *Politická ekonomie* 37:5 (1989): 523-35.

Komunistická strana Československa. *Akční program kommunistické strany československa priatý na plenarím zasedání úv KSČ dne 5, dubna 1968*. Prague, 1968.

—— 'Zpráva ústředního výboru Komunistické strany Československa o plnění závěru XVI. sjezdu strany.' *Rudé právo*, March 27, 1986, supplement.

'Koncepce bezpečností.' *Svobodné slovo*, February 11, 1991, p. 1.

'Konec mnoha fam.' *Mladá fronta*, April 28, 1990, pp. 1, 2.

Königová, Marie. 'Doktrína večí nejen generální.' *Rudé právo*, October 4, 1990, p. 5.

'Konkretizaca zásad přestavby hopodářského mechanismu ČSSR.' *Příloha Hospodářskych novin*, March 27, 1987, pp. 1-16.

Korbel, Josef. *The Communist Subversion of Czechoslovakia: 1938-1948: The Failure of Coexistence*. Princeton, NJ: Princeton University Press, 1959.

—— *Twentieth-century Czechoslovakia: The Meanings of Its History*. New York, NY: Columbia University Press, 1977.

Korbonski, Andrzej. 'Bureaucracy and Interest Groups in Communist Societies: The Case of Czechoslovakia.' *Studies in Comparative Communism* 4:1 (January 1971): 57–79.

—— 'The Politics of Economic Reforms in Eastern Europe: The Last Thirty Years'. *Soviet Studies* 41:1 (January 1989): 1–19.

Korcak, Joseph. 'Z discuse na 12. zasedani UV KSČ.' *Rudé právo*, December 7, 1984.

Kosický vládní program. Prague: Nakladatelství svoboda, 1974.

Košnár, Jozef, Okáli, Ivan, and Šikula, Milan. 'Politická ekonómia socializmu a proces přestavby hospodářského mechanizmu.' *Ekonomický časopis* 36:8 (1988): 716–27.

Kostelancik, David J. 'The Gypsies of Czechoslovakia: Political and Ideological Considerations in the Development of Policy'. Unpublished manuscript, Ann Arbor, MI, 1987.

Kostka, Antonín. 'Pioneers of Historical Progress.' Prague Domestic Service. January 29, 1987. As reported in 'Prague Comments on Significance of CPSU Session.' FBIS-EEU-87-020 (January 30, 1987): D1–D3.

Koubská, Libuše. 'Jaderný poprask.' *Lidové noviny*, July 21, 1990, pp. 1, 16.

Kovač, Peter. 'Představy—a možnosti.' *Rudé právo*, May 15, 1990, pp. 1, 2.

Kozová, M., and Bedrna, Z. 'Prediction and Evaluation of Agricultural Nonpoint Source Pollution and Water Resource Conservation.' *Ekologia CSSR* 8:3 (1989): 307–14.

Král, Milan. 'Výmenou za ropu.' *Národná obroda*, October 10, 1990, p. 1.

Kramer, Alexandr. 'Kudy do Ameriky?' *Lidové noviny*, January 27, 1990, p. 4.

Kramer, John K. 'The Policy Dilemmas of East Europe's Energy Gap.' In *East European Economic Assessment*, Part 2. Joint Economic Committee, Congress of the United States. Washington, DC: US Government Printing Office, 1981, pp. 459–75.

—— 'Soviet-CEMA Energy Ties.' *Problems of Communism* 34:4 (July/August 1985): 32–47.

Kraus, David. 'Czechoslovakia in the 1980's.' *Current History* 84 (November 1985): 373–6, 39–93.

Krejčí, Jaroslav. *Social Change and Stratification in Postwar Czechoslovakia*. New York: Columbia University Press, 1972.

—— 'Classes and Elites in Socialist Czechoslovakia.' In *The Social Structure of Eastern Europe: Transition and Process in Czechoslovakia, Hungary, Poland, Romania, and Yugoslavia*, edited by Bernard Lewis Faber. New York: Praeger Publishers, 1976.

—— *National Income and Outlay in Czechoslovakia, Poland, and Yugoslavia.* New York: St. Martin's Press, 1982.

Kress, John H. 'Representation of Positions on the CPSU Politburo.' *Slavic Review* 39:2 (June 1980): 218-38.

Kriseová, Eda. *Václav Havel: The Authorized Biography.* New York: The Atlantic Monthly Press, 1991.

Kříž, Karel. 'Cenové zemětřesení.' *Lidové noviny.* December 29, 1990 (a), pp. 1, 3.

—— 'Řekneme to nahlas.' *Lidové noviny.* October 31, 1990 (b), p. 1.

Kříž, Karel, and Kotrba, Josef. 'Tentokrát na ostro.' *Lidové noviny*, January 2, 1991, pp. 1, 2.

Krno, Martin. 'Nestačí byt' pasívnym divákom...' *Pravda*, June 28, 1988, p. 5.

Kroulik, Barbara. 'Czechoslovak Arms Trade.' *RFE/RL Daily Report*, No. 58, March 22, 1991, p. 2.

Kroupová, Alena. 'K projednání zprávy o společensky závažných tendencích v rodinné problematice.' *Demografie* 30:3 (1988): 243-4.

Křovák, Jiří. 'Problémy v sociálně ekonomických systémech a úloha expertů při jejich řešení.' *Ekonomický časopis* 36:7 (1988): 669-83.

Krýl, Pavel. 'Rozchod se stranou OF.' *Rudé právo*, January 21, 1991, pp. 1, 2.

'KSČ vrátí majetek.' *Svobodné slovo*, October 16, 1990, p. 1.

'Kto najviac doplatí?' *Práce*, December 28, 1990, p. 5.

Kučera, Milan. 'Domácnosti a bydlení cíkánského obyvatelstva.' *Demográfie* 26:2 (1984): 172-8.

Kuchař, Ivan, and Pavlík, Zdeněk. 'Optimalizace kvality populace.' *Demografie* 4 (1987): 289-98.

Kuchařová, Věra. 'Specifické a obecné ve vzdělanostně kvalifikačním rozvoji dělnické třídy v socialistickém Československu.' *Sociologický časopis* 20:6 (1984): 598-610.

Kuchařová, Věra, and Kuchař, Pavel. 'Proměny společenského postavení a uplatněni delnické mládeže v socialistickém Československu.' *Sociologický časopis* 21:5 (1985): 501-13.

Kulčarová, V., and Gomboš, M. 'Water as a Distributor of Undesired Substances in Ecosystems.' *Ekológia* ČSSR 8:4 (1989): 337-60.

'Kultura na přetřesu.' *Svobodné slovo*, February 1, 1991, p. 1.

Kunstová, Alena. 'Možnosti zjišťování a měření negativních jevů ve vědomí lidí.' *Sociologický časopis* 22:5 (1986): 514-25.

Kurková, Marie. 'Rovnat křivou hůl—ne stin.' *Mladá fronta*, January 23, 1990, p. 3.

Kusin, Vladimir V. *The Intellectual Origins of the Prague Spring: The*

Development of Reformist Ideas in Czechoslovakia, 1956-1967. Cambridge: Cambridge University Press, 1971.

—— *Political Grouping in the Czechoslovak Reform Movement.* New York, NY: Columbia University Press, 1972.

—— ed. *The Czechoslovak Reform Movement 1968.* Santa Barbara, CA: ABC-Clio, 1973.

—— *From Dubcek to Charter 77: A Study of 'Normalization' in Czechoslovakia, 1968-1978.* New York, NY: St. Martin's Press, 1978.

—— 'Challenge to Normalcy: Political Opposition in Czechoslovakia.' In *Opposition in Eastern Europe,* edited by Rudolf Tokes. London: Macmillan, 1979.

—— 'Husak's Keynote Address.' Radio Free Europe Czechoslovak Situation Report/7 (April 30, 1981): 8-11.

—— 'How to Reform the Economy without a Reform.' Radio Free Europe Czechoslovak Situation Report/4 (February 22, 1982 [a]): 1-4.

—— 'Husak's Czechoslovakia and Economic Stagnation.' *Problems of Communism* 31 (May/June 1982 [b]): 24-37.

—— 'Dissent in Czechoslovakia after 1968.' In *Dissent in Eastern Europe,* edited by Jane Leftwich Curry. New York: Praeger, 1983, pp. 48-59.

—— 'Husak's Speech.' Radio Free Europe Czechoslovak Situation Report/6 (April 16, 1986): 11-14.

—— 'Reform and Dissidence in Czechoslovakia.' *Current History* 86 (November 1987): 361-4, 383.

—— 'The Leadership Taken Aback by the Ground Swell of Opposition.' Radio Free Europe Czechoslovak Situation Report/2 (January 26, 1989): 9-10.

Kussi, Peter. 'Havel's "The Garden Party" Revisited.' In *Czech Literature Since 1956: A Symposium,* edited by William E. Harkins and Paul I. Trensky. New York: Bohemica, 1980.

Kusý, Miroslav, and Šimecka, Milan. 'Dialogues With the Young Generation: A First Dialogue.' In *Cross Currents: A Yearbook of Central European Culture,* volume 6. Edited by Ladislav Matejka. Ann Arbor, MI: Michigan Slavic Materials, 1987.

kva and ctk. 'Ministr přípomíná bibli.' *Svobodné slovo,* September 4, 1990, p. 1.

Kvacková, Radka. 'Co s tolika dětmí?' *Svobodné slovo,* February 23, 1990, pp. 1, 4.

Kwiatkowski, Stanislaw. 'Attitudes Towards Political Leaders and Institutions.' Report of the Center for Research on Public Opinion, Warsaw, 1989.

Kysilka, Pavel. 'Počátky úsilí o ekonomické reformy.' *Politická ekonomie* 2 (1989): 219-33.

'Kyslík pro všechny!' *Práce*, November 15, 1989, p. 5.

la. 'Odchod co nejdřivě.' *Zěmědelské noviny*, January 24, 1990, p. 2.

Labudová, Hana, and Wlater, Karel. 'Co říkáme a co děláme.' *Rudé právo*, July 29, 1986, p. 3.

Lacko, Jindřich. 'Podmínky jsou stále náročnější.' *Svět hospodářství*, April 5, 1989, p. 1.

Lane, David. *The End of Inequality? Stratification under State Socialism.* Harmondsworth, UK: Penguin Books, Ltd., 1971.

Lapidus, Gail Warshofsky. 'Political Mobilization, Participation, and Leadership: Women in Soviet Politics.' *Comparative Politics* 8 (October 1975): 90-118.

Lavíčka, Vaclav. 'Good Accounts Make Good Friends.' *Hospodářské noviny*, June 8, 1990, p. 1. As reported in FBIS-EEU-90-117 (June 18, 1990), p. 26.

lb. 'Pokles důvěry pokračuje.' *Lidové noviny*, October 9, 1990. pp. 1, 2.

Leff, Carol Skalnik. *National Conflict in Czechoslovakia: The Making and Remaking of a State, 1918-1987.* Princeton, NJ: Princeton University Press, 1988.

Lesná, Luba. 'Dovolite otázku?' *Verejnost'* 36 (May 8, 1990): 7.

Levcik, Friedrich. 'Czechoslovakia: Economic Performance in the Post-Reform Period and Prospects for the 1980's.' In *East European Economic Assessment*, Part 1. Joint Economic Committee, Congress of the United States. Washington, DC: US Government Printing Office, 1981, pp. 377-424.

—— 'The Czechoslovak Economy in the 1980's.' In *East European Economies: Slow Growth in the 1980's*, volume 3. Joint Economic Committee, Congress of the United States. Washington, DC: US Government Printing Office, 1986, pp. 85-108.

—— 'Economic Reforms in Czechoslovakia.' In *Pressures for Reform in the East European Economies*. Joint Economic Committee, Congress of the United States. Washington, DC: United States Government Printing Office, 1989, pp. 215-29.

'Liberalization Does Not Mean Arbitrariness.' *Zemědělské noviny*, December 29, 1990, pp. 1, 3.

Liehm, Antonin J. *Closely Watched Films: The Czechoslovak Experience.* White Plains, NY: International Arts and Science Press, 1974.

—— 'Milan Kundera: Czech Writer.' In *Czech Literature Since 1956: A Symposium*, edited by William E. Harkins and Paul I. Trensky. New York: Bohemica, 1980 (a), pp. 40-55.

—— 'Some Observations on Czech Culture and Politics in the 1960's.' In *Czech Literature Since 1956: A Symposium*, edited by William E. Harkins and Paul I. Trensky. New York: Bohemica, 1980 (b).

—— 'Milos Forman: the Style and the Man.' In *Politics, Art and Commitment in the East European Cinema*, edited by David Paul. London: The Macmillan Press, Ltd., 1983, pp. 211-24.

Lihocký, Julius, ed. *The Forty Years of Slovak Educational System in the Socialist Czechoslovakia*. Bratislava: Slovak Pedagogical Publishing House, 1989.

Likařová, Zdenka. 'Cesta z temnoty.' *Tvorba* 25 (June 20, 1990): 4.

Linhart, Jiří. 'Názorová kulturní pluralita.' *Sociologický časopis* 26:4 (1990): 313-16.

Linhart, Jiří, Tuček, Milan, and Vodáková, Alena. 'Šetření 'Třídní a sociální struktura obyvatelstva ČSSR v roce 1984.' *Sociológia* 17:2 (1985): 189-96.

—— 'K problematice hodnotových orientací a ekonomického vědomí obyvatel ČSSR v období intenzifikace národního hospodářství.' *Sociologický časopis* 22:6 (1986): 630-43.

Liška, Petr. 'Tolerancí místo sporů.' *Lidové noviny*, July 10, 1990, p. 1.

ln. 'Generál Vacek odvolán.' *Lidové noviny*, October, 18, 1990, pp. 1, 2.

Loebl, Eugen. *My Mind on Trial*. New York, NY: Harcourt Brace Jovanovich, 1976.

Lohmeyer, Michael. 'Interview with Environmental Minister Bedrich Moldan.' *Die Presse*, February 27, 1990, p. 4. As reported in 'Minister Advocates Phasing Out Nuclear Power.' FBIS-EEU-90-040 (February 28, 1990): 25.

Lovaš, Ladislav and Jurečková, Viera. 'Postoje súčasnej učňovskej mládeže k jej budúcim povolaniam.' *Sociologický časopis* 22:2 (1986): 164-76.

Lowenthal, Richard. 'Development vs. Utopia in Communist Policy.' In *Change in Communist Systems*, edited by Chalmers Johnson. Stanford: University Press, 1970, pp. 33-116.

Ludz, Peter Christian. *The Changing Party Elite in East Germany*. Cambridge: Massachusetts Institute of Technology Press, 1972.

Luers, William H. 'Czechoslovakia's Road to Revolution.' *Foreign Affairs* 69:2 (Spring 1990): 77-98.

Lukas, Zdenek. 'Agricultural Reforms and Trade in the CSSR.' *Osteuropa und Wirtschaft*, March 1989, pp. 33-48. As reported in 'Agricultural Reforms and Trade in the CSSR.' JPRS-EER-89-069 (June 15, 1989): 38-42.

Luža, Radomír. *The Transfer of the Sudeten Germans: A Study of Czech-German Relations, 1933-1962*. New York, NY: New York University Press, 1964.

—— 'Czechoslovakia Between Democracy and Communism.' In *A History of the Czechoslovak Republic, 1918-1948*, edited by Victor S. Mamatey and

Radomír Luža. Princeton, NJ: Princeton University Press, 1973.

ma. 'Jak se změní ceny.' *Rudé právo*, December 29, 1990, p. 1.

Mácha, Dalibor, and Sirota, Igor. 'Hrad moderním úřadem.' *Rudé právo*, July 12, 1990, pp. 1, 2.

Macháček, Jan, and Marcela, Jiří. 'Kdy přijde školství na řadu.' *Respekt* 35 (November 7-13, 1990): 7.

Macháček, Ladislav. 'Sociálno-profesionálna orientácia mládeze a rodina.' *Sociologický časopis* 18:2 (1982): 193-203.

—— 'Aktuálne otázky socialistickej výchovy mladej generácie robotníckej triedy.' *Sociologický časopis* 21:5 (1985): 490-500.

—— 'Hnutie mládeže a formovanie jej socialistickej hodnotovej orientácie.' *Sociológia* 20:2 (1988): 129-40.

Machonin, Pavel. *Sociální struktura socialistické společnosti*. Prague: Svoboda, 1966.

Macková, Marta. 'Abychom si nevyčítaly . . .' *Vlasta* 27 (July 6, 1990): 6.

mag. 'Pod světí, bez zábran.' *Svobodné slovo*, January 16, 1991, p. 4.

Magocsi, Paul R. *The Rusyn-Ukrainians of Czechoslovakia*. Vienna, Austria: Wilhelm Braumuller, 1985.

'Malá privatizace žacne v Praze.' *Hospodářské noviny*, December 28, 1990, p. 4.

Malý, Václav, and Herc, Svatopluk. 'Příspěvek k pojetí systému plánovitého řízení v období intenzifikace.' *Politická ekonomie* 36:1 (1988): 17-28.

Mamatey, Victor S. 'The Development of the Czechoslovak Democracy.' In *A History of the Czechoslovak Republic, 1918-1948*, edited by Victor S. Mamatey and Radomír Luža. Princeton, NJ: Princeton University Press, 1973 (a).

—— 'The Establishment of the Republic.' In *A History of the Czechoslovak Republic, 1918-1948*, edited by Victor S. Mamatey and Radomír Luža. Princeton, NJ: Princeton University Press, 1973 (b).

—— 'The Birth of Czechoslovakia: Union of Two Peoples.' In *Czechoslovakia, the Heritage of Ages Past: Essays in Memory of Josef Korbel*, edited by Hans Brisch and Ivan Volgyes. New York, NY: Columbia University Press, 1979.

Mamatey, Victor S. and Radomír Luža, eds. *A History of the Czechoslovak Republic, 1918-1948*. Princeton, NJ: Princeton University Press, 1973.

Mannová, Daniela. 'O státním rozpoctu ČSSR na rok 1987.' *Rude pravo*, December 10, 1986, pp. 1, 2.

Marek, Tomaš. 'Pole pro sociální demagogy.' *Mladá fronta dnes*, December 6, 1990, pp. 1, 2.

Maršal, Petr, and Stupavský, Milan. 'Co naznačily volby.' *Svobodné slovo*, December 28, 1990, p. 7.

Martin, Peter. 'Church-State Relations.' Radio Free Europe, Czechoslovak Situation Report/22 (December 27, 1988): 19-24.

—— 'Economic Results for 1988 Disappointing.' Radio Free Europe, Czechoslovak Situation Report/3 (February 16, 1989 [a]): 7-10.

—— 'Economists Discuss Reform.' Radio Free Europe, Czechoslovak Situation Report/9 (April 27, 1989 [b]): 13-16.

—— 'Signs of Rapprochement with the Vatican.' Radio Free Europe, Czechoslovak Situation Report/9 (April 27, 1989 [c]): 7-11.

—— 'Pope John Paul II in Czechoslovakia.' *Radio Free Report on Eastern Europe* 1:19 (May 11, 1990 [a]): 8-12.

—— 'Scenario for Economic Reform Adopted.' *Radio Free Europe Report on Eastern Europe* 1:42 (October 19, 1990 [b]): 5-8.

—— 'Tough Choice Faced on Nuclear Power.' *Radio Free Europe Report on Eastern Europe* 1:34 (August 24, 1990 [c]): 11-13.

—— 'Privatization: A Balance Sheet.' *Radio Free Europe Report on Eastern Europe* 2:5 (February 1, 1991): 7-11.

Martinek, Peter. 'Nekrológ Varšavskej zmluve.' *Smena*, February 13, 1991, p. 6.

Mašek, M., and Strapec, M. 'Územné plánovanie vo vnútri mesta.' *Životné prostredie* 23:6 (1989): 319-23.

Mastny, Vojtech. *The Czechs Under Nazi Rule: The Failure of National Resistance*. New York, NY: Columbia University Press, 1971.

Matejka, Jaromir. '1,134 New State Enterprises.' *Hospodářské noviny*, January 1989, p. 2. As reported in JPRS-EER-89-044 (April 20, 1989): 10-11.

Matějovský, Vladimír. 'Všude jen za tvrde.' *Mladá fronta dnes*, January 3, 1991, p. 1.

Matějů, Pavla, and Šulcová, Barbara. 'Težko vybirat.' *Mladá fronta*, March 15, 1990, p. 4.

Matějů, Petr. 'Demokratizace vzdělání a reprodukce vzdělanostní struktury v ČSSR ve světle mobilitních dat.' *Sociologický časopis* 22:2 (1986 [a]): 131-51.

—— 'Vzdělání—mzda—životní úroveň.' *Sociologický časopis* 22:6 (1986 [b]): 599-613.

—— 'Role vzdělání a kvalifikace ve výkonové společnosti.' *Sociologický časopis* 26:4 (1990): 290-7.

Matuška, Peter. 'Disputes and Protests Over the New Abortion Law.' Radio Free Europe, Czechoslovak Situation Report/1 (January 17, 1987): 41-3.

—— 'Relations between Czechs and Slovaks.' Radio Free Europe, Czechoslovak Situation Report/6 (March 30, 1989): 3-8.

—— 'Czechs and Slovaks Critical of Parliament.' Radio Free Europe/Radio Liberty Daily Report/61 (March 27, 1991): 2.

'Maximum možného.' *Svobodné slovo*, December 18, 1990, pp. 1, 2.

mb. 'Smutné bilancie minulosti.' *Rozhlas a televizia*, July 8, 1990.

McDonough, Peter; Lopez Pina, Antonio; and Barnes, Samuel H. 'The Spanish Republic in Political Transition.' *British Journal of Political Science* 11:1 (January 1981): 49-75.

Melichařková, Jana. 'Chranit' a zveladovat' talent.' *Čas*, July 16, 1990, p. 5.

Menke, Henrich. 'Differentiated Compensation in Practice.' *Práce a mzda*, December 1988, pp. 6-11. As reported in 'Transition to Pay According to Performance Viewed.' JPRS-EER-89-037 (April 4, 1989): 33-7.

Merhaut, Boris. 'Udaje dřivě tabu.' *Svobodné slovo*, March 16, 1990, p. 6.

Merta, Vladimír. 'Hrozí kolaps hudebního trhu.' *Hospodářské noviny*, January 9, 1991, p. 13.

Meyer, Alfred G. 'The Comparative Study of Communist Political Systems.' *Slavic Review* 26:1 (March 1967): 3-28.

Mezřický, Václav. 'Problems of Political Reforms in Central and Eastern Europe.' Paper presented at roundtable, 'Political Changes in Central and Eastern Europe,' San Francisco, August 1990.

mf. 'Svátek matek proti MDŽ.' *Lidové noviny*, April 1988, p. 5.

Michalová, Tereza. 'Menej bilancovania, viac výkričníkov.' *Pravda*, November 30, 1988, p. 4.

Michalová, Valéria. 'Postavenie a úloha služieb pri urýchl'ovaní sociálno-ekonomického rozvoja.' *Ekonomický časopis* 36:7 (1988): 612-29.

Milbrath, Lester W. *Political Participation*. Chicago: Rand McNally, 1965.

'Miliardar z USA ako sponzor.' *Čas*, May 3, 1990, p. 3.

Millar, James, ed. *Politics, Work, and Daily Life in the USSR*. Cambridge: University Press, 1987.

min. 'Moja penazenka spl'asla.' *Verejnost'*, November 13, 1990, p. 2.

Minar, Imrich. 'Vrat'me národu dejiny.' *Nové slovo*, February 8, 1990, p. 20.

Ministerstvo životního prostředí České republiky. 'Koncepce ekologické politiky České republiky.' *Územní plánovaní a urbanismus* 3 (1990 [a]).

—— *Životní prostředí České republiky*. Prague: Academia, 1990.

'Ministr přípomina bibli.' *Svobodné slovo*, September 4, 1990, p. 1.

'Ministří v Budapeští.' *Svobodné slovo*, January 22, 1990, pp. 1, 2.

Míšková, Věra. 'Karlovy Vary za devet dni.' *Rudé právo*, June 28, 1990, p. 4.

Mišovič, Jan. 'Názory na vzt'ahy národov a národností ČSSR.' *Informace*, March 1990.

——— 'Názory čs. veřejnosti na vztahy Čechů a Slováků a na federaci.' *Informace*, n.d.

'Místo na Javaj do Prahy.' *Zěmědelské noviny*, March 7, 1990.

Mlýnář, Vladimír. 'Povedená dohoda.' *Lidové noviny*, December 1, 1990, p. 2.

Mlýnář, Zdeněk. *Nightfrost in Prague: The End of Humane Socialism.* Translated by Paul Wilson. New York, NY: Karz Publishers, 1980.

Mojžíšková, Soňa. 'Záruka pro zahraniční.' *Hospodářské noviny*, April 13, 1990, p. 4.

Moldan, Bedřich. Interview. 'It is Peaceful Across the Bleached Out Peaks.' *Profil*, April 17, 1990, pp. 74-8. As reported in JPRS-EER-90-092 (June 26, 1990): 7.

'More Companies Setting Up Offices in Czechoslovakia.' *Business Eastern Europe* (July 31, 1989): 243-4.

'Moric se distancuje.' *Lidové noviny*, October 31, 1990, p. 2.

Móricová, Marta. 'Vláda musí chránit' občana.' *Národná obroda*, November 16, 1990 (a), p. 3.

——— 'Prvé dražby vo februári.' *Národná obroda*, January 4, 1990 (b), p. 1.

——— 'Sociálne dopady: prioritná otázka.' *Národná obroda*, January 3, 1991, p. 3.

Morrisson, Christian. 'Distribution of Incomes and Rights in the West and in the East.' In *Equality and Inequality in Eastern Europe*, edited by Pierre Kende and Zdenek Strmiska. New York: St. Martin's Press, 1987, pp. 198-245.

Mošnová, Eva. 'Hlavní směry jeho přestavby v etapě urychlení hospodářského a sociálního rozvoje.' *Podniková organizace* 3 (1987): 98-101.

'Most Members New: the Czech National Council Presidium Appointed a New Czech Republic Government.' *Rudé právo*, June 30, 1990, pp. 1, 2.

M.P. 'The Case of Augustin Navratil.' Radio Free Europe Czechoslovak Situation Report/10 (July 11, 1986 [a]): 21-4.

M.P. 'Prague Exercises Firm Control Over Religious Activists and Dissidents.' Radio Free Europe Czechoslovak Situation Report/1 (January 7, 1986 [b]): 27-31.

M.P. 'Cardinal Tomasek Calls upon the West for Help.' Radio Free Europe Czechoslovak SR/4 (March 10, 1986 [c]): 9-12.

M.P. 'Protestent Churches in Czechoslovakia: Less Than Complete Loyalty?' Radio Free Europe Background Report/93 (July 10, 1986 [d]): 1-8.

Mrázová, Helena, and Kučerová, Vladka. 'Brutalita vzrusta.' *Mladá fronta*, June 30, 1990, p. 4.

ms. 'Kroky ke směnitelnosti koruny.' *Hospodářské noviny*, October 26, 1990 (a), pp. 1, 16.

ms. 'Strategie dozná úprav.' *Hospodářské noviny*, December 19, 1990 (b), p. 1.

ms. 'Vedle moralního i finanční odškodnění.' *Hospodářské noviny*, November 21, 1990 (c), pp. 1, 4.

Musil, Jiří, and Linhart, Jiří. 'Naše mravní krize a politický pluralismus.' *Sociologický časopis*, April 1990, pp. 303-12.

Myant, Martin. *The Czechoslovak Economy, 1948-1988*. Cambridge: University Press, 1989.

Nadvorník, Lukaš. 'Konečně nezavislá televize a rozhlas.' *Lidová demokracie*, June 15, 1990, p. 3.

'Nahlas o životním prostředí v Bratislavě.' *Lidové noviny*, January 1, 1988, p. 7.

'Náměty jsou Ted' je uskutečnit.' *Mladá fronta*, October 24, 1988, pp. 1, 3.

'Národnost posluchačů československých výsokých skol 1970-1986.' *Demografie* 30:3 (1988): 267.

Navarová, Hana. 'Impact of the Economic and Political Changes in Czechoslovakia for Women.' 1990, MS.

Navářová, Ružena. 'Občané české republiky o svém vztahu k národním výborům základního stupne.' *Národní vybory*, February 1990, pp. 20-1.

'Návrh cenového stropu.' *Rudé právo*, December 28, 1990, p. 1.

'Návrh zákona.' *Zěmědelské noviny*, January 31, 1991, p. 7.

'Několik vět.' *Svobodné slovo*, November 30, 1989, p. 5.

Nelson, Daniel N. 'On Political Participation in Communist Systems.' *East European Quarterly* 14:1 (Spring, 1980): 315-22.

—— *Communism and the Politics of Inequalities*. Lexington, MA: Lexington Books, 1983.

Nelson, Daniel N., and White, Stephen, eds. *Communist Legislatures in Comparative Perspective*. London: Macmillan, 1981.

Nemec, F., and Moudry, V. *The Soviet Seizure of Subcarpathian Ruthenia*. Westport, CT: Hyperion Press, Inc., 1981.

Nemec, Ludvík. 'Solution of the Minorities Problem'. In *A History of the Czechoslovak Republic, 1918-1948*, edited by Victor S. Mamatey and Radomir Luža. Princeton, NJ: Princeton University Press, 1973.

Neovesky, Martina. 'The 14th National Congress of Women.' Radio Free Europe Czechoslovak Situation Report/15 (July 14, 1989).

'Nesouhlasí s liberály.' *Občanský deník*, December 18, 1990, p. 3.

Nešporová, Alena. 'K vývoji zaměstnanosti v socialistických zemích.' *Hospodářské noviny*, April 17, 1989, pp. 8-9.

'New Private Farmers are Rarer than Hen's Teeth for Now; More Interest in Private Plots.' *Zěmědelské noviny*, August 18, 1990, pp. 1, 3. As reported in 'Lack of Interest in Private Farming Slowing Privatization.' JPRS-EER-90-141 (October 16, 1990): 36-7.

'Nezamestnanost' narastá.' *Čas*, February 1, 1991, p. 1.

Nežna revolúcia. Bratislava: ČSTK, 1989.

nig. 'Složení parlamentu.' *Rudé právo*, February 21, 1990, p. 11.

no. 'Právomoc nad vlastnými zdrojmi.' *Národná obroda*, September 26, 1990, pp. 1, 2.

no and st. 'Will There Be Oil From Iran.' *Národná obroda*, December 15, 1990, p. 1. As reported in 'Iranians Offer Oil in Return for Slovak Goods.' FBIS-EEU-90-246 (December 21, 1990): 16.

'Notes on the Margin of General Forecast of the RandD, Economic, and Social Development in the CSSR until 2010.' *Lidové noviny*, April 1989, p. 22. As reported in 'CPCZ Economic Commission Rejects Proposed Reforms.' JPRS-EER-89-087 (August 3, 1989): 16-17.

Nováček, Petr. 'A Decisive 'No' to the Blackmailers.' *Zěmědelské noviny*, November 2, 1990, p. 2. As reported in 'Hunger Strikers Called Democracy "Blackmailers".' FBIS-EEU-90-218 (November 9, 1990): 12.

Novak, Arne. *Czech Literature*. Translated by Peter Kussi. Edited by William E. Harkins. Ann Arbor, MI: Michigan Slavic Publications, 1976.

Novák, Pavel. 'Co nového ve školách.' *Rudé právo*, June 7, 1990, pp. 1, 2.

'Novela Hospodářského zákoníku.' *Příloha hospodářských novin* 20 (1990).

'Novozvolené ústredné organy strany slovenskej obrody.' *L'ud*, February 2, 1988: p. 1.

'Now Official: CSSR Signs Its First Official Joint Venture.' *Business Eastern Europe* (October 6, 1986): 316.

'Number of CSSR's Joint Ventures Up; Most Gains in Tourism.' *Business Eastern Europe* (June 26, 1989): 204-5.

Nyrop, Richard F. *Czechoslovakia: A Country Study*. Washington, DC: The American University (Foreign Area Studies), 1982.

'O novém hospodářském mechanismu v zemědělsko-potravinářském komplexu.' *Rudé právo*, March 24, 1989, p. 4.

'O podnikání není zájem?' *Lidová demokracie*, January 22, 1991, p. 3.

'O přestavbě RVHP.' *Svobodné slovo*, January 4, 1991, pp. 1, 2.

'O "případu Moric".' *Lidové noviny*, November 1, 1990, p. 3.

'Občanské fórum politickou stranou.' *Zěmědelské noviny*, January 14, 1991, p. 1.

Obrman, Jan. 'The Wastage of Talent.' Radio Free Europe Czechoslovak Situation Report/19 (December 30, 1987): 31-4.

—— 'Czechoslovakia.' In 'Alienation and Protest: Students in Eastern Europe.' Radio Free Europe RAD Background Report/119 (June 28, 1988 [a]): 9-11.

—— 'Efforts to Limit Increase in Gypsy Population'. Radio Free Europe Czechoslovak Situation Report/20 (November 18, 1988 [b]): 35-6.

—— 'The Authorities Legalize the Art Forum.' Radio Free Europe Czechoslovak Situation Report/15 (July 14, 1989): 11-13.

—— 'Civic Forum Surges to Impressive Victory in Elections.' *Radio Free Europe Report on Eastern Europe* 1:25 (June 22, 1990 [a]): 13-16.

—— 'New Youth Groups and Movements.' *Radio Free Europe Report on Eastern Europe* 1:13 (March 30, 1990 [b]): 6-10.

'Odčiňme křivdy na dětech.' *Práce*, March 22, 1990, p. 3.

O'Donnell, Guillermo, Schmitter, Phillippe C. and Whitehead, Laurance, eds. *Transitions from Authoritarian Rule: Prospects for Democracy*. Baltimore, MD: Johns Hopkins University Press, 1986.

Oliver, James H. 'Citizen Demands and the Soviet Political System.' *American Political Science Review* 43:2 (June 1969): 465-75.

Olivová, Věra. *The Doomed Democracy: Czechoslovakia in a Disrupted Europe, 1914-1938*. London: Sidgwick and Jackson, 1972.

'Omezený pohraniční styk s Polskem.' *Lidové noviny*, October 31, 1990, p. 4.

Ondera, Peter. 'Spoločnosti i sebe.' *Pravda*, March 22, 1988, p. 2.

Ondrejkovič, Peter; Ondrašíková, Viera; Slany, Jaroslav; and Ivaničková, Margita. 'Prestiž na pretase.' *Nové slovo* 23 (June 14, 1990): 7.

orf. 'Neprodejný exil.' *Večerní Praha*, March 16, 1990, p. 6.

os. 'Hierarchie zájmu.' *Hospodářské noviny*, November 23, 1990, p. 8.

Osecká, Lída, and Macek, Petr. 'Životní plány a cíle dnešních adolescentů.' *Sociologický časopis* 23:1 (1987): 92-101.

Ošmerová, Jozefína, and Blaho, Vladimír. 'Kultúrné aktivity robotníckej a rolníckej mládeže.' *Sociologický časopis* 18:2 (1982): 204-10.

Oswald, Eduard. 'Co není zakázáno, je dovoleno.' *Hospodářské noviny*, January 10, 1991, pp. 1, 16.

Otava, Jiří. 'Public Opinion Research in Czechoslovakia.' *Social Research* 55: 1-2 (Spring/Summer 1988): 247-60.

'Otvorený list Slovenskej vytvarnej unie vytvarným umelcom kritikom a historikom umenia.' *Kulturný život*, July 4, 1990, p. 12.

Parížek, Michal. 'Spat' do Europy.' *Verejnost'*, April 10, 1990.

Parížek, Michal, and Kamenický, Peter. 'Mrtvá krajina, suzovaní l'udia.' *Verejnost'* 19 (May 15, 1990): 1, 2.

Parkin, Frank. *Class Inequality and Political Order: Social Stratification in*

Capitalist and Communist Societies. New York: Praeger Publishers, 1971.

Paro, Rudolf. 'Report on Interview with Czechoslovak Prime Minister Marian Calfa.' *Hufvudstadsbladet,* March 10, 1990, p. 14. As reported in 'Calfa Reviews Trends in Foreign Relations.' FBIS-EEU-90-057 (March 23, 1990): 21.

Pastier, Oleg. 'Samizdat daval slobodu.' *Ahoj Europa,* July 4, 1990, p. 1.

Paul, David W. *The Cultural Limits of Revolutionary Politics: Change and Continuity in Socialist Czechoslovakia.* New York: Columbia University Press, 1979.

―― *Czechoslovakia: Profile of a Socialist Republic at the Crossroads of Europe.* Boulder, CO: Westview Press, 1981.

―― *Politics, Art and Commitment in East European Cinema.* London: Macmillan Press, Ltd., 1983.

―― 'Czechoslovakia's Political Culture Reconsidered.' In *Political Culture and Communist Studies,* edited by Archie Brown. London: Macmillan, 1984, pp. 134-48.

Pavelka, Zdenko. 'Člověk v situaci.' *Tvorba,* June 26/27, 1990, pp. 16, 17.

Pavlík, Zdeněk. 'Na okraj sociálních procesů.' *Demografie* 30:3 (1988): 235-6.

Pecháčková, Marčela. 'Naslouchejme!' *Mladá fronta,* March 24, 1990, p. 2.

Pecháčková, Marčela, and Ševčik, Libor. 'Pánev pod pokličkou.' *Mladá fronta,* November 18, 1989, pp. 1, 2.

Pechota, Vratislav. 'Czechoslovakia and the Third World.' In *Eastern Europe and the Third World: East vs. South,* edited by Michael Radu. New York: Praeger, 1981, pp. 77-105.

Pehe, Jiří. 'Independent Movements in Eastern Europe.' Radio Free Europe RAD Background Report/228 (November 17, 1988).

―― 'The Czech Branch of the International PEN Club is Revived.' Radio Free Europe Czechoslovak Situation Report/17 (August 18, 1989 [a]): 21-3.

―― 'Growing Ferment in Czechoslovak Culture.' Radio Free Europe Czechoslovak Situation Report/23 (November 30, 1989 [b]): 37-43.

―― 'The Independent Peace Association and the Authorities.' Radio Free Europe Czechoslovak Situation Report/3 (February 16, 1989 [c]): 21-3.

―― 'A Secretary of the Union of Czech Writers Rejects 'Doctored Literature.'' Radio Free Europe Czechoslovak Situation Report/15 (July 14, 1989 [d]): 15-17.

―― 'Who are the Banned Writers in Czechoslovakia?' Radio Free Europe Czechoslovak Situation Report/6 (March 30, 1989 [e]): 19-23.

―― 'Who Issued the Ban on Many Czech Writers of the 1960s?' Radio Free

Europe Czechoslovak Situation Report/1 (January 20, 1989 [f]: 27-9.

—— 'Activities of the National Front Suspended.' *Radio Free Europe Report on Eastern Europe* 1:9 (March 2, 1990 [a]: 7-10.

—— 'Changes in the Communist Party.' *Radio Free Europe Report on Eastern Europe* 1:48 (November 30, 1990 [b]: 1-5.

—— 'The Controversy Over Communist Managers.' *Radio Free Europe Report on Eastern Europe* 1:36 (September 7, 1990 [c]: 6-10.

—— 'Culture under New Economic Conditions.' *Radio Free Europe Report on Eastern Europe* 1:36 (September 7, 1990 [d]: 11-14.

—— 'The New Federal Assembly: The Balance Sheet After One Month.' *Radio Free Europe Report on Eastern Europe* 1:33 (August 17, 1990 [e]: 7-11.

—— 'The Return of Philosophy.' *Radio Free Europe Report on Eastern Europe* 1:34 (August 24, 1990 [f]: 21.

—— 'The Agenda for 1991.' *Radio Free Europe Report on Eastern Europe* 2:3 (January 18, 1991 [a]: 11-16.

—— 'The Civic Forum Becomes a Political Party.' *Radio Free Europe Report on Eastern Europe* 2:5 (February 1, 1991 [b]: 1-3.

Pehe, Jiří, and Obrman, Jan. 'Hard-line Chairmen of the Writers' Union and Press Agency Resign.' Radio Free Europe Czechoslovak Situation Report/4 (March 2, 1989 [a]: 13-16.

—— 'More Changes in Czechoslovak Party Leadership.' Radio Free Europe Research (December 8, 1989 [b]: 41-4.

—— 'Recent Public Opinion Polls.' *Radio Free Europe Report on Eastern Europe* 1:21 (May 25, 1990): 17-19.

Pelikán, Jiří. *The Czechoslovak Political Trials, 1950-1954*. Stanford, CA: Stanford University Press, 1971.

pen and la. 'Občanské forum politickou stranou.' *Zěmědelské noviny*, January 14, 1990, pp. 1, 2.

—— 'Rozvod bez skandálu.' *Zěmědelské noviny*, February 25, 1991, pp. 1, 2.

Pergl, Václav. 'Dnes začina 18 s'jezd KSČS.' *Rudé právo*, November 3, 1990, p. 1.

Perman, Dagmar. *The Shaping of the Czechoslovak State: A Diplomatic History of the Boundaries of Czechoslovakia, 1914-1920*. Leiden: E.J. Brill, 1962.

Petráček, Zbyněk. 'Visegrad: Společná cesta, nikoliv aliance.' *Respekt*, February 18-24, 1991, p. 2.

Petránek, Jan. 'Bez Varšavské smlouvy.' *Lidové noviny*, February 26, 1991.

Petránek, Jan. 'Partneři zcela jinak.' *Lidové noviny*, October 31, 1990, pp. 1,3.

Petrušek, Miloslav. 'Jsme vážně z klece venku.' *Přítomnost'* 3 (1990): 14-15.

Piekalkiewicz, Jaroslav. *Public Opinion Polling in Czechoslovakia, 1968-1969: Results and Analysis of Surveys Conducted During the Dubcek Era.* New York, NY: Praeger Publishers, 1972.

Pilátová, Agáta. 'Trezor jen na zámek.' *Občanský deník*, May 12, 1990 (a), p. 5.

—— 'Stav ohrožení?' *Lidové noviny*, September 26, 1990 (b), p. 5.

Plávková, Ol'ga. 'Postavenie ženy v socialistickej spoločnosti.' *Sociólogia* 17:3 (1985): 337-9.

'Počet soukromých podnikatelu zaregistrovanýchy v obdobi od 1.5. do 30.7.1990.' *Zěmědelské noviny*, August 25, 1990, p. 9.

'Pohyb obyvatelstva v Československu v letech 1982-1988.' *Demografie* 30:2 (1988): 161-3.

Pohl, Frank. 'The Czechoslovak Economy from its Communist Takeover to Perestroika.' Radio Free Europe Czechoslovak Situation Report/5 (March 25, 1988 [a]): 17-22.

—— 'The Failure to Tackle Wage Egalitarianism.' Radio Free Europe Czechoslovak Situation Report/8 (June 3,1988 [b]): 19-22.

Poliaková, Eva. 'Zdravie—hodnota abstraktna?' *Nové slovo* 40 (October 6, 1988): 14.

'Politická platforma strany zelených.' *Zelení*, May 24, 1990, p. 6.

'Pomalu nás ubývá.' *Lidové noviny*, December 29, 1990, p. 3.

'Poselství dobré vůle.' *Lidové noviny*, April 23, 1990, pp. 1, 2.

'Poslanci federálního shromáždění.' *Rudé Právo*, May 18, 1986, pp. 1-3.

Pospišilová, Magda, and Tvarožek, Michal. Bratislava Domestic Service. March 6, 1991. As reported in 'Meciar Interviewed on VPN Problems.' FBIS-EEU-91-045 (March 7, 1991): 15-16.

Pospišilová, Věra. 'Kdy bomba vybuchne?' *Lidové noviny*, March 17, 1990, pp. 1, 2.

Possaner, Georg. 'Cooperation Instead of Neutrality.' *Der Standard*, October 5, 1990. As reported in 'Views Security Structures.' FBIS-EEU-90-197 (October 11, 1990): 14-15.

'Potiže středoskoláků.' *Rudé právo*, July 2, 1990, p. 4.

pp. 'Obrat dosud nenastal.' *Rudé právo*, December 9, 1988, p. 8.

Prague Domestic Service. June 7, 1990. As reported in 'Havel, Delegation News Conference on Pact Summit.' FBIS-EEU-90-111 (June 8, 1990): 18-21.

—— June 10, 1990. As reported in 'Parties Percentages in Assembly.' FBIS-EEU-90-112 (June 11, 1990): 32-3.

—— July 16, 1990. As reported in 'Government Approves Local

Administration System.' FBIS–EEU–90–137 (July 17, 1990): 19.

—— September 21, 1990. As reported in 'Holds Press Conference With Calfa.' FBIS–EEU–90–186 (September 25, 1990): 26-7.

—— September 24, 1990. As reported in 'Gulf Aid to be Entirely Defensive.' FBIS–EEU–90–187 (September 26, 1990): 5.

—— September 27, 1990. As reported in 'Pithart Outlines Tripartite Talks.' FBIS–EEU–90–189 (September 28, 1990): 10.

—— November 6, 1990. As reported in 'Duties of Local Government Officials Outlined.' FBIS–EEU–90–217 (November 8, 1990): 19-20.

—— January 3, 1991. As reported in 'Government Passes Arms Accords, Wage Levies.' FBIS–EEU–91–003 (January 4, 1990): 10.

—— January 4, 1991. As reported in 'Vales Says Exports to Soviet Union to Decline.' FBIS–EEU–91–004 (January 7, 1991): 19.

—— January 8, 1991. As reported in 'IMF Approves $1.783 Billion in Financial Aid.' FBIS–EEU–91–006 (January 9, 1991): 16.

—— February 21, 1991. As reported in 'Country Officially Admitted to Council of Europe.' FBIS–EEU–91–35 (February 1991): 19.

Prague Television Service. October 4, 1990. As reported in 'Economy Minister Announces Gasoline Sale Measures.' FBIS–EEU–90–194 (October 5, 1990): 13-14.

—— December 16, 1990. As reported in 'Economic Cooperation Agreement Signed with Poland.' FBIS–EEU–90–242 (December 17, 1990): 35.

—— December 21, 1990. As reported in 'Slovakia's Miklosko on Final Soviet Withdrawal.' FBIS–EEU–90–247 (December 24, 1990): 22.

'Právní předpisy pro podnikatele.' *Příručka Hospodářských novin,* May 1990.

Prazanová, Daniela. '. . . a rušily se školy.' *Zěmědelské noviny,* May 29, 1990, p. 5.

'Press Reacts to Havel's 10 December Proposal.' FBIS–EEU–90–244 (December 19, 1990): 13.

'Prezidentův návrh ústavy.' *Lidové noviny,* March 6, 1991, pp. 1,2.

'Přijímací řízení na vysoké školy'. *Hospodářské noviny,* July 22, 1988, p. 2.

'Přírůstek národního důchodu loni téměř tři procenta.' *Rudé právo,* January 26, 1989, pp. 1, 3.

'Problems in Economic Transition.' Radio Free Europe Czechoslovak Situation Report/14 (June 3, 1980): 5-8.

'Problémy s kursem zůstávají.' *Hospodářské noviny,* September 13, 1990, pp. 1, 8.

Probostová, Drahuše, and Kramer, Alexandr. 'Trvá kumulace moci?' *Lidové noviny,* December 20, 1990, p. 8.

Procházková, Katarína Krčméry, Vladimír, *et al.* 'Indicators of Quality of Surface Water in an Industrially Polluted Country.' *Ekologia* 8:3 (March 1989): 263-73.

'Profit.' *Národná obroda*, October 3, 1990. As reported in FBIS-EEU-90-195 (October 9, 1990): 27.

'Program Československé Sociální Demokracie.' Mimeograph, Československé Sociální Demokracie, 1990.

'Program odstránenia obmedzení.' *Pravda*, May 8, 1990, p. 8.

'Program SSM "Volný čas".' *Mladá fronta*, October 24, 1988, p. 3.

'Programové prohlášení vlády ČSSR.' *Rudé právo*, May 4, 1988, pp. 3, 4.

Prokop, Jozef. 'Gypsy Citizens, Too, Can Be Helped'. *Smena*, July 30, 1987.

'První aukce.' *Lidové noviny*, December 29, 1990, p. 3.

'První rady pracovních kolektivů vstupují do života.' *Rudé právo*, April 26, 1988, p. 1.

Pryor, Zora P. 'Czechoslovak Economic Development in the Interwar Period.' In *A History of the Czechoslovak Republic, 1918-1948*, edited by Victor S. Mamatey and Radomir Luza. Princeton, NJ: Princeton University Press, 1973.

Ptáčník, Stanislav. 'Liberalizace neznamená libovůli.' *Zěmědelské noviny*, December 29, 1990, pp. 1, 2.

'Public on Constitutional Arrangements of the State.' *Hospodářské noviny*, August 29, 1990, p. 1. As reported in 'Survey on Constitutional Arrangement of State.' FBIS-EEU-90-174 (September 7, 1990): 7-8.

Putnam, Robert D. *The Comparative Study of Political Elites*. Englewood Cliffs, NJ: Prentice-Hall, 1976.

r. 'Pražská demonstrace na Žižkově.' *Lidové noviny*, December 1988, p. 2.

'Rada vzájemné dohody.' *Lidové noviny*, October 4, 1990, p. 2.

Ramet, Pedro. 'Christianity and National Heritage among the Czechs and Slovaks.' In *Religion and Nationalism in Soviet and East European Politics*, edited by Pedro Ramet. Second Edition. Durham, NC: Duke University Press, 1989, pp. 264-85.

Rasocha, Milos. 'Kultura na přetřesu.' *Svobodné slovo*, February 1, 1991, p. 1.

rd. 'Vznikla tajná FIS.' *Mladá fronta*, December 22, 1990, p. 1.

rd and khv. 'Několik otázek pro nového ministra obrany.' *Mladá fronta dnes*, October 30, 1990, p. 2.

Reboun, Ota. 'Long Shadows of the Economy.' *Práce*, June 18, 1988, p. 3. As reported in 'Official on Scale of 'Shadow Economy.'' FBIS-EEU-88-122 (June 24, 1988): 23-5.

Remington, Robin Alison. *Winter in Prague: Documents on Czechoslovak Communism in Crisis*. Cambridge, MA: MIT Press, 1969.

—— *The Warsaw Pact: Case Studies in Communist Conflict Resolution.* Cambridge, MA: MIT Press, 1971.

'Report of the Federal Statistical Office on Socioeconomic Development in 1989.' *Statistika* 4 (April 4, 1990): 178-84. As reported in 'Federal Statistical Office 1989 Report Published.' JPRS-EER-90-085 (June 15, 1990): 17-33.

Ričalka, Michal. 'Rozvoj vzdelanostnej úrovne ukrajinského obyvateľstva v ČSSR od roku 1945.' In *Socialistickou cestou k národnostnej rovnoprávnosti.* Bratislava: Pravda, 1975.

Rice, Condoleezza. 'Czechoslovakian Secret Police.' In *Terror and Communist Politics: The Role of the Secret Police in Communist States*, edited by Jonathan R. Adelman. Boulder, CO: Westview, 1984 (a).

—— *The Soviet Union and the Czechoslovak Army, 1948-1983: Uncertain Allegiance.* Princeton, NJ: Princeton University Press, 1984 (b).

Rigby, T. H. 'The Soviet Politburo: A Comparative Profile, 1951-71.' *Soviet Studies* 24:1 (July 1972): 3-23.

—— 'Hough on Political Participation in the Soviet Union.' *Soviet Studies* 28 (April, 1976): 257-61.

Robinson, Anthony. 'Winding-up of Comecon delayed.' *Financial Times.* March 16, 1991, p. 2.

Rod, Rostislav. 'Výchozí bod pro demokracii.' *Mladá fronta*, August 27, 1990, p. 1.

'Rok hledání.' *Lidové noviny.* January 16, 1991, p. 2.

Roncek, Joseph S. 'Czechoslovakia and Her Minorities.' In *Czechoslovakia*, edited by Robert J. Kerner. Berkeley, CA: University of California Press, 1949.

Rothschild, Joseph. *East Central Europe Between the Two World Wars.* Seattle, WA: University of Washington Press, 1974.

—— *Ethnopolitics: A Conceptual Framework.* New York: Columbia University Press, 1981.

'Rules in Poland, CSFR Hamper JV Acquisitions.' *Business Eastern Europe* (December 3, 1990): 393-4.

Ruttkay, Jozef. 'Na armády rozostrený obraz.' *Verejnosť*, September 3, 1990, pp. 1, 16.

Rúžička, Jiří. 'Vroli sirotků.' *Rudé právo*, January 18, 1991, p. 3.

Ružička, Milan. 'Ekologické rizika VD Gabčíkovo.' *Práca* (December 5, 1990): 1.

Růžickova, Blanka. 'Chránit přírodu.' *Hospodářské noviny*, July 27, 1990, p. 3.

Růžková, Alena. 'Vyplnia medzery?' *Pravda*, December 20, 1990, p. 3.

Rychtařík, Karel. 'Drama idejí.' *Rudé právo*, May 7, 1989 (a), p. 5.

—— 'Názory na aktualní politickou situaci.' *Zpráva z operativního výzkumu c. 89-14*. Prague: Ústav pro výzkum veřejného mínění pri Federálním statistickém úřadu, December 1989 (b).

'S optimismem a odhodláním do další práce.' *Rudé právo*, December 11, 1984, pp. 1, 2.

Šabata, Petr. 'Co se vlastně stalo?' *Mladá fronta dnes*, December 14, 1990 (b), p. 2.

—— 'Prezident chce víc.' *Mladá fronta dnes,* December 12, 1990 (a), p. 2.

Sadykiewicz, Michael. 'The Transformation of the Warsaw Pact.' *Radio Free Europe Report on Eastern Europe* 1:13 (March 30, 1990): 47-8.

Samková, Klára. 'Prohlášení Romské občanské iniciativy.' *Respekt* 16 (July 3, 1990): 16.

Samson, Jan. 'Koncert na uvítanou.' *Lidové noviny*, February 1988, p. 17.

Šamudovský, Juraj. 'Ešte dva názory.' *Učitelské noviny*, January 10, 1991, p. 6.

Sartori, Giovanni. 'Concept Misformation in Comparative Politics.' *American Political Science Review* 64:4 (December, 1970): 1033-53.

šc. 'Novinka pro drobné podnikatele.' *Hospodářské noviny*. November 8, 1990, p. 5.

'Scénář ekonomické reformy.' *Hospodářské noviny*, September 4, 1990, příloha.

Scheuch, Richard. 'Religiozita okresů ČSSR.' *Duchovní paostýř*, no. 5, May 1989, pp. 97-8.

Schulz, Donald E. and Adams, Jan S., eds. *Political Participation in Communist Systems*. New York: Pergamon Press, 1981.

Schuster, Roman. 'Skola zacina.' *Rudé právo,* September 3, 1990, pp. 1, 2.

Scott, Hilda. *Does Socialism Liberate Women?* Boston, MA: Beacon Press, 1974.

Sekot, Aleš. 'K sociologickým dimenzím náboženství a religiozity.' *Sociologický časopis* 21:1 (1985): 34-52.

'Semiannual Czech Statistical Report Published.' JPRS-EER-90-138 (October 5, 1990): 36-8.

'Sen o Evropě se naplňuje.' *Lidové noviny*, May 11, 1990, pp. 3, 4.

'Serious Crime in Czech Republic Doubles.' FBIS-EEU-90-l06 (June l, 1990): 22.

Seton-Watson, Hugh. *The East European Revolution*. New York, NY: Praeger Publishers, 1956.

Seton-Watson, R.W. *A History of the Czechs and Slovaks*. Hamden, CT: Archon Books, 1965.

Sharlet, Robert S. 'Concept Formation in Political Science and Studies: Conceptualizing Political Participation.' In *Communist Studies and the Social Sciences: Essays on Methodology and Empirical Theory*, edited by Frederic J. Fleron. Chicago: Rand McNally, 1969.

Šibl, Jaromír. 'Gabičkovo očami odborníkov.' *Práca*, March 10, 1990, p. 5.

Siemiéňska, Renata. 'Women and Social Movements in Poland.' *Women and Politics* 6:4 (Winter, 1986): 5–36.

Šík, Ota. *Plan and Market under Socialism*. Translated by Eleanor Wheeler. White Plains, NY: International Arts and Sciences Press, Inc., 1967.

Šiklová, Jiřina. 'Are Women in Middle and Eastern Europe Conservative?' 1990, MS.

Silhavý, Jiří. 'Zkvalitnováním členské základny násobit síly strany.' *Život strany* 24 (1988): 11–13.

Silver, Brian. 'Levels of Sociocultural Development among Soviet Nationalities: A Partial Test of the Equalization Hypothesis.' *American Political Science Review* 68:4 (December 1974 [a]): 1618–37.

—— 'Social Mobilization and the Russification of Soviet Nationalities.' *American Political Science Review* 68:1 (March 1974 [b]): 45–66.

Šimek, Miroslav. 'Projekce obyvatelstva ČSSR do roku 2010.' *Demografie* 30:1 (1988): 18–24.

Simon, Bohumil. 'Nove sliby—stare navyky.' *Lidové noviny*, December 1988, p. 9.

Šimonovičová, Alžbeta. 'Čísla nad osudmi.' *Nové slovo* 48 (December 1, 1988): 2.

Šindelařová, Milena. 'Čí bude půda.' *Respekt*, February 18–24, 1991, p. 8.

Singer, Daniel. 'Czechoslovakia's Quiet Revolution.' *The Nation* 250:4 (January 29, 1990): 122–30.

Singleton, Frederick B. *Twentieth-Century Yugoslavia*. New York: Columbia University Press, 1976.

Sirota, Igor. 'Vláda národního porozumění.' *Rudé právo*, December 11, 1989, pp. 1, 3.

—— 'Zákon o majetku KSČS ve čtvrtek znovu do vlády.' *Rudé právo*, October 16, 1990, pp. 1, 2.

—— 'Nejsem eminence grise.' *Rudé právo*, March 1, 1991, pp. 1, 3.

'Sjezd KSČS k vývoji společnosti.' *Rudé právo*, November 8, 1990, p. 3.

ska. 'Aukční seznamy dostupné.' *Svobodné slovo*, January 12, 1991, p. 1.

Skalicky, Jaroslav. Prague Domestic Service. December 17, 1990. As reported in 'Vales Interviewed on Moscow Trade Agreement.' FBIS-EEU-90-244 (December 19, 1990): 22.

368   *Bibliography*

Skalková, Olga, and Denemark, Martin. 'S mačetou v džungli.' *Svobodné slovo*, October 4, 1990, pp. 1, 4.

Skilling, H. Gordon. 'Interest Groups and Communist Politics.' In *Interest Groups in Soviet Politics*, edited by H. Gordon Skilling and Franklyn Griffiths. Princeton, NJ: Princeton University Press, 1971, pp. 3-18.

—— 'Czechoslovak Political Culture: Pluralism in an International Context.' in *Political Culture and Communist Studies*, edited by Archie Brown. London: Macmillan, 1984, pp. 115-33.

—— *Czechoslovakia's Interrupted Revolution*. Princeton, NJ: Princeton University Press, 1976.

—— 'Stalinism and Czechoslovak Political Culture.' In *Stalinism: Essays in Historical Interpretation*, edited by Robert C. Tucker. New York: W.W. Norton and Company, 1977.

—— Charter 77 and Human Rights in Czechoslovakia. Boston, MA: Allen and Unwin, 1981.

—— 'Independent Currents in Czechoslovakia'. *Problems of Communism* 34 (January/February 1985): 32-49.

—— *Samizdat and an Independent Society in Central and Eastern Europe*. Columbus, OH: Ohio State University Press, 1989.

Skilling, H. Gordon and Griffiths, Franklyn. *Interest Groups in Soviet Politics*. Princeton, NJ: Princeton University Press, 1971, pp. 3-18.

Škorík, Jaroslav. 'Slováci v Prahe.' *Smena*, August 23, 1990, p. 4.

Škvorecký, Josef. *All the Bright Young Men and Women. A Personal History of the Czech Cinema*. Toronto: Peter Martin Associates, Ltd., 1971.

Sládková, Mária. 'Slovenské národné povstanie a česko-slovenské vzt'ahy.' *Sociológia* 16:4 (1984): 377-85.

Slavíková, Jitka. 'Zpráva z operativního výzkumu č. 89-13.' Prague: Ústav pro výzkum veřejného minění při Federálním statistickém úřadu, December 1989.

Slejška, Dragoslav. 'Hodnotová sféra pod vlivem stagnace a tendence jejího dalšího vývoje po listopadu 1989.' *Sociologický časopis* 26:4 (1990): 317-20.

Slezáková, Alena, and Pokorný, Zdeněk. 'Svoboda je nedělitelná.' *Lidové noviny* (January 17, 1991) pp. 1, 2.

—— 'Pilíř právního státu.' *Lidové noviny*, February 28, 1991, pp. 1, 2.

'Slovak Council Results.' FBIS-EEU-90-112 (June 11, 1990): 31-2.

Slovenskej vytvarnej unie. 'Otvorený list Slovenskej vytvarnej unie vytvarným umelcom, kritikom a historikom umenia.' *Kulturný život*, July 4, 1990.

Slovenský národopis 36:1 (1988).

Slušná, Nataša. *Postavení ženy ve společnosti: K problematice postavení ženy v socialistické společnosti.* Prague: Univerzita Karlova, 1988.

Šmíd, J. 'V. Klaus: Možna odstoupím.' *Zěmědelské noviny*, February 14, 1991, pp. 1, 2.

Šmídová, Jana, and Veis, Jaroslav. 'Pragmatický doprava.' *Lidové noviny*, December 10, 1990, pp. 1, 2.

—— 'OF: Hnutí stranou.' *Lidové noviny*, January 14, 1991, pp. 1, 2.

Šmidová, Maja. 'Šanca nastupujucej generacie.' *Čas*, July 3, 1990, p. 2.

Smola, Josef. 'Co přinese samospráva.' *Rudé právo*, October 17, 1990, pp. 1, 5.

Smrčka, Jaroslav. 'K přestavbé hospodářského mechanismu.' *Politická ekonomie* 36:8 (1988 (a)): 785-98.

—— 'Perspektivy vývoje organizačních struktur podnikohospodářské sféry.' *Politická ekonomie* 36:7 (1988 (b)): 715-24.

—— 'Enterprise Management: Law on Enterprises with Foreign Ownership Participation.' *Moderní řízení* 2 (1989): 49-53. As reported in 'Law on Enterprise With Foreign Participation.' JPRS-EER-89-067 (June 12, 1989): 19-21.

Smutný, Svatopluk. 'Máme si co závidět?.' *Rudé právo*, February 4, 1989, p. 3.

'SNS je za Moricem.' *Lidové noviny*. November 3, 1990, p. 3.

Sobell, Vlad. 'Czechoslovakia on the Eve of the CPCS Congress.' Radio Free Europe Czechoslovak Situation Report/4 (March 10, 1986 [a]): 3-8.

—— 'Outlook for Trade with the West.' Radio Free Europe Czechoslovak Situation Report/8 (May 26, 1986 [b]): 9-14.

—— 'Czechoslovakia: The Legacy of Normalization.' *East European Politics and Societies* 2:1 (Winter, 1988): 36-69.

—— 'East European Economies at a Turning Point.' *Radio Free Europe Report on Eastern Europe* 1:18 (May 4, 1990 [a]): 40-3.

—— 'In search of a new CMEA.' *Radio Free Europe Report on Eastern Europe* 1:6 (February 1990 [b]): 39-42.

Socialistickou cestou k národnostnej rovnoprávnosti. Bratislava: Nakladatel'stvo Pravda, 1975.

'Sociológia vidieka a pol'nohospodárstva.' *Sociológia* 16:2 (1984): 265-7.

Sodaro, Michael J., and Wolchik, Sharon L. *Domestic Policies in Eastern Europe in the 1980s: Trends and Prospects.* New York: St. Martin's Press, 1983.

Sokolová, Gabriela. 'K některým otázkám bilingvismu v etnicky smísených regionech ČSSR.' *Sociológia* 17:2 (1985): 213-23.

—— *Soudobé tendence vývoje národností v ČSSR.* Prague: Academia Praha, 1987.

Šolcová, Miroslava. *Postavení ženy v socialistické společností.* Prague: Horizont, 1984.

—— 'Úloha a postavení ženy v soudobých podmínkách.' *Život strany* 5 (1988): 35-8.

'Soubor opatření ke zdokonalení soustavy plánovitého řízení národního hospodářstvi po roce 1980.' *Příloha Hospodářských novin,* November 1980.

'Soukromé podnikání.' *Hospodářské noviny,* December 18, 1990, p. 1.

Soukup, Lubomír. 'Dva dny ve svobodné Evropě, z návštévy pracovníků ČS rozhlasu v Mnichovském sidel RFE.' *Rozhlas,* March 12, 1990, p. 3.

Sourek, Stanislav. 'New Agricultural Tax.' *Finance a úvěr,* January 1989, pp. 793-6. As reported in 'Purpose of New Agricultural Tax Discussed.' JPRS-EER-89-044 (April 20, 1989): 14-17.

Špak, Dušan. 'Provizórium na ceste k trhu.' *Hospodářské noviny,* February 1, 1991, p. 10.

Špáni, Ivan. 'With Entrepreneurship Against Inflation,' *Práce,* April 26, 1989, p. 5. As reported in JPRS-EER-89-067 (June 12, 1989): 30.

—— 'Otázky, ktoré sme si nekládli.' *Nové slovo,* July 19, 1990, p. 5.

'Společně o životních prostředéch.' *Hospodářské noviny,* July 30, 1990, p. 2.

'Spor o Bohunice.' *Rudé právo,* December 15, 1990, pp. 1, 2.

Šporer, Peter. 'V záujme kvality života.' *Práca,* August 7, 1990, p. 5.

Spurný, Jaroslav. 'Still Without Public Supervision.' *Respekt,* August 14, 1990, pp. 4-5. As reported in 'Lack of Information Persists.' JPRS-EER-90-148 (October 26, 1990): 17-19.

Srb, Vladimír. 'Některé demografické, ekonomické a kulturní charakteristiky cikánského obyvatelstva v ČSSR 1980.' *Demografie* 26:2 (1984): 161-72.

—— 'Sborník o československých romech.' *Demografie* 30:3 (1988 [a]): 236-8.

—— 'Soudobé tendence vývoje národností v ČSSR.' *Demografie* 30:2 (1988 [b]): 137-9.

Srb, Vladimír, and Bulíř, Michal. 'Národnost posluchačů československých vysokých škol 1970-1986.' *Demografie* 30:3 (1988): 267-71.

Srb, Vladimír, and Vaňo, B. 'Některé demografické charakteristiky čs politické reprezentace 1990.' *Statistika* 12 (1990): 555-7.

Sršňová, Milena. 'Kniha v pasti.' *Respekt,* July 17, 1990, p. 14.

st. 'Balance of the CSFR Payments in the First Semester; Reasonable Level of Debts.' *Hospodářské noviny,* September 13, 1990, pp. 1, 8. As reported in 'Balance of Payments for First Semester Reported.' FBIS-EEU-90-184 (September 21, 1990): 13-14.

st. 'Waiting for an Apology.' *Hospodářské noviny*, February 28, 1991, p. 2. As reported in 'Moravian Deputies Return to Czech Legislature.' FBIS-EEU-91-043 (March 5, 1991): 18.

Staněk, Karel. 'Devět slovenských stran žádá samostatný stát.' *Občanský deník*, August 15, 1990, pp. 1, 2.

'Statistics Office Issues 1986 Economic Report.' As reported in FBIS-EEU-87-020 (January 30, 1987): D3-D5.

'Statistics Office Releases Economic Report.' As reported in FBIS-EEU-88-033 (February 19, 1988): 13-14.

Státní úřad statisticky. *Statistický ročenka republiky československé*. Prague: Orbis, 1937.

Státní úřad statisticky. *Statistický ročenka republiky československé*. Prague: Orbis, 1951-9.

Státní úřad statisticky. *Statistický ročenka republiky Československé socialisticke republiky*. Prague: SNTL, 1960, 1967, 1968.

Steiner, Eugene. *The Slovak Dilemma*. London: Cambridge University Press, 1973.

Štětina, Jaromír. 'Poslední zvonění RVHP.' *Lidové noviny*, January 7, 1991, pp. 1, 2.

Stevens, John N. *Czechoslovakia at the Crossroads: The Economic Dilemmas of Communism in Postwar Czechoslovakia*. Boulder, CO: East European Monographs, 1985.

Ševulová, Mária. 'Pošleme naše deti na ulicu?' *Národná obroda*, October 2, 1990, p. 3.

Stloukal, Libor. 'Potratovost v ČSR v regionálním pohledu.' *Demografie* 30:3 (1988): 212-19.

štp. 'Rozkazy nebyly.' *Lidové noviny*, September 11, 1990, p. 1.

Stránský, Frantisek. 'Realistic View as an Alternative, Adaptation as a Necessity.' *Hospodářské noviny* 43 (1985). As reported in JPRS-EER-86-021 (February 14, 1986): 8-9.

'Středoevropska universitá od roku '91.' *Mladá fronta*, June 4, 1990, p. 2.

Strmiska, Zdeněk. 'Social Mobility in Soviet-type Societies in Comparative Perspective.' in *Equality and Inequality in Eastern Europe*, edited by Pierre Kende and Zdeněk Strmiska. New York: St. Martin's Press, 1987, pp. 143-97.

'Struktura obratu čs. zahraničního obchodu.' *Hospodářské noviny*, March 16, 1990, p. 18.

Šubert, Jan. 'Federální tajná služba.' *Zěmědelské noviny*, September 13, 1990, p. 3.

Suda, Zdeněk. *The Czechoslovak Socialist Republic*. Baltimore, MD: Johns

Hopkins University Press, 1969.

—— *Zealots and Rebels: A History of the Ruling Communist Party of Czechoslovakia.* Stanford, CA: Hoover Institution Press, 1980.

—— 'Czechoslovakia.' In *United States – East European Relations in the 1990s*, edited by Richard F. Staar. New York: Taylor and Francis, Inc., 1989.

Šulc, Zdislav. 'Snaha rozdávat nikam nevede.' *Hospodářské noviny*, May 4, 1990, pp. 8–9.

Šulcová, Olga. 'Žena jako prácovní síla.' *Lidové noviny*, September 1988, p. 9.

'Suroviny za zboží.' *Lidové noviny*, September 3, 1990, pp. 1, 8.

'Světová banka nám věří.' *Lidové demokracie*, October 20, 1990, p. 1.

'Svoboda je nedělitelná.' *Lidové noviny*, January 17, 1991, pp. 1, 2.

Švirloch, Stanislav and Ševčík, Dušan. 'Vol'ny čas a protispoločenská činnost' mládeže.' *Sociální politika* 14:10 (1988): 232–4.

Szomolányiová, Soňa. Interview, June 14, 1990, Bratislava.

Szporluk, Roman, ed. *The Influence of East Europe and the Soviet West on the USSR.* New York, NY: Praeger Publishers, 1975.

—— *The Political Thought of Thomas G. Masaryk.* New York, NY: Columbia University Press, 1981.

Taborsky, Edward. *Communism in Czechoslovakia, 1948-1960.* Princeton, NJ: Princeton University Press, 1961.

—— 'Tragedy, Triumph and Tragedy: Czechoslovakia 1938-1948.' In *Czechoslovakia, the Heritage of Ages Past: Essays in Memory of Josef Korbel*, edited by Hans Brisch and Ivan Volgyes. New York, NY: Columbia University Press, 1979.

Taussig, Pavel. 'I lživé filmy jsou pravdivé.' *Lidové noviny*, July 9, 1990, p. 5.

Teichová, Alice. *The Czechoslovak Economy 1918-1980.* London and New York: Routledge, 1988.

'Ted' už opravdu činy.' *Svobodné slovo*, April 6, 1990, p. 1.

'The Territorial Structure of Czechoslovakia's Foreign Trade.' *Czechoslovak Foreign Trade* 1 (1988): 38.

Thomson, Samuel Harrison. *Czechoslovakia in European History.* Second Edition. Princeton, NJ: Princeton University Press, 1953.

Tihlařík, Jan. 'Příliš těsná košile.' *Rudé právo*, January 31, 1989, p. 7.

tma. 'Další vyjasnění v OF.' *Mladá fronta*, December 15, 1990, p. 1.

Tökés, Rudolf L. *Opposition in Eastern Europe.* Baltimore, MD: Johns Hopkins University Press, 1979.

—— 'Hungary's New Political Elites: Adaptation and Change, 1989-90.' *Problems of Communism* 39:6 (November–December 1990): 44–65.

Tománek, Stanislav. 'In Eighteen Months.' *Národná obroda*, December 10, 1990 (a), p. 1. As reported in 'CHISSO, Slovnaft to Build Gasoline Installation.' FBIS-EEU-90-246 (December 21, 1990): 20.

—— 'There are Four Possibilities.' *Národná obroda*, August 23, 1990 (b), pp. 1, 2. As reported in 'Slovak Industry Ministry on Crude Oil Issue.' FBIS-EEU-90-171 (September 4, 1990): 19-20.

Tomašek, František, and Ruml, Jiří. 'Dostal jsem přes pul milionu podpisů' *Lidové noviny*, June 1988, pp. 4-5.

Tomek, Ivan. 'K problematice výzkumu světového názoru a světonazorové orientace československé mládeže.' *Sociologický časopis* 21:5 (1985): 539-51.

—— 'Co si lide myslí o průběhů volební kampane.' *Informace*, May 29, 1990 (a).

—— 'Názory československé mládeže na politický systém ČSSR v letech 1986-1989.' *Veřejné míñeni v ČSSR*. Prague, 1990 (b).

Tomek, Ivan, and Forst, Václav. 'Postoje čs. veřejnosti k základním politickým institucím.' *IVVM*, January 1991 (a).

—— 'Postoje čs. veřejnosti k základním politickým institucím.' *IVVM*, February 1991 (b).

Tomiček, Jan. 'Songy prohibiti.' *Tvorba* 8 (February 21, 1990): 6.

Trávníčková, Ivana. 'P. Vojna a kol: Kriminalita—skutečnost a právní vědomí.' *Sociologický časopis* 22:1 (1986): 86-8.

Treglová, Jaroslava. 'The Edges of the Green Circle.' *Práce*, January 22, 1990, p. 3. As reported in 'Spectrum of Ecological Movements Viewed.' FBIS-EEU-90-019 (January 29, 1990 [a]): 42-3.

—— 'Luxusní dovolena?' *Práce*, August 23, 1990 (b), p. 5.

—— 'Volby '90 v číslech.' *Práce*, November 28, 1990 (c), p. 1.

Trensky, Paul I. *Czech Drama Since World War II*. White Plains, NY: M.E. Sharpe, 1978.

—— 'Havel's "The Garden Party" Revisited.' In *Czech Literature Since 1956: A Symposium*, edited by William E. Harkins and Paul I. Trensky. New York: Bohemica, 1980 (a).

—— 'The Playwrights of the Krejca Circle.' In *Czech Literature Since 1956: A Symposium*, edited by William E. Harkins and Paul I. Trensky. New York: Bohemica, 1980 (b).

trg. 'clo tři sta procent.' *Práce*, March 8, 1990, pp. 1, 2.

Triska, Jan F. 'Messages from Czechoslovakia.' *Problems of Communism* 24 (November/December 1975): 26-42.

'Třístranná rada.' *Rudé právo*, October 4, 1990, p. 1.

Truncová, Dagmar. 'Naděje na ropu?' *Hospodářské noviny*, September 28, 1990 (a), p. 1.

—— 'Zásobování plynem komplexně.' *Hospodářské noviny*, September 25, 1990 (b), p. 1.

—— 'With Prime Minister Calfa in Africa, But Not Only About Africa; Sitting in a Lounge.' *Hospodářské noviny*, December 11, 1990 (c), p. 7. As reported in 'Calfa Comments on Trade With Algeria, Gas, Oil.' FBIS-EEU-90-244 (December 19, 1990): 24–5.

Tuček, Milan. 'Sociální souvislosti restrukturalizace národního hospodářství.' *Sociologický časopis* 26:4 (1990): 297–302.

Tuček, Josef. 'Špióny už nemáme.' *Mladá fronta dnes*, September 7, 1990, pp. 1, 2.

Turek, Otakar. 'Hospodářská politika v období přestavby hospodářského mechanismu.' *Politická ekonomie* 36:6 (1988): 575–92.

Turek, Otakar, and Ježek, Tomáš. 'Strukturální změny a hospodářský mechanismus.' *Politická ekonomie* 37:5 (1989): 580–91.

'TV Interview of State Planning Official Vertelar.' As reported in FBIS-EEU-86-146 (July 30, 1986): D2–4.

Uhde, Jan. 'The Film World of Jan Švankmajer.' In *Cross Currents: A Yearbook of Central European Culture*, volume 8. Edited by Ladislav Matejka. Ann Arbor, MI: Michigan Slavic Materials, 1989.

Ulč, Otto. *Politics in Czechoslovakia*. San Francisco, CA: W.H. Freeman and Co., 1974.

—— 'The Normalization of Post-Invasion Czechoslovakia.' *Survey* 24:3 (1979).

—— 'Gypsies in Czechoslovakia: A Case of Unfinished Integration.' *Eastern European Politics and Societies* 2:2 (Spring 1988): 306–32.

UNESCO. *Literary Statistics from Available Census Figures*. Paris: Education Clearing House, 1950.

Unger, Aryeh L. 'Political Participation in the USSR, YCL and CPSU.' *Soviet Studies* 33:1 (January 1981): 107–24.

Urban, Bohumil. 'Úkoly plánu 1989.' *Hospodářské noviny*, December 23, 1988, pp. 1, 5.

Urban, František. 'Česky les.' *Přitomnost'*, June 4, 1990, pp. 26–7.

'Usnesení předsednictva ÚV KSČ a vlády ČSSR k Souboru opatřeni ke zdokonalení soustavy plánovitého řízeni národního hospodářství.' *Příloha Hospodářských novin*, November 1980.

'Usnesení ústředního výboru KSČ o komplexní přestavbě hospodářského mechnaismu ČSSR a jejím zabezpečeni.' *Rudé právo*, December 22, 1987, pp. 3–5.

'Ústavní zákon o československé federaci.' Prague, 1990.

'Ustavující schůze ústředního vyborů', *Svobadné slovo*, February 23, 1987, p. 2.

Ústřední komise lidové kontroly a statisticky. *Statistická ročenka Československé socialistické republiky.* Prague: SNTL, 1963-66.

Ústřední úřad státní kontroly a statisticky. *Statistická ročenka Československé socialistické republiky.* Prague: SNTL, 1961, 1962.

'ÚV strany.' *Svobodné Slovo,* February 23, 1987: 2.

'V ČNR diskuse na pokračování.' *Hospodářské noviny,* September 5, 1990, pp. 1, 4.

'V nových šatech.' *Lidové noviny,* November 5, 1990, p. 12.

Valach, Vladimir. 'Establishment of State Enterprises—Only the First Step.' *Hospodářské noviny,* January 1989, p. 3. As reported in 'State Enterprise Formation Said to be Only First Step.' FBIS, *JPRS Report, East Europe,* JPRS-EER-89-044 (April 20, 1989): 11-14.

Valašek, Rotislav. 'Atestace v plném proudu.' *Rudé právo,* August 28, 1990, pp. 1, 5.

Valenta, František. 'Na přelomu k nové kvalitě rozvoje.' *Politická ekonomie* 35:5 (1987): 457-67.

—— 'Únor 1948 o socialismu a společenských vědách.' *Politická ekonomie* 36:2 (1988): 113-18.

Valenta, Jiří. *Soviet Intervention in Czechoslovakia, 1968: Anatomy of a Decision.* Baltimore, MD: Johns Hopkins University Press, 1979.

Valenta, Jiří and Rice, Condoleeza. 'The Czechoslovak Army.' In *Communist Armies in Politics,* edited by Jonathan R. Adelman. Boulder, CO: Westview Press, 1982.

Valík, David. 'Vstupní zkouška—Universita Karlova—nové formy.' *Lidové noviny,* January 17, 1991, p. 9.

Vaňous, Jan. 'East European and Soviet Fuel Trade.' In *East European Economic Assessment,* Part 2. Joint Economic Committee, Congress of the United States. Washington, DC: United States Government Printing Office, 1981, pp. 541-60.

—— 'East European Economic Slowdown.' *Problems of Communism* 31:4 (July/August 1982): 1-19.

vc. 'Náš dluh poroste.' *Rudé právo,* December 19, 1990, p. 2.

Večerník, Jiří. 'Sociální faktory příjmové diferenciace.' *Sociologický časopis* 20:5 (1984): 503-15.

—— 'Dynamika mzdové diferenciace v socialistých zemích a postavení dělnické třídy.' *Sociólogia* 17:2 (1985): 143-56.

—— 'Mzdová diferenciace: odkud a kam.' *Hospodářské Noviny,* October 31, 1990 (a), priloha.

—— 'Sociální souvislosti přechodu k tržní ekonomice.' *Sociologický časopis* 26:4 (1990 [b]): 276-83.

vej. 'Zpřísněná restriktivní politika.' *Lidové noviny*, October 9, 1990, p. 3.
'Veřejné mínění o půdě.' *Lidová demokracie*, January 16, 1991.
'Více ropy pro ČSFR.' *Rudé právo*, October 11, 1990, p. 1.
Víšek, Petr. 'K některým novým aspektům společenské integrace Romů v socialistickém Československu.' *Slovenský národopis* 36:1 (1988): 35-44.
Vítečková, Jana. 'Změny ve způsobu využití času obyvatel ČSSR v letech 1961-1980.' *Sociologický časopis* 21:4 (1985 [a]): 372-91.
—— 'Způsob využití časového fondu mládeže v ČSSR.' *Sociologický časopis* 21:5 (1985 [b]): 566-74.
—— 'Tendence a problémy vývoje hmotných podmínek života.' *Sociologický časopis* 23:1 (1987): 40-54.
vl. 'Decline, but in Expected Limits.' *Hospodářské noviny*, October 12, 1990 (a), p. 2. As reported in 'Nine-Month Economic Report Shows Decline.' FBIS-EEU-90-202 (October 18, 1990): 8.
vl. 'Nadále pod loňskou úrovní.' *Hospodářské noviny*, September 20, 1990 (b), p. 2.
vl. 'The Outlook on Statistical Scales.' *Hospodářské noviny*, December 11, 1990 (c), p. 2. As reported in 'Statistician on Prospects for Economy in 1991.' FBIS-EEU-90-244 (December 19, 1990): 21-2.
vl. 'Record Retail Turnover.' *Hospodářské noviny*, December 17, 1990 (d), p. 1. As reported in 'Statistics Office Issues 11-Month Economic Report.' FBIS-EEU-90-246 (December 21, 1990): 15.
vl, hm *et al.* 'Ze stávky spíš groteska.' *Mladá fronta*, September 27,1990. pp. 1,2.
'Vláda o tancích.' *Svobodné slovo*, January 4, 1991, pp. 1, 4.
Vladislav, Jan, and Prečan, Vilém. *Horký leden 1989 v Československu*. Prague: Vydavatelstvi novinář, 1990.
Vlček, Josef. 'O místě ČSSR v Evropě.' *Rudé právo*, March 6, 1990, p. 2.
Vodička, Milan. 'Přemety lásky nenávisti.' *Mladá fronta*, February 8, 1990, p. 5.
'Volby 1990.' *Hospodářské noviny*, June 14, 1990, příloha.
vrz. 'O krok ke komunálním volbám.' *Svobodné slovo*, September 5, 1990, p. 1.
vt. 'Mliečne tabu.' *Verejnost'* 13 (February 13, 1990): 5.
'Výkonný výbor ÚV KSČ.' *Rudé právo*, January 8, 1990, p. 1.
'Výkročení do Evropy.' *Svobodné slovo*, January 2, 1991, p. 2.
'Výskum naznačuje strach a obavy.' *Národná obroda*, November 28, 1990, p. 2.
'Výsledky voleb do FS a ČNR podle jednotlivých krajů.' *Svobodné slovo*, June 12, 1990, p. 4.

'Význam generálnej dohody.' *Práca,* November 24, 1990, p. 1.

'Výzva československé vláde.' *Lidové noviny,* May 2, 1990, p. 2.

'Vzhledem k úbytku.' *Lidové noviny,* January 5, 1991, p. 3.

Wadekin, Karl-Eugen. *Agrarian Policies in Communist Europe, A Critical Introduction.* The Hague/London: Allanheld, Osmun and Co., 1982.

Wallace, William V., and Clarke, Roger A. *Comecon, Trade and the West.* London: Pinter Publishers, 1986.

Wechsberg, Joseph. *The Voices.* Garden City, NY: Doubleday, 1969.

Wellek, Rene. 'Modern Czech Criticism and Literary Scholarship.' In *Essays on Czech Literature.* The Hague: Mouton and Co., 1963 (a), pp. 179-93.

—— 'Recent Czech Literary History and Criticism.' In *Essays on Czech Literature.* The Hague: Mouton and Co., 1963 (b), pp. 194-203.

—— 'Twenty Years of Czech Literature, 1918-1938.' In *Essays on Czech Literature.* The Hague: Mouton and Co., 1963 (c), pp. 32-45.

—— 'The Two Traditions of Czech Literature.' In *Essays on Czech Literature.* The Hague: Mouton and Co., 1963 (d), pp. 17-31.

de Weydenthal, Jan B. 'Religious Pilgrimages: A Step Toward Public Self-Assertion.' Radio Free Europe Background Report/98 (July 11, 1986), 3 pp.

White, Stephen. *Political Culture and Soviet Politics.* New York: St. Martin's Press, 1979.

Wightman, Gordon and Brown, Archie. 'Changes in the Levels of Membership and Social Composition of the Communist Party of Czechoslovakia, 1945-1973.' *Soviet Studies* 27:2 (July 1975): 396-417.

Wilson, Paul. 'Religious Movement in Czechoslovakia Faith or Fashion?' *Cross Currents: A Yearbook of Central European Culture,* volume 7. Edited by Ladislav Matejka. Ann Arbor, MI: Michigan Slavic Materials, 1988, pp. 109-19.

Wiskemann, Elizabeth. *Czechs and Germans: A Study of the Struggle in the Historic Provinces of Bohemia and Moravia.* London: Oxford University Press, 1938.

Wolchik, Sharon L. 'Politics, Ideology, and Equality: The Status of Women in Eastern Europe.' Unpublished Ph.D. Dissertation, The University of Michigan, 1978.

—— 'The Status of Women in a Socialist Order: Czechoslovakia, 1948-1978.' *Slavic Review* 38:4 (December 1979): 583-603.

—— 'Demography, Political Reform and Women's Issues in Czechoslovakia.' In *Women, Power and Political Systems,* edited by Margherita Rendel. New York: St. Martin's Press, 1981 (a), pp. 135-50.

—— 'Eastern Europe.' In *The Politics of the Second Electorate: Women and Public*

Participation, edited by Jane Lovenduski and Jill Hills. London: Routledge and Kegan Paul, 1981 (b): pp. 252-77.

—— 'Elite Strategy Toward Women in Czechoslovakia: Liberation or Mobilization?' *Studies in Comparative Communism* 14:2/3 (Summer/Autumn 1981 [c]): 123-42.

—— 'Ideology and Equality: The Status of Women in Eastern and Western Europe.' *Comparative Political Studies* 13:4 (January 1981 [d]): 445-76.

—— 'Regional Inequalities in Czechoslovakia.' In *Communism and the Politics of Inequalities*, edited by Daniel J. Nelson. Lexington, MA: Lexington Books, 1983 (a): pp. 249-70.

—— 'The Scientific-technological Revolution and the Role of Specialist Elites in Policy-making in Czechoslovakia.' In *Domestic Policy in Eastern Europe in the 1980s: Trends and Prospects*, edited by Michael J. Sodaro and Sharon L. Wolchik. New York, NY: St. Martin's Press, 1983 (b): pp. 111-32.

—— 'Ethnicity and Politics in Communist States.' *Studies in Comparative Communism* 18:2/3 (Summer/Autumn 1985 [a]): 181-9.

—— 'The Precommunist Legacy, Economic Development, Social Transformation, and Women's Roles in Eastern Europe.' In *Women, State, and Party in Eastern Europe*, edited by Sharon L. Wolchik and Alfred G. Meyer. Durham, NC: Duke University Press, 1985 (b): 31-46.

—— 'Economic Performance and Political Change in Czechoslovakia.' In *Prospects for Change in Socialist Systems: Challenges and Responses*, edited by Charles J. Bukowski and Mark A. Cichock. New York, NY: Praeger Publishers, 1987, pp. 35-60.

—— 'Prospects for Political Change in Czechoslovakia.' Paper presented at the 1989 meeting of the Midwest Political Science Association, Chicago, IL, April 1989 (a).

—— 'Women and the State in Eastern Europe and the Soviet Union.' In *Women, the State and Development*, edited by Sue Ellen Charlton, Jana Everett, and Kathleen Staudt. Albany, New York: SUNY Press, 1989 (b), pp. 45-65.

—— 'The Crisis of Socialism in Central and Eastern Europe and its Future.' Paper presented at 'Conference on the Future of Socialism in Eastern Europe,' University of North Carolina, April 1990 (a).

—— 'Women and the Collapse of Communism in Central and Eastern Europe.' Paper presented at the World Congress of Slavic Studies, Harrogate, England, July 1990 (b).

—— 'Central and Eastern Europe in Transition.' In *Asia and the Decline of Communism*, edited by Young C. Kim and Gaston Sigur. New Brunswick, NJ: Transaction Publishers, 1991 (a), forthcoming.

—— 'Czechoslovakia in Transition.' In *Instability in Eastern Europe After Communism*, edited by Trond Gilberg. Boulder, CO: Westview Press, 1991 (b), forthcoming.

—— 'Czechoslovakia in the Twentieth Century.' In *The Columbia History of East Central Europe in the Twentieth Century*, edited by Joseph Held and Stephen Fischer-Galati. New York: Columbia University Press, 1991 (c), forthcoming.

—— 'Women and Work in Communist and Post-communist Central and Eastern Europe.' In *Women's Work and Women's Lives in Modernizing and Industrial Countries*, edited by Hilda Kahne and Janet Z. Giele. Boulder, CO: Westview Press, 1991 (d), forthcoming.

—— 'Women's Issues in Czechoslovakia.' In *Women and Politics Worldwide*, edited by Barbara Nelson, 1991 (e) forthcoming.

Wolchik, Sharon L. and Curry, Jane. *Specialists and Professionals in the Policy Process in Czechoslovakia and Poland*. Report for the National Council for Soviet and East European Research, 1984.

Wolchik, Sharon L. and Meyer, Alfred G., eds. *Women, State, and Party in Eastern Europe*. Durham, NC: Duke University Press, 1985.

Wurmova, Anna and Kana, Miroslav. 'We Will Not Let Prices Get out of Hand.' *Hospodářské noviny*, no. 15 (1989): 1, 6. As reported in 'Price Bureau Minister Rejects Market Pricing.' JPRS-EER-89-077 (July 7, 1989): 49-53.

Yazdgerdi, Tom. 'Changes in the Educational System.' *Radio Free Europe Report on Eastern Europe* 1:34 (August 24, 1990): 14-18.

Yazdgerdi, Tom, and Obrman, Jan. 'The Disintegration of National Front Organizations.' *Radio Free Europe Report on Eastern Europe* 1:31 (August 3, 1990): 21-8.

Zábojníková, Marcela. 'Cirkevné školy od septembra?' *Rol'nické noviny*, August 6, 1990 (a), p. 1.

—— 'Radikálne zmeny i do nášého školstva.' *Rol'nické noviny*, August 11, 1990 (b), pp. 1, 2.

'Základ pro širší vývoz do NSR.' *Rudé právo*, January 30, 1989, p. 1.

'Základá se demokratická mládež.' *Lidová demokracie*, November 30, 1989, p. 3.

'Zákon o akciových společnostech.' *Příloha Hospodářských novin* 18 (1990).

'Zákon o bytovim, spotřebním, výrobním, a jiném družstévnictví.' *Příloha Hospodářských novin* 23 (1990).

'Zákon o soukromém podnikání občanů.' *Příloha Hospodářských novin* 17 (1990).

'Zákon o státním podniku.' *Příloha Hospodářských novin* 17 (1990).

Žantovský, Petr. 'Přátelstvi nikoliv na pokyn.' *Práce*, March 13, 1990, p. 7.

'Zásady přebudování hospodářského mechanismu ČSSR.' *Rudé právo*, January 9, 1987, p. 3.

'Zasedala vláda ČSSR.' *Rudé právo*, May 12, 1989, pp. 1, 2.

Zavarský, Pavol. 'Dozvieme sa pravdu?' *Verejnost'*, July 16, 1990, pp. 1, 2.

'Záverecné slovo soudruha Miloše Jakeše.' *Rudé právo*, January 29, 1987, p. 5.

zč. 'Cenová houpačka začíná.' *Svobodné slovo*, December 29, 1990 (a), pp. 1, 7.

zč. 'Konec Svazu spisovatelů.' *Svobodné slovo*, December 17, 1990 (b), p. 1.

Zeman, Rudolf and Mlynář, Vladimír. 'Jsem člověk konzervativní.' *Lidové noviny*. November 2, 1990, p. 2.

'Žiadajú spolkovú republiku.' *Pravda*, January 28, 1991, p. 2.

Žiarska, Anna. 'O nás je reč.' *Nové slovo* 16 (April 21, 1988), p. 14.

Zich, František. 'Hlavní rysy stavu společenského vědomí naší společnosti.' *Sociologický časopis* 22:5 (1986): 434–49.

Ziegenfuss, Vladimír, and Skružná, Jana. 'Rodinný stav obyvatelstva ČSSR.' *Demografie* 30:3 (1988): 203–65.

Zima, Jaroslav. 'Kvalita ovzduší v Praze.' *Lidové noviny*, April 1988 (a), p. 7.

—— 'Životní prostředí a politika.' *Lidové noviny*. Summer 1988 (b), p. 11.

Zimmerman, William. 'Issue Area and Foreign-Policy Process: A Research Note in Search of a General Theory.' *American Political Science Review* LXCII: 4 (1973).

—— 'Soviet-East European Relations in the 1980s and the Changing International System.' In *East-West Relations and the Future of Eastern Europe: Politics and Economics*, edited by Morris Bornstein, Zvi Gitelman, and William Zimmerman. Boston: Allen and Unwin, 1981, pp. 87–104.

Zinner, Paul. *Communist Strategy and Tactics in Czechoslovakia, 1918-1948*. New York, NY: Praeger Publishers, 1963.

'Život není jen práce nebo škola.' *Mladá fronta*, October 18, 1988, pp. 1–3.

'Životopis J. Svobody.' *Rudé právo*, October 15, 1990, p. 2.

zn. 'Zájem spíše o záhumenky.' *Zěmědelské noviny*, August 18, 1990, pp. 1, 3.

zn. 'K návrhu zákona o půdě.' *Zěmědelské noviny*, January 31, 1991, p. 1.

'Zpráva federálního statistického úřadu o vývoji národního hospodářství a plnění státního plánu ČSSR v roce 1985.' *Rudé právo*, January 25, 1986, pp. 1, 2, 3.

'Zpráva ze zasedání předsednictva ÚV KSČ.' *Rudé právo*, May 14, 1988, p. 1.

zr. 'Odbory: Životní minimum 1600-1700 korun.' *Rudé právo*, November 14, 1990 (a), p. 2.

zr. 'Statistika roku 1989.' *Rudé právo*, February 10, 1990 (b), pp. 1, 2.

Zvára, Juraj. 'Príspevok k prognóze vývoja národnostných vzt'ahov v ČSSR.' *Sociológia* 20:1 (1988): 3-14.

Zvosec, Christine. 'Environmental Deterioration in Eastern Europe.' *Survey* 28:4 (Winter 1984): 117-41.

Index